SOUTHERN HERO

Matthew Calbraith Butler. COURTESY PHOTOGRAPHIC HISTORY OF THE CIVIL WAR.

SOUTHERN HERO

MATTHEW CALBRAITH BUTLER

*Confederate General, Hampton Red Shirt,
and U.S. Senator*

SAMUEL J. MARTIN

STACKPOLE
BOOKS

Copyright © 2001 by Stackpole Books

Published by
STACKPOLE BOOKS
5067 Ritter Road
Mechanicsburg, PA 17055
www.stackpolebooks.com

Printed in the United States of America

10 9 8 7 6 5 4 3 2 1

FIRST EDITION

Library of Congress Cataloging-in-Publication Data
Martin, Samuel J.
    Southern hero : Matthew Calbraith Butler, Confederate general, Hampton Red
Shirt, and U.S. senator / Samuel J. Martin.—1st ed.
        p. cm.
    Includes bibliographical references and index.
    ISBN 0-8117-0899-3
    1. Butler, M. C. (Matthew Calbraith), 1836–1909. 2. Legislators—United States—
Biography. 3. United States. Congress. Senate—Biography. 4. Generals—Confederate
States of America—Biography. 5. Confederate States of America. Army—Biography.
6. United States—History—Civil War, 1861–1865—Cavalry operations.
I. Title.
E664.B98 M37 2001
973.7′092—dc21
[B]
                                                                    00-058824

CONTENTS

ACKNOWLEDGMENTS

Many people were a great help to me in researching and writing General Butler's biography, and I would like to acknowledge their contributions.

I am greatly indebted to Dr. Allen Stokes, Director of the South Caroliniana Library, University of South Carolina, who read the entire manuscript and offered me encouragement as well as many good suggestions.

Dr. George C. Rable, Professor of Southern History for the University of Alabama, read the chapters covering the Reconstruction and provided me with guidance toward understanding the conflicting interpretations for that period of time.

Ellen Adams Gutow, Butler's great granddaughter, was an astute contributor. She read and edited the manuscript, added intimate detail regarding family relationships, and furnished a number of the photographs used in the book.

I especially appreciated the cheerful and competent assistance of Chris Wilhelm at the National Archives. She was a godsend, a public servant who patiently led me through the bowels of that dusty institution to find answers to my questions.

Isabel Vandervalde, the Chief Researcher for the Aiken County (South Carolina) Historical Museum, heard of my project and without my asking, sent me details of the Hamburg Massacre.

Several Edgefield (South Carolina) residents graciously spent time with me during my several visits, and provided me with local facts about General Butler. They included Bettis Rainsford, Carrie Clark, Bonnie Drewry, and Ruth Nicholson.

David Parker, also a resident of Edgefield, a relative of General Butler's, sent me many letters, each containing a new "gem" of information.

Research must often be done by mail, and the following were quick to provide timely input: Judith Sibley, Archives Curator for the U.S. Military Academy at West Point; Peggy Hollis of the National Society of Colonial Dames of America, Columbia, South Carolina; Carl Esche, a Special Collections Assistant for Seeley G. Mudd Manuscript Library, Princeton University; Sarah D. McMaster, Librarian at the Fairfield County Library, Winnsboro, South Carolina; and David Beachman, the Executive Director of Developments for Wofford College, Spartanburg, South Carolina.

Clarke B. Hall shared an important Robert E. Lee letter from his Brandy Station collection.

I visited many universities and libraries, where I was always greeted with friendly assistance. I particularly recall Linda McCurley with the Special Collections Library at Duke University in Durham, North Carolina; Jessica Pigza of the Maryland Historical Society in Baltimore; and Edith Hayes with the South Caroliniana Library in Columbia.

My trips to the Hilton Head (South Carolina) Library; the Virginia Historical Society in Richmond; Armstrong Coastal University in Savannah; the Beaufort (South Carolina) Library; the South Carolina Department of Archives and History, Columbia; Georgia Historical Society, Savannah; the University of North Carolina, Chapel Hill; the University of Virginia, Charlottesville; the Charleston (South Carolina) Library Association; and Library of Congress, Washington, D.C., were all highlighted by helpful personnel.

And I am most appreciative of the professional help of my copy editor, Barbara Rossi, and Associate Editor Leigh Ann Berry, of Stackpole Books.

PROLOGUE

Col. Matthew Calbraith Butler, leader of the 2nd South Carolina Cavalry, had been in many a tight spot during his service in the Civil War, but never one quite so precarious as that he faced the morning of June 9, 1863. Matthew and his mounted troops were positioned just east of Stevensburg, Virginia, and anticipating the arrival of a superior Federal force. The battle of Brandy Station had been raging for almost five hours to the northeast. The rattle of muskets and the bellow of artillery filled the air with an ever increasing crescendo.

Butler had not taken part in the main engagement. His command had started the day in reserve, "standing to horse," Matthew noted, "when a courier . . . came at full speed [and reported] the enemy was at Stevensburg [in our rear]."[1]

Without waiting for orders, Matthew gathered his small force of about 200 men and rushed toward the point of peril. He posted Capt. Frank Hampton, younger brother of the brigade commander, Wade Hampton, with twenty-five riders along the Culpeper Road, just east of Stevensburg, then dismounted the rest of his regiment to form a defensive line in the woods above the pickets on the pike. The Union cavalry soon came in view.

Alfred N. Duffié led the Federal force, 1,600 troopers supported by a battery of six cannons, toward Butler's north flank. "[They] made a vigorous attack," Matthew wrote. "A volley from our Enfields soon sent them back."[2] The Yankees mounted a second charge, but again Butler's fire forced the enemy to retire.

Duffié then turned his attention to the south, to the pike. He sent his men galloping up the road, and they swept past both Hampton's small band and the 4th Virginia, who had just arrived to assist Butler. The Rebel reinforcements were not only routed, they "took to their heels towards Culpeper," and were no longer a factor in the battle.[3] Williams C. Wickham, their commander, stated later that "the conduct of my regiment [was] . . . disgraceful."[4]

As the enemy pressed into and past Stevensburg, Butler was already countering their just won advantage. He wheeled his line like a gate to the right until his men were facing south. The Federals quickly reorganized and started coming north. Their superior numbers overlapped both of Matthew's flanks. Seeking better ground, he fell back several hundred yards across a small creek (Mountain Run) and assumed a new position at the crest of a ridge. Astride his horse, a silhouette against the blue sky, Butler shouted directions to his men where to fall in. He offered an attractive target to the Federal cannoneers, who were advancing with the cavalry. They took aim and sent a missile screaming toward him.[5]

The shell struck the earth about thirty yards in front of Butler, skipped, and then veered forward. The shrapnel sliced through Butler's right leg at the ankle, disemboweled his horse, and then smashed into Capt. William Farley, who was mounted beside Butler. The metal severed Farley's right leg before burrowing into his steed, killing the animal.

"My house bounded in the air," Butler wrote, "and threw me, saddle and all, flat on my back in the road."[6] Although he was certainly in shock, Matthew had the presence of mind to take a silk handkerchief and wind a tourniquet around his leg. His foot dangled from the limb, held on by a shred of skin. Butler then called to Farley to follow his example in stopping the flow of blood from his terrible wound.[7]

Matthew's men, of course, rushed up to their commander. "Go at once to Farley," Butler exhorted, "since he needs you more than I do."[8] This was the typical, chivalrous gesture of a Southern gentleman. This was Matthew Calbraith Butler.

Butler's troopers held their ground that day, and were a major factor in the Confederate victory at Brandy Station. Although his limb was amputated at the ankle, Matthew recovered from his wound, and served with distinction to the end of the War between the States. He was a Southern hero.

The Civil War, however, was not the climax of Butler's life. He went on to become an outstanding lawyer, a Hampton Red Shirt who helped halt the injustices of Reconstruction in South Carolina, a U.S. senator, and finally a major general during the Spanish-American War. Few have led such an interesting and accomplished life. Fewer still have done so while securing both the love and respect of their fellow men. His story is worth the telling.

CHAPTER 1

Boyhood

THE MAPLES HAD STARTED TO BUD NEAR EAGLE'S CRAG, SOUTH CAROLINA, in early March of 1836, but the pasture grass still held its hue of winter's brown. Dark shadows from the mountains soaring to the west crept over the hamlet and hastened the approaching darkness the afternoon of the eighth. The wail of a newborn then pierced the chilly air. Matthew Calbraith Butler, the sixth son and seventh living child of Jane Perry Butler and her husband, William, had safely arrived. Everyone was relieved and happy because three earlier babies had died at birth.[1]

Both parents could take pride in their ancestral roots. William's great-grandfather, also named William, had come to America from England in 1737. He settled in Prince William County, Virginia, and then married "Miss Mason," who bore him three children: James, Sarah, and Susan.[2]

James Butler married Mary Simpson; in 1772 he took his wife, his children (six boys and two girls), and his two sisters to South Carolina. He worked as a trader, but soon found himself embroiled in military affairs. First he led a company in the "Snow Camp" expedition against the Cherokee, then joined in America's War for Independence. When Charles Town fell to the British, James was captured and imprisoned on a ship in the harbor. Soon after his release, he and his son (also named James) were killed in the battle of Cloud's Creek.[3]

William Butler, James's oldest boy, also fought the English in the Revolutionary War. Although just a teenager at the onset, William began his service as a lieutenant of cavalry. He earned acclaim from his commanders for his efforts in the clashes with the Tories at Stono, Augusta, Ninety Six, Dean Swamp, and Orangeburgh, and as a result, was promoted to captain of the Mounted Rangers in February 1781.[4]

In 1788 William was a representative at the convention to consider South Carolina's adoption of the federal Constitution. He voted against the pact. In 1790, he helped draw up his state's constitution. One year later, he was elected sheriff for the District of Ninety Six. William was chosen major general of militia in 1796 and in 1800 won a seat as representative to Congress. He relinquished his post in 1810 to make way for a promising young politician named John C. Calhoun. When the United States went to war against the British in 1812, Pres. James Madison asked William to be a brigadier general in the regular army, but Butler refused the honor. His interests were now limited to South Carolina.[5]

William was married to Behethland Foote Moore in 1784, and they had eight children (seven boys and one girl). Their third son, yet another William, Matthew's father, graduated from South Carolina College and became a surgeon in the U.S. Navy. He served in that capacity with Andrew Jackson during the battle of New Orleans. In 1819 while he was stationed in Rhode Island, William met, courted, and then married Jane Tweedy Perry. He resigned his commission in 1825 and moved to Greenville, South Carolina, where he became a country doctor.[6]

Jane's ancestors emigrated to America in 1639. Edward Perry, a Quaker, fled Devonshire, England, to elude religious persecution. Settling outside of Sandwich, Massachusetts, a Pilgrim community on Cape Cod, he took up farming, and by 1654 was wealthy enough to woo Mary Freeman, a daughter of the local magistrate. Although Edward was a Quaker, his feisty personality often resulted in conflict with his associates. On one such occasion, he refused to be married by his father-in-law, preferring his church's ritual of joining hands. Edward paid an annual fine for not having a legal wedding. In 1659 Edward was fined for threatening the town marshal. And in 1663 he was "called to account . . . for a rayling letter which he wrote to the Court."[7] At the same time, however, Edward held the respect of his peers. Twice he was elected surveyor of Sandwich, and in 1671 Edward was named inspector of the local "ordinary" to control drinking.

Edward's son, Benjamin, moved to Rhode Island in 1704, where he became a planter. His community, Narragansett, was similar to tidewater Virginia in that the many estates were large and worked by slaves. Benjamin prospered greatly over the years, and when his first wife died he married Susanna Barber. She bore him five offspring, the third of which was a son, born in 1733, whom they called Freeman.[8]

Freeman Perry became both a doctor and a surveyor, serving the area around his home at Matunuck. He married Mercy Hazard, a daughter of a rich planter, in 1755. During the War of Independence, Freeman was appointed chief justice for the Court of Common Pleas for Washington County, a position that he held until his death in 1813.[9]

Freeman and Mercy had a son Christopher, born in 1761. The boy inherited Edward's pugnaciousness. While still a teenager, Christopher joined the Kingston Reds, a military company organized to support the American Revolution. He was involved in murdering Simeon Tucker, a Quaker neighbor who refused to pay taxes financing the War. Forced by shocked and angry townspeople to flee from home, Freeman first went to sea with a privateer, then in 1778 joined the Continental army as a private. His service as a soldier was brief. Christopher claimed that he was captured and put in prison by the British; more likely he deserted to again become a privateer.[10]

Christopher's sailing experience was hardly a success. His second privateer, the *Mufflin,* was soon captured and he went to Charleston in irons. He escaped from prison and sped north where he joined the Continental navy. He served on the frigate, the *Queen of France,* which sailed to Charleston, only to be trapped in the harbor by the British. The captain decided to scuttle his vessel. Eluding capture by the enemy, Christopher again hurried north, where he signed on with the *Trumbull.* In June 1780 this ship fought a battle with the *Watt,* an English privateer. Badly damaged, the *Trumbull* returned to Boston for repairs. Christopher then volunteered his services to a privateer headed for Ireland to intercept merchant vessels supplying England. This ship and her crew were easily captured by the British, and Christopher was imprisoned in the Newry, County Down, near Belfast.[11]

The twenty-year-old disheartened sailor soon found his luck had turned. The warden granted Christopher parole, and he spent his hours hunting, riding, and drinking with local Irish youth. During one boisterous party, two teenage girls burst into the room by mistake. Christopher was captivated by the dazzling blue eyes and raven tresses of Sarah Wallace Alexander. As she and her friend, both giggling with embarrassment, backed out of the door, he pointed after Sarah and declared, "There goes my future wife!"[12]

Christopher soon broke his parole and fled back to the United States, where he found that the Revolutionary War had ended. He quickly signed on as a master's mate on the ship, *Favorite,* and set sail for Dublin. Christopher's plans were to desert his post upon reaching Ireland, locate Sarah, and marry her. When he arrived in port, Christopher was shocked to see her waiting on the dock. Her parents had died in an epidemic, and she was about to board his vessel and emigrate to Philadelphia to live with relatives. Christopher stayed with his ship, and despite the close watch of Sarah's guardians (a Mr. Calbraith and his young son, Matthew),[13] wooed and won her heart during their six week passage back to the United States. They were wed on August 2, 1784, in Philadelphia.

Christopher led his sixteen-year-old wife to South Kingstown, Rhode Island. His happy father greeted Christopher as a prodigal son, and gave him a suite in a nearby mansion.[14]

Christopher could have farmed one of his father's many estates, but he chose instead to become a ship captain, and through the following years, built a substantial fortune through his life at sea. Sarah bore him eight children: five boys and three girls. All of the sons were sailors. The eldest, Comdr. Oliver Hazard Perry, was a hero during the War of 1812 for winning the battle of Lake Erie. Comdr. Matthew Calbraith Perry, their third boy (who was named for Sarah's long-ago guardian), gained fame for conducting the naval expedition which opened Japan to the world. Their third girl and sixth child, Jane Tweedy Perry, married Dr. William Butler. They were the parents of Matthew Calbraith Butler.[15]

Matthew (his family and boyhood friends usually called him "Calbraith") spent his early years living in a home atop Butler Hill, four miles north of Greenville, South Carolina. The house was by necessity quite large because by 1844, Jane had given birth to twelve children: four girls (Behethland, Sally, Emmala, and Elise); eight boys (George, Christopher, William, James, Pickens, Matthew [named for his illustrious uncle], Thomas, and Oliver). Their father was both a physician and a planter, farming the fields that lay adjacent to his mansion. Slaves provided the manual labor.[16]

Like most Southern boys, young Matthew learned to ride at an early age, and one of his favorite jaunts was no doubt to the heights close by the family home where a cool spring flowed between huge boulders. His older brothers had carved their names in the smooth-faced rocks.[17] From this vantage, Matthew could see for miles. The flat farmland stretched to the north, overshadowed by Hog Back Mountain. In the solitude of his peaceful environs, the lad must have contemplated what the future held for him.

Butler was well aware that he would not live a life of leisure. Although many Southern parents coddled their sons, allowing them to hunt and fish while slaves performed their chores, William Butler was a hard nosed disciplinarian. "As soon as we were able to work," Matthew said when recalling his youth, "my father required [us] to go to the field."[18] He himself began plowing fields at age thirteen. And in the winter, when he spent weekdays in school, Matthew was given tasks for Saturdays. None of the boys was allowed to "order a servant to saddle or hitch up a horse," Matthew recounted. He did not understand then why the slaves should not perform menial duties, but later admired his father for his "wisdom in inculcating habits of self-reliance in his sons."[19]

Jane Butler agreed with her husband's methods for rearing their children. "She was a woman of remarkable force of character," Matthew noted, then added no doubt with a smile, "and impressed her strong personality on . . . [us]. She used a peach tree switch liberally on the boys . . . never hit one . . . a lick amiss . . . but allowed the girls to do pretty much as they pleased."[20] He later related, "Whatever I have achieved in my life . . . I owe it to the training, example and character of my much revered father and mother."[21]

In 1849 Pres. James Polk offered Matthew's father a post as agent for the Cherokee. William's younger brother, Pierce Mason Butler, former governor of South Carolina, had held this position from 1840 to 1846. He resigned to join the war against Mexico, where he was killed at Churubusco.[22] William accepted the president's offer and Jane and eleven of their offspring (their oldest boy, George, had already left home and settled in Missouri) accompanied him to Fort Gibson, Arkansas. Thirteen-year-old Matthew drove a wagon, pulled by a mule named "Jerry," on the trek.[23] Every other night, while his brothers and sisters rested, he spent hours greasing the wheels of his cart.

Life was certainly difficult on the primitive frontier. None, however, anticipated the crisis that came on September 24, 1850. William Butler died. George hastened south from Missouri to assume both his father's post as Indian agent as well as head of the family.[24] Matthew, however, was placed in limbo. Both William's younger brother, Andrew P. Butler, and Jane's brother, Matthew Calbraith Perry, had made offers to raise and educate the lad. The boy was forced to choose between his two uncles; whether he would spend his life as a genteel Southern gentleman or as a Yankee sea captain. He elected to live with Andrew. In the fall of 1851 Matthew rode east for Edgefield, South Carolina.[25]

CHAPTER 2

Manhood

ALTHOUGH JUST FIFTEEN-YEARS-OLD, MATTHEW WAS ALREADY A MAN, ONE who fit the later descriptions of him as being "tall and striking . . . molded like an Apollo . . . with a face as sweet as any god of old."[1] Others would call him "the handsomest man in South Carolina if not in the country . . . a most gracious gentleman."[2] Matthew had piercing eyes, a straight nose, and the jet-black hair of his grandmother, Sarah. He would grow bald in his old age, and already showed this tendency with widow's peaks on both temples.[3]

The uncle that Matthew had opted for a guardian, Andrew P. Butler, was a lawyer, admitted to the bar in 1819. After serving in both the South Carolina House and Senate, he was appointed a judge in 1833. In 1848 Andrew was first elected to the U.S. Senate, and he still held that position when Matthew arrived at "Stoneland," the Judge's plantation, four miles above Edgefield. Andrew had married twice but he had fathered only one child, a daughter, Eloise, the product of his second union. She was now seventeen, two years older than her cousin, Matthew.[4] Andrew had lost his second wife, too, and so his mansion was kept by his aged mother, Behethland, who lovingly welcomed young Matthew.[5]

Although Edgefield itself was a small community, the area surrounding the hamlet was heavily populated. Almost 40,000 people (15,653 whites, 24,233 blacks) resided within a day's drive to the county seat. Only the cities of Charleston and New Orleans had more inhabitants in the South.[6] And most of Edgefield's people, as the slave population indicates, farmed for a living.

Matthew attended school in Edgefield at first, then he boarded at George Galphin's Bethany Academy at Liberty Hill, situated on the county line to the north, through 1853. He came home late that year to study at William Leitner's Edgefield Academy.[7] He not only made good grades but also took part in a number of outdoor sports. Matthew captained every team for which he played.[8]

C.S.A. General Matthew Calbraith Butler. COURTESY LIBRARY OF CONGRESS

The lad's promise caught the attention of his mother's brother, Comdr. Matthew Calbraith Perry, who asked Butler to accompany him as his private secretary on his coming voyage to Japan. He was sailing east to "make arrangements for the [United States] to gain entree there. . . . I had consented to do so and had packed my trunk," Matthew recalled, "but at the last moment, my mother [who had come back to South Carolina to live in nearby Greenville] . . . would not let me go."[9]

Matthew headed instead for Columbia, the state capital, to attend South Carolina College. The eighteen-year-old boy did well in his studies and was popular with his classmates. He pledged the Delta Kappa Epsilon (DKE) fraternity.[10] In 1856, however, two years short of graduating, he dropped out of school and came home to Edgefield to read law at the offices of James P. Carroll.[11] Matthew had two reasons for this sudden change in plans. The first dealt with a family crisis: Judge Butler had been insulted!

The slander evolved from the arguments over extending slavery into the Kansas Territory. Attempting to defuse the issue, Illinois senator Stephen A. Douglas introduced legislation calling for "Popular Sovereignty," a concept which permitted the residents of a territory to choose whether to be slave or free, thereby relieving Congress from making this decision.[12] His act was passed in 1854, but the results were disastrous. Thousands rushed into Kansas, not to settle but to vote on the slavery issue. Their angry words soon turned into gunfire.

Speaking in the Senate on May 19, 1856, Charles Sumner, the abolitionist from Massachusetts, professed that the violence in Kansas was a crime precipitated by slaveholders in general and South Carolina's Andrew P. Butler in particular. "He is the Don Quixote of slavery," Sumner thundered, "who has chosen a mistress to whom he has made his vows, and who, though ugly to others, is . . . lovely to him; though polluted in the sight of the world, is chaste to his sight."[13]

The next day Sumner continued his personal assault on Butler. He charged his counterpart from South Carolina, who was at home where he was recovering from a labial paralysis, with uttering "incoherent phrases, [discharging] the loose expectoration of his speech" against the free men of Kansas. "He cannot open his mouth," Sumner sneered, "but out . . . flies a blunder."[14]

Butler's friends and family (Matthew included) were no doubt incensed by Sumner's slander, but their path of response was not clear. A gentleman, of course, could not just idly accept an insult. Nor could he carry his personal grievance into a court of law. To do so would "degrade the plaintiff in the estimation of his peers, [putting] the whole case beneath the value of society."[15] The field of honor beckoned; but a duel could only be fought between equals, two gentlemen, and Sumner was obviously not a gentleman.

According to the Southern Canon of Honor (an unwritten but rigid code, "hedged in by strict conventions and proprieties as any of stilted social conduct"), a person of lower estate who has delivered an insult should be horsewhipped or even better, pommeled with a cane.[16] Andrew Butler was too old and feeble to flog anyone, much less a strapping man the size of Sumner. Someone would have to stand in his stead.

Preston S. Brooks, a second cousin of Matthew, a member of the House of Representatives from South Carolina, decided on his own to act in behalf of his kinsman. On the morning of May 22, he charged into the Senate Chamber where Sumner was sitting. "I am come to punish you!" Brooks stated, and then proceeded to batter the abolitionist senseless with his gutta-percha cane.[17] Over three years would pass before Sumner found the health (or the courage) to resume his seat in the Senate.

People in the North were vehement in denouncing Brooks for his assault on Sumner. The South, however, saw him as a hero. He received scores of new canes to replace the gutta-percha that he had shattered on Sumner's skull.[18] Unsettled by the unwanted attention, including a failed House attempt to expel him, Brooks resigned his seat. The voters in his district soon sent him back to Congress, but his return was marred by ill-

Maria Pickens.
COURTESY ELLEN ADAMS GUTOW

ness.[19] Brooks, who was only thirty-nine-years-old, died suddenly that fall from throat cancer.

Matthew, like most of his fellow Southerners, no doubt approved of Brooks's assault on Sumner, and his impression of the North must have been jaundiced by the incident. But he was distracted by other events. His uncle, Judge Butler, whose health had been failing for some time, finally died on May 25, 1857. Six months after the funeral, Matthew was admitted to the bar. "More lawyers," the *Edgefield Advertiser* reported laconically.[20] Matthew opened his own office, promoting his services via weekly insertions at a cost of fifty cents each in the local newspaper. But what took up most of his time was his second reason for leaving college. He was in love.

Her name was Maria (pronounced "Marīah") Pickens, twin sister to Eliza, and one of four daughters born to a wealthy planter and politician, Francis W. Pickens. She was twenty-three, almost three years older than Matthew. Although pretty and trim, Maria was at an age where she was in danger of becoming an old maid, and was perhaps somewhat desperate to be married. Matthew was probably in love with Maria, but he might have been overly impressed with her father's resources and social status. Sensing that the two were ill matched, Pickens opposed a wedding. He told Maria that Matthew "had few prospects."[21]

Pickens was surely influenced by an incident that took place at a masked ball at the home of Arthur Simkins, editor of the local newspaper. During the festivities, Butler led his partner (probably Maria) to the dance floor to take part in a quadrille. There was only one position available, and Thomas J. Lipscomb claimed it as his. When Matthew refused to step aside,

Matthew C. and Maria Butler (wedding photo). COURTESY ELLEN ADAMS GUTOW

a bitter argument ensued, and a challenge to duel was finally given and accepted.

"For . . . days business matters were subordinated to the Butler-Lipscomb embroglio," an observer recalled. "Everybody talked about it; everybody became a partisan of one or the other."

A field of honor near Augusta was selected, and Butler took up temporary residence in the home of Thomas Barrett, a Georgia banker, to prepare for the ordeal. At the last minute, however, friends intervened and convinced the young men to reconcile. The duel was canceled.[22]

Maria must have admired Butler for his obstinacy. And she had reason to suspect her father's motives for objecting to her suitor. Her wedding might upset his own romantic designs. Fifty years old, twice a widower, Pickens was wooing twenty-six-year-old Lucy Holcombe. His letters revealed a shameless passion. "I love you with painful solitude," he wrote her, "wildly, blindly, madly . . . it is for you to bless or turn me . . . without hope . . . upon a dark and dreary world."[23]

Lucy, however, was not swayed by florid rhetoric. She was an opportunist, attracted to Pickens because she thought he was about to be elected U.S. senator from South Carolina.[24] When the state legislature, meeting in December 1857, named a rival, James Henry Hammond, to the seat,[25] Lucy broke off the engagement. His romance seemingly over, Pickens finally gave Maria his permission to marry. She and Matthew wed on February 25, 1858.[26]

The couple moved onto land adjacent to "Edgewood," her father's plantation. The farm, a wedding gift from Pickens, was valued at $7,000. Matthew's assets, now including a number of slaves, part of his wife's dowry, totaled $17,000.[27] The couple assumed a typical gentry life: he practiced law; she took charge of the home; they both joined the elite Trinity Episcopal Church, where Butler was soon elected a vestryman.[28] Then on December 8, 1858, Maria gave birth to a son, Francis Wilkinson Pickens Butler, named in honor of her father.[29]

In June 1859 Matthew joined and was elected second lieutenant of the Edgefield Hussars, a militia cavalry group founded by his uncle, Andrew, in 1833. He led the troopers in their parades, "[occupying] a prominent place in the picture," the local newspaper said, "and right soldierly did . . . [his] devoir."[30]

That fall Matthew helped organize the Edgefield Literary Club. He was elected secretary of the circle, which met fortnightly to present speeches and to debate their content. Only men were allowed to stand before the group, but Matthew, showing a proclivity for the fair sex, encouraged wives to attend, too. "[Our] meetings . . . should be illuminated by the sparkling eyes and beaming faces of . . . ladies," he professed. "Give us your countenance and encouragement, and there is no such word as fail."[31]

And in October Matthew was one of the judges for fine arts at the annual Edgefield District Agricultural Fair. He also entered a stallion in the horse competition, which won the silver cup for best three-year-old colt.[32]

These halcyonic days for Butler and Maria, in fact the lives of almost every Southerner, were forever changed later that same month. John Brown, a wild-eyed abolitionist from Kansas, invaded Harpers Ferry, Virginia. He led a group of twenty-one, armed with pikes, intent on inciting a slave insurrection. The raid was foolish and easily quelled. Local militia quickly trapped the marauders in the firehouse and then a U.S. Army contingent, headed by Col. Robert E. Lee and Lt. James Ewell Brown Stuart, captured the small band of fanatics. Brown was tried, convicted, and on December 2, 1859, executed by hanging.[33]

Although John Brown's attempt to incite slaves against their masters had failed, it had a profound effect both above and below the Mason-Dixon line. A highly vocal minority in the North, sympathetic with his goals, proclaimed Brown a martyr. Southerners, appalled by the prospect of murderous Abolitionists, embraced secession in numbers approaching a majority. John Brown's raid widened the rift between North and South, serving as one of the principal causes of the Civil War.

On a more personal note, fears of a slave insurrection, always unspoken, had been terrorizing the Southern mind over the years. John Brown's ludicrous foray surfaced this consternation. "[He]," Steven A. Channing related, "plunged a knife deep into the psyche of Southern whites."[34] Those in South Carolina responded in two ways. The state legislature passed several bills, one that banned any contact between a slave and all possible sources of disaffecting ideas, e.g., a play, books, pictures, even a whispered phrase, and another law that required licenses for any businessman visiting from the North.[35] The intent of the latter was to hinder the mobility of future "John Browns." And in every community, the citizens formed vigilant committees, groups of young men to watch for and "test the soundness" of itinerants.[36] Matthew no doubt belonged to the band covering Edgefield.

Butler was, of course, already involved in public life, and in April 1860 he moved to expand that role. He joined in the race for the Edgefield County seat in the South Carolina House of Representatives. But first, he had to free up time for that role. Matthew formed a new legal partnership with S. McGowan and G. A. Wardlaw, who would serve the needs of his clients;[37] and he sent Maria with the baby to Greenville to live with his mother. His wife was pregnant again, due to deliver in early October, and since he would be away most evenings campaigning, Butler wanted to make sure that she had kin at hand if he was not there.

This was their first lengthy separation, and it set an example of what would follow throughout their years of married life. Butler wrote her newsy and affectionate letters almost every day; Maria seldom replied. When she did, it was only to complain. "I hope," Matthew said in his August 7 note, "[your] rather gloomy strain is induced by nothing more serious than a fit of the 'blues'. . . . You say not one word about Frank. I presume by that he is well."[38]

Maria also spent more money than Matthew could afford. "We will have to economize . . . more," he was forced to reprove her, "until the times are easier."[39]

Although Butler had problems at home, his campaign was running well. "I reached Shatterfield about 12 o'clock, and had to 'take the stump' soon after my arrival," he reported in a note to Maria. "They told me I made fifty votes."[40] A few days later, he boasted, "The election is just six weeks off, and my prospects are very flattering."[41] He was right. That October, shortly after the birth of a second son named William Wallace for Matthew's father,[42] Butler won the election. He attended the Special Session that started in Columbia on November 5.[43]

Gov. William H. Gist had called the legislators to the capital to name electors who would cast the state's vote for U.S. president. In October balloting, the citizens of South Carolina and the other slave states had given their support to John C. Breckinridge, one of two Democrats vying for the nation's highest office. He received sparse backing up north, however, where Abraham Lincoln, candidate for the "Black Republicans," outpolled both Stephen A. Douglas, also a Democrat, and John Bell, who ran under the Constitutional Union banner. He thus captured most of the states above the Mason-Dixon line and the presidency. Gist intended to keep the Special Session in Columbia until Lincoln's election was confirmed so the members would be available to "consider and determine the mode and measure of redress [to an administration that was] hostile to our institutions and fatally bent on our ruin."[44] He would ask the representatives to approve the secession of South Carolina from the federal Union.[45]

This drastic step was proposed because Lincoln and his Republican cohorts would no doubt seek to end slavery, using peaceful ways if possible but force if necessary. "A house divided against itself cannot stand," Lincoln said. He then predicted: "This government cannot endure . . . half slave and half free."[46] And William H. Seward, a leading spokesman for the Republicans, stated that an "irrepressible conflict" to abolish the South's "particular institution" was bound to come.[47] With the North now positioned and powered to carry out this threat, which would not only destroy the South economically but also subject her people to the horror of free blacks in her midst intent on exacting revenge for years of servitude, the states below the Mason-Dixon line recognized that they could no longer remain in the Union.

The electoral college sanctioned Lincoln's election on November 7; three days later, the South Carolina assembly approved a secession convention. The representatives would be elected on December 6; they would meet on December 17, 1860.[48]

When the Special Session adjourned, Butler returned to Edgefield to report on his activities. "[He is] fully up to the mark of separate-State action," the local newspaper proclaimed, "[marching] to independence, in double-quick time."[49]

Two days later, on November 26, Butler raced back to Columbia. He faced two issues: the selection of the representatives to the secession convention, and the election of the new governor by the legislature. The latter was of particular interest because Francis W. Pickens, his father-in-law, was among the leading contenders for the office, and he had asked Matthew to manage his campaign.

Pickens, who had finally wed young Lucy Holcombe, enticing her father with money to pay off his debts and winning Lucy with the promise of an exciting life in Russia, where he had been appointed U.S. minister, had just returned home. Lucy had hated Moscow. She "begged him on her knees" to leave, thus he had resigned his post.[50] Upon arriving in Edgefield, Pickens was thrilled by the frenzy for secession, and he immediately added his voice to the clamor. "Southern Independence now and forever," he

roared in a speech to the townsmen, "rather than bear in peace the igno-
minious bondage whose shadow is already thrown insultingly in our path."[51]

On November 30, Pickens repeated these same words in an address to
the general assembly in Columbia. The members were so impressed, they
nominated him for governor. On the first ballot, counted on December 12,
Pickens and Benjamin J. Johnson led the pack with fifty-two votes each.
Through the ensuing polls, with Matthew cajoling supporters to hold firm,
Pickens remained in the running. And on the seventh show of hands, he
won the seat.[52]

Pickens was inaugurated December 17. He immediately called the
Secession Convention, whose members had been nominated on December
6, to order. But before the delegates could address the issue of South Carolina leaving the Union, an outbreak of smallpox threatened Columbia.
The assembly hurriedly moved to Charleston. On December 20, the representatives voted to secede.[53]

Matthew participated in the assembly's meeting, January 8 through the
28, then rode home to resume his law practice. While in Columbia, however, he and the other members of the Edgefield Hussars had offered their
unit to be a part of the state's army, just now being formed. Their services
were accepted, but they were told to wait in place until the need arose for
duty and probably war.[54]

Within weeks of South Carolina's secession, six of the cotton states,
Alabama, Georgia, Florida, Mississippi, Texas, and Louisiana, had followed
her out of the Union. Although each was independent to itself, all knew
that their survival required joining hands as a new nation. And they had to
combine before Lincoln's inauguration, before the federal government
would be positioned to dispute this forming of a Southern Confederacy.[55]

Representatives from the seven seceded states gathered in Montgomery,
Alabama, in early February. They prepared articles for a confederation,
which were approved on February 8, and the following day, elected their
president, Jefferson C. Davis, from Mississippi.[56]

While the Southern states were consolidating, attempts to close the
schism and return the dissidents into the Union arose across the land. Plans
proffered by statesmen such as Kentucky senator John J. Crittenden, former
president John Tyler, and Illinois senator Stephen A. Douglas, were
debated. But the one man who could have really made a difference, the
incoming president Abraham Lincoln, refused to budge. He had won the
election and was determined to cash in on the fruits of victory, the
prospective abolition of slavery. "The tug has come," he wrote, "and better
now than later."[57] Lincoln at this time in his life was only a politician, lack-
ing the courage to stand up to his party for the greater good of the nation.
He would change through the coming years, but this noble transformation

into one of our greatest presidents would come too late to avoid the stain of civil war on American history.

Lincoln was inaugurated on March 4. Upon taking his office, he immediately became involved in a controversy over Fort Sumter, the bastion protecting Charleston harbor. The South considered this stronghold theirs; Lincoln refused to cede Federal property to a "country" he would not recognize. The controversy peaked on April 12, when the Rebels opened a sustained bombardment on the fort. Two days later, Maj. Robert Anderson, the Union defender, raised a white flag and surrendered his post.[58]

Northerners were outraged by the South's firing on the national flag and Lincoln asked for 75,000 volunteers to put down what he dubbed "a rebellion." Virginia, Tennessee, Arkansas, and North Carolina were all mortified by his call to arms against their sister states. They seceded from the Union and joined the Confederacy.[59] The Civil War began.

Most thought the conflict would be brief. Matthew was no exception. "Your Pa [Governor Pickens] told me," he said in a note to Maria, "that he did not think the fight . . . will last longer than three weeks."[60] But the men from Edgefield were not about to miss even a short war. Cicero Adams, who had formed an infantry company in January, left at once for Charleston. Another band of foot soldiers, raised by Elbert Bland, also started for the coast.[61] Butler's Hussars, however, remained in town. "This arm of the State service [is] dormant," a reporter wrote, "because there is no duty suited to them."[62]

On April 19, the opportunity that Butler had been so long awaiting finally came. An ad in the *Charleston Courier* announced the forming of a "Legion" of all arms, consisting of six companies of infantry, four troops of cavalry, and an artillery battery. All thousand volunteers had to be "ready at an early date," according to the organizer, Wade Hampton, a wealthy South Carolina planter, "as I have every reason to hope that it will be ordered into active service."[63]

Grandson of a Revolutionary War hero, Hampton was well known throughout the nation. Forty-three-years-old, a tall, broad-shouldered man, he was famed as a cotton planter, who managed both the family plantation, "Millwood," located near Columbia, and extensive fields in Mississippi. He was also a huntsman, scholar, and a state senator. Hampton was opposed to slavery, despite owning thousands of blacks.[64] He was a model for Matthew's personal aspirations, and the young lawyer moved at once to gain a spot for himself in the Legion.

Matthew quickly petitioned Hampton to include the Edgefield Hussars as one of his cavalry companies. Other groups from the local area (Jefferson Nullifiers, Saluda Sentinels, and Edgefield Raiders) also applied to Hampton for a post in the Legion, but Butler's band was the only one of these com-

Gen. Wade Hampton, C.S.A. COURTESY LIBRARY OF CONGRESS

petitors accepted.[65] After meeting on May 27 to reelect Butler as their captain, the Hussars assembled in Edgefield to prepare to ride for Columbia.

"They arrived in our village on Friday evening about 6 o'clock [June 5]," the newspaper said. "They then took up . . . quarters at the two hotels, where entertainment had been prepared for them. [At] 9 o'clock, Captain Butler was called on for a speech, and he responded in a clever manner [possibly using a double entendre], paying some compliments to the . . . ladies who were present, encouraging them on to duty."[66]

The troops formed in front of the Planter's Hotel about 10:30 A.M. the next morning. After speeches by Capt. A. J. Howard and Maj. George Boswell, venerable prior commanders of the outfit, whose words brought tears to the eyes of many of the women in the audience, Matthew stepped forward. "In these ranks, many of you have sweethearts, brothers and husbands," he said. "We go to the tented fields in the defense of our homes and firesides against the invasion of the hireling foe, whose only desire is for beauty and booty." After applause, he averred, "We will return as honored soldiers or fill a soldier's grave. It is ours to act and not to speak. You will hear from us. Farewell!"[67]

Wheeling his horse about, Matthew led his troop out of town and on to the Civil War. "A mingled sentiment of pride and grief pervaded the whole assemblage," an observer wrote, "as the Hussars filed off amid a weeping adieu of their many friends."[68]

CHAPTER 3

Early Days

THE HUSSARS TROTTED LEISURELY WHILE COVERING THE SIXTY PLUS MILES from Edgefield to the state capital. On June 12, 1861, six days after the ceremonies in the town square, the troopers finally rode into Camp Hampton, located three miles east of Columbia.[1] The extended journey was due in part to delays along the way to add to their roster (thirty more men joined during the trek) and by an excess of baggage and servants. Matthew, for example, had brought a number of trunks filled with clothing and a slave (Edmund) with him.[2]

On June 14, 1861, Matthew's company formally enlisted in the Confederate service for one year. As captain, Butler received a salary of $140 per month. His horse, insured by the government, was valued at $240. And he was given credit for personally supplying $30 worth of equipment, such as his saddle.[3]

Matthew's eighty-man troop included himself as captain and three lieutenants (J. J. Bunch, J. J. Crafton, and J. M. Lanham), five sergeants (Thomas W. Glover, J. M. Wise, F. L. Butler, a distant relative of Matthew's, A. J. Anderson, and P. M. Butler, Matthew's cousin), five corporals (J. B. Ryan, F. B. Walker, W. A. Glover, N. L. Griffin, and J. L. Nicholson), a farrier (Alex Rutherford), a bugler (M. A. Markert), a chaplain (J. Wesley Barr), and sixty-three privates. Among the latter were three more relatives of Matthew's: his two cousins, Andrew and Edward, and another remote kin, Harrison Butler.[4]

The Hussars were one of four cavalry units included in Hampton's Legion. The other three were the Congaree Mounted Rifles under Capt. John Meigher, a second Columbia outfit led by Capt. James P. McFie, and the troopers captained by Thomas Taylor.[5] Matthew's band was clearly the best of the lot. "They rode with military primness," a witness related, "and were mounted on steeds of delicately shaped limbs, with glistening eyes and full of fire and motion."[6]

The Hampton Legion's six infantry companies were built around a first-class element from Charleston, the Washington Light Infantry, captained by B. J. Johnson. Because of his experience, he was promoted to lieutenant colonel, Hampton's second-in-command; his men were given to James Conner.[7]

The artillery battery selected Stephen D. Lee, an 1854 graduate from West Point and an experienced cannoneer, to be their captain. He was serving as the quartermaster for Gen. Pierre G. T. Beauregard in Charleston at that time, but had expressed his interest in the Legion. "I would like to get into active service," he related to influential friends.[8] Hampton approved Lee's nomination, but Beauregard would not release the young officer, the only one familiar with the Creole's accounts. This post was held open until late July, when after paying off Beauregard's vendors, Lee was finally allowed to join the Legion.

Camp Hampton was a lovely spot with "beautiful oaks, a good spring, and spacious . . . parade grounds."[9] Both officers and privates ate from a common mess. Bread was supplied by a Columbia bakery, and black cooks stewed fresh beef in huge kettles.

Although the troopers supplied their own horses, their weapons were furnished by Hampton, who paid for their swords from his own pocket. Each received a "two-edged blade that was forty inches long . . . weighing about six pounds. Plain of hilt and guard, sharpened on both edges, and finished with a loop for forefinger to give a firm grip, it was a weapon for a giant."[10] Hampton plied his saber at will in battles, but Butler often left his in camp. He would earn a "reputation for carrying no weapon in battle, but [leading] his men with only a silver mounted riding whip in hand."[11]

Hampton also provided uniforms, "rich gray with gilded buttons and braid."[12] Dressed in a snug jacket with a jaunty kepi perched on his dark head, Matthew looked no doubt like the perfect cavalier.

Each day was spent in drilling the men, who trained as a unit, learning to act as one under battle conditions. And in the evening, the entire camp took part in a dress parade. "Fine ladies and gentlemen from the city," a participant recalled, "came out to see us."[13]

After two weeks of such duty, the Legion was called to Richmond. The Rebels had taken up a position below Washington, D.C., and the Federals were expected to challenge them at any time. Beauregard had come north to take command, and he was pleading for reinforcements. Hampton broke his camp on June 28, bringing his force by train to the Confederate capital.

A reporter described the departure of Butler's cavalry:

> [They] came bounding through the town as if the horses were
> inspired by the summons to Virginia, so ardently desired by

their masters. And even the [officer's] servants . . . seemed to feel that they were about reaching the destination so devotedly wished.

They are a gallant looking band. I never saw a brighter or braver-looking set. [After] the Governor [Butler's father-in-law] addressed a few words . . . the train moved off. Cheers and shouts were heard until lost in the distance.[14]

The bulk of Hampton's Legion reached their new bivouac, an area called "Rocketts," located on the edge of Richmond at the foot of Main Street near the tracks of the York River Railroad, by July 1. The capital opened its arms to the troops, especially to the tall, handsome, aristocratic Matthew Butler. "[Hampton's Legion] was recognized as the elite of the regiments," Edward Pollard related, "and obtained the best of the social honors that were then . . . so profusely distributed among military men."[15] Most evenings, Matthew probably went to a soiree to meet pretty girls wearing low-cut gowns. When they smiled adoringly, he may have rued that he was a married man and the father of two babies. Maybe the temptation to take advantage of his situation was too strong to resist.

Although life in Richmond was courtly, the Legion camp existence was primitive. One noncommissioned officer published a complaint in the local paper in which he grumbled about the cold, poor food, and what he considered an infringement on his freedom of speech.[16]

The misery did not last long. On July 10, Matthew's troopers galloped north to Ashland to attend cavalry school, run by former officers of the Regular army. "We [sleep in] a long shed latticed on all sides," Butler wrote in a letter to Maria, "something that we have not been accustomed to for some time."[17]

On July 17, the Legion's infantry, still in training outside of Richmond, received orders from Robert E. Lee (the president's military adviser) to break camp and "proceed . . . to Manassas Junction, and join the Army of the Potomac under Brigadier General Beauregard."[18] Other troops summoned forward included the men led by Gen. Joseph E. Johnston, who were stationed in the Shenandoah Valley. The reason for the concentration was because a Yankee army of 37,000 under Gen. Irwin McDowell had come out of Washington to probe the Rebel line arrayed along Bull Run.

Early in the morning of July 19, while still in camp, the Legion infantrymen were roused by the cries of newsboys. "Latest news!" they piped as they hawked their papers. "Big battle at Manassas!"[19] The Union had mounted a weak attack on Beauregard at Blackburn's Ford the previous day. The Rebels had repelled the Yankee thrust, but the need for Hampton at the front had become dire. He moved swiftly. His men rushed to pack

Joseph Eggleston Johnston. COURTESY
PHOTOGRAPHIC HISTORY OF THE CIVIL WAR

their equipment, and by 10:00 P.M., they were boarding trains headed for Manassas. Butler and the cavalry remained at Ashland.

Hampton and the infantry reached Manassas on July 21, in time to participate in the first major battle of the Civil War. McDowell tried to flank the Rebels, but the Confederates, after an all-day, exhausting fight, held fast and then sent the Federals reeling back to Washington. Hampton and his troops were in the thick of the fray. They suffered 121 casualties (including the death of Lt. Col. B. J. Johnson), 20 percent of their force.[20]

Matthew Butler and his troopers did not reach Manassas until the night of July 26. "An awful sight," he wrote in a letter to Maria. "There are still many of the Federalist lying [unburied] upon the field . . . in a state of the most repulsive putrifacation . . . their faces perfectly black. I presume they are of such a class that nobody cares whether they are interned or not."[21]

Butler also learned that Hampton has reorganized the Legion. J. B. Griffin had replaced Johnson, who died in the battle, as second in command; James Conner was assigned responsibility for all six of the infantry companies; Stephen Lee still led the artillery battery; and Matthew now headed the four cavalry companies.[22] He was promoted to major and his salary was raised to $162 per month.[23]

With the Federals cowering in Washington, Joe Johnston took over command from Beauregard. A native of Virginia, he graduated from West Point in 1829, fought and gained brevet promotions in both the Seminole and Mexican Wars, spent time as a topographical engineer, then rose through the ranks to become quartermaster general of the U.S. Army in 1860. When Virginia seceded, he resigned his post to join the Confederacy.[24]

Johnston set up a defensive line, ranging almost fifty miles from the mouth of the Occoquan River to Leesburg. The army headquarters were at Fairfax Court House; the cavalry, first a regiment, then a brigade under Jeb Stuart, occupied outposts close to the Federal capital, where they could see and report the enemy's activities.[25] Butler's horsemen were located along Broad Run, close to Manassas Junction. On August 15, they changed camp to Bacon Race Church.[26]

While settling into his new quarters, Matthew received a disturbing letter from Maria. She had decided that living at home was too tiresome, so she had moved to Greenville to stay in a boardinghouse. His brother, Pierce Butler, would manage the plantation during her absence. Adding to her expense, Maria had taken his favorite team of horses with her. The high cost was a shock to Butler. "I want you to be comfortable," he grumbled, "but . . . in these uncertain [times], it behooves us all to economize, economize!"[27]

A few nights later, as Butler was sleeping in his tent, he was wakened by a shout. "Captain, Captain!" a picket was yelling, "The enemy is out!"

Butler leaped from his cot, called for Edmund his servant to bring his horse, and was soon mounted and ready for action. "The moon was shining," Butler recalled, "and as I looked down the streets of tents, I saw groups . . . standing together . . . not knowing what to make of it." They awaited his orders. He told them to mount. "Such scampering you never saw," he told Maria, "I could not refrain a hearty laugh at the scene, one hunting his bridle, another his saddle, and a third pulling at [his] wet boots, but all [were] ready in an astonishingly short time."

The "assault" proved to be just a single spy, who when challenged by a sentinel, fled the area. "I sent patrols on every road approaching the camp," Butler wrote, "but all returned [to] report . . . quiet. We were all disappointed that the 'enemy was not out,' but it will do the men good as they will now [keep] . . . bridles, saddles, and arms where they can put their hands on them."[28]

Matthew also worked hard to indoctrinate discipline in his command, a difficult task given the elite upbringing for many of his troops. Those with black servants at hand felt it beneath them to dig ditches. Butler showed no favoritism in punishing those refusing his orders. He sent his cousin, Sgt. Pierce Butler, to the guardhouse on a number of occasions. "He has become very respectful and correct in his deportment," Matthew would later note.[29]

Throughout the fall, the army practiced drill. Butler kept busy running his troopers through their paces, but from time to time, he rode forward to help Stuart in reconnoitering the Union positions in front of Washington.

CONFEDERATE LINE
NORTHERN VIRGINIA
JULY 1861–MARCH 1862

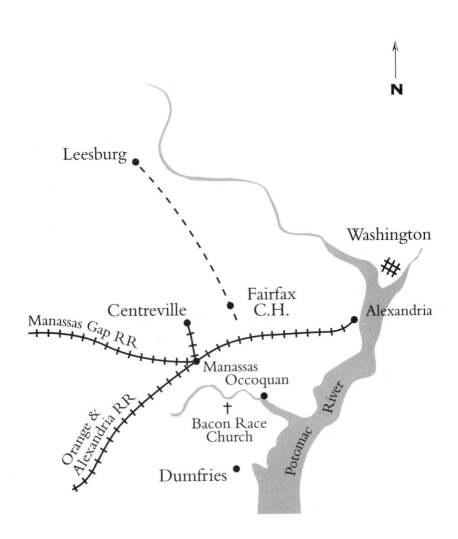

On one such sally in September, he and his men routed enemy pickets from two different posts, then rode almost to Alexandria. They captured four horses, three prisoners, two wagons, eight muskets, and camp equipment during the raid. "After this day's sharp work," a participant gloated, "[we were back] in camp at Bacon's Race Church . . . the next morning . . . [by] eleven o'clock."[30]

On September 22, Butler moved to Dumfries, and three weeks later, he set up his winter quarters near the mouth of the Occoquan River. When told that spies were operating in the area, Matthew decided to look for them. "I took a small boat and some men and [rowed] to Colchester on the opposite of Occoquan Bay," he noted. "We surrounded [a] house and . . . I went in and represented myself as a Lincolnite . . . the inmates were delighted to see [me]. . . . Upon my inquiring who were the best and most reliable Republicans in the neighborhood, they gave us a list. . . . We arrested one of the parties they had informed upon and returned to Occoquan at 3 o'clock in the morning."[31]

On another foray Butler and his troopers failed to encounter any Federals, but did have a profitable venture. On a cold, rainy night, they galloped east toward the lower Potomac area. When it grew dark, Pvt. John Gaston, who had a habit of wandering away from the command, left the column and rode into the small village of Dumfries. He spotted and confiscated a team of horses hitched to a covered wagon. He then started back for the regiment with his unknown spoils.

When Gaston finally caught up with the rest of the column, Butler took no interest in his prize. "Cut the horses' throats and burn the wagon," he snapped. His errant trooper protested.

"[Why?]" Butler demanded. "What's it loaded with?"

"I don't know."

A hasty search uncovered two barrels of whiskey. "You never saw such a scramble," Gaston recalled fondly. "Butler [filled] two bottles [for himself]. [And soon] the command wanted to go back and fight Sickles' [whole] division."

Second, but not especially sober, thought prevailed, and the troop headed back toward camp. Not trusting the whiskey team to anyone else, Matthew insisted on driving it himself. He only managed a few dozen yards before he turned the wagon over and toppled into the mud. He shook the slime from his hands, tried to brush his now soiled uniform, and called out for Gaston. "Take the damn horses and drive them," he said groggily, "I want nothing more to do with them."[32]

Although Butler had a fleeting thought of engaging the Yankees, they had no interest in offering battle. They were fully occupied with drilling,

George B. McClellan. COURTESY LIBRARY OF CONGRESS

learning to be soldiers under their new commander, Gen. George B. Mc-Clellan.

The president had summoned McClellan to Washington the day after the Confederates had routed the Union at Manassas. Lincoln wanted a winner in command, and the West Point graduate, hero of the Mexican War, and later railroad executive, had led the Ohio volunteers in driving the Rebels from western Virginia. His was the most significant Federal victory up to that time.[33]

McClellan's first task was to take charge of the force that had fled the field at Manassas. But when Congress approved thousands of additional troops to coerce the Southern states back into the Union, he assumed responsibility for these volunteers, too. He was an extraordinary administrator, and under his guidance, the once raw recruits who filled the Army of the Potomac were rapidly becoming superb soldiers.[34]

But the Yankees remained within their camps. The only attack that Butler's troopers faced was typhoid fever, which raged from late summer through January 1862. Matthew, too, came down with "camp fever," as it was called. "He will be sick a good while," James B. Griffin predicted in a note to his wife, but Butler quickly recovered.[35] The best description for the times came from Hampton. "There is nothing to tell you," he wrote his wife, "except we are quiet."[36]

With winter at hand and all thought of battle gone, Butler asked for and received permission to go home to South Carolina in early December. His visit, however, was marred by arguments. Prior to his gallop to Edgefield, Matthew had complained frequently about Maria's lack of writing letters. "I have been surprised and disappointed," he grumbled in his September 16 note, "that I have not heard from you for so long a time."[37] This was probably the issue that led to the exchange of insults that Matthew continued after his return to duty. "While I overlook and forgive your impatient irritability," he related, "it is but fair that you should make some allowances for my shortcomings."[38] Although the couple grew somewhat estranged during his stay, they did not spend all the time fighting. Maria became pregnant before Matthew rode back to Virginia.

Shortly after returning to camp, Butler started out on a raid into Federal territory. He shared command with James Conner, leading 200 infantrymen, who trudged behind Matthew's 150 riders. The force headed north, crossed the Occoquan River, and then divided into two wings: the foot soldiers heading northeast, the cavalry trotting to the northwest. They planned to converge on a Union bivouac lying ahead.

Butler was not happy to be serving with Conner. There was no personal animosity; he simply felt that since the infantryman had already seen battle at First Manassas, he had seniority. The command and commendations, if the two forces acted as one, would go to his rival. "He thought to make a bold stroke," Conner later said, "act independently, and get all the credit for the cavalry."[39]

So instead of swerving to the right as planned, Butler continued northward, hoping to find and fight the Yankees on his own. He galloped on until it became obvious he had not only ridden past the enemy's camp but also too far to return to Conner before sunset. He could not risk roaming through the countryside in the dark, so Butler and his now weary men spent a cold night deep behind the Federal line.

Come morning, Butler retraced his steps, and about one o'clock that afternoon, finally found Conner. The infantryman had his troops concealed in a woods, located just short of the Union camp. He proposed that he and Matthew lead the cavalry in a timid charge, pretend to be routed, and retire past the dense forest where his foot soldiers lay in ambush. They would blast away at any enemy pursuers. Butler agreed to the plan.

The two officers rode at the head of the cavalry ranks. "A picket fired on us [from] only about forty yards," Conner related. "Butler's horse slipped and fell, and bruised him so badly . . . he could not remount."[40]

Conner took over the charge, but the Yankees fell back in an obvious attempt to draw the Rebels into an ambush. "I refused to follow," Conner wrote in his report. "The thing was quickly done and quickly over."[41] The Confederate force returned to camp, where Butler nursed his battered body and probably thought better of his seeking glory through independent action.

With spring still in the distance, pressure mounted on McClellan to take the offense. Congressmen grumbled because of his continuing inactivity; "On to Richmond!" newspapers blared; and Lincoln even issued orders to McClellan that he must "seize and occupy Manassas Junction on or before February 22, 1862."[42] McClellan refused to budge.

Other Union generals, however, were not as reticent as the leader of the Army of the Potomac. On February 6, 1862, Ulysses S. Grant captured Fort Henry on the Tennessee River, and ten days later, he took Fort Donelson, a bastion on the Cumberland River.[43] His triumphs in Tennessee opened waterways into the deep South, which the Federals soon exploited. Nashville surrendered on February 25. Ambrose E. Burnside led the expedition that seized Roanoke Island off the North Carolina coast on February 8.[44] And on March 8, Yankees under Samuel R. Curtis defeated Earl Van Dorn and the Rebels in battle at Pea Ridge, Arkansas.[45]

Johnston recognized that these Federal conquests would soon shame McClellan into moving against Richmond, and as he studied his adversary's alternatives, he concluded that two were available: a direct confrontation over land to assault the Confederate capital from the north; or a flanking movement by sea, proceeding toward the city from the east, up the peninsula between the York and James Rivers. "I determined to move to . . . the south bank of the Rappahannock," he related in his memoirs, "[where] we should be better able to resist the Federal army advancing by Manassas . . . as well as to unite with any Confederate force that might be sent to oppose him should he move by . . . Fort Monroe."[46]

The retrograde began on March 9. The roads were bad and few wagons were available, so Hampton found that much of the equipment and individual belongings, amassed during the months, had to be destroyed. He could not just leave things for the enemy to acquire. "The loss of public property was remarkably small," he wrote, "but my greatest regret is that I cannot say the same as to private property."[47] Matthew's troopers lost most of their trunks, loaded with clothing and personal items, in the retreat to the Rappahannock. Butler took advantage of the movement to slip home for a fast visit with Maria.[48] Their relationship remained icy.

McClellan opted for the Peninsula Campaign, but before he could board his men on ships for the trek south, the Confederates unveiled an innovation that promised to upset his strategy. They seized the Union warship, *Merrimack,* covered her with iron plates, and called her *Virginia.* She

AREA OF
LOWER PENINSULA CAMPAIGN
APRIL–MAY 1862

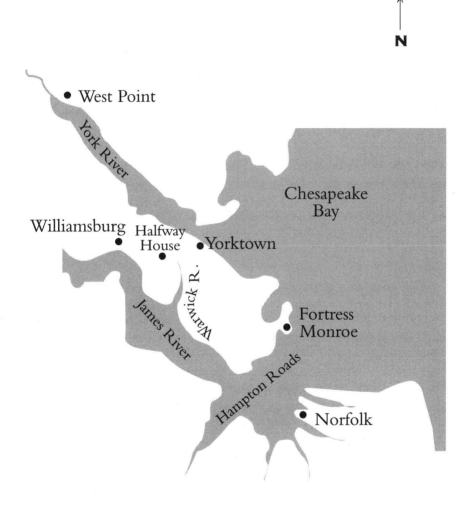

steamed out of her base at Norfolk on March 8 to assault the enemy fleet in Hampton Roads. The Federals' wooden ships were no match for the armored Rebel vessel. It seemed nothing could stop the *Virginia* from sailing through Chesapeake Bay, then up the Potomac River to shell Washington. And moving troops by sea past this goliath would be impossible.

On March 9, however, the same day that Johnston withdrew from Manassas, the Union unveiled the *Monitor,* a bantam ironclad armed with twin guns mounted on a revolving turret. She fought the *Virginia* in Hampton Roads, and in a clamorous two-hour duel, the two fired shell after shell at the other. The missiles only bounced off the iron plates attached to the sides of each ship, and the battle ended in a stalemate.[49] But with the *Monitor* now serving as a buffer against the *Virginia,* the sea-lane to Richmond opened for McClellan, and he started to sail south on March 17.

McClellan arrived at Fortress Monroe on April 2, and although he had only half his force, 66,700 men, at hand, he displayed unusual vigor by ordering an immediate advance up the Peninsula. He hoped to use the York River as his supply channel, but first he had to take Yorktown, whose forts protected the stream. McClellan sent one corps under Samuel P. Heintzelman directly toward the village. Their task was to hold John B. Magruder and his 12,000 troops in place while a second corps, led by Erasmus D. Keyes, took a parallel path toward Halfway House in the Confederate rear. Upon reaching their destination, they would flank the Rebels ensconced in Yorktown and force their surrender.[50]

McClellan assumed that Magruder had concentrated all of his men behind the Yorktown forts, but soon learned that the Rebels were spread along the Warwick River, a marshy stream wandering from below Yorktown to the James River, the entire twelve-mile width of the peninsula. Their position was further strengthened by dams that Magruder had erected to flood the five available fords across the water. The Confederate commander had placed artillery at these points, and as Keyes approached, he was met by a barrage of fire.[51]

With a six-to-one-man advantage, McClellan should have easily punched through the Rebels' weak front. But Magruder had a surprise for him. He paraded his few troops back and forth in front of the enemy, thereby creating the impression that the Confederates had large numbers at hand. "It was a wonderful thing," Mary Chesnut wrote, "how he played his ten thousand before McClellan like fireflies and utterly deluded him."[52]

Assuming that his flank assault was stymied, McClellan changed his strategy. He set out to lay siege to the village.

When McClellan had landed at Fortress Monroe, Richmond was unsure of his intentions. He was probably planning to march up the Peninsula, but he could have been only stopping before proceeding farther south to join Burnside at Roanoke Island. They had to wait to ascertain his objectives before reacting. But when McClellan moved on Yorktown, there were no longer any questions about his aims. "Enemy advancing in force," Lee wrote to Johnston on April 4, 1861, "Troops . . . from your line must immediately be [sent] to this place."[53]

Johnston reacted quickly. The divisions led by Daniel H. Hill and William H. C. Whiting boarded trains heading for the peninsula.[54] The Hampton Legion and Butler's cavalry were part of the latter's force. On April 9, the first of these reinforcements, Jubal Early's brigade, arrived at the front. Matthew and his troopers rode up a few days later.

As they filed into position to face the Federals under McClellan, Butler no doubt heard about the just-ended battle at Shiloh, Tennessee.[55] The South had not only been routed but also had suffered massive casualties, including the loss of their leader, Albert Sidney Johnston. The dead, wounded, and missing total for both adversaries exceeded 24,000, over 20 percent of the numbers engaged. Matthew must have been sobered by the numbing realization that the war would be bloody, and that before it ended, he and many of his friends might die.

CHAPTER 4

The Peninsula Campaign

WHILE THE CONFEDERATES RUSHED SOUTH TO SHORE UP THE DEFENSE OF Yorktown, McClellan slowly carried out his siege of the historic site. He brought up over 100 heavy artillery pieces, built breastworks for these weapons, and dug a network of trenches to provide coverage for his troops as they inched forward toward the Southern works protecting the front.[1] The corps led by Gens. Edwin V. Sumner, William B. Franklin, and Fitz-John Porter had all landed at Fortress Monroe and come forward, giving McClellan about 110,000 men at hand.[2]

Johnston, who had taken over command of the defense of Yorktown from Magruder, had 60,000 soldiers in place. James Longstreet and G. W. Smith had brought their divisions from the Rappahannock to the Richmond area. Richard S. Ewell, in charge of Johnston's reserve division, had been sent into the Shenandoah Valley to reinforce Thomas J. "Stonewall" Jackson in his confrontation with the enemy forces led by Nathaniel P. Banks.[3]

On April 14 Johnston went to Richmond for a meeting with President Davis and his advisors to discuss their plans for dealing with McClellan. Johnston urged that they leave their position at Yorktown and concentrate all available men near the capital for a winner-take-all fight with the enemy. Robert E. Lee disagreed. He argued that abandoning Yorktown would also mean giving up both Norfolk and the *Virginia*. He also noted that the Confederacy needed more time to build up their forces. Holding Yorktown for as long as possible was essential. The debate lasted for fourteen hours, and in the end, Davis stood by Lee. Johnston must fight McClellan at Yorktown. Although he appeared to accept the president's decree, Johnston had no intention of ever obeying the order. "Events on the Peninsula," he related in his memoirs, "would soon compel the . . . government to adopt my method of opposing the Federal army."[4] In other words, as soon as possible, he would withdraw from the confrontation.

By May 3 McClellan was finally positioned to launch his attack. And on that same day, Johnston started to withdraw toward Williamsburg. G. W. Smith was in charge of the force leaving Yorktown; Longstreet led his division along the James River. To cover their movement, Johnston ordered his cannons to open a desultory fire upon the entrenched Yankees and to keep on shelling until 9:00 P.M. The army would use this interlude to assemble. When they heard their artillery stop their bombardment, this was their signal to march.[5]

Along the Yorktown front, D. H. Hill's brigades would be the first to go, followed by Whiting's men, then the Hampton Legion. The gunners, of course, would be the last to leave, and Matthew Butler's cavalry was assigned as their escort.

Whiting's brigade commanders and their principal aides (including Butler) waited north of Yorktown that night. The weather was cool, so they built a bonfire to keep warm. To the south, the sound of cannons was clearly heard. Soon it was 9:00 P.M., but the guns continued to roar. At midnight, General H. C. Whiting asked Butler to take some men back to Yorktown to find out why the artillery was still firing.[6]

"There was not a sound, not a light . . . on the principal street," Butler related. "The stillness and darkness of the place was dismal, oppressive, aggravated and intensified by the contrast with the scene . . . [at] sunset, when all was bustle and haste."[7]

"As I rode along the street," he went on, "a small boy . . . yelled out to me at the top of his voice, 'Look out, sir, a torpedo has been planted in front of you.' I looked down and, sure enough, just in front of me I discovered the fresh earth. . . . My horse's foot could not have missed it [by more than] twelve inches." The Southerners had buried land mines through the area to harass the enemy when they took over Yorktown. "I gave it a wide berth afterwards," Butler said, "and required no further admonitions [about] fresh earth."[8]

Butler soon found that the artillery had ceased firing at 9:00 P.M., and moved out as scheduled. The salvos he had heard came from Union gunboats on the river, which were blasting away at the empty Confederate bastions below the town.

Leading his troops northward to report his findings to Whiting (and watching out for torpedoes), Matthew had barely left town when a challenge cried out of darkness.

"Who goes there?" an ominous voice rumbled.

Butler clapped hands three times, then waited for the answering three whistles—the password response for the night. Instead, he heard again the curt words, "Who goes there?"

"A friend with the countersign," he bellowed, adding language not "as gentle as would be used in the boudoir of a fair lady."[9]

As Butler carefully advanced toward his challenger, he heard the "click" of a carbine. Before the sentry could fire, he was at his side, and they recognized each other as fellow Confederates. The soldier was a vedette with the 10th Virginia Cavalry, who were destroying matériel stored along the river. Butler passed on, but he had ridden no more than several hundred yards when a thundering explosion, followed by a burst of musketry, exploded to his rear. Thinking that an enemy force was assaulting the comrades he had just left, Butler wheeled his squad about and galloped back to join the fray. He found, however, no fighting. One of the Virginia troopers had entered a warehouse crammed with ammunition and accidentally triggered an "infernal machine" (torpedo), set to catch the enemy. He had blown himself and the building's contents to bits. "It went off in volleys," Butler related, "and waked the echoes for miles."[10]

Butler and his force were challenged by Rebel sentries twice more before they finally reached Whiting's camp to report their findings. Dawn was just now breaking and in the dim light, Matthew saw all three Confederate brigades posted for battle. They, too, had heard the explosion and assumed that the Yankees were advancing. When apprised of the true situation, Whiting quickly formed his infantry into columns and started for Williamsburg. Butler and his cavalrymen returned toward Yorktown to watch the enemy and, if necessary, head off any attempts to disrupt Whiting's retreat.[11]

When he reached the hills overlooking the town, Butler noted that the village was filled with Yankees, drawn to the scene by the inadvertent explosion. But although McClellan had learned of the Confederate withdrawal from Yorktown just hours after it started, he was content to let the Rebels go. And when Butler deduced there would be no immediate pursuit, he turned his men around and trotted to rejoin the army.

"We moved leisurely the entire day," Butler remembered, "frequently halting for long intervals."[12] Late that afternoon, May 4, he reached Williamsburg and pitched his camp behind Fort Magruder, a bastion located about two miles east of the village and in advance of the main Rebel line, which lay behind a meandering creek. The brigade led by Lafayette McLaws occupied the bulwark. The weather was chilly, and a light drizzle was falling.

"We had scarcely dismounted," Butler recalled, "when a messenger came at full speed, saying Gen. Johnston wanted the cavalry."[13] Matthew hurriedly mounted his troopers and rushed to the front. He reported to Johnston, who then sent him forward to McLaws. The infantry leader pointed to four squadrons of Yankee horsemen drawn up to the north and

WILLIAMSBURG FRONT

MAY 1862

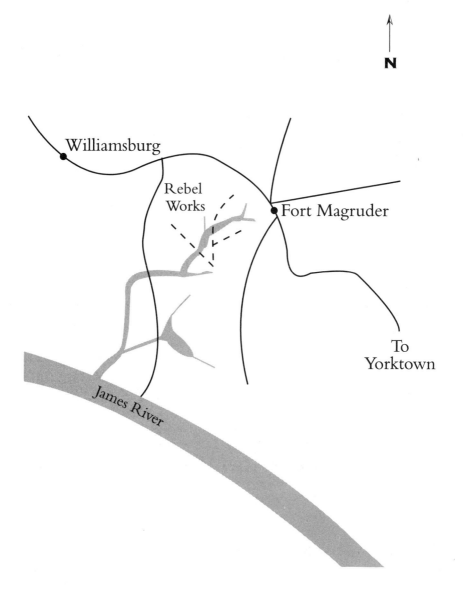

N

Williamsburg

Rebel
Works

Fort Magruder

To
Yorktown

James River

said, "I want you to drive that cavalry away." Butler, joined by horsemen under J. Lucius Davis and Williams C. Wickham, rode ahead.

"We made at them," Butler stated, "put them to flight, and drove them pell mell across a [swampy] ravine. . . . Many of their horses [floundered] in the mud. . . . [We] captured seventeen men and horses." Pursuing the Federals up the opposite slope, Matthew came face to face with the Yankees' reserves. Although he would later acknowledge, "It was our time to get back," he rashly charged this superior number, too. "At one time," he related, "we were mixed up with the [Yankees], and it was one of the very few occasions during the war . . . I ever saw an opportunity to use the sabre."[14] And wield it he did! Pvt. John Gaston testified that Butler "cut a man off his horse."[15]

With the enemy routed, Butler returned to the plaudits of friendly lines. "Much praise must be given," McLaws said in his official report, "[to Matthew and his men] for their inspiring hand-to-hand encounter with the cavalry of the enemy. Their gallantry was rewarded . . . by enthusiastic cheers of those who saw the charge."[16] Jeb Stuart gloated over the "signal success" of his horsemen, and then added, "emulated by . . . the Hampton Legion under Major Butler."[17] Even General Johnston had a kind word. In his congratulatory message to the troops, he lauded the "manner in which . . . Major Butler of Hampton's Legion . . . repulsed the Federal advance guard."[18]

Matthew had finally "seen the elephant," and performed heroically in front of the whole army. He became that day a man marked for future glory.

That glory, however, would have to wait since Johnston had no intention of opposing McClellan east of Williamsburg. He was determined to follow his plan to retreat to Richmond, concentrate his forces, and confront the Yankees there. And since Davis and Lee were opposed to this strategy, Johnston opted not to send word to them that he was on his way to the capital.[19]

That night a heavy rain started, and it was still pouring in the morning of May 5. The muddy roads pitifully slowed the progress of the Confederate retreat out of Williamsburg. "March or wade two minutes," E. Porter Alexander described their trek, "and [then] halt ten or longer."[20] And unlike the Yankees pursuing him, Johnston was encumbered by long, winding wagon trains carrying his supplies. If he did nothing to stop McClellan and his army, they might overtake him and force a battle. To avoid such a confrontation, Johnston sent ahead all of his divisions except the brigades under Longstreet. He was instructed to hold off the enemy to give Johnston some time to open space between it and himself.

Longstreet watched as the Federals approached his line from the south along the Yorktown Road. They advanced their skirmishers to develop his position, began to lob artillery shells toward him, and started to form the two divisions led by William F. "Baldy" Smith and Joseph Hooker into a battle formation. Longstreet decided that rather than await an enemy attack, he would take the initiative. He sent forward six brigades under Richard H. Anderson against Hooker's position. The Yankees were pushed backward, leaving a ten-gun battery in their wake. "We took their ammunition," a Rebel gloated, "and shot it back at them."[21] Longstreet's charge halted when Philip Kearny's division rushed up and stabilized the Union line.

Although the Rebels had stymied the enemy to the south, they soon found themselves threatened from the north. Smith had not participated in the battle, but he had sent a flanking brigade under Winfield Scott Hancock toward the unmanned bulwarks above the Confederate line. He filed into position about 3:00 P.M. Just as Hancock was ordered to retire (the Federals had accepted defeat in the battle), Jubal Early led his brigade in a foolhardy charge against the enemy's easily defended post. He suffered a bloody and needless repulse.[22]

Longstreet's success gave the Rebels the time Johnston needed to escape the enemy's pursuit, and he proceeded without obstruction on the road to Richmond. Matthew's men had not taken part in the battle of Williamsburg, but one of his troopers, Private Boggs, who was probably acting as a courier, had been killed. Late the next afternoon after the fray, Butler spotted a soldier riding his dead comrade's mount.

"Who are you?" he demanded.

"I am First Sergeant Y. J. Pope," came the answer, "of Company E., Third South Carolina Infantry, of Kershaw's Brigade."

"Where did you get that horse?"

"Colonel William Drayton Rutherford . . . captured him on the battlefield of Williamsburg, and knowing that on account of a spell of typhoid fever I was unable to walk a long distance, he turned the horse over to me [so] that I might keep up with my regiment."

"That horse belonged to one of my men . . . who was killed at the battle. . . . That horse could be sold and the money sent to his widow at her home in Greenville. . . . Keep him until tomorrow, when I will send for him."[23]

Pope surrendered the horse. Despite his youth, Butler's imposing presence exacted submission to his will. His men were no doubt thrilled by the regard that Matthew so often showed for them. His leadership qualities were inspiring.

The Confederates continued to retreat up the Peninsula. After his bloody reversal at Williamsburg, McClellan tried a different tactic to impede Johnston's withdrawal. On May 7 he landed Franklin's infantry division at the mouth of the York River. They had planned to rush south to intercept the Rebel rear, but G. W. Smith charged their line near Eltham's Landing, where he held them in place until the rest of Johnston's army had slipped past on their way back toward Richmond.[24] They reached the Chickahominy on May 9, where Johnston halted to assess his situation.

He stood above the river, a wide, languid stream more like a bog than a waterway, which ran southeast. Two bridges lay to his rear offering a means for further retreat. Both flanks were protected by mire. And reinforcements (Benjamin Huger's force of 10,000) were coming up from Norfolk. They had been isolated when Johnston gave up Yorktown, and he had ordered them to abandon the harbor with its extensive naval works. Their departure left the *Virginia* stranded without a port, and since the behemoth drew too much water to use the shallow James River and was too unstable to take to the open sea, the Rebels were left with no choice but to scuttle the formidable vessel. She sank on May 11.[25]

Johnston remained in place for six days. His infantry dug in, and Matthew's cavalry were most likely occupied with performing as couriers and reconnoitering the front, reporting on McClellan's slow but steady progress toward the Rebel position. Butler did, however, have some free time, and he spent much of it writing to Maria. Two themes dominated his thoughts: her lack of letters to him; and her shortcomings as a wife. "I was most grievously disappointed yesterday in not getting a letter from you," he said on May 14.[26] "It is now ten days since . . . your last letter," he groused on May 24.[27] And later he would complain, "My fourth letter and yet no response [from you]. I suppose I had as well despair of ever hearing from you again."[28]

Maria's reluctance to write was possibly the result of her being upset by frequent criticism from Matthew. He felt that she had been spoiled by her parents, and was unwilling to perform housework. "I have made many allowances, knowing as I do . . . the manner in which you have been raised," he complained in a May 11 note, "[but still] you do not manifest sufficient activity."[29] In a later letter, he chided Maria for having both a "tone of depression" and a "disinterest in the future."[30]

What Butler wanted most to hear from Maria, but seldom received, was news about Frank and Willie. Each of his many letters begged for details on his sons' daily lives, and he always ended with a plea for Maria to "kiss the darling boys for Papa."[31]

All the while McClellan continued to slowly advance on Richmond. He stopped momentarily to establish a supply base at White House along the Pamunkey River, a tributary of the York, then resumed inching forward. As the enemy approached Johnston's line on May 15, he retreated across the Chickahominy to take up a position in the entrenchments outside of the Confederate capital.[32]

"I think [Johnston] will fight [here]," McClellan said in a letter to his wife, "and if he is badly thrashed (as I trust he will be) . . . he will begin to cry *peccavi* . . . [meaning] he has enough of it."[33]

McClellan now prepared for his assault on the Confederate capital. He divided his army into two wings, one posted above the Chickahominy, the other below the stream, forming a north-south line fronting the Rebels. Missing was a force of 38,000 under Irvin McDowell—who led the Federal army at the battle of Bull Run—located fifty miles to the north at Fredericksburg. McClellan wanted the troops shipped to him by sea to strengthen his push from the east, but Lincoln insisted that McDowell move overland, keeping his men between the Rebels and Washington. He would swoop south and assault Johnston's left just as McClellan charged from the east.[43]

The Federal strategy was sound, but it did not account for Stonewall Jackson. Maneuvering northwest of Richmond in the Shenandoah Valley, he attacked the force under Banks at Winchester on May 25. The routed Yankees were sent reeling across the Potomac River.[35] Jackson's victory opened a path to Washington, and a panicked Lincoln recalled the men under McDowell to protect the Northern capital. This change in plans trapped McClellan. Anticipating McDowell's coming in from the north, he had extended his right to connect with these reinforcements. His line was now strung out, and his left flank (two corps led by Keyes and Heintzelman) was isolated from the rest of the army by the swollen waters of the Chickahominy River. Johnston reacted quickly to take advantage of the Union's vulnerability. He planned an attack on the enemy at Seven Pines.

Johnston's strategy was simple. On May 31 he would send his troops down three parallel paths toward the Federal position. Longstreet, in overall command, would follow the Nine Mile Road; D. H. Hill wold charge in the center along the Williamsburg Road; and Huger would attack below on the Charles City Road. Smith and Magruder would lie in reserve.[36] The cavalry would act as couriers and reconnoiter the front. Probably seeking to achieve optimum coordination between his troopers, Johnston also decided that all of the horse units, including Butler's, should report directly to Jeb Stuart.[37]

Clouds gathered the afternoon of May 30, and a heavy rain began to fall. The storm continued through the night, but by dawn, as the Rebels advanced, the downpour slackened. The troops moved out on schedule. Hill proceeded as planned down the Williamsburg Road, but Longstreet made a fatal mistake. Instead of marching down the Nine Mile Road, he swung south to take up a position behind Hill. This move blocked Huger, who waited hour after hour for the way to the Charles City Road to clear. Johnston's attack was supposed to open at 8:00 A.M., but by 1:00 P.M., neither Longstreet nor Huger was yet in position. Hill finally attacked on his own.[38]

BATTLE OF
SEVEN PINES

MAY 31–JUNE 1, 1862

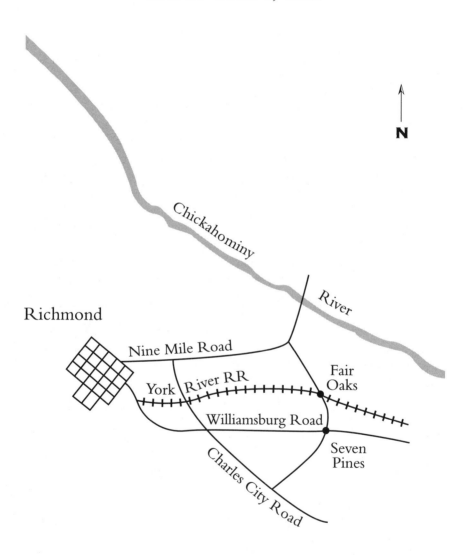

Despite a ferocious charge, Hill's troops were too few to penetrate the enemy line. Longstreet finally came up and reinforced Hill, but fed his regiments piecemeal toward the center of the Union position. The Yankees continued to hold their ground.[39] Late in the afternoon, Johnston rode ahead down the Nine Mile Road, where the South had finally charged the Federals' right flank at Fair Oaks, to watch the battle. Just as he reached the front, a bullet ripped into his right shoulder. "A few moments after," Johnston recalled with understatement, "[I] was unhorsed by a heavy fragment of shell which struck my breast."[40] Bleeding and gasping for breath because of several broken ribs, he was carried to the rear.

G. W. Smith took command of the army. He continued to fight the next morning, but by now, McClellan had managed to bring reinforcements, first Sumner's corps, then the troops under Franklin, south over the Chickahominy. The fray ended in a stalemate.[41]

Butler's cavalry was not assigned a role in the battle, but on the afternoon of May 31, his troops (probably on the Rebel flank) were approached by a Union force. The infantry fell back, leaving only Butler to face the Federals. "Then, Palmetto boys," he cried, "we will do it ourselves."[42] And he led the charge that routed the Yankees. This tale of his cool valor soon found its way back to Richmond, where ladies repeated it over and over with excited admiration.

The day after the battle of Seven Pines, Robert E. Lee took over command of the forces defending Richmond. The son of Revolutionary War hero "Light-Horse" Harry Lee, he graduated from West Point in 1829, then married Mary Anne Randolph Custis, step-granddaughter of George Washington. He was given three brevets for gallantry in the Mexican War. After years as a brilliant engineer, he was designated superintendent of West Point in 1852. Just prior to the Civil War, Lee had been a lieutenant colonel with the U.S. 2nd Cavalry. He was the preeminent officer in the army, which led Winfield Scott to offer him command of the Union ground forces. Lee, however, turned to the South and his native state, Virginia.[43]

Lee quickly saw that by strengthening his left against the Confederates' recent onslaught, bringing the corps under Sumner and Franklin below the Chickahominy River, McClellan had weakened his northern flank. This was particularly significant since the Federal supply base was located at White House, behind and above the Yankee line. If Lee could drive a wedge between McClellan and his provisions, his adversary could not sustain his siege and would be forced to quit the campaign against Richmond.[44]

Before taking this decisive step, however, Lee knew he had to be sure of the disposition of the Federal forces. He called Jeb Stuart to his headquarters and asked him to make a reconnaissance of the enemy position.

Robert E. Lee. COURTESY LIBRARY OF CONGRESS

Stuart, now leading all of the cavalry, including Butler's command, hand-picked 1,200 horsemen, most from Virginia, for the ride. He headed north on June 12, leaving Butler and his men in camp.[45]

Stuart galloped in a wide circle completely around the Federal army. Upon his return to Richmond on June 15, Jeb reported that the enemy's right was "in the air" and vulnerable to attack. Lee made his plans. He would bring Jackson, who earlier that month had routed the Federals confronting him in the Shenandoah Valley, John C. Frémont at Cross Keys, then James Shields at Port Republic,[46] to the front to join in a grand assault on McClellan. The main army would charge from the west; Stonewall's troops would come down from the north to pounce on the Union's open flank.

Lee opened his campaign on June 26. The men under Ambrose Powell Hill attacked Fitz-John Porter's isolated corps at Mechanicsville. Jackson, however, was late, and without his expected help from the north, Hill was unable to shatter Porter's line. The Union commander retreated that night to a stronger position at Gaines' Mill. The battle was renewed the next day,

Gen. James Earl Brown Stuart. COURTESY LIBRARY OF CONGRESS

and this time, Jackson was there to assist in the bitter fighting that drove Porter south over the Chickahominy. McClellan's supply line was severed, and the Union commander was forced to retire for the James River, where he planned to establish a new base of operations.[47]

Lee pursued the Yankees, hoping to find them in column where he could devastate their army. The adversaries fought June 29 near Savage's Station, June 30 at Frayser's Farm, and July 1 at Malvern Hill. In this last battle, Butler's cousin, Edward, was killed. Each of the confrontations was indecisive, however, and the Union eluded Lee's trap. When they reached Harrison's Landing on the James River, the Federals found their gunboats in place, protecting against any further harrying.[48] Lee's offensive saved Richmond, but the enemy had survived to fight again.

The stalemate lasted for weeks. The cavalry, still reporting to Stuart, spent its time either picketing the front east of the capital or training on the open fields near Hanover Court House, a few miles above Richmond. At the latter location, the horsemen often paraded in review for admiring ladies, most of whom remained for the evening for the inevitable party that followed at Jeb's headquarters.[49] The men confiscated chairs and sofas from a nearby home and arranged them into a great circle under a tent fly. The women drank cold milk and ate gingersnaps; the officers sipped juleps. After a night of "animated talk and patriotic songs," everyone agreed that camp life [with the cavalry] was no so bad after all."[50] Given his estrangement from Maria, Butler no doubt attended and enjoyed many of these soirees.

During this interim, Lee began to reorganize his force, and his first step was the consolidation of his cavalry. He promoted Stuart on July 28 to division command of all the horsemen. The scattered units were formed into two brigades—one led by Fitzhugh Lee, the second by Wade Hampton.[51] A few days later, a third brigade, troopers serving in the Shenandoah Valley under Beverly Robertson, were added to Stuart's charge, giving him control over 15,000 men.[52]

After graduating from West Point in 1854, Stuart spent most of his service time with the cavalry in Kansas. He was in Virginia in 1859 when John Brown descended upon Harpers Ferry, and he helped Lee capture, then hang the abolitionist devotee. He fought well at First Manassas, for which he received a general's star. Jeb was a serious soldier, but he was also a "ladies' man," and his partying would soon become the envy of all the army.[53]

Each brigade leader was responsible for organizing his force into regiments, and Hampton nominated Butler for chief of the South Carolina Cavalry. A recommendation by the brigade commander was generally accepted, but Lee was reluctant to accept Matthew's advancement. "I have some doubts as to the propriety of promoting . . . Butler," Lee wrote to President Davis, "for reasons known to his Excellency."[54] Butler had proved himself in battle, so Lee's objection, which was not recorded, must have been personal in nature. Youth may have been a factor, or perhaps Lee was peeved with Matthew's participation in Stuart's soirees or similar affairs in the capital. "There were gay parties every night," according to Alfred Bill, "with music, dancing and wine."[55] Butler must have taken advantage of such opportunities for fun.

Hampton, however, was not rebuffed, and he pressed for Butler's advancement. "I am tired of the suspense," Matthew wrote to his wife, "and prefer to have the question decided one way or the other, and know whether or not I am to have a regiment." Probably feeling a bit guilty over his partying and possibly seeking a reconciliation, he added, "I enclose a piece of poetry . . . and address the lines to you, especially that portion that says:

> Oh! Who can tell the depths of light
> Which from those orbs devine

So crystal clear, so starry bright
So lovingly outshine."[56]

Hampton's brigade (with Butler in limbo with his small band of troopers) was assigned to Longstreet's infantry, who were keeping watch on
McClellan at Harrison's Landing. The rest of the cavalry had moved north
with Jackson to confront a new Union army, led by John Pope. On August
22 scouts reported that McClellan was abandoning the Peninsula, taking his
troops by sea to unite with Pope. Butler led the reconnaissance that proved
that the Federals were in fact leaving the area.[57]

Longstreet hurried north, arrived before the Yankee reinforcements
reached the scene, and combined with Jackson to crush Pope in the battle of
Second Manassas.[58] Butler rode up the coast in pursuit of the slow-moving
McClellan. Along the way, he received two bits of good news. Maria had
given birth to a third child, another boy. Matthew suggested they call the lad
"Perry," his mother's family name, but perhaps as a peace offering, Maria
insisted on Matthew C. Butler II.[59] And Lee had finally consented to his
promotion to colonel in charge of the 2nd South Carolina Regiment,
Hampton's brigade, Stuart's division.[60] He and his men reported for duty
outside of Washington, D.C., on September 2, just in time to join Lee's
army in its invasion of Maryland.

CHAPTER 5

Sharpsburg

AFTER DEFEATING POPE AT SECOND MANASSAS, ROBERT E. LEE FACED A quandary: he could not stay in place. Northern Virginia had been so stripped of food and forage, he could not feed his men. Lee did not want to return south, which would draw the Federals after him to once again threaten Richmond; going east to assault Washington made no sense as the Yankee capital was protected by impregnable bulwarks; and although withdrawing westward into the Shenandoah Valley was a viable move, doing so would cede the strategic advantage to McClellan, who had resumed command of the Union army. His actions would dictate the Rebels' response. The only reasonable alternative was to wheel north and invade Maryland, whose lush farmlands could sustain his troops.[1]

Although a process of elimination imposed Lee's course, there were positive aspects to the invasion. Maryland was a Southern state, and its occupation by the Rebels might draw much needed recruits into the Confederate force. The Yankee troops would have to come after Lee, and this would prevent their interfering with the farmers' fall harvest of crops in Virginia. And when the Federals finally caught up with Lee, he would offer them battle. A victory would allow the South "to propose . . . the recognition of our independence," Lee submitted to Jefferson Davis. "Such a proposition . . . could in no way be regarded as suing for peace . . . made when it is in our power to inflict injury."[2]

Lee's army entered Maryland on September 5, crossing the Potomac River east of the Catoctin Mountains. Jackson's corps led the way, followed by Longstreet's divisions. The men, described by one as "the dirtiest, lousiest, filthiest, piratical-looking cut-throats . . . I ever saw,"[3] were plodding toward Frederick City. As the infantry moved north, west of the Monocacy River, Stuart's cavalry, including Butler's regiment, protected their flank by picketing along the eastern bank of the stream. Fitz Lee's troopers were posted to the north of the twenty mile line; Hampton's riders guarded the

44

SHARPSBURG CAMPAIGN

SEPTEMBER 1862

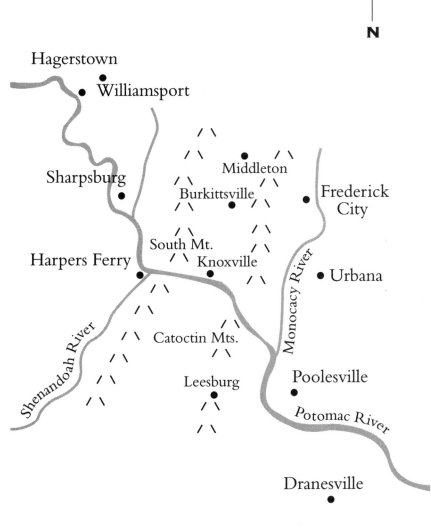

N

Hagerstown

Williamsport

Middleton

Sharpsburg

Burkittsville

Frederick City

South Mt.

Harpers Ferry

Knoxville

Monocacy River

Urbana

Shenandoah River

Catoctin Mts.

Poolesville

Leesburg

Potomac River

Dranesville

center at Urbana; and Robertson's force was located to the south at Poolesville.[4]

Jackson reached Frederick City on September 6; Longstreet arrived the following afternoon. The army paused for several days to enjoy the "hospitality" of the locals. Most were not happy to find Rebels in their midst. "The houses were all shut up," James Shinn reported, "and nearly all the people . . . looked as if they had lost a dear friend."[5] Lee's hopes that Marylanders would rush to his cause had proved to be false.

Lee had other reasons for holding his men in Frederick City. He had anticipated that entering Maryland would force the Union to withdraw their troops posted at Harpers Ferry, located at the entry to the Shenandoah Valley. The town was surrounded by mountains and indefensible. With the Yankees out of the way, Lee could use the Valley as a supply line to provide his army with ammunition, making it safe to advance into Pennsylvania, up to Harrisburg, where he wanted to burn the railroad bridge over the Susquehanna River. This would seriously disrupt the shipment of supplies to the Union from the Midwest.[6] But the Federals stationed at Harpers Ferry had not budged, so Lee needed time to rethink his strategy.

Jeb Stuart grew impatient with the delay. His pickets had not been seriously challenged by inquisitive Yankees, so to liven things up, he decided to have a ball. Invitations to the dance were sent to all the pretty girls living in the area and on the evening of September 9, everyone gathered at a schoolhouse near Urbana where Butler was posted. "The large halls of the Academy," Heros von Borcke stated, "were aired and swept and festooned with roses."[7] The battle flags of the different cavalry regiments were draped on the walls. The 18th Mississippi band provided the music.

Matthew Butler was no doubt one of the handsome Rebels, who after hanging up their sabers, took the hand of a lovely lass and led her onto the dance floor. "Just as everything had become well started, " William Blackford recalled, "there came shivering through the night air the boom of artillery."[8] After begging their partners to wait while they took a brief leave to tend to the war, the men grabbed their weapons, mounted up, and dashed toward the battle.

After skirmishing with the Yankees, who were only probing their front, the troopers returned to Urbana. "Dancing was resumed," Blackford wrote, "and was at its height again when, alas, it was doomed to a final interruption."[9] Some of the men injured in the fight had been brought on litters to the school for treatment.

"It was no use talking to them of any more dancing that night," Blackford related. "Like a flock of angels in their white dresses, [the ladies] assembled around the stretchers. They bent over the wounded men, dressing their wounds . . . ministering to their wants, with their pretty fingers . . . stained with blood. All that was left . . . was to escort [our partner] home . . . and to bid [her] a last, tender farewell."[10]

The next morning, the army was on the move. Lee had decided on his strategy. While Jackson took half of his force southwest to dislodge the Yankees from Harpers Ferry, Longstreet would conduct the rest northwest to Hagerstown. Once Harpers Ferry had fallen, opening the supply route through the Shenandoah Valley, Jackson would advance north to rejoin the army in its thrust into Pennsylvania.[11]

Lee knew that dividing his army was risky, but he was confident that McClellan, once more in command of the Yankee forces, would be cautious in pursuing him. Only three days were envisioned for the operation, and the enemy would never move that fast. Orders outlining the plan were written and forwarded to only two officers, Longstreet and Jackson. The latter, however, made a copy for D. H. Hill, whose division had just been assigned to Stonewall. This breach of secrecy would cost the South dearly.[12]

While the infantry moved for their assigned objectives, Stuart's cavalry consolidated toward Frederick City in their rear. Only Butler stayed in position, stationed on the Monocacy River west of Urbana. Later that afternoon, September 11, enemy foot soldiers approached the only bridge in the area, where Matthew had posted some troopers under Lt. John Meighan. The Yankee infantry spotted the Rebels ahead. Looking to disperse Butler and his men without a fight, they brought up a lone cannon, which started a desultory fire on the Southern horsemen. The Federals then advanced as shells soared over their heads. They assumed that their adversary across the stream would soon wheel and run.

Matthew, however, was not about to withdraw peacefully. "Like lightning," von Borcke recalled, "he darted across the bridge, [took] the piece of artillery . . . and [fell] upon the regiment, [who] were dispersed in a few seconds."[13] Butler's troopers spiked the gun, then galloped back over the stream and fired the span. "The conflagration . . . of course, checked [the enemy's] forward movement," von Borcke stated, "and we quietly continued [to] retreat under the annoyance only of a spirited shelling, which did us very little harm, and of an irregular fusillade . . . by bush-whackers and citizens from the houses."[14]

Matthew and his men rejoined the rest of Hampton's Brigade in Frederick City. They slept there that evening, then prepared to move out the next morning. When Butler started to leave town, he found his path blocked ahead by Yankee infantry, Col. Augustus Moor's 28th Ohio. "Come on boys," Moor shouted when he saw Butler's oncoming troopers, "let's give 'em hell!"[15] The Yankees charged.

Some might have scattered under the onslaught, but Butler ordered a countercharge. The two foes clashed, and soon the Yankees were running and Moor was a prisoner. "I . . . commend most favorably the conduct of the 2nd South Carolina . . . ably and gallantly led by Colonel Butler . . . on this occasion," Hampton lauded in his official report.[16] Stuart, too, praised Butler's performance in his summary of the action.[17]

The cavalry withdrew over Catoctin Mountain that afternoon and bivouacked in Middletown that night. At sunrise on September 13 (the day when Stonewall was scheduled to capture Harpers Ferry), Hampton's troopers took up a defensive position and awaited the enemy. The Federals soon appeared, and a lively skirmish followed as the Rebels contested their foe's advance. That evening Hampton (and Butler) galloped south and camped at Burkittsville.[18]

The next morning, Butler learned that Jackson was late in getting into position to take Harpers Ferry. His troops had followed a roundabout route, circling below the village, and were now approaching from the west; the division led by John G. Walker was posted to the south atop Loudoun Heights; and Lafayette McLaws was assembling his men on Maryland Heights to the north. He would make the key assault, now set for tomorrow, September 15.[19] To shield McLaws from any Union excursions from the east, Hampton's brigade headed toward Knoxville on the Potomac River, then crossed South Mountain at Crampton's Gap to take up a position west of the pass and protect that flank. As Butler dismounted about noon, he heard the sounds of battle to the north.[20]

Jackson was late, but McClellan was unexpectedly early. His army was pressing forward with unusual vigor, attempting to push through D. H. Hill's infantrymen, guarding Turner's Gap in South Mountain. McLaws had positioned two of his ten brigades on guard at Crampton's Gap, but when he heard that the Federals were approaching this pass, too, he sent Howell Cobb's soldiers back as reinforcements. This released Hampton's troopers to come further west to shield McLaws when he attacked Harpers Ferry with the remainder of his force.[21]

McClellan's change in character (Lincoln described him as having "the slows")[22] was because he had learned of Lee's plans to divide his army and was hoping to catch the Confederates before they could regroup. One of D. H. Hill's aides had copied the secret orders. The never-identified officer wrapped three of his cigars in the document, then carelessly left the package behind upon leaving Frederick City. A Federal soldier (Cpl. Barton W. Mitchell) found the packet and smoked the cigars, but sent the revealing papers up through channels to McClellan. "If I cannot whip Bobbie Lee [now]," the Union leader exclaimed after seeing the orders, "I will be willing to go home."[23]

Fortunately Lee soon received word through a local sympathizer that McClellan knew about his perilous position. He did not call off the impending foray against Harpers Ferry, but Lee did take steps to consolidate his force. Longstreet was ordered to start south from Hagerstown. And the troops in the gaps were told to hold their position at all costs.

Despite a fierce resistance by the Rebels, the Yankees came through both Turner's Gap and Crampton's Gap on September 14. Lee was prepared to give up his campaign at this point and retreat back to Virginia. But when Stonewall took Harpers Ferry the following day, he changed his mind. Lee ordered his army to concentrate at Sharpsburg and prepare to fight McClellan, who had reverted to form. After his burst of aggressive action, he had slowed just west of South Mountain and was now advancing with his usual caution.[24]

Butler and his troopers remained in the Harpers Ferry area throughout September 15. The next morning, they rode northward and took up a position between Crampton's Gap and Sharpsburg, where they guarded the Confederate rear. And on September 17, they galloped toward the tiny Maryland town, where a battle was raging.[25]

Lee had aligned his troops along a low ridge, parallel to Antietam Creek, that ran north to south. Just after sunrise on September 17, McClellan assaulted Lee's left from above. Hooker's corps drove the Rebels as far as the Dunker Church, then fell back under John Bell Hood's counterattack. Joseph Mansfield's infantry pressed forward to force Hood to retreat, but his charge was turned by Walker's brigade, who had come up from the south. Sumner's corps attacked Walker, but they were repelled by McLaws, who had just arrived from Harpers Ferry. By 10:00 A.M., this phase of the battle had ended in a stalemate. The Yankees suffered more than 7,000 casualties; the South lost about 5,000.[26]

Butler arrived on the scene about this time and joined Jeb Stuart on Nicodemus Hill, located along the flank of the enemy's line of assault.[27] Except for their artillery, which had punished the Federals until exhausting their ammunition, the troopers had not been engaged. They continued to watch as the scene shifted to the Rebel center.

D. H. Hill's troops, posted in front of the ridge along a sunken road that faced east, were assaulted at midmorning by elements of Franklin's and Sumner's corps. This natural bulwark give Hill's men an advantage, and their first volley "brought down the enemy," one observer testified, "as grain falls before a reaper."[28] The Federals took huge casualties until finally enveloping the Rebels' position. All at once, Hill's troops were caught in a death trap that they later called the "Bloody Lane," and they were forced to fall back to the refuge of the ridge. The Yankees, however, were so battered by their efforts, they were unable to pursue their foe. By 2:00 P.M., the center stage of the battle had reached an impasse, too. The Union lost over 3,000 men here; the Rebels suffered about 2,600 killed or wounded.[29]

To Lee's right, 14,000 Northern troops led by Burnside had been attempting since sunrise to cross Antietam Creek to enter the fray. They could have waded through the water in a number of places, but instead had concentrated on the only bridge, a stone span, defended by just 550 Rebels. The Confederate sharpshooters' musket fire stymied the Federals until 1:00 P.M., when Burnside finally forced a crossing. He then took almost two hours to form his command. By the time Burnside was finally advancing in what should have been the decisive charge of the day, A. P. Hill's division had reached the scene after a seventeen-mile forced march from Harpers Ferry. He crashed into Burnside's flank, drove him from the field, and brought the battle to a close.[30] The Union lost over 2,300 men on this front; the Rebels about 1,000.[31] In an unnecessary battle, fought for pride instead of position, the total casualties for both foes totaled almost 23,000—the bloodiest day in the Civil War.

All the next day, the Rebels waited in position, ready to renew the battle. Lee had no desire to fight and probably could not have held off a determined Union attack, but he felt that his leaving the field would be an admission of having been defeated. McClellan, however was unwilling to initiate any further action, and so when darkness finally came, the Confederates withdrew across the Potomac into Virginia. Butler and his cavalry lingered in the rear to guard against a Federal pursuit. When it became obvious that the enemy was not about to come after Lee, Matthew, too, retired and set up camp at Sulpher Spring.[32]

CHAPTER 6

Chambersburg

President Lincoln issued his Emancipation Proclamation on September 22. He decreed that on January 1, 1863, "All persons held as slaves" within any state or part of a state still in rebellion will be "thenceforward and forever free."[1] He claimed that his presidential power allowed him to do so, and that his purpose was "only to restore the constitutional relations between the United States, and each of the states, and the people thereof."[2] Two days later, Lincoln made sure that there would be no public outcry against his new policy. He suspended the writ of habeas corpus throughout the North, authorizing arbitrary arrest of anyone engaged in "disloyal practice, offering aid and comfort to the Rebels."[3]

Lincoln later claimed that the decree was the crowning achievement of his administration, and most historians agree with him.[4] Freeing the slaves was, of course, a momentous edict. But just as the altruistic pronouncements of today's politicians are often suspect, Lincoln's goals at that time should also be questioned. His orders applied to only those held in servitude in the South, where Lincoln had no authority to dictate their freedom. Black bondmen in the Northern states (Delaware, Missouri, Maryland, and Kentucky) whom he might have released from their masters were not included in his proclamation. He was more likely planning to shift the objective of the Civil War from preserving the Union to ending slavery. If this became the main issue, foreign powers such as Britain and France would find it embarrassing to support the Confederacy.

Jefferson Davis pointed out a diabolical goal that Lincoln might also have envisioned. Davis saw the proclamation as an invitation to Southern slaves to rise in insurrection, to riot and massacre women and children while their husbands were away at war. "The measure," he said, "was the most execrable recorded in the history of guilty man."[5]

As the military and political battles continued in the East, so too did the war in the West. Two campaigns were in progress. The first involved

51

western Tennessee, where Grant had divided his force among three strong-holds: Memphis under William T. Sherman; Jackson under Edward O. C. Ord; and Cornith under William S. Rosecrans. The Rebels led by Earl van Dorn assaulted Rosencrans on October 3, but despite having superior numbers, were routed in the two-day battle.[6]

To the north, the Rebels had invaded Kentucky with two separate forces led by Braxton Bragg and E. Kirby Smith. Bragg halted at Bards-town; Smith stopped at Frankfort, the state capital, where the two generals met to install a Confederate government. They had planned on combining their armies for an assault on Louisville, but before they could act, Federal troops under Don Carlos Buell came southeast from that city on October 1 toward Bardstown. Bragg, in overall command, retreated to Perryville, but unsure of where Buell intended to attack, sent Smith's army toward Ver-sailles. The Yankees charged Bragg's portion on October 8, but despite out-numbering the Rebels two to one, were soundly thrashed. Bragg, like Lee at Sharpsburg, found his victory hollow. He had no choice but to retreat the next day.[7]

Back in camp, Butler knew of the impending battle in the West, but did not learn the result until much later, because on October 9, he rode north into Pennsylvania on a cavalry raid.

"An expedition into Maryland . . . is desirable," Lee said in his October 8 orders to Jeb Stuart. "Form a detachment of from 1,200 to 1,500 well-mounted men . . . cross the Potomac above Williamsport . . . and proceed to the rear of Chambersburg [Pa.]." Lee went on to outline the objectives for the raid: to destroy the Cumberland Valley Railroad bridge across Conococheague Creek, which would seriously disrupt the Union flow of supplies from the West; to gain information regarding McClellan's position, force, and probable intentions; to gather up civilian hostages, preferably local government officials, whom Lee would then exchange for their coun-terparts being held captive by the enemy; and to appropriate "horses and other necessary articles" to replenish the cavalry.[8]

Stuart received Lee's orders the morning after hosting a magnificent ball at The Bower, the plantation where he was headquartered. The dance had lasted until sunrise. Butler was probably there, and possibly was one of those engaged in "public kissing . . . a feature of every gathering."[9] Stuart immediately began preparing for the raid, but before embarking northward, he threw yet another party. "We had . . . music and dancing until 11 o'clock," Channing Price related, "and then retired to our tents."[10]

The troopers assembled at Darkesville the next morning. Hampton, William H. F. "Rooney" Lee, and William E. "Grumble" Jones each had about 600 riders from their commands with them. Butler was present with

175 of his South Carolina horsemen; the other groups under Hampton included the 1st North Carolina, led by Lt. Col. J. B. Gordon; the 10th Virginia under Maj. J. T. Rosser; and the Phillips Legion, led by Capt. S. S. Dunlap.[11] In addition to their cavalry, the Rebel entourage had four cannons and their squads under Capt. John Pelham.

Stuart led his raiders north toward Hedgesville, where most spent the night. Hampton and his men, however, rode up to the banks of the Potomac River. They slept in the woods to stay out of sight of the Federals, patrolling the opposite bank.[12]

At 3:00 A.M., Hampton roused his troopers to carry out a plan for crossing the Potomac. Using the cover of a thick fog, twenty-five men of the 10th Virginia, under Lt. H. R. Phillips, forded the river and made contact with the Federal pickets on the far shore. The foray exposed the Union's position, a signal for Butler and his troopers to dash through the water. He quickly routed the Union sentries and opened a path for Stuart's force to advance into Yankee territory.[13]

The Rebels rode north until reaching the National Road running west out of Hagerstown, where they halted to capture a small band of Federal signalmen, perched on a nearby hill. The prisoners revealed that Jacob D. Cox's six Ohio infantry regiments had just passed by, headed east toward Cumberland. Stuart had planned to wheel right here to attack and destroy the Union supply depot at Hagerstown. But since this large Yankee force stood between him and his objective, he decided instead to push north to Chambersburg. Butler still led the way.[14]

As Matthew and his men galloped into Mercersburg, they spotted a shoe store along the main street. Butler stopped, entered the shop, and "purchased" the merchant's full stock of boots for his cavalry. The seller, "who had no suspicion of the character of his liberal customers," was dumbfounded when Matthew handed him a Confederate receipt as payment for the goods.[15]

The Rebels usually did not appropriate military supplies without "payment," but now Stuart commenced to forage. He divided his column into three groups: Hampton's brigade was up front; Rooney Lee's men brought up the rear; Grumble Jones's riders in the center ranged left and right gathering up horses.[16]

Butler reached Chambersburg about 8:00 P.M. The night was dark and a cold drizzle was falling. Wary that the town might be defended by Union troops, Hampton decided to bluff his way into the village. He sent Lt. T. C. Lee under a flag of truce into Chambersburg to demand a surrender. If the citizens did not capitulate, he would begin an artillery barrage. The local officials, whom Stuart had hoped to take hostage, had all fled, but those

ROUTE OF STUART'S CHAMBERSBURG RAID

OCTOBER 10–12, 1862

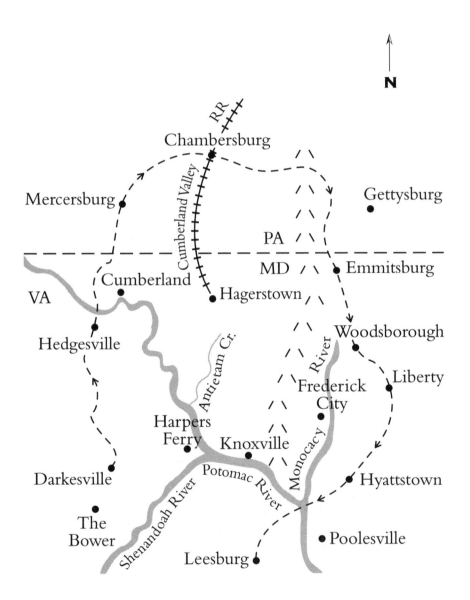

remaining in charge were quick to accept Hampton's terms. Butler and his men galloped into the village square.[17]

Butler's first stop was the bank to confiscate all the funds at hand. The cashier, however, had been warned of the approaching Rebels, and had earlier that day sent the money to safety out of town. "He opened the vault and drawers for inspection," one of the Confederates recalled. During this exchange, Butler had acted with great courtesy, and the bank official was so impressed, he voluntarily summoned his wife and had her bring dinner for Matthew and his staff.[18]

When Stuart reached the village, he named Hampton "Military Governor for Chambersburg." The honor was then passed to Butler, who in turn put Capt. J. P. Macfie in charge of keeping the peace. "I am happy to say," Hampton said in his official report, "that good order was maintained during the whole of our [time] in the city."[19]

That night, while Butler stayed in town, Grumble Jones took a detachment north to set fire to the Cumberland Valley Railroad bridge, a target that Robert E. Lee had identified. Jones found, however, that the trestle was constructed with iron, and his efforts to burn it failed.[20]

Stuart started his retreat the next morning. Assuming that the Federals would be expecting him to return home along the same path by which he had invaded Pennsylvania, he opted instead to go east and then south, encircling McClellan in the process. Butler remained in town. He had been told to destroy all the military stores, then catch up to the column.[21]

Butler found a huge supply of goods at hand. Stuart's men had already taken all the blue overcoats, revolvers, and muskets they could carry. About 5,000 new rifles, a number of sabers, more clothing, and a large quantity of ammunition had been left behind. He gathered all of this in one storehouse, alerted nearby residents to flee, struck a match, lit a slow-burning fuse, and then retired to a safe distance to await the result. "A loud explosion announced that the fire had reached the fixed ammunition," a Rebel related, "and in another instant the whole building was wrapped in flames."[22] In addition to these stores, Butler torched the railroad depot, various machine shops, and several railroad cars on a siding.[23] He started after Stuart about 9:00 A.M.

The Rebel cavalry was headed toward Gettysburg. Their presence in Pennsylvania was now well known, and the Yankees were determined to capture everyone. "Not a man should be permitted to return to Virginia," Henry W. Halleck, the Federal general in chief, declared. "Use any troops in Maryland or Pennsylvania against them."[24]

The problem was that no one knew where Stuart had gone. Because of yesterday's rain, the roads were muddy: there was no billowing cloud of dust to divulge the location of 1,800 cavalrymen. The ruse of circling the enemy was working.

The Yankee effort to nab Stuart's troopers centered on surrounding Chambersburg. At 3:00 A.M. on October 11, shortly after the Rebels entered the village, a Federal cavalry brigade led by William W. Averell galloped northeast from Green Spring to oppose any further Confederate advancement to the west;[25] three hours later, John E. Wool boarded four regiments of infantry in Baltimore on a train, heading for Harrisburg to front the raiders from the north;[26] about 8:00 A.M., the 6th Pennsylvania left Frederick to ride toward Gettysburg and block Stuart's retreat to the east;[27] and at 11:00 A.M. the cavalry division under Alfred Pleasanton raced west out of Hagerstown to bar the Rebels' path to the south.[28]

"I have given every order necessary to insure the . . . destruction of these forces," McClellan declared in a telegram sent to Washington from his headquarters in Knoxville. "[I will] teach them a lesson they will not . . . forget."[29]

McClellan spoke too soon. After crossing the Catoctin Mountains west of Gettysburg, Stuart turned south and slipped past the rear of the 6th Pennsylvania, hurrying northward. Jeb must have known that the Yankees were after him, yet he had the audacity to delay his escape by continuing to forage for his horses until he crossed into Maryland. His cavalry reached Emmitsburg at sunset, where they halted for supper. Their meal was eagerly provided by locals, sympathetic with the Southern cause. As darkness fell, Stuart remounted his force and started again toward the Potomac.[30]

The Rebels rode at a trot all through the night. "The monotonous jingle of arms and accoutrements mingled with the tramp of horses' feet into a drowsy hum all along the marching column," Blackford remembered, "and to be sleepy and not to be allowed to sleep [was] exquisite torture."[31]

By dawn the column had reached Hyattstown, only a few miles from the river. McClellan knew by now that Stuart had eluded the encirclement he had set at Chambersburg. And although he was unsure of the Rebels' current location, scouts had reported that the raiders were approaching the fords of the Potomac near Poolesville. To keep Stuart from returning safely to Virginia, McClellan sent the infantry division under George Stoneman to block the four most likely crossings. Stoneman posted about 600 men at each and kept a like number in reserve at Poolesville, where they would be ready to run to the first sound of confrontation.[32]

A second threat to Stuart was the cavalry under Alfred Pleasanton. They had started west out of Hagerstown yesterday, were redirected north toward Gettysburg, then hurried south once Stuart's route had been detected. They, too, had ridden all night, and were actually moving in parallel with the Rebels.[33]

Mindful of the danger ahead, Stuart turned off the main road at Barnesville to approach the Potomac on a seldom used wagon path. The trail cut through a dense forest, and the men had to stop from time to time to slash an opening in the underbrush. When they finally broke into a clearing just a few hundred yards from the stream, they suddenly encountered Pleasanton's cavalry, whose number had been greatly reduced by straggling during their all-night pursuit of the Rebels. Stuart immediately ordered a charge, which forced the Union riders to retire to a nearby mound. Rooney Lee, leading the column, quickly dismounted a few men to hold the Yankees at bay. Pelham rushed up and added three of his cannons to the fray. Union infantry, posted at White's Ford ahead, ran up to support Pleasanton, but this combined force was unable to dislodge Pelham and Lee's sharpshooters. Stuart took advantage of the stalemate to start his force across the Potomac.[34]

When he heard the skirmish break out up ahead, Matthew, riding at the tail of the column, stopped and assumed a defensive stance facing the rear, where he expected the enemy to appear. He did not know that Stuart had stymied the Federals and that the Rebels were already crossing the stream. He waited for word to join his compatriots.[35]

Stuart got all of his cavalry but Butler, Pelham, with now just one gun, and Lee's skirmishers over the stream. He had sent four separate messages to call Butler forward, but none of his couriers had been able to locate the South Carolinians. "We are going to lose our rear guard," he groaned to Blackford.

"Let me try [to find them]," Blackford urged.

"All right," Stuart replied. "Tell Butler if he can't get through, to strike back into Pennsylvania and try to escape through West Virginia."[36]

Blackford scurried back through the woods, and after a three-mile sprint, finally located Butler, still entrenched, still faced north. "Withdraw at a gallop," Blackford cried out as he rode up to Butler, "or you'll be cut off."

"I don't think I can bring off that gun," Butler noted, pointing out the artillery piece that Stuart had assigned to his care. "The horses can't move it."

"Leave the gun! Save your men!"

"Well," Butler answered, showing coolness under pressure, "we'll see what we can do."[37]

Butler turned to his men, calmly ordered the cannon hitched to a team of horses, and then began his dash for the Potomac. He could hear the skirmishing continuing up ahead, and anticipating that he might have to fight his way across the water, Butler told his troopers to draw sabers so they could cut their way through the enemy lines. When the regiment reached the clearing by the river, they found Pelham and Lee's riflemen still holding the Union at bay. Yankee bullets zipped overhead as the column began fording the water. Pelham and Lee's riders followed them.[38]

When Stuart on the Virginia bank saw Butler's troopers coming across the river, he entered the Potomac and splashed to the middle of the stream. He watched as Butler directed traffic, waiting until all had passed by before he (the last man) made his escape. Matthew advanced to meet Stuart.

"Well done, my brave boy," Stuart greeted him, doffing his plummed hat in a salute to Butler's cool behavior.[39] Stuart's raid was a great success. He had destroyed a huge quantity of military and railroad supplies at Chambersburg, his foragers had captured about 1,200 horses, and via conversations with local citizens, he had discerned all that Lee wanted to know about McClellan's dispositions. And his ride around the Union's encampments had proved an embarrassment for the Federal commander. During the three-day sally, Stuart lost just two troopers to straggling and had only one man wounded.[40]

Butler, of course, got his share of the glory. Stuart specifically lauded him in his official report, saying that he was "entitled to my lasting gratitude for . . . coolness in danger and cheerful obedience to orders."[41]

CHAPTER 7

A Cold Winter

THE REBELS REMAINED IN PLACE BY THE POTOMAC ON OCTOBER 13.
They spent most of their time exchanging friendly insults with the Federals, who lined the opposite shore. The next morning, the raiders rode to
Leesburg, where they slept that night. After crossing the Blue Ridge on the
15th, the column separated, each brigade returning to its old bivouac. That
evening, Stuart hosted a ball to celebrate the success of his raid. Butler
would not have missed this dance at the Bower, despite the twenty-five
mile gallop from his camp at Martinsburg to cavalry headquarters.[1]

On October 16, as if to spite Stuart, McClellan sent two waves of
infantry and cavalry across the Potomac in an armed reconnaissance to
locate Lee's position. One group crossed at Harpers Ferry and headed
towards Charlestown; the second forded the stream at Shepherdstown and
moved south for Smithfield. The tired troopers led by Rooney Lee skirmished with the enemy throughout that day; Hampton and Butler joined
the fray on the 17th. The enemy soon retreated, and the men again settled
in camp.[2]

While resting at Martinsburg, Matthew further strengthened the bond
he had with his command. One of his scouts, Hugh Scott, had brought
him a message from Hampton. After delivering his note, Scott left to visit
the regiment. Soon shots rang out. Butler quickly sent a guard to investigate, and they returned with a few culprits, one of whom was Scott—
noted for getting into mischief.

"Were you shooting, too?" Butler demanded of Scott.

"Yes, Sir."

"What were you shooting at?" Butler queried. He added, "You are
always getting into trouble."

"I am not in . . . trouble. I was shooting at a squirrel."

"If you didn't kill that squirrel," Butler decided, "I will put you in the
guardhouse."

"Put the balance in the guardhouse, Colonel; I killed the squirrel."

Scott's cohorts loudly disputed his claim. Butler (no doubt with a smothered smile at the noisy furor) shipped the whole lot to the stockade. Soon, however, he released them. "I couldn't catch you," Butler said later to Scott, "to save my life."[3]

Butler probably flew his old company's flag, presented to him by the ladies of Edgefield, at his headquarters. The banner was a copy of the national emblem, having a palmetto, capped by a crescent, to the left in the circle of stars on the blue square; the company's motto, "Our cause, our home, our honor," was to the right, written on the white stripe.[4]

The placid days at Martinsburg soon ended. On October 26, McClellan started his army across the Potomac, east of the Blue Ridge. He had resisted advancing, but Lincoln via a series of snide notes had insisted upon his breaking camp. "If you [saw] the mean & dirty character of the dispatches I receive," McClellan wrote to his wife, "you would boil over with anger."[5] The president had relieved Buell from command in the West on October 24—naming William S. Rosecrans in his place—because his slow pursuit had allowed Bragg to escape from Kentucky. McClellan saw a similar fate ahead for him if he did not comply with Lincoln's demands.[6]

Lee had no choice but to counter McClellan's move. He started his army over the mountains with the cavalry leading the way. Stuart spread his forces, including Butler, across the Federals' front, and by skirmishing daily, blocked their further progress. The Yankees halted in the Loudoun Valley. When Lincoln learned that Lee was impeding the Union's route south, he lost patience and relieved McClellan of duty. Ambrose Burnside was given command of the Northern Army of the Potomac on November 5.[7]

"This I believe is the best thing for us," Butler said about the change in Union commanders, "for whatever they may say of McClellan as general, they will not [get] a man in whom the whole Northern army have such confidence."[8]

Knowing that Lincoln wanted him to bring the Rebels to battle, Burnside prepared his plans for the coming campaign. The muddy roads and rickety railroads in Virginia precluded provisioning the army by land if he proceeded directly south toward Richmond, so Burnside proposed heading for the coast, where the inland rivers offered a supply route. He expected Lee to follow and confront him at Fredericksburg. On November 15 Burnside turned left and moved southeast.[9]

Lee, of course, shifted his army right, too. Burnside won the race to Fredericksburg, but found himself stymied by the Rappahannock River. He had expected to see pontoons, shipped south from Washington, in place for crossing the wide and deep-running water, but they were late in arriving. As Burnside agonized with frustration, Lee slipped into place atop the tall hills on the south shore, above the town. Butler was posted near Stevensburg, twenty some miles west of Fredericksburg, where he protected the Rebel left flank.[10]

"You can form no conception of the desolation of [this] magnificent country," Butler wrote Maria. "Splendid estates are ruined . . . and the fields which have luxuriated [with] the finest grapes and pastured herds . . . are [now filled] with broom sage . . . not a vestige of prosperity or comfort remains. I could not resist feelings . . . [of] melancholy as I rode thru this rich and beautiful [land, which has been] desolated and desecrated by an army of plunderers and vandals."[11]

The Union supply depot for the campaign was located at Aquia on the Potomac, but the sutlers used an overland route that passed through Occoquan and Dumfries. These towns and the roads through them to the front offered an inviting target for the cavalry. Hampton led a probe in that direction on November 28, while Butler remained in camp. He captured a hundred Federal pickets, their horses and weapons, plus two regimental colors.[12] Having proved he could invade Northern territory at will, Hampton looked forward to striking a more decisive blow. His opportunity arose early that December.

Scouts reported that a caravan of sutler wagons loaded with "Christmas things" was coming south from Washington for Dumfries. Hampton decided to capture the train. After sunset on the evening of December 10, he led about 500 riders eastward. Butler and a detachment of his men were included in the party. It was snowing, the weather "intensely cold," one of the participants recalled. "The night [was] as dark as Erebus."[13] The raiders advanced slowly the next day, hid that evening in the woods west of Dumfries, and then charged into the town just after dawn on December 12.

Butler, riding at the head of the column, found twenty-four loaded wagons parked in a vacant lot, the teamsters and their military escort asleep in a large shed along the main street. A volley of shots woke the Yankees. Matthews first gathered up captives, then hitched up the wagons and headed north to find Hampton with the rest of the brigade, guarding against a Union retreat. After they met, they proceeded to divide the spoils.[14]

"[We found] almost every variety of goods," a Confederate stated, "eatables, drinkables, confectionaries, buckskin gauntlets, boots, shoes, hats, [and the] choicest underware, etc."[15] Butler's lot included a four-horse team and covered wagon. "Tired of the saddle and having a . . . fancy to drive," Butler wrote Maria, "I mounted the seat just at dusk and got on swimmingly until it got very dark, when I struck a stump and over went the

THE
FREDERICKSBURG CAMPAIGN

DECEMBER 1862

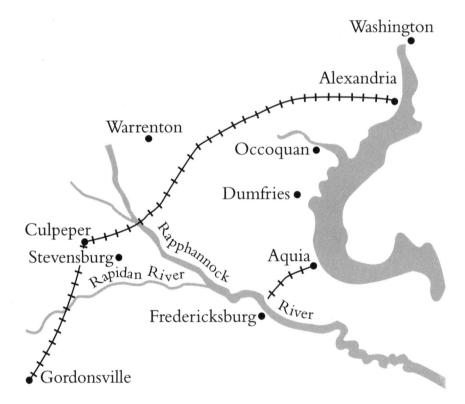

N

Washington

Alexandria

Warrenton

Occoquan

Dumfries

Culpeper

Stevensburg

Rappahannock

Rapidan River

Aquia

Fredericksburg

River

Gordonsville

wagon, driver, passengers, plunder and all. My foot caught in the reins and dragged me . . . in the reddest sort of Culpeper mud. . . . I never laughed so [much] in my life as when I found nobody hurt."[16]

Before starting to drive the wagon back to his bivouac, Butler was approached by its owner, who requested that he be allowed to keep at least some part of its contents. "Every cent [I] own," he cried, "is invested in that wagon, team and goods. I [can] make a small fortune . . . from Burnside's [army when I reach Fredericksburg]."

"Inasmuch as [you will] be a prisoner in Richmond in a very short time," Butler noted unkindly, "it is not clear to me how [these] goods will be of any benefit to [you]." His words opened the poor sutler's eyes to the depth of his predicament.[17]

Butler, driving his captured team, was the last man to leave the area. As he pushed through the column to seek the van, he saw a rider who was balancing a barrel of butter on his mount's back. "What is this?" Butler demanded.

"Plunder we took from the Yankees at Dumfries. I am carrying it back to camp to divide among the boys."

"[Your] poor horse has burden enough without that keg," Butler snorted. "Dump it on the ground." Matthew cared for his mounts as much he did his men.[18]

When Hampton's cavalry reached Stevensburg, they found that during their absence, a ferocious battle had erupted at Fredericksburg. Burnside had crossed the river on December 11, positioned his troops the next day, and then ordered a charge against the heights defended by Lee. Six successive waves of Yankees clambered up the slopes. And six times the Rebels, protected by entrenchments, one a sunken road reminiscent of Antietam, slaughtered the attackers. The Federal losses totaled over 12,500; the Confederates suffered only 5,300 casualties. The Union finally retired back across the Rappahannock on December 15.[19]

Hampton led a third foray without Butler on December 17. His objective was Occoquan. Despite his encountering a large Federal force, he captured 150 prisoners, twenty wagons, and a quantity of infantry arms. "General Hampton has again made a brilliant dash into enemy [territory]," Stuart wrote in his report of the raid, "and I cordially commend his conduct."[20]

Although Stuart said he was proud of Hampton's efforts, he was more likely jealous of his subordinate's success. He decided he would gain some glory for himself by leading the next intrusion against the Yankees. Stuart rode west on December 26 with a grandiose plan in mind. He would attack Dumfries with Fitz and Rooney Lee's commands; Hampton, this time with Butler, would assault Occoquan.[21]

While galloping toward Occoquan, Hampton and Butler developed a strategy for attacking the Yankees. Matthew would charge into the town and drive the enemy wagon trains southward. Hampton would post the remainder of his brigade below Occoquan, where he could gobble up the sutlers and their escorts as they fled from Butler. The assault was launched at sunset on December 27. Matthew surprised the Federals and sent them racing toward Dumfries. Their flight was so fast, however, the caravan slipped past Hampton before he got into position. When Butler came up with seven wagons and twelve prisoners that he had nabbed in town, Hampton realized that the enemy had escaped his trap. He took his command west to rendezvous with Stuart at Cole's Store.[22]

Stuart, too, reported little success. He had found the Federals in force at Dumfries, and he could only watch with frustration as a long train of wagons left the village under the protection of overwhelming Union numbers.[23]

In part because Hampton had accomplished so much in his earlier raids, Stuart could not accept failure. He probably should have gone home essentially empty-handed, but instead, Stuart decided to foray above Occoquan. Fitz Lee would lead the advance, followed by Hampton, then Rooney Lee. The column headed northeast through the darkness.[24]

"The night was terrifically cold, and nearly every man in my regiment traveled on foot [through] the night, leading their horses to keep from freezing," Butler wrote in his report. "We were . . . exhausted, having been in the saddle [for] two days and nights."[25]

In the early dawn, scouts reported an enemy detachment up ahead to the left. Stuart ordered Butler to take his regiment north toward Bacon Race Church, the site of his camp during the fall of 1861, and flank the Yankees. The rest of the column would soon wheel, too, to assault the enemy from his right.[26]

As Butler came within a mile of Bacon Race Church, his van encountered Federal pickets. "I confidently expected an attack . . . by . . . our cavalry division on the roads parallel to [mine]," Butler later wrote, "[so] I ordered a charge." The Union skirmishers retreated rapidly, but as Matthew pressed his advance, he found himself facing superior numbers of enemy horsemen, supported by cannons. "They opened upon me a terrific fire of grape and canister," he related. "I halted and retired a short distance."[27]

Unknown to Butler, Stuart was no longer heading toward Bacon Race Church. He had run into a small force of Federal cavalry and was chasing them across the Occoquan River. He left Matthew and his men isolated in enemy territory.[28]

"[After] waiting as long as I thought prudent," Butler wrote, "I endeavored to retrace my steps, and found the road by which I had advanced occupied by the enemy." He was surrounded! But once again, Matthew proved imperturbable under pressure. He took to the fields and slipped through the Union snare. With the aid of a guide, sent by Stuart, he rode northeast, forded the Occoquan, and caught up with the column.[29]

By now, of course, the Federals were well aware of the presence of Stuart's cavalry, and were mounting an effort to capture his force. As he did at Chambersburg, Stuart chose the most unlikely path home. Instead of retracing his steps south or wheeling west, he continued to gallop north toward Burke's Station on the Orange and Alexandria Railroad, a depot only nine miles from Washington, D.C. Upon arriving at the tracks, Stuart entered the telegraph office and read the many messages relating to his raid. "[They] were very ludicrous," Channing Price chortled. "The Federals were in great alarm, and orders were [sent] to destroy everything in case of our attacking them."[30]

Stuart could not resist sending a wire of his own. In a telegram to Washington, he complained about the quality of the Northern mules. "They are so inferior," he said, "that when put to captured wagons, they will scarcely pull the vehicles within Confederate lines."[31]

Continuing his ride north, Stuart finally stopped near Fairfax Court House, where he found Federal infantry huddled behind bulwarks. He built bonfires as if planning on spending the night, then quietly left, hurrying west. The Rebels passed slowly through Middleburg and Warrenton, stopping often for food and rest. They arrived at Culpeper on December 31.[32]

When Stuart wrote his report of the raid, which had accomplished little, he gave special mention to Butler. "The manner in which [he] brought his command . . . from the crucial situation [at Bacon Race Church]," Stuart praised, "reflects great credit upon his coolness and presence of mind."[33]

Returning to camp, Butler and his men suffered through the cold weather. "The severe winter privations around this dingy hamlet," one man said, "will long be remembered." Shelters of every description were erected to get away from the continuing sleet and snow. "From the different modes of construction," the above writer added, "one . . . supposed that the confused builders of Babel's tower had taken the contract."[34]

As they shivered in their primitive huts, Butler's men no doubt reviewed the war out West. Rosecrans had occupied Nashville on November 10, and Bragg hoped to drive the enemy from the Tennessee capital. He gathered his forces near Murfreesboro below the metropolis. The Union, however, did not wait for his assault. Rosecrans moved south, and on December 31, he attacked Bragg. The contest raged for three days, and finally, the Rebels were forced to withdraw. The bloody affair cost the Federals over 13,000 casualties; the South lost almost 10,000 men.[35]

Farther west, Grant had attempted to take Vicksburg, a bastion on the Mississippi River. While he headed overland, east of the stream, Sherman took 40,000 troops by boat down water toward the mouth of the Yazoo, only twelve miles above the city. The two-pronged campaign ended with disaster for the Federals. Earl Van Dorn attacked Holly Springs, Grant's supply depot, on December 20 and completely destroyed the base. Grant had no choice but to retire.[36] And on December 29, Sherman's move on Vicksburg was repulsed at Chickasaw Bayou.[37]

The Union's problems were not limited to the West. On January 19, Burnside attempted to flank Lee's position below the Rappahannock. Butler must have expected to be soon summoned from his snug hut to battle, but as the enemy moved west above the river, the skies overhead clouded and drenching rain began to fall. The storm continued all through the next day, then it started to snow. The roads turned into a bog, and Burnside's force became mired in the mud. They abandoned their offensive and trudged wearily back to camp.[38] The "Mud March" was a fatal ignominy for Burnside. On January 25, he was replaced as head of the Federal Army of the Potomac by Joe Hooker.[39]

About this same time, Butler learned that friends from Edgefield had nominated him to represent the district in the state legislature. He wrote at once to turn down the honor. "I am profoundly grateful," he said, "but as long as the war lasts and I am spared, I will remain in the field."[40]

Butler had expected to spend the rest of the winter in Stevensburg, but in the middle of February, Hampton's brigade was ordered to southern Virginia on recruiting duty. The troopers were responsible for supplying their own mounts. If a man lost his horse in a battle or injured the animal while raiding, he was reassigned to the infantry. Butler and the other regimental leaders had seen their ranks reduced through this process during the past few months, and they had to rebuild their organizations. Hampton led them to Lynchburg, where they began looking high and low for fresh men and mounts. "We went from one point to another, whippaty, whoppaty, flippaty, floppaty," one of the troopers recalled, "riding around over the land."[41]

Matthew no doubt enjoyed this respite from the war and the opportunity to relax at parties, hosted by pretty girls. Butler perhaps developed a guilty conscience, because late that month, he sent a strange love letter to Maria. "I have seen, fondled and admired the dark-eyed beauties of the Tropics. . ." he confessed, "have sported with the beautiful well developed blondes of the North, [have] enjoyed the charming [company] of the gay, handsome, frank, intelligent daughters of the Old Dominion and the reserved, languid, gentle belles of our sunny land, yet none, no not one have I [found] equal to thee in loveliness and purity."[42] Since he never set foot outside of South Carolina (except for the time spent in Missouri as a child) prior to the Civil War, the trysts that Butler described must have taken place after his marriage to Maria. She was no doubt shocked by his admission, and perhaps realized that her marriage was in danger.

In early April Matthew found reason to leave Virginia for South Carolina for a brief time. The Union had gathered a fleet of warships outside of Charleston, and on April 7, they steamed single file into the harbor. The armada led by Admiral Samuel F. DuPont included seven single-turreted monitors plus four ironclad vessels. As they came in range of the shore batteries and Fort Sumter, the Confederates opened their fire. The Yankee flotilla replied, and a battle raged for two hours and twenty-five minutes. Matthew's older brother, William, a colonel commanding the 1st South Carolina infantry, directed the Rebel bombardment from Fort Moultrie.[43]

About 5:30 P.M., the Union vessels had had enough and retired to Port Royal, minus the *Keokuk*, who sank after taking repeated hits from the accurate Confederate gunners. Everyone anticipated that DuPont would attack again, perhaps supported by infantry, so reinforcements were rushed to the scene. When Hampton learned of the Union threat to his home state, he asked permission to move his cavalry to South Carolina. "Lead your . . . men . . . to Charleston," James A. Seddon, the secretary of war, replied, "and God speed you."[44]

Butler accompanied the 200 riders who galloped to the coast, but upon his arrival, he found that DuPont had abandoned his effort to capture Charleston.[45] Matthew then went home to see Maria. He found her not only elated to see him but also determined to travel north to spend the summer with her husband (so she could keep an eye on him). His admissions of infidelity had produced a most positive effect. Butler was thrilled with her decision, and looked forward to her being with him. "I have been thinking of you constantly for . . . days," he wrote her after returning to Lynchburg, "and have experienced the most melancholy depression at our being separated. I have never felt it so intensely before."[46]

With the snow melted and the trees in bloom, it was time to return to the front. But before Butler had begun to gallop north, Hooker assaulted Lee. On April 28 he sent three infantry corps to the Rapidan River, where they forded the water and then moved southeast into an area filled with scrub oak and brambles called "The Wilderness." At the same time, two other Union corps crossed the Rappahannock at Fredericksburg to feign a frontal attack on Lee, to hold him in place for the charge from the west.

"My plans are perfect," Hooker had pronounced, "and when I . . . carry them out, may God have mercy on Bobby Lee; for I shall have none."[47]

Lee was not fooled. When he learned that the Federals were on his left flank, he, too, divided his troops, sending the bulk of his force west to confront Hooker in The Wilderness. The move so shocked Hooker, he cancelled his assault to assume a defensive position at Chancellorsville, where he awaited a frontal charge from Lee. The Confederate general, however, split his army for a second time, sending Stonewall Jackson in a wide arc to attack Hooker's right flank. This late afternoon blow on May 2 shattered the Union line, and the Yankees fell back along the Rappahannock. Lee sent them reeling over the river the following day.[48]

Although the South was elated over Lee's brilliant victory, they were devastated with the loss of Jackson, wounded by shots from his own force during the height of battle. He was seemingly recovering after the amputation of his left arm, but died of pneumonia on May 10.[49]

With Hooker now on the defensive, Lee planned his next move, an invasion of Pennsylvania. He had ample reason for entering Union territory: Virginia was devoid of provisions, which would be plentiful up north; such an offensive would threaten Washington and might force Lincoln to recall troops from Vicksburg, where Grant was besieging the bulwark; and Lee envisioned a battle in which he would annihilate his enemy. If he could slip by Hooker and gain a lead of several days march, he could concentrate his army while the trailing Yankees were still in column. Lee would then pounce on his unsuspecting foe, sending wave after wave of Rebels into the melee, driving the Northern corps back on each other. This decisive triumph could end the Civil War.[50]

Stuart's cavalry would, of course, play a crucial role in the campaign, and Lee ordered the horsemen to assemble at Culpeper. Butler started for the area on May 4, 1863.[51]

CHAPTER 8

Brandy Station

INSTEAD OF REPLACING STONEWALL JACKSON, LEE DECIDED TO SPLIT HIS corps in two. Richard S. Ewell was put in command of one half; Ambrose P. Hill took charge of the other. Hill remained at Fredericksburg to confront Hooker; Ewell headed west on a roundabout route toward Pennsylvania. Longstreet fell in behind Ewell.[1]

The Confederate columns were headed for the Shenandoah Valley. Lee hoped to surprise Hooker with his movement, and meant to keep out of sight by going north, west of the Blue Ridge. Stuart was charged with guarding the passes, to prevent the Yankees from crossing the mountain and discovering the Rebel advance. To make sure that the cavalry had enough manpower, two brigades of horsemen (Jones's and Robertson's) were transferred to Jeb's command. He established new headquarters, first at Orange Court House on May 10, then at Culpeper on May 20.[2]

All was quiet, but Stuart was not content to just rest his men. He kept his troopers busy with parades. The first, in which Butler participated, was held May 22, 1863. Then, on June 5, when all 10,000 of his command had arrived, Jeb scheduled another grand review. It was preceded, of course, by a magnificent ball. Hundreds of pretty women poured into Culpeper. First they filled the hotels, then private homes, and those who arrived late had to sleep in tents. The dance hall was lit by only a few tallow candles. Emory M. Thomas recounted that this "heightened the romantic mood—if that was possible."[3]

Butler probably did not attend this party. He instead eagerly anticipated Maria's imminent visit to the front. "I look forward to your arrival with . . . thrilling pleasure," he wrote in a May 21 letter, "and will spend many a sleepless hour thinking of it."[4] On June 1 he stated, "I think and dream of you almost constantly, and as the time draws nearer for your arrival, I [become] more and more impatient to see you."[5]

On June 6 the cavalry mounted and stood in formation as Stuart rode by to inspect their ranks. They waited while he retired to a podium to view the artillery pass in review. The horsemen trailed at a walk. The cannoneers dispersed to prechosen points on the field and unlimbered their weapons. When they were all in position, the cavaliers started riding past the dais, first at a trot, then at a gallop as the regiments peeled off, each attacking an emplaced piece. The guns greeted the chargers with a thundering response. "[It] seemed to convert the pageant into real warfare," the corps adjutant, Henry B. McClellan, said. "Pomp and circumstance . . . was fully satisfied."[6]

That evening Stuart held yet another ball. "We danced in the open air . . . by the light of enormous woodfires," Heros von Borcke said, "the ruddy glare of which . . . gave the whole scene a wild and romantic effect."[7] Taking advantage of the moonlight, some couples took private walks to get away from the eyes of the crowd. Matthew again probably stayed in his tent that night.

Stuart had expected Lee to come to the review, but the commanding general was unable to attend. When he arrived at Culpeper on June 7, however, Lee wanted to inspect the cavalry, so Jeb assembled his force for yet another parade the next afternoon. The women had all gone home, but Stuart did not lack an audience.

"You invited me and my people," John B. Hood said with a grin as he pointed to his 10,000 troops, "and you see I've brought them."

"Well," Fitz Lee grumbled, expecting to be harassed by the infantry, "don't let them holler, 'Here's your mule!'"

"If they do," Hampton warned Hood, "we'll charge you."[8]

This review was subdued compared to the one held three days ago. The artillery did not participate and the cavalry did not race their horses. Lee wanted to avoid taxing both the men and their mounts as they were due to depart the next day for their stations in the gaps of the Blue Ridge. That night the troopers abandoned their old camps and spread out toward the Rappahannock River. They slept in the formation that they would assume the next morning.[9] This change saved Stuart's cavalry.

About 3:00 A.M., one of the pickets on the stream woke his compatriots. "Yankees!" he cried. "Great God, millions of 'em!"[10]

Hooker was aware that Lee was shifting his forces (Ewell and Longstreet were both near Culpeper), and he suspected an enemy flanking movement, starting with a Rebel cavalry raid on his rear. Determined to thwart the Confederates, he sent his horsemen, led by Alfred Pleasanton, to attack Stuart before he could start his foray.[11]

"Disperse and destroy the rebel force assembled in the vicinity of Culpeper," Hooker told Pleasanton. "Destroy its trains and supplies. . . . If you should succeed in routing the enemy . . . . follow them vigorously."[12]

Pleasanton's plan of attack was to divide his force at the Rappahan-nock. The cavalry divisions, led by David McMurtrie Gregg and Alfred N. A. Duffié plus the infantry brigade under David A. Russell, would cross the stream at Kelly's Ford; John Buford's horsemen and the infantry under Adelbert Ames would head upstream to wade the water at Beverly Ford. Heading west, the two elements would converge at Culpeper, where they thought Stuart was sleeping.[13]

The pickets that saw the Union (Buford and Ames) crossing the stream were from Grumble Jones's brigade. He quickly roused his troopers and began to dispute the Yankee advance. Stuart, alerted by the sound of mus-ket fire, ordered Hampton and Rooney Lee to the front. Butler, however, was excepted. He remained in the rear, posted about halfway between Brandy Station and Stevensburg. The Rebels set up their defensive line at the base of Fleetwood Hill near St. James Church.[14]

Buford and Ames attacked the Confederate position, but were unable to dislodge the Rebels. While this battle raged in stalemate, Gregg, Duffié, and Russell were going west along the Culpeper Road. They heard the fight to their right, but when they turned north to join the fray, they met Robertson, blocking their way. Russell entrenched his men and began to duel with this force; Gregg and Duffié returned to the pike and pressed on toward Culpeper.[15]

When he reached the road to Brandy Station, Duffié continued riding toward Culpeper; Gregg, however, turned right and headed for the fray. He arrived at the railroad tracks, where he found the area deserted. The fight still boiled to the north, but he could not see the battle because of Fleet-wood Hill. Gregg decided to climb the knoll, but just as he started forward, a lone Rebel cannon appeared on the summit, unlimbered, and began fir-ing at him. This was a petty threat because the piece was using solid shot, but Gregg suspected a trap ahead. He stopped to call his own artillery to the fore to reply to the Confederate weapon. This delay proved fatal to the Union cause. Warned that the Federals were in his rear, Stuart had started both Hampton and Jones to the scene; Lee remained to the north still fac-ing Buford and Ames.[16]

Gregg finally charged the heights, where he was met by Jones and Hampton, who were just now reaching the new front. The rivals collided, and the hand-to-hand fighting that followed was furious. A trooper re-membered the contest as "indescribable clashing and slashing, banging and yelling."[17]

Butler waited southwest of the fray. He had sent his horses into a clover field to graze at dawn, but when he heard battle explode to the east, Butler called his men to mount. "We knew that we had to get busy," he recalled.

BATTLE OF
BRANDY STATION

JUNE 9, 1863

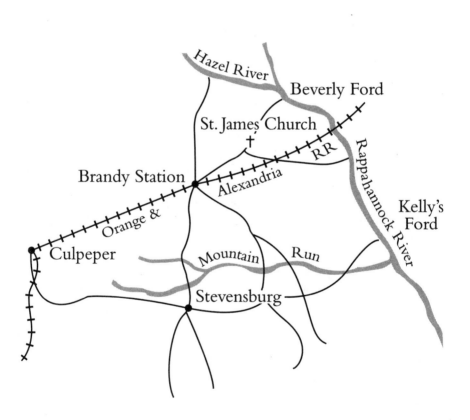

Butler soon received orders to start toward Brandy Station. Shortly after his arrival, a courier rushed up and reported that the enemy (Duffié's division) was approaching Stevensburg to the south. "There was nothing left for me to do," Butler went on, "but to move without orders as rapidly as our horses could carry us, and . . . check the advance of the [Federals]. . . . This separated my regiment four or five miles from the [rest of our] cavalry, engaged . . . in front of Brandy Station."[18]

When he reached Stevensburg, Butler found that the Federals had not yet reached the small village. He quickly set up a defensive line: Frank Hampton, Wade's younger brother, took twenty-five men to the pike, where they blocked the way into town; the rest of the regiment, fewer than two hundred troopers, dismounted into a north-to-south position in the pine wood above the road. While they awaited the enemy, Capt. William Farley, one of Stuart's scouts, arrived and reported that the 4th Virginia was coming to reinforce the 2nd South Carolina. Butler sent word for them to go to Hampton, the weakest point in his line.[19] The Yankees soon appeared.

Duffié wheeled northwest, off the pike, to try to turn Butler's left flank. The first attack failed. "They came a second time," Butler related, "and were repulsed [again]."[20]

During this assault, one of Butler's men took aim at a Union cavalryman and fired. The mounted blue-coated trooper slid down off his horse. "Colonel," the Rebel shouted with glee, "I got that fellow!"

"Get him, the devil," Butler reported. "He has [only] dismounted to get you; load your gun!" He discovered later that the marksman had in fact killed a Union officer.[21]

Duffié returned to the road, where he mounted a charge against the tiny band of twenty-five guarding Butler's right flank. They were no match for the thousand or more Yankees, who blew through the Rebel's position, killing Frank Hampton in the process. The Union riders stormed on toward Stevensburg.[22]

The 4th Virginia had just left the village and were riding toward the front. They had not expected to be met by the enemy, and the sight of the oncoming Yankees proved to be frightening. Williams C. Wickham's troopers broke ranks and scattered, most fleeting all the way back to Culpeper. "[We] were obliged to retire," Wickham wrote later, "and stand not on the order of [our] going."[23]

When Butler learned that Duffié's force had gained his rear and that Wickham had departed the scene, he calmly made the best of his situation. He swung his right flank like a gate until his line faced south, ready to resume the battle. Duffié advanced toward him. His riders overlapped the ends of Butler's position. Seeking better ground, Butler retired across Mountain Run to the crest of a hill on the road. He was mounted on "Old Bench Legs," a favorite horse whose hind legs were crooked, hence the nickname.[24] As he hurried his men into place, the Yankee gunners, who had unlimbered their cannons, spotted Butler, outlined against the postnoon sky. One took careful aim and fired. The shell hit the ground thirty yards in front of Butler, skipped, and then sped toward its target. Both Matthew and his horse were hit. As Butler toppled from the saddle, the missile continued to strike Farley, who was mounted nearby, slicing off his leg before thudding into his animal.

As Butler lay on the ground, his right foot hanging by only a shred of skin from the limb, he saw his horse stagger back toward the clover field where he had been grazing that morning. "Poor fellow," Butler sadly remembered, "[had] his entrails hanging out."[25] "Old Bench Legs" soon died.

The two officers were bleeding profusely. "I directed Farley to get out his handkerchief and [strap] his leg above the wound," Butler said, "and we were doing our best in the tourniquet business when [several men] came to our relief."[26]

They went first to Butler. "Go at once to Farley," he insisted, "he needs you more than I do."[27] Those tending the mortally wounded captain laid him on a makeshift litter. As they were about to tote him to the rear, Farley asked for his limb. "It's an old friend," he said with a grin, pressing it to his bosom as one would a child. "I do not wish to part from it."[28]

Once Farley was removed from the scene, the men turned to Butler. "I was placed on a blanket," Matthew wrote, "and with a man at each corner . . . they walked with every possible care. The grating of the bones was anything but pleasant."[29]

The troopers carried Butler into a nearby glade, where he was lowered into a horse trough. "We then cut two sticks sufficiently long to pass under and across the box," one of the men recalled, "and resumed our way through fields and woods by the shortest route towards Culpeper."[30]

"Almost at the moment we started," the trooper went on, "a force of the enemy were reported to be crossing . . . between us and Brandy Station . . . all was excitement and anxiety . . . our chances of getting safely off with our burden seemed [to be] very slim."[31] And for once, probably the only instance during the Civil War, Butler lost his cool. Racked with pain, disheartened with expectations that the Federals would soon gain Stuart's rear, and perhaps expecting that he would die, Matthew showed fear. "Don't let them take me, boys!" he cried.[32] As he was carried toward the rear, each jolt causing excruciating pain from his almost severed foot, Butler may have considered his Civil War experiences: the camaraderie with his men and their present devotion; the battles in which his daring and coolness had saved his command; and the parties and the ladies. Butler may have wondered if the pretty girls would still see him as handsome and dashing if his lost his leg. And what about his wife? Would Maria love him despite his mutilation or would an amputation cost him his marriage?

Matthew may have even thought that his days were about to end. He could never have envisioned the fullness of life that lay ahead.

CHAPTER 9

Recuperaton

Just prior to being carried to the rear, Butler called his second-in-command, Maj. Thomas J. Lipscomb, the boyhood rival he had once challenged to a duel, to his side. "Continue the fight," Matthew urged, "fall back slowly toward Culpeper. . . . If you can save us from capture, do it."[1]

Lipscomb waited for Duffié's advance. But much to his surprise, the Union retired, and this phase of the battle of Brandy Station ended. The explanation was ludicrous. Just as he was about to charge, Duffié received a desperate order from Gregg to rush north, "retracing your steps."[2] Instead of easily blasting through Lipscomb's undermanned line (the Federals held a nine-to-one advantage) and taking the shortest route to the front, Duffié elected to obey his instructions explicitly. He wheeled about and galloped south to Stevensburg, then hurried east on the Culpeper Road to where Gregg had started north to Brandy Station. By the time he reached this intersection, however, the fray was finished. Pleasanton, unable to dislodge Stuart, was retreating, returning to the Rappahannock.[3]

While Duffié was winding his curious way to the battle, Butler continued his painful route to the rear. His bearers took him to a farmhouse owned by a widow, Mrs. Fitzhugh, where he was given brandy. Although it was obvious he would lose his right foot, the amputation had to be delayed until chloroform could be obtained. A messenger was sent to Culpeper for the anesthetic, and upon his return, they laid Matthew on a table. Dr. B. W. Taylor performed the surgery.[4]

When he awoke, Butler asked the surgeon if he had said anything during the operation. "Yes," Taylor answered (probably with a grin), "You strongly admonished W. C. Swaffield to keep his sorrel mare . . . in line while drilling."[5] Perhaps Matthew was worried that he mentioned a woman, not his wife. Maria, of course, soon learned of her husband's wounds, and on June 12, she hurried north with her father, Francis Pickens, to be at his side.[6]

Although Butler was out of action, he did look forward to returning to duty. He had been promised a brigade (and a general's star), and so he took steps to make sure that his promotion was not denied because of his wounds. Butler gave an aide, U. R. Brooks, the necessary forms, and asked him to locate Stuart and obtain his approval. "I felt the responsibility of being in charge of these papers," Brooks related, "and at every fight we went into, this responsibility seemed to grow heavier, [thinking] of the danger of their loss. . . . I drew a long sigh of relief when [I finally] presented [then] to General Stuart."[7]

Butler and Maria returned to Edgefield, where he would recuperate from his amputation. He stored his embalmed foot in the attic, saving it to be buried with his body when he died. His children used the loft as a playroom, and the dried up appendage became a feature of many of their games.[8]

Although he was no doubt weak and disoriented from the operation, Matthew must have followed the war with great interest. Lee had invaded Pennsylvania as planned, his troop movements screened by Stuart's cavalry, who blocked the gaps in the Blue Ridge from enemy eyes. Hooker's horsemen tried to break through to discern Lee's intention, but in a series of skirmishes at Aldie, Middleburg, and Upperville, the Confederate riders held them off.[9] Stuart, however, then made a terrible mistake.

Jeb had been ordered by Lee to advance north into Pennsylvania to continue screening the army and to keep watch on the following Union forces. He was given a choice of routes: he could cross the Blue Ridge to ride along the western edge of the mountain; or he could slip through the gaps between the Federal corps, camped along a twenty-five-mile line from Thoroughfare Gap to Leesburg, turn north to proceed between the enemy's force and Washington, and then gallop west ahead of the van of the Yankee column to rejoin Lee's command. The latter course was more risky, as Stuart's cavaliers would be isolated from the rest of the Rebels. It was also, however, the more glamorous gambit. Jeb's presence between the enemy and their capital was sure to panic the politicians in Washington. Stuart found this thought so tempting, he could not resist taking that path. At 1:00 P.M. on June 25, Stuart started east with his three best brigades, those led by John R. Chambliss Jr., Hampton, and Fitz Lee.[10]

Stuart passed between the enemy's lines with ease, but when he turned northward, he encountered a problem. Jeb had based his plans on the assumption that Hooker's corps would remain stationary. They had, however, started to move after Lee toward Pennsylvania, and Stuart found that he could not get around the van of the Union force. He remained to their right, unable to slip through their marching columns to get back to his compatriots.[11]

Stuart's absence left Lee without word as to the enemy position, which doomed his hopes of catching the Federals in column where he could devastate their force. When George C. Meade, who on June 27 had replaced Hooker as leader of the Army of the Potomac, reached Pennsylvania, he found the Confederates scattered. Both foes hastily concentrated, and from July 1 to 3, they fought the great battle of the War at Gettysburg.

Stuart did not reach the field until the second day of the conflict. The Confederates, under the effective efforts of Ewell, had prevailed the first day, but the Union had assumed high ground in an impregnable position below the town. Longstreet's attempt to dislodge the Yankees on July 2 had failed.[12]

Stuart, posted on the Rebel left flank, saw the chance to attack the Yankee rear and perhaps force them into ceding their heights, and on the afternoon of July 3, he led his cavalry into battle. Butler, had he still been with his regiment, would have participated in this assault. The Union horsemen, led by David Gregg, met the challenge. "So sudden and violent was the collision," a participant stated, "that many of the horses were turned end over end [crushing] their riders beneath them."[13] Stuart's desperate charges were repulsed. He suffered 181 casualties, one of whom was Hampton—slashed in the head by a saber.[14]

At the same time that Stuart was dueling Gregg, George Pickett sent his Rebel infantry division in a massive charge against the center of the Federal line along Cemetery Ridge. His assault, too, was rebuffed.[15] The Confederates had been defeated at Gettysburg, and Lee was left with no choice but to retreat back to Virginia.

Butler saw Gettysburg with both patriotic and personal sorrow. Not only had the South lost the battle, but on July 2, his younger brother, Thomas, a Confederate infantryman, had been killed.[16]

Gettysburg was not the only Southern disaster that summer. On July 4, John C. Pemberton surrendered to Grant at Vicksburg.[17] And four days later, when Nathaniel P. Banks captured Port Hudson, the Federals gained control of the entire length of the Mississippi River.[18] The Confederacy had been cut in two.

The news from the war front was certainly discouraging, but Matthew faced personal problems, too. He was recovering his physical strength, but would his ego survive the mental blow of losing his foot? Psychologists who deal with male amputees report that they often "view the amputation as castration," a devastating mind-set for a man who flaunted his attractiveness to the ladies.[19] "Grief, self-pity, and despair are almost inevitable [in an amputee]," Dr. Lawrence W. Freeman, professor for Rehabilitation Medicine at the State University at Stony Brook, New York, reports. "Fear for the future and panic . . . are frequent later."[20]

Butler found an answer to this problem in Clara Dargan, a vivacious, twenty-year-old girl from Winnsboro, South Carolina. She had moved to Edgefield in the summer of 1862, where she joined Arthur Simkin's family as governess to his children. The two formed a relationship that August, which Butler would describe as "the tenderest memories of the days of 'lang syne' . . . possessed of all the freshness and bouyancy of that charming period of our lives."[21] Clara was just as enthralled. "Oh," she inscribed in her diary, "shall I ever walk those same paths with him again."[22]

Their mutual captivation might well have been platonic, but Matthew must have been relieved to find that despite the loss of a foot, he still had appeal to women. The relationship no doubt contributed to his complete recovery.

Another contributing factor was the reorganization of the cavalry. On September 9 Stuart combined his troopers into two divisions: one led by Fitz Lee, the second by Wade Hampton. The latter commanded three brigades under William E. Jones, Laurence S. Baker, and a just-commissioned general—Matthew Calbraith Butler. His four regiments included the Jeff Davis Legion, Cobb's Legion, the 2nd South Carolina, and the Phillips Legion.[23] While Butler was recovering from his Brandy Station wound, a distant relative, Col. Pierce Manning Butler Young, would lead the brigade.[24]

Prior to promoting Butler, officials in the War Department were concerned over his recuperation. Would he be able to lead in the field again? They sent him a wire, asking, "Can you ride a horse?" Matthew limped outside, mounted a favorite mare, jumped a fence or two, then telegraphed a one word reply. "Yes." His commission came in the next mail.[25]

That same month, the fortunes of the South took a turn upward. In the West the Rebels led by Braxton Bragg, reinforced by Longstreet, routed Rosecrans at Chickamauga Creek. The Federals retired into Chattanooga, where they came under siege.[26] And at Charleston, P. G. T. Beauregard refused to bow to the combined effort by the Yankees under Adm. John A. B. Dahlgren and Gen. Quincy A. Gillmore to take the port city.[27]

While Butler was convalescing at home, he was probably confused by the continuing changes in his division. Hampton had returned to South Carolina to recuperate from the saber gash suffered at Gettysburg, so Stuart had assumed temporary command of his men.[28] And none of the brigade chiefs named in September remained on duty. After a bitter argument with Jeb, Jones had been transferred to southwest Virginia. Thomas L. Rosser took over his post. Baker, wounded in the withdrawal from Gettysburg, was replaced by James B. Gordon; Young remained as head of Butler's command, but the brigade had been expanded by the addition of yet another regiment, the 1st South Carolina.[29]

Butler could take pride in his men's performance. The opposing armies in Virginia had fought only one major battle, Bristoe, and although neither could claim a clear victory, the cavalry, especially Matthew's troopers, had stood out in the October campaign. They lured the Yankee horsemen under Judson Kilpatrick into a trap at Buckland, and sent him running in disarray from the field. Kilpatrick, a man so vain he would file false reports rather than admit failure, could not gloss over his total rout. "This is the only . . . victory" he said, "that the enemy can boast over my command."[30]

Success in the field, however, proved fleeting for the Confederacy. Grant took over command from Rosecrans, and on November 14, he assaulted Bragg outside Chattanooga. Despite holding the heights that encircled the city, the Rebels were driven from their peaks and back into Georgia.[31] In a few months, this Federal triumph would set the stage for the end of the war. Joe Johnston would replace Bragg; Sherman would take charge from Grant in the west, freeing the latter to come east to face Robert E. Lee.[32]

When Hampton finally reported for duty on November 3, he was appalled by the deterioration of his command. A lack of forage had dismounted over half his men. He appealed to Lee to send his riders to winter in North Carolina, where they could not only feed their horses but also add recruits to their depleted ranks.[33]

This plea was denied. Rosser's brigade and Fitz Lee's division were shipped to the Shenandoah Valley to help Jubal Early meet a Federal cavalry raid by William W. Averell.[34] They stayed there, enjoying ample forage, but both Young and Gordon remained along the bleak shores of the Rapidan River to picket the front. This service further weakened Butler's brigade.

Lee, of course, recognized the problem, and in January, he asked Richmond if recruits from the cavalry regiments now serving on the coast of South Carolina could be transferred north to augment Butler's brigade. Lee noted that the ranks of hussars reporting to Beauregard at Charleston were "overflowing [with men] not called upon for very active duty."[35]

Secretary of War Seddon asked Beauregard to comment on Lee's proposal, and he naturally resisted any thought of losing men under his command. His reticence angered Stuart. He wrote the War Department and demanded that they order the Creole to provide the much needed reinforcements. He noted further that Butler, now convalescent from his wounds, could go to Charleston to "inspect those regiments so much beyond the proper proportion, and take out . . . a sufficient number to increase the First and Second South Carolina."[36]

No decision were made and the situation worsened. On February 1, Hampton reported that in Butler's brigade, "not 500 men can be mounted on serviceable horses . . . the alarming decrease in this command . . . will soon dismount every man."[37]

Ten days later Young joined the clamor by proposing a unique solution to the problem. He advocated a swap of brigades between Lee and Beauregard. Butler's men would go to Charleston; they would be replaced by the regiments on duty along the coast. "I cannot see how General Beauregard's department would be loser in this exchange." he said. "In less than a month . . . this brigade being . . . near their homes, would be full."[38] Hampton liked Young's idea, but Stuart would not agree to the loss of an experienced brigade. "We need more cavalry here," Jeb wrote, "but cannot spare any."[39] Lee was willing to consider the plan, but insisted on first knowing which regiments would be sent north.

On February 28 the risk of picketing the front with undermanned cavalry was revealed to the Confederacy. Judson Kilpatrick and 4,000 Federal troopers slipped past the thin Rebel line and rode for Richmond. They were bent on freeing the thousands of Yankee soldiers imprisoned in the Southern capital. When Hampton learned of the raid, he started after the Union horsemen, but he had only 300 men available for the pursuit. His chances for thwarting the enemy's efforts were slim. Fortunately for the Confederacy, Kilpatrick proved a coward. Upon arriving at the outskirts of the essentially defenseless city, he halted, then decided to retire. Hampton finally caught up with Kilpatrick east of the capital, and in a nighttime attack, despite the huge disparity in numbers, sent him flying down the Peninsula.[40]

Stuart, still hoping for recruits rather than a switch of brigades with Beauregard, made the next proposal for adding to his command. On March 14 he suggested that since Rooney Lee was available for duty (he, too, had been wounded at Brandy Station, taken captive while recuperating at home, and just now exchanged), a third division be created for him in the corps. Rosser would be transferred to Rooney; Hampton could replace this loss by splitting Butler's command in two, one half led by Matthew, the other under Young. Not so incidentally, this change would bring Stuart a promotion.[41]

Hampton was infuriated by Stuart's brazen ploy to gain the stars of lieutenant general. "I have received no orders . . . to break up one of my brigades," he wrote in a letter to Stuart, "and until such orders come, I shall not divide Butler's brigade."[42] Jeb's scheme was put on hold.

On March 18 the War Department finally decided on a means for strengthening Butler's brigade. The swap proposed by Young was accepted.

Gen. John Dunovant.
COURTESY CONFEDERATE VETERAN

The 1st and 2nd South Carolina were reassigned to the coast; the 4th, 5th, and 6th South Carolina would go to Virginia. Since the latter were at full strength (about 1,500 riders), they would constitute Butler's entire command. His three legions, augmented with troopers from Georgia, were passed to Young, who now led his own brigade. This opened the way for Gordon from Hampton's command and Chambliss from Fitz Lee's division to be grouped together to form a unit for Rooney Lee. Stuart thus got his third division, but not the expected promotion.[43]

Matthew went to Charleston on March 29, where he met with his three regimental chiefs. The 4th South Carolina was led by Col. Benjamin Huger Rutledge. Born in Statesburg, South Carolina, in 1828, he graduated with honors from Yale University, then returned to Charleston to set up a law practice. Rutledge married Eleanor Middleton in 1858. Noted for his rhetorical skills, he entered politics and won election to the state legislature. Rutledge was also a delegate to the Secession Convention. He joined the military as captain in the Charleston Light Dragoons in 1861.[44]

The 5th South Carolina was led by John Dunovant. He was born in Chester, South Carolina, in 1825, joined the army in 1846 to fight in Mexico, and rose in rank to sergeant by the end of that war. He remained in the military and gained a captaincy before resigning to join the Confederacy. Dunovant was given charge of the 1st South Carolina infantry in 1861, and assigned garrison duty at Charleston. He must have found this duty dull, because in June 1862, Dunovant was cashiered for drunkenness. The governor, Francis Pickens, Matthew's father-in-law, stepped in to salvage his career by appointing him commander of the 5th South Carolina. Dunovant was unmarried.[45]

Col. Hugh K. Aiken.
COURTESY BUTLER AND HIS CAVALRY

Hugh Kerr Aiken led the 6th South Carolina. Born in Winnsboro in 1822, he graduated from South Carolina College. He married Mary Gayle, daughter of Judge John Gayle, twice governor of Alabama, a representative to Congress, and later a United States judge, in 1852. Aiken was a brother-in-law to Josiah Gorgas, head of the Confederate Ordnance.[46] Prior to the war, Aiken owned a cotton plantation near Charleston, but he was not without military experience, having served in the South Carolina militia, rising to the rank of major general. He started the war as commander of the 16th Battalion of Partisan Rangers, assigned to coast duty.[47]

Although Butler was no doubt pleased by both the experience of his commanders and the sight of their men, dressed in clean uniforms and mounted on fresh horses, he must have had some trepidation. Few if any of the troopers had ever been in battle. Would they be good soldiers?

Hampton had anticipated this question and taken action to assure that at least some experienced cavalry would be in the command. "As General Butler will have a brigade of new troops," he requested of Richmond, "let me have ten men from each [old] regiment as scouts and guides . . . I do not care to have them mounted as they [can] soon mount themselves in the lines of the enemy."[48] His appeal was granted.

Butler spent the next month in Columbia, where his men were assembling for the ride north. His main concerns, however, lay with Maria. She was pregnant and having problems. "I will try to return home before my final departure for the Army," he said in an April 28 letter, "and hope to heaven I may reach there in time for your confinement."[49]

On May 1 Maria gave birth to yet another boy. When asked to name the child, she suggested they call him "Johnny Simpkins" in honor of one

CENTRAL VIRGINIA
JUNE 1864

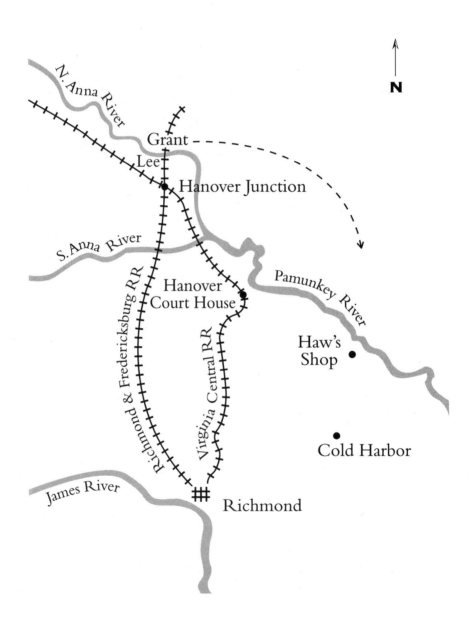

of her relatives, a former editor of the *Edgefield Advertiser,* Butler countered with "Andrew Pickens" as his choice. Neither accepted the other's offering, so the baby remained unnamed until late July, when they finally agreed on "Matthew Calbraith Butler," seeing him as a replacement for their third child, named after his father, whom they had lost in 1863, shortly after Matthew's injury in battle.[50]

On May 4 Grant, now commanding the Yankee armies in the East, crossed the Rapidan River to begin the summer campaign. Lee immediately attacked his exposed columns in The Wilderness, the area of scrub oak and thick brambles west of Fredericksburg. The foes fought furiously, but after three days of battle, neither had gained the advantage. The enemy lost almost 18,000; Lee's casualties, including Longstreet, wounded by his own troops, were about 8,700.[51]

Grant now faced a decision: he could retire, as the other Union leaders had done before him; or he could shift east, then south to flank Lee out of his immovable position. He took the latter course.

Lee, however, discerned Grant's strategy, and although the Federals marched throughout the night of May 7 to 8, when they finally reached Spotsylvania Court House the following morning, they found the Rebels in position, awaiting battle. The fighting was renewed and another stalemate evolved.

Frustrated by his failure to dislodge Lee, Grant tried a different strategy. On May 9 he sent his troopers, now under Philip H. Sheridan, into the Confederate rear. "Our move," Sheridan recalled, "[was] a challenge to Stuart for a cavalry duel behind Lee's lines."[52] He led 15,000 men in a column that stretched for thirteen miles.

Stuart assumed that the enemy was heading for Richmond, so he split his 4,000-man force in two: half approached the Union rear to harass and slow their advance; the rest rode for the van of the Northern column to block their entry into the Southern capital. They achieved their objective on May 11 at Yellow Tavern, six miles outside the city, where the Confederates dug in for battle. Sheridan charged their hastily prepared line, and easily thrashed his outmanned rival. During the fray, Stuart was shot in the stomach. He suffered excruciating pain for hours before finally dying about 8:00 P.M. on May 12.[53]

After routing Stuart, Sheridan's men galloped north to rejoin Grant, still engaged with Lee near Spotsylvania. But before they reached the front, that contest had ended. The Union had again failed to dislodge the Rebels. The Federals suffered almost 18,000 casualties, twice as many as the Confederates (half of whose losses fell on May 12 during the enemy's assault on a point along Lee's line dubbed the "Mule Shoe"), in their unsuccessful efforts to batter through the Southern defenses.[54] On May 21 Grant started yet another turning movement, heading east, then south in an attempt to gain Lee's rear.

About the same time that the Union was leaving Spotsylvania, Butler headed north from Columbia for the front. The 4th South Carolina led the parade, followed by the 5th, and finally the 6th. Matthew accompanied the troopers who brought up the rear.

When Grant reached the North Anna River, he found that Lee had once more anticipated his strategy and entrenched in an inverted "**V**" below the water. He crossed the stream to probe the Confederate position, but soon learned that it was so strong, offering battle was out of the question. The enemy broke camp on May 27 to embark on still another flanking march around Lee's right.[55]

Portions of Butler's new brigade, the 5th South Carolina and about half of the 4th, arrived at the front that evening. The veterans (probably envious of the "new issues" in their clean uniforms and astride sleek, well-bred horses) teased the green riders. Their rifles, long-range Enfields, were a special object for ridicule. "I say," one of the old hands said, "let me have your long-shooter and I'll bite off the end."[56]

Butler was still en route, unavailable to lead his men, but Lee immediately sent the inexperienced troopers into the field. He wanted to know where Grant's infantry was headed. They joined Rosser's and Wickham's riders under Hampton in a reconnaissance, trotting southeast along the Pamunkey River.

At the same time, the Yankee army had turned south and was also approaching this stream. Sheridan's horsemen, just returned from their contest with Stuart, were screening the infantry's march. Grant sent his horsemen across the waters to probe the front to see if Lee had countered his shift in position. They soon collided with Hampton's Rebels near Haw's Shop.

Hampton quickly formed a defensive line with Rosser on the left, Wickham in the center, and Butler's South Carolinians on the right. The enemy charged, but were thrown back. In the melee, a few Yankee infantrymen who had joined in the assault were captured. Their presence confirmed Grant's location, so Hamtpon, having achieved his mission, ordered his force to retire. Both Rosser and Wickham withdrew, but the call to retreat failed to reach the South Carolinians. They continued the battle.

The enemy pressed forward against Butler's small group, charging them from the left, the center, and the right. The inexperienced Rebels, however, never flinched. No doubt determined to prove to Rosser's and Wickham's veteran troopers that they, too, could fight, they stayed cool and took careful aim before firing volley after volley toward the Federal assaulters. "Our loss was greater than in any other engagement in the campaign," George Custer said after the contest. The Union cavalry chief was so impressed by the accurate and fast fire of the Confederates, he thought that his force had faced superior numbers.[57] Even Sheridan was impressed. "It is the first time we have met those Carolinians of Butler's," he said, "and I wish to God it might be the last."[58]

Hampton himself finally extracted Butler's troops from the front. He personally galloped into their midst to guide them to the rear.[59] They joined the rest of Lee's force as it assumed a position west of Cold Harbor where they awaited Grant's next gambit. Matthew rode up that night (May 28) and took command of his brigade.[60]

CHAPTER 10

Trevilian Station

WHEN BUTLER REPORTED FOR DUTY IN LATE MAY 1864, HIS TROOPS were amazed by his robust appearance. He was as tall and handsome as before, and although he now had a cork foot in place of the one he lost at Brandy Station, it was hidden inside a spurred, polished boot. "I am not much of a pedestrian," he noted, "but in the saddle, I am as good as ever."[1]

In a meeting with his three regimental chiefs, Matthew reviewed the situation at their front. Lee faced Grant east of Richmond; Beauregard had come up from South Carolina to confront a Union force under Benjamin Butler, who had landed men from the sea into an area below the capital near Petersburg. Held at bay, the latter was shipping troops north to Grant, who was again moving eastward, hoping to hook up with the oncoming soldiers. Lee wanted to halt his adversary until he received reinforcements from Beauregard. He had sent Jubal Early, now in command of the Second Corps, camped near Bethesda Church, to assault Grant's ranks.[2] Early asked for horsemen for reconnoitering. He was referred to Butler, who gave the assignment to Rutledge.

The head of the 4th South Carolina soon returned in shame. In his meeting with Early, he had become confused by the complicated maps being used, and the surly, profane Virginian had sent Rutledge and his men back to Butler.[3]

Matthew mounted up and hurried to Early. He knew that Jubal could be obnoxious, but Butler was not about to accept any guff. "I have been ordered to picket your [front]," he snapped to Jubal, "and if you don't assist me in getting into position, I will take this cavalry back to camp and you can go to hell and do your own picketing."

"Well, get down, Butler," Early replied, "and we will talk this over."

Butler dismounted, and the two sat astride a log, each with his own map. But before starting a discussion of the mission, Early made a peace offering. "Wouldn't you like a drink?"

"Well, yes," Butler answered. "It's about the time of day that a cavalry-man enjoys a little something."[4]

Early produced a flask from an inside pocket, and with a nodding smile, each took a healthy swig. They then agreed that Butler would ride to Knowles' Cross Roads, where Jubal thought he would find the enemy. Matthew encountered Yankee infantry opposition prior to reaching the intersection, but he and his men pushed the Union soldiers backward until they finally arrived at their desired position. They skirmished from early afternoon until dusk, when Early finally came up. The Federals retired as the Second Corps came into view.[5]

"I told you," Early said with a wink to one of his generals, Stephen Ramseur, "as soon as [our] infantry appeared, the Yanks would travel." He was baiting Butler.

"Infantry be damned," Butler fumed. "Here we have been fighting all afternoon . . . against about ten to one, while you have been lounging . . . in the woods . . . smoking your pipe while we have been catching the devil."[6]

Butler, in his first skirmish since being wounded, had been personally conspicuous in the fighting. "My troops all being fresh," he explained in a note to his wife, "I had to expose myself more than ever before." He offered himself as a target to the enemy, hoping his men would draw courage by his display of bravery.[7] A Yankee prisoner later stated, "I shot at that man six times," pointing to Matthew, astride a gray horse. Butler's staff of couriers and orderlies wanted to chip in to buy him a different animal, one that would be less distinct on the battlefield, but Matthew would not give up his mount.[8]

That evening, Butler was reinforced by a Georgia troop, whom he immediately assigned to picket duty. Their chief, a captain, asked if there was a doctor nearby. He said he was feeling bad. "No, Sir!" Butler explod-ed. He thought that the officer was a shirker, too cowardly to face the Yan-kees. "You have no use for a doctor tonight," Matthew snapped with cold fury, "go on picket and, if necessary, see a doctor tomorrow, if you [still] need one."[9]

Early charged the enemy at Bethesda Church on May 30, but was rebuffed. Grant continued to shift his force to the east. Richard Anderson's First Corps attacked the Federals on June 1, but they, too, were thrown back. Grant stopped sidling, however, because his reinforcements had finally arrived. It was his turn to initiate battle. On June 3, he mounted a massive assault along a three-corps front against Lee's lines at Cold Harbor. The Rebels were ready and waiting for the Union, and during the first eight minutes of the early morning blitz, the Yankees suffered most of the 7,000

Fitzhugh Lee. COURTESY. PHOTOGRAPHIC
HISTORY OF THE CIVIL WAR

casualties they took that day. Lee's losses were fewer than 1,500. Grant was
defeated almost as the contest began.[10]

Once again a stalemate ensued. But on June 8 a new threat was discovered. Northern cavalry led by Sheridan had left the front and were rushing
northwest, seemingly headed for the Shenandoah Valley. Their force was
large, estimated at about 8,000 troopers, arrayed in two divisions: one led
by Alfred T. A. Torbert, whose three brigades included those under George
A. Custer, Thomas C. Devlin, and Wesley Merritt; the second by David
Gregg, whose two brigades were led by Henry E. Davies and J. Irvin
Gregg.[11] They were thought to be reinforcing the Union infantry led by
David Hunter, who had just taken Staunton, and was now going south to
invest Lynchburg. After the two combined to capture this city, they would
then move on Richmond. Jubal Early had started west to confront Hunter;
Hampton was ordered to stop Sheridan.[12]

The expedition forced Lee to make a decision about his cavalry leadership. He had avoided choosing between Hampton and Fitzhugh Lee to
replace Stuart, but now he had to face this issue. He could not order his
horsemen into the field under dual commanders. Lee assigned Hampton as
temporary head of the corps.[13]

Fitz Lee was probably unhappy with this decision because he, too, was
well qualified to lead the corps. Born in 1835 in Fairfax County, Virginia,
he graduated from West Point in 1856 and served as a cavalry officer in
Indian Territory until 1861 when he returned to the Academy as an assistant
instructor of tactics. He resigned the post in May 1861 to join his uncle,
Robert E. Lee, and the Confederacy. At the start of the war, Fitz found

duty with Joe Johnston's staff, but he soon transferred to the cavalry. He won a brigadier general's star in July 1862. About a year later, the bushy-bearded officer was elevated to major general plus division command.[14]

Five cavalry brigades, totaling almost 5,000 men, left the Richmond area about sunrise on June 9: Butler, Young, and Rosser from Hampton's division; Wickham and Lunsford L. Lomax from Lee's. They moved north until 12:00 P.M., halted for two hours near Hanover Junction, then trotted west along the Virginia Central Railroad until midnight. After resting for just two hours at Beaver Dam Station, they continued on through the night into the next morning. The men stopped at noon for another short breather, then galloped to Trevilian Station.[15] Their desperate pace had put them ahead of Sheridan's troopers, who had ridden much slower and were camped to the north. The tough trek should have exhausted Matthew, but he had held up extremely well. "Butler seemed to be in his glory," an admiring participant noted.[16]

Rosser camped above Trevilian Station, Butler near the depot, Young's brigade, led by Col. Gilbert J. Wright, who had replaced Young, wounded in the battles near Richmond, below Butler. Lee's troopers, who had brought up the rear, halted at Louisa Court House.[17]

Once his troops were settled, Butler rode to Hampton's headquarters, situated in a handsome mansion along the South Anna River. Rosser, too, was there. They met with Hampton and the plantation owner in his sitting room, where they viewed the lay of the surrounding country. No plans for the morrow were made except to be ready to fight at first light. "After supper our teacher played the piano," Alice West, the landlord's daughter, remembered, "and the soldiers and young ladies danced and sang all the war songs."[18] One wonders if Butler with his corked foot dared join in the festivity.

At sunrise Rosser rode into Matthew's camp to find out if he had any further news about their orders. "Butler," he called, "What is Hampton going to do here today?"

"Damned if I know," Matthew replied. "We have been up mounted since daylight . . . my men and horses are being worsted by non-action."[19]

The two decided to go back to Hampton, who had finally decided to mount a charge. Butler, trailed by Wright, would advance north on the left; Fitz Lee would come up from the right; they would converge to take on Sheridan at Clayton's Store. Rosser's brigade would cover the left flank, making sure that the enemy did not slip past them into the Valley.[20]

Both Rosser and Butler returned to their camps to wait for the signal to start. And when Lee soon reported that he was on the move, Butler, accompanied by Hampton, started his advance toward Clayton's Store. He

TREVILIAN STATION

JUNE 11–12, 1864

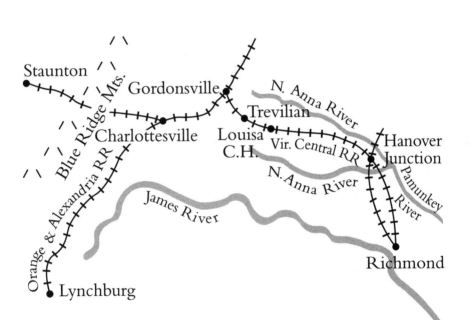

soon met a Rebel picket, who reported that the Yankees were coming south in force.

Hampton hurried back to the rear where he would direct the battle; Butler ordered his men to dismount. One out of four was assigned to stay in place and hold the horses; the others formed in line: Rutledge with the 4th Carolina on the left; Maj. Joseph H. Morgan, in charge while Dunovant recovered from wounds received at Haw's Shop, and the 5th South Carolina in the center; Aiken leading the 6th Carolina to the right. They moved ahead on foot, and were soon engaged with Devin's Union brigade.[21]

At first Butler's men held the upper hand, driving the enemy backward about half a mile. But as the combat raged into its second hour, Sheridan pressed Merritt, Davies, and then Irvin Gregg into the battle. The four Federal brigades, also fighting on foot, soon overlapped both ends of the Rebel line. "I am being flanked!" Rutledge cried in a frantic note from the left. "Send reinforcements."

Butler had no men to spare, but he remained as cool as always. "Flank back!" he replied. Rutledge would later recall with a grin that this was the "cheekiest" order he had received during the war.[22]

Matthew did, however, ride to his left, where he found a squadron giving way. Although he was typically restrained during battle, the sight of cowardice always broke Butler's usual reserve. He exploded with anger. "You damn rascals," he thundered, "if you don't turn back, I will murder the last damn one of you!" The men immediately wheeled and returned to the front.[23]

Butler, of course, had already advised Hampton that he was in peril, and the commander had pushed Wright's troopers ahead. They arrived at the front just in time to stabilize Rutledge's line.

Suddenly word came from Hampton that a disaster was unfolding. Fitz Lee had not come up on the east. With no one to stop him, George Custer had led his Yankee riders around Butler's right and into his rear. The Federals had captured the brigade's wagons and led horses. Butler must disengage at once and return to Trevilian Station.[24]

Butler, per usual, did not panic. "It is hell to hold on," he advised Hampton, "and hell to let go." He would retire, but at a safe speed. He mounted his men one regiment at a time (without regard to whose horse was whose), sending them in column toward Trevilian Station. Upon reaching the rear, Butler found that Custer was gone. Rosser had come in from the left to rout the enemy. He had not only recovered Butler's wagons and mounts, but also relieved the Federals of their own vehicles.[25]

Although Custer had been driven away, he remained near the railroad, between Hampton and Lee, blocking the latter's route to the front. And the

enemy who had pursued Butler's withdrawal were at hand, eager to continue the battle. They advanced en masse on foot toward the station.
Matthew, however, was waiting for them, and he led a mounted charge that
scattered the oncoming Yankees. Butler chased the fleeing Union, but he
was soon recalled by Hampton. Another Federal contingent had gathered
on the left, threatening the ground where the Confederate wounded had
been assembled.[26]

The Federals attacked just as Butler reached the scene. Matthew had
only a small detachment with him, and this group under Lieutenant Long
were a poor match for the hundreds of Yankees marching elbow to elbow.
Butler had no choice. He had to order Long to mount a suicidal charge. It
was "an act of gallantry and dash," Butler stated later, "[that] I have never
seen surpassed."[27] Their audacity shocked the enemy, who halted, allowing
ambulances to whisk the wounded to safety. Most of Long's saddles, however, were emptied during the assault.

Butler's troopers were all rushing to the area, and as they arrived,
Matthew put them in a line west of the station to engage the Yankees. The
two adversaries fought in place until sunset. Butler then withdrew farther
west about three miles into Green Springs Valley, where his force spent that
night.[28]

"This day's operations ended disastrously to our arms," Matthew admitted.[29] Hampton's plan for a converging assault on Sheridan at Clayton's
Store had gone awry. Butler's men had charged on the left, but when Fitz
Lee failed to advance on the right, Matthew found himself without support
and facing superior numbers. He was just barely holding his ground when
the enemy exploded into his rear. Butler quickly withdrew, and although
Rosser did drive Custer's Yankee troopers eastward, the Federals had opened a wedge between Hampton's ranks and were positioned to finish off the
Rebels tomorrow. The only advantage the South held was in attitude,
"Sheridan *supposing* the battle was over," one observer said, "Hampton
knowing that it had not been fought yet."[30]

In the darkness, Butler and Hampton met to decide on a strategy for
the next morning. Their first problem was Fitz Lee. Hampton had allowed
him to operate independently, but Fitz seemingly would not follow orders.
Hampton had to gain control, but in giving Lee his full attention, he could
not retain command of his own division. He put Butler in charge of his
three brigades and their deployment.

Matthew elected to assume a defensive line parallel to the railroad
embankment about one mile north of the station. His three South Carolina
regiments would take a position on the left, where the track turned at a
sharp angle; Wright's brigade would cover the center; and Rosser's troop-

ers, now under Col. Richard H. Dulany due to the former being shot in the knee late the day before, would be on the right. His eight cannons would be "stationed at convenient points" along the line.[32] Fitz Lee, still posted to the east near Louisa Court House, would circle south around the Yankees to report to Hampton and form the reserve.

At first light Butler took the division to the tracks, where they built an entrenchment made of loose railroad ties and earth. "With nothing to work with but tin cups, frying pans, or bare hands," one related, "we threw up a protective shield against the enemy's bullets."[33] The men then waited for the arrival of both the Yankees and Fitz Lee's troopers.

Fitz's men reached the front about noon, and they took up their position as the reserve. Sheridan, however, failed to show. Perhaps thinking that Hampton had been so bruised by yesterday's beating that he would soon slink away without a fight, the Northern commander spent the morning and early afternoon ripping up the tracks eastward toward Louisa Court House. Finally, after 3:00 P.M., Torbert's division headed for Butler's line. One assault, they must have assumed, and Hampton would scatter. Then on to Lynchburg.[34]

Butler was on the far left, sitting on some loose ties, talking with Rutledge, when the Federals advanced toward his post. A Yankee sharpshooter, moving with the skirmish line, saw the two officers, and he fired a shot that plowed with a thud into the wood close to Butler. "That is the opening of the ball," Matthew drawled as he rose, then ambled toward the center of his position to direct the battle.[35]

Merritt made the first charge on foot against Butler's weakest point, the swerve in the track where his "new issue" South Carolinians lay awaiting. The enemy was greeted with a hailstorm of lead. "Those raw men didn't know anything . . . about being whipped," an observer said, "and had no idea of anything but killing all the Yankees in sight. . . . [They] made their rail piles look as if they were on fire, so incessantly did they burn their powder."[36]

The Federal charge was thrown back. Infuriated by the stubborn resistance of Butler's men, Torbert sent wave after wave toward the Rebel left, Merritt, Devin, and then Custer; but every time, the green troops stood fast. After six such assaults, the enemy gathered for one final attempt to break through Butler's lines. The sun was setting, and as the sky darkened with each minute, the Yankees mounted their attack. "Before the canister and still steady fire of our . . . rifles," Butler remembered with great pride, "the enemy fell back for the last time before the deadly aim of our troops."[37]

Butler's brigade had born the brunt of the battle, and they drew their inspiration from him. A soldier offered the following description of

Matthew during the critical moment of one of the Yankees' charges. "He was quiet as if . . . facing a party of ladies in a parlor," the man related, "his right leg cast unconcernedly over the pommel of his McClellan saddle, and with a neatly cut switch in hand, tapping [on] his boot heel."[38] He showed no fear and his confidence was contagious.

Hampton later stated his praise. "Butler's defense at Trevilian was never surpassed," he related. "He was as good a soldier as we had."[39]

As the Yankees disengaged, they were suddenly assailed on their right. Hampton had sent Fitz Lee with Lomax's brigade to charge the Union flank. The effect was devastating. Sheridan realized that he was in desperate peril. He was in enemy territory, low on both provisions and ammunition, and facing a determined foe who was bent on and capable of annihilating his command. He ran, leaving his dead and wounded on the field. "It was," one Rebel gloated, "a regular 'Bull Run' on a small scale."[40]

Sheridan fled through the night, heading for the North Anna River, hoping to put the water between his force and an angry, pursuing enemy. But Hampton had not left camp. His men were exhausted by the fight, and did not start after the Union until the next morning. Of the 4,700 Rebels who came to Trevilian Station, almost 1,100 had been killed, wounded, or were missing. Among their casualties was Aiken, shot in the chest. His lung was pierced, but he was expected to recover.[41]

The Union had sent over 8,000 into the fray, and their casualties exceeded 1,000. The combined losses for the combatants were 40 percent more than those incurred at Brandy Station, often deemed the "greatest" cavalry battle of the war.[42]

The Federal retreat headed northeast, more toward Washington, D.C., than a return to Grant's camp. Hampton trailed after the enemy, skirmishing with their rear but never able to bring the Yankees to battle. Upon reaching Spotsylvania, Sheridan turned southeast, following the north shore of the Mattapony River, galloping through Bowling Green, Walkerton, King and Queen Court House, and then Dunkirk. He rode into White House on June 20.[43]

Hampton continued to follow, remaining below the water, keeping between the Yankee riders and their goal of reaching Grant. He found it difficult to keep up because Sheridan's men were confiscating fresh mounts as they moved. The wornout animals were killed to prevent local farmers from using them to raise crops for the Confederacy. "In his retreat of one hundred miles," a Rebel stated, "[Sheridan] left, on an average, twelve dead horses to the mile."[44] Cruelty of this sort was shattering to men like Butler, who like many Southerners, loved their mounts almost as if they were human beings. Sheridan's butchering of horses helped to fan the hatred for Yankees that permeated the Confederacy to the end of the war and beyond.

Protected by the gunboats on the James River, Sheridan remained at White House for several days to rest his troops. He also contemplated how he would get past Hampton and back to Grant, who had embarked on yet another flanking maneuver. On the night of June 12 the Yankees had slipped by Lee's right and started crossing the Peninsula, heading toward the James River. They used pontoons to traverse the stream on June 14, and the next day, assaulted Petersburg, twenty miles below Richmond. Grant sought to isolate the capital from its supply points to the south by seizing this key railroad center.[45]

Lee was caught unawares, but Beauregard, despite being badly out-numbered, managed to fend off the Federals' charges until June 18, when the Army of Northern Virginia arrived to stabilize the new front. Both sides started to build entrenchments. The war in the East had evolved into a siege.[46]

On June 23 Sheridan left White House, heading south in two columns, Torbert and the trains on the left, Gregg on the right. As he cut across the Peninsula toward the James River and Petersburg, Hampton moved in parallel, keeping his force between the Union and Richmond. To prevent an attack that would disrupt his march, Sheridan sent Gregg's troopers westward the following day to occupy the Rebels, and Butler, still commanding Hampton's division, accepted the challenge at Samaria Church. He dismounted his men and opened a slow fire to hold the Yankees in place. At the same time, Butler asked for reinforcements to attack Gregg's right. His plan was to mount an assault from the front at the same time his riders hit the Yankees' flank. Fitz Lee came up, asked that he be put in charge, and when Hampton agreed to his request, carried out Butler's tactics. This attack drove the enemy from the field. "We realized for the first time," one of the Union horsemen confessed, "how it felt to get a good sound thrashing and then be chased for our lives."[47]

This skirmish ended the fighting. Sheridan's troopers crossed the James River on June 26 and spent a month resting from the campaign. Hampton followed, but he would have no time to recuperate. Another Yankee cavalry troop, led by James H. Wilson, was deep in Southern territory, and Robert E. Lee ordered a pursuit by the weary Rebel horsemen.

━•━ ≡✦≡ ━•━

In his report to Grant, Sheridan claimed that he won a victory at Trevilian Station. He considered the battle only a one-day affair, and that his repeated charges and rebuffs on June 12 were just a "reconnaissance." He further noted that Hunter had not performed his role in the campaign, and that was why he had elected (not been forced) to retreat.[48]

His compatriots knew better. Wilson later pointed out that Sheridan "neither joined Hunter . . . nor returned directly to the army, but made a wide detour to the northeast . . . [following] a circuitous . . . route. . . . He finally pushed Hampton aside . . . but this was with much heavy fighting and no substantial fruits of victory."[49]

And even amid his crowing over having beaten Hampton, Sheridan did admit that he had failed to meet the objectives of his mission. "I regret," he said to Grant, "my inability to carry out your instructions."[50] He blamed Butler for his failure. "That damned man," he grumbled during his retreat, "[gave me] more trouble with his South Carolina brigade than all the rebel cavalry put together."[51]

CHAPTER 11

Wilson

WHEN THE REBEL CAVALRY NEARED THE CAPITAL, BUTLER TOOK TEM-porary command of the corps. Hampton rode into Richmond to visit political leaders there; Matthew led the men through the city, then south to Petersburg where he reported to Robert E. Lee.

Butler reached Lee's headquarters at noon on June 27. When Matthew entered the commander's tent, Lee invited him to share his meal, a small ham sandwich. "I was as hungry as a college boy," Butler related, but seeing that there was only enough for one, he refused Lee's generous offer. "You will require this lunch yourself," he answered. "I can manage to get along."[1]

"But I insist," Lee replied, handing Butler an elegant linen napkin. The two munched in silence, then Lee outlined a problem. Provisions into the capital came via three railroads: the Richmond & Danville, which entered the city from the southwest; the Southside, which began at Burkeville, a junction of the Richmond and Danville, then ran due east to Petersburg; and the Petersburg & Weldon, which came up through Petersburg and on to Richmond from the south. Union cavalry under Gen. James Wilson had entered this general area in order to destroy as much of all three tracks as possible.[2]

The Federals had left their camp on June 22. Wilson had a force of about 5,500 troopers, which included both his division plus the men led by Gen. August V. Kautz. They had slipped around the Confederate line to follow the Southside westward, tearing up tracks and burning depots as they progressed. Rooney Lee's cavalry was in pursuit, but he had been held off by Wilson's men, leaving Kautz free to carry out the destruction. The Union riders arrived at Burkeville on June 24, where they wheeled south-west. The ravaged the rails of the Richmond & Danville for over thirty miles. When they arrived at the trestle over the Staunton River on June 26, however, they were met by local militia, defending the overpass. Wilson was unable to drive the citizen soldiers away. He then decided to end his

AREA OF
SIEGE OPERATIONS

JUNE 1864

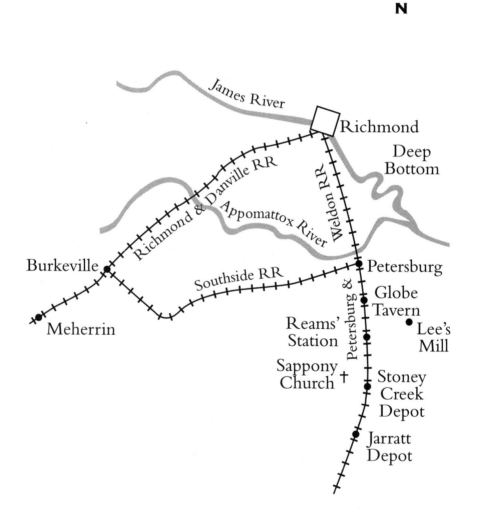

raid, and was now headed back for his own lines. The Yankee horsemen were following a course toward Stoney Creek Station on the Petersburg & Weldon. Lee asked Butler to intercept Wilson and annihilate his force.[3]

Having already ridden about twenty miles since morning, the troopers were tired, and Matthew decided to rest his men as much as possible before confronting the enemy. The column passed through Petersburg, then halted and camped for the night.

The next morning, June 28, Butler headed south along the Weldon tracks for Reams' Station, where Fitz Lee's force dropped out to defend this post. Butler took the remaining cavalry on to Stoney Creek Station. Both Hampton and Rooney Lee soon joined the command. Chambliss's brigade (from Lee's division) was posted to the west along Sappony Creek to look for Wilson's anticipated approach.[4]

The Union rode up about dusk. Chambliss charged their column, forcing Wilson to fall back to Sappony Church, where he entrenched. Hampton then advanced and formed a line confronting the enemy. Over the next few hours, Wilson ordered a number of attacks, trying to press through the Rebels' position, but in each instance, his men were thrown back. The two foes continued to skirmish until past midnight. Seeing that he could not get by Hampton, Wilson started Kautz north for Reams' Station; the rest of his cavalry would follow at daybreak. To conceal this diminishing of his force, Wilson resumed his assaults on Hampton's line at sporadic intervals throughout the remaining darkness. "It was a night," he recalled, "of unusual peril and excitement."[5]

The Rebels, too, were making plans. During one of the quieter moments, Butler was told that one of his men, Young Epps, had grown up in the area and knew of a route through a morass that protected the Federal left. He went to Hampton to ask permission to take 100 hand-chosen men through the bog and into the Yankee rear. He would assault Wilson from behind at dawn. Hampton agreed to the foray.

The men were quietly selected, and the group moved off on horseback toward the mire. Epps, however, soon got lost. He would lead the column into the marsh, then back off when the morass proved impassable. Butler finally concluded that Epps was afraid, and Matthew would never tolerate cowardice. "Young man," he snapped, "if you do not conduct this column over this swamp, I will have you tied to your horse and send you in front."[6] The threat proved sufficient, and on their next sally, the troopers rode through into the enemy rear.

When Matthew opened fire at dawn on June 29, Hampton ordered a frontal charge. The Yankees panicked, losing all semblance of order. Hit from two different directions, they scattered every man for himself, most following Wilson north toward Reams' Station. The Federal casualties totaled more than 800 killed, wounded, or captured. Butler lost about twenty men.[7]

Hampton did not pursue Wilson. He instead returned to Stoney Creek Station to reset his lines. Fitz Lee would be sure to fend off the Yankees at Reams' Station; they had to return south, and when Lee sent word of the retreat, Hampton would be waiting for them.[8]

Late that afternoon, Butler visited the field hospital to check on his wounded. Once he was satisfied that the men were in good hands, he turned to the doctor and asked if he had anything to drink. Matthew explained that he was "about to expire from loss of sleep, hunger, thirst, and heat."

"Only some sorghum whiskey," the physician offered.

"Any port in a storm," Butler answered. He took a sip, but found the liquor so fetid, he could not swallow it. "If the Yankee bullets don't kill these poor fellows," he stated with a grimace, "that stuff will."[9]

When Wilson joined Kautz at Reams', they tried to push through the Rebel line, but found they could not get by Fitz Lee's cavalry, reinforced by William Mahone's infantry from A. P. Hill's corps. Wilson was so thoroughly routed, he had to abandon his artillery (twelve field cannons and four howitzers) and his wagons, many filled with personal items that his men had stolen during the raid. The Rebels were infuriated when they found women's clothing, furniture, and even a silver communion service among the Union's booty.[10]

The Federals suffered over 500 casualties before escaping to the south, back toward Butler and Hampton. The enemy losses would have been greater, but when the Rebels started chasing after them they encountered hundreds of slaves who had fled from their plantations to look for freedom by falling in behind the retreating ranks. "The [Southern] cavalry would leave pursuing a 'Yankee' at any time for the pleasure of [killing] a negro," a Northern soldier bitterly recalled. "Men were shot without mercy. . . . [W]omen and children were made prisoners, after being beaten and abused."[11] Butler was not involved in this carnage, but had he been there, he probably would not have stopped the bedlam. He would have been upset by the blacks' betrayal of their masters, and no doubt felt that their "punishment" was well deserved.

Fitz Lee was supposed to have sent a courier to Butler and Hampton to inform them that Wilson was on the run toward their position, but he elected instead to mount his own pursuit, which had little chance for success. "The country was covered . . . by an unbroken forest. . . . The trees were large and the underbrush almost unpenetrable," Wilson wrote. "The roads were obscure and difficult to follow."[12] The Yankees were soon out of

Fitz's sight. That night Kautz turned east ten miles below Reams' Station and passed through Hampton's net and back to the Federal line. Wilson crossed the Weldon tracks, too, but he headed south, past Stoney Creek Station and on to Jarrett Station, where he spent that evening.[13]

Hampton had waited all day June 29 for word from Lee, but none came. Finally, at 9:00 A.M. on the thirtieth, a courier from Fitz rode into camp and reported that Wilson's cavalry was at Jarratt Station. Hampton and Butler raced south, but they were too late. The enemy had started east, and before the Rebels could catch them, they had passed into Union territory.[14]

Butler was incensed with Fitz for allowing the Federal cavalry to escape, and he went to Hampton to suggest that he file charges against Lee. Butler was convinced that Fitz's inaction at Trevilian Station and his failure to communicate from Reams' Station were proof that Lee was striving to discredit Hampton so he could gain command of the cavalry corps for himself. Hampton refused. Noting that Fitz was Robert E. Lee's nephew, his requesting a court-martial would embarrass the commanding general, something he would never do to a man he admired so much. All trust of Fitz Lee was gone, however, so Hampton used him as little as possible in the campaigns to come.[15]

With Wilson's return to his own lines, the fighting between opposing cavalries ended. The Union horsemen had been whipped at both Trevilian Station and below Petersburg, and many were fatigued and demoralized. Few were left who would risk further action.

Hampton's riders moved into camp above the James River, where they rested and recuperated for about a month. Butler continued in temporary command of the division, but he felt that he was being used, not rewarded for his recent triumphs in the field. "General Hampton telegraphs General Lee . . . 'I turned the flank of the enemy and routed him,'" he said in a note to Maria, "when the truth is he did not order it . . . but had nothing to do with the execution. . . . I ought to have the rank as well as the trouble."[16]

Butler's frustration rose on July 2, when Robert E. Lee proposed that Hampton be given permanent charge of the cavalry corps, Army of Northern Virginia. His promotion, without a change in rank, was confirmed on August 11.[17] His former post of division commander was left unfilled, so Butler remained in limbo.

CHAPTER 12

Siege

DURING THIS PERIOD OF REST, BUTLER MUST HAVE FOLLOWED THE WAR IN other theaters with great interest. Early had chased Hunter out of the Valley, then moved north into Maryland. He fought the Federals led by Lew Wallace at the Monocacy River on July 9, defeated them, and two days later stood on the outskirts of Washington, D.C. Lincoln was forced to ask Grant to send reinforcements to defend the capital. Horatio Wright rushed his VI Corps to the scene. Early, however, knew that he had too few troops to capture the city, so after a day or so of teasing the enemy with his presence, he withdrew to head back toward the Valley.[1]

To the south Johnston was using a strategy of pacific retreat in dueling with Sherman. He would assume a position as if to fight, but when the Yankees came up, he would withdraw, moving ever deeper into Georgia. Several inconclusive battles had been fought with neither side gaining the advantage. By July 9 the Army of Tennessee had their backs to Atlanta. President Davis shuddered over Johnston's willingness to cede territory; the general was proud of his having conserved the strength of his army. The two were at loggerheads. On July 15 Davis settled their differences with a decisive move. He replaced Johnston with John B. Hood.[2]

Many in the South were shocked by Johnston's dismissal. He was considered among the best Confederate generals, even equal to Lee. Butler, however, agreed with the president. "I . . . thought Mr. Davis was right," he professed, "in placing a more aggressive man in command."[3] War to him meant fighting the enemy. Maneuvering was just a form of retreat.

There was, however, still levity to life near Richmond. Butler's mischievous scout, Hugh Scott, had disappeared from camp in early July. He appeared one evening in the capital, where he reported to Butler, meeting with fellow officers in the Exchange Hotel.

"Where have you been?" Butler demanded.

"Fredericksburg."

"Did you bring that hat?" Scott had promised Butler he would get him a new hat if he ever left the lines.

"Yes, Sir."

"Where is it?"

"Out here in the office."

"Go and get it."

"No, Sir," Scott declared. He had not received permission to wander off, and was fearful that Butler was about to arrest him. "If I go to the guardhouse," he bargained, "you don't get the hat, General."

"Go and get the hat," Butler repeated.

"I have got to have [your] promise whether I go to the guardhouse or not," Scott persisted.

When Butler grudgingly agreed to overlook Scott's failure to follow orders, the scout left the room, then returned with an elegant hat, trimmed in gold cord. "It . . . fitted him 'jam up,'" Scott recalled with glee.

The other officers, who had enjoyed this insubordinate exchange, were jealous of Butler, and demanded that he order his scout back to Fredericksburg to get them hats, too. He refused, and the scene perhaps became a little testy. Scott resolved the problem.

"General," he intervened, "I have got a canteen of rye liquor in the office."

"Bring it up," Butler replied.

Scott brought the whiskey to the room. "They stayed up there a good while," he remembered, "having a good time."[4]

The quiet outside of Richmond was about to end. Grant had Lee besieged, but he was not encircled. Provisions continued to pour into the capital. To defeat the Confederacy, Grant had to sever the railroads that were supplying his adversary. His initial target was the Weldon tracks, south of Petersburg. The Union, however, could not overlook a chance to smash through the Rebel line and capture Richmond. These two options led Grant to a unique strategy.

Knowing that he had twice as many men as Lee, Grant decided to use his excess numbers to advantage. He would send a striking force to one end of Lee's line. If the Confederates strengthened this point with reinforcements, drawn from another post, Grant would attack the ground that the Rebels had just weakened. He had the surplus in soldiers to follow this course. If Lee, however, did not rise to the bait and left those threatened on their own, Grant would proceed with his assault.

The first phase of this strategy was initiated on July 26 when Grant ordered two infantry corps, those of Robert S. Foster from Benjamin Butler's army and Hancock, plus two divisions of horsemen northwest across the James River at Deep Bottom toward Richmond. Lee quickly countered the next day, sending Kershaw's brigade, Henry Heth's infantry division, plus Rooney Lee's cavalry to the scene. The two foes met and began skirmishing. Expecting an assault, Lee then reinforced his front on July 29 with Charles W. Field's foot soldiers and Fitz Lee's riders.[6] The Confederates awaited battle.

Grant attacked on July 30, not above the James River but below Petersburg where Lee had drawn his reinforcements. The charge was both unexpected and at first, unseen. Ingenious former miners, solders from Pennsylvania, had dug a tunnel 586 feet from their line to a point under an opposing Rebel earthwork. They filled the passage with 8,000 pounds of explosives, and then detonated the powder. The blast opened a path for their troops to exploit. The crater (30 feet deep, 135 feet long, and 97 feet from front to rear) proved, however, a death trap for the hordes of Federal soldiers, who had been waiting since before dawn for the order to attack.[7]

After swarming into the yawning breach, the lead ranks discovered that they could neither climb the opposite slope, nor could they retreat. They were pressed from the rear by thousands of following comrades. The crowded mass presented an inviting target to the Confederates, drawn to the rim of the hole. A disaster was in the making. The enemy suffered 3,500 casualties before they could extract their men.[8]

On the day when the Federals threatened Lee's left but instead attacked at the Crater, Butler was hurrying south on a foraging mission. A farmer behind the enemy line had promised to sell the Rebels 45,000 pounds of hay and fifty beef cattle, and Matthew had gone to acquire the needed supplies. The 6th South Carolina was on the left, guarding the flank of the train; Butler accompanied the 4th and 5th regiments and the empty wagons they would fill upon reaching the farm in the Yankee rear. "The whole affair proved an entire success," one participant recalled, "[We] brought off everything without firing a gun."[9]

But on the return trip, just after Butler passed Lee's Mill, Gregg's entire division of Federal troopers approached from the east, starting out on a raid of Weldon, North Carolina. The Union riders quickly mounted a charge against the 6th South Carolina, still positioned along the flank. The assault was repelled, but the Yankees did not retreat. They dug in and began firing at long range.

"The battle raged nearly two hours," a Rebel combatant stated, "when a lull occurred. . . . Strategy was taking place." Gregg had divided his force, attempting to encircle the Confederates. When his men were in position, he attacked "from the front, right, and rear." The Federal assault was on the verge of success when suddenly "a cyclone of musketry struck the flanking enemy." Matthew had come back with the rest of his brigade. He stopped Gregg in his tracks. The Union remained in place until darkness before finally returning to their line. Butler then continued with the filled wagons toward his camp.[10]

Also on the same day as the crater battle, Jubal Early was creating trouble. Northern infantry units led by George Crook, Franz Sigel, and Hunter (plus Averell's cavalry) had trailed him into the Shenandoah Valley. On July 24, Early had whirled at Kernstown, charged the leading element under Crook, and sent the Yankee soldiers scampering back over the Potomac.[11] Early then moved into Pennsylvania, and on July 30, burned the town of Chambersburg to retaliate for prior torchings of key Confederates' houses.[12] The Federals were exasperated by this affront, and took steps to deal with the menace to the west. The four departments covering the area were combined into one military district with Philip Sheridan in command. "Put [yourself] south of the enemy," Grant wrote, "and follow him to death."[13] When he left Petersburg for the Valley in early August, Sheridan took both Wilson's and Torbert's cavalry divisions with him.

Since the main portion of the Federal cavalry had left the front, Lee felt that he had to support Early by shifting his troopers to the Valley, too. Fitz Lee started north in early August, Butler, still in temporary charge of Hampton's division, followed on August 11. Only Rooney Lee's horsemen remained near Richmond and Petersburg. On August 14, just as he reached Beaver Dam, Hampton (accompanying Matthew) received a desperate message from Lee. "Halt your command and return to Richmond," the note stated. "Gregg's Division is crossing at Deep Bottom."[14]

The reason for Hampton's recall was that the Union had again posed a threat north of the James River. The infantry corps under David B. Birney and Hancock and Gregg's cavalry had crossed the water and were heading for Richmond. Birney was advancing along the Varina Road; Hancock was moving between the New Market and Darbytown Roads; Gregg covered the right flank.[15]

Those blocking the enemy's path into the city included the artillerymen and government clerks, who left their desks in the capital during the emergency to fill the forts along the outer defensive line, under Ewell; Fields's infantry division; and the independent cavalry brigade, led by Martin Gary, one of Butler's Edgefield neighbors. Lee sent his oldest son Rooney's troopers to the front, but did not call more infantry to meet the threat. When Grant learned that Lee was not really strengthening this position, he ordered an immediate assault. The Federal infantry charge on August 16 was repelled, but Gregg's cavalry, galloping down the Charles City Road, blew past both Gary and Rooney Lee. A path into Richmond

was opened for the Union. But at that critical moment, Hampton and Butler arrived on the scene.[16]

"The men quickly dismounted," a participant remembered, "and . . .
were immediately thrown into action, striking the enemy on his flank and
rear."[17] Gregg's troopers were driven from the field, and the front was stabilized. The following morning, Lee brought up reinforcements. The Yankees stayed in place for three days. Lee could not dislodge them; they were
unable to push through the Rebel defense. Finally, on August 20, the Federals retreated back over the James, and the threat to Richmond was over.
Butler's orders to follow Fitz Lee to the Valley were cancelled, so he led his
cavalry to their old camp below Petersburg.[18]

Grant had been waiting for Lee to reinforce his troops above the stream.
"I have relieved the Fifth Corps from the trenches," he wrote Washington,
"and have it ready to march around Petersburg if the enemy . . . throw
troops enough [above] the James to justify it."[19] When Lee complied with
Grant's wishes on August 1, he sent Gouverneur K. Warren ahead to
attacked the Weldon Railroad. The Union captured almost four miles of
track near Globe Tavern.[20] Lee's lifeline to the south had been severed.

On August 19, Lee tried to regain the railroad. The infantry divisions
led by Henry Heth and William Mahone assaulted Warren. Although he
was battered (over 3,000 of his troops were taken prisoner), the Yankee
commander managed to hold his position. Grant then reinforced Warren
with Hancock's II Corps, just returned from above the James River. They
took up a post below Warren at Reams' Station, then started south to tear
up track.[21]

Hampton, too, had come south. On August 23 he sent Butler to
reconnoiter the Yankee stronghold along the Weldon tracks. Matthew
approached from below, on the right of the roadbed; Rosser, who had
returned from sick leave that day, advanced to Butler's left.

"Find the Yankees in [my] front," Butler barked to one of his scouts,
"and tell [me] how many there [are]."[22] When the man returned, he
reported 1,200 enemy soldiers ensconced to the left. "Very well," Butler
replied, "I know what's on the right." He led his dismounted riders forward, galloping fifty yards in front of the line, exposing himself to the fire
of both friends and foe. Hancock's men were unable to withstand this
charge, and they fell back into their entrenchments at Reams' Station.

Butler followed, and he remained in position, fronting they enemy,
until night came. He then called for a messenger to tell his men to retire. A
shaken soldier reported for the mission. He was shivering with fear of the
bullets that whizzed overhead.

"Young man," Butler said with disgust, "you're scared. Go back to
[your] Captain . . . tell him to send me a *courier*."

A replacement soon appeared. Butler asked if he could carry a dispatch to the men at the front. "God!" he gasped, looking into the hailstorm ahead, where the bark of muskets was marked by blinking red lights, like a swarm of fireflies on a June night. "I'll start," he said with a gulp, "[but] don't know so much about going."

"You'll do," Butler replied with a chuckle.[23] The man made it to the front, and Butler's troops safely withdrew to the rear.

As a result of Butler's scouting report, Hampton noted that Hancock's left flank was "in the air." He suggested to Lee that if the infantry attacked the Yankees from the west, holding them in position at Reams' Station, he could come up from the south to drive the Federals away from the railroad and back to their lines. Lee agreed with the plan.[24]

Heth and Cadmus M. Wilcox, A. P. Hill's corps, located their infantry west of Reams' Station on the night of August 24; Hampton placed Rooney Lee's division, temporarily under Rufus Barringer, and Butler's riders south of the depot. The next morning, shortly after sunrise, while Barringer remained in position to cover Hill's right flank, Butler drove the Yankee skirmishers back toward their lines, then waited for the infantry attack.[25]

The enemy, of course, was uncomfortable with Butler on their flank, so they opened an artillery barrage toward his ranks. The shells flew low overhead.

"They are disposed to be rather familiar this morning," Butler observed calmly to Rosser.

"Politeness is the order this morning," Rosser replied. Turning to his staff, he added, "Don't bow too low, boys, it isn't becoming."

"Yes it is!" one answered. "It's becoming a little too damn hot here, if that's what you mean."[26]

Hill took seemingly forever to prepare for his assault. When he finally advanced about 3:00 P.M., Matthew dismounted his men and moved east across the tracks, then turned north, then west to approach his adversary from the rear. "The enemy, taken on the front and flank, fell back pell mell," one stated, "through trees cut down, fence rails, breastworks of every kind . . . thrown up as a defense against us."[27]

"Just at the time when a few minutes would have secured the repulse of the enemy," Hancock wrote, "a part of [my] line gave way in confusion. . . . The [enemy] advanced along the rifle pits, taking possession of the battery and turning one gun on our troops."[28]

The Rebels captured the artillery, but no one knew how to fire the pieces. An enemy prisoner saw the problem. "If you boys will allow me," he called, "I can mow those Yankees down." The astonished Confederates moved aside, and the Union gunner quickly opened a devastating fire on

Gen. Thomas L. Rosser. COURTESY
PHOTOGRAPHIC HISTORY OF THE CIVIL WAR

his former friends (many of whom were foreigners who did not speak English, some of whom had only recently arrived from overseas). "[He] seemed to enjoy the sport very much," one of Matthew's men recalled.[29]

Beset from both the front and rear, Hancock was forced to fall back to the Yankee line east of Petersburg. Warren, however, was not dislodged. The enemy's grip on the Weldon tracks remained firm. The Confederates could bring supplies by rail only up to Reams' Station, then had to transfer the goods to wagons for delivery into Petersburg. Yankee losses in the battle were over 2,300 men killed, wounded, or taken prisoner, nine cannons, and more than 3,000 small arms. The Rebel casualties were fewer than 800 soldiers.[30]

Butler remained on the field through that night. When morning came, he retired southward and made camp at Malone's Crossing. His troopers were both tired and dirty, but they had no soap available for washing. Matthew solved this problem by organizing a company of soap makers. They used the bark of trees for lye, mixing this with bacon grease and the fat from dead horses to complete the process. "We soon had an amply supply," a soldier recalled, "with some to spare to our neighbors the infantry."[31]

While camped at Malone's Crossing, Butler learned that Atlanta had fallen to Sherman's forces. President Davis had wanted an aggressive general who would assault the Federals; Hood had obliged with a series of battles: Peach Tree Creek, Atlanta, and Ezra Church. In each, however, the Rebels were routed. On September 1 Hood abandoned the city.[32]

Matthew, perhaps for the first time, seemed to realize that the South would lose the Civil War. He was distraught, and he passed his feelings on to Maria. "I sometimes think of leaving the service," he stated, "and return

Gen. Pierce Manning Butler Young.
COURTESY CONFEDERATE MILITARY HISTORY

home for the balance of my days. . . . What say you, my darling? Shall I resign or not? Would you prefer a man at home in relative obscurity or [a husband] constantly absent with reputation and distinction?"[33]

Maria would have preferred Butler at home, because she complained constantly about the hardships she had to endure. "You should be thankful," Matthew wrote her, "that you have shelter, food, and rainment . . . and your husband spared, mutilated tho he be." He, too, seems to have been feeling sorry for himself. Butler went on to scold Maria for moans of being alone. "You have your father, sisters, and friends near you, my own brothers, mother, and sisters not far off," Matthew noted. "How many poor, miserable women . . . have lost all and are [now] left refugees? You are fortunate, and should beware of how you complain."[34]

On September 14, as Butler lay sick in his tent, probably suffering from his problems with Maria and the army as much as the lingering effect of his amputation, Hampton led the cavalry east in a raid behind Federal lines. He planned to steal Grant's herd of beef, over 2,400 animals. The venture appeared ludicrous on the surface, but the Confederates were successful. They slipped past the Union left flank to Ruffin's farm (only ten miles from Grant's headquarters near City Point), quickly rounded up the steers, then drove them back without significant enemy interference.[35]

Although Matthew could take pride in his men and their roles during the raid, a more personal award came his way on September 19. He was promoted to major general in charge of one of the three divisions in Hampton's corps. He finally had the title as well as the trouble.[36]

Matthew was, of course, very pleased at being advanced, and his thoughts of going home vanished. Dunovant was given charge of Butler's troopers. Rosser and Young continued to lead the division's other two brigades.

Rosser's command was composed of the 35th Virginia Battalion and the 7th, 11th, and 12th Virginia Regiments. He was born in the "Old Dominion," but at an early age, his parents moved to Texas. He was appointed to West Point in 1856. He spent five years at the Academy, but in May 1861, just two weeks prior to his scheduled graduation, Rosser resigned and joined the Confederacy. He started the war as an artillery lieutenant, was wounded at Mechanicsville in 1862 during the Peninsula Campaign, and upon returning to service, switched to the cavalry. Rosser received his general's stars and brigade command on September 23, 1863 (about three weeks after Butler's date of rank).[37]

Pierce Manning Butler Young was born in South Carolina, but he grew up in Georgia. His command was composed of five small legions (Cobb's, Phillips's, Jeff Davis's, Millen's, and Love's) plus the 7th Georgia Regiment. His service prior to and during the war was very similar to Rosser's. He entered West Point in 1857, resigned at the outbreak of hostilities, began with the artillery, and then joined the cavalry. Even their date of rank as general was the same.[38]

Both Rosser and Young were upset by Butler's promotion. Having served through his recuperation, each felt that his having spent more time in the field offset Matthew's earlier date of rank, a key consideration in Butler's advancement. They viewed Butler as being Hampton's pet and undeserving of his new rank. "Hampton has [pushed] his claim," Young wrote his sister, "it is all a political click [sic]."[39]

Hampton visited both Young and Rosser in an attempt to persuade them to accept Butler as their new chief. Although Young grudgingly dropped his objections, Rosser remained adamant. "I am unwilling to serve under Butler," he explained in a note to his wife, "[and] want to get out of this mess."[40]

Hampton would not be dissuaded. He solved the problem by sending Rosser and his brigade into the Shenandoah Valley to support Early. "I am not anxious to go," Rosser wrote his wife, "but I'm very desirous to get away from . . . *Butler & Hampton!*"[41] He and his troopers left the Richmond front on September 27, leaving Matthew with only his former command and Young's cavalry at hand for the fall campaign.

—+—≣✦≣—+—

Matthew's promotion was not based on favoritism. Ever since returning to duty, he had "opened the ball" in each of Hampton's battles. "We went in first at Totopotomoy Creek," Matthew recalled, "opened the battle at Trevilian Station . . . were first in the attack on Gregg's Division [near] Samaria Church . . . among the first in the all night fight with Wilson, and so and so on."[42] He had commanded the division starting with Trevilian Station and had done well. Butler had earned his stars during the past three months.

CHAPTER 13

Mcdowell's Farm

Rosser's leaving for the Valley was only partly because of his bitter feelings about Hampton having supported Butler for division command. There was trouble in the Shenandoah.

Earlier that month, Lee had called Anderson's infantry back from the Valley to Richmond. He needed more men to defend his thin line facing Grant. This left Early outnumbered by the enemy four to one, and although Sheridan had been reluctant to offer battle, he moved quickly to take advantage of the changed odds. On September 19 the Yankees charged Early's position outside Winchester, and not only drove the Rebels southward but also dealt them over 4,000 casualties—40 percent of their force. Early retired to Fisher's Hill, twenty miles below Winchester. Sheridan followed, and on September 23, renewed his assaults. Jubal was again routed, losing about 1,200 more men. He staggered further south to Waynesboro. On September 27 Rosser's brigade headed northwest to help shore up Early's beleaguered ranks.[1]

Rosser left just as Grant began another ploy. He sent two infantry corps led by Birney and Edward Ord plus Kautz's cavalry above the James River to threaten the Rebels' outer line, which started near Chaffin's Bluff and ran north. The area was defended by Ewell, who had only Gary's cavalry and two of Field's brigades at hand. Since the Federals usually waited to see if reinforcements were rushed to the scene before committing to battle, Lee may have thought he had a day to consider his options. But this time Grant did not hesitate. He attacked on September 29. The Federals captured Fort Harrison, the Rebels' main bulwark. Rather than hurrying on into Richmond, however, the Yankees decided to charge both Southern flanks, where Ewell had concentrated his tiny force. He managed to hold his ground until troops, summoned from Petersburg, arrived to stabilize the front. New earthworks were then built closer to the capital, maintaining the integrity of his line.[2]

As soon as Lee's reinforcements left Petersburg, Grant mounted a threat below the James where Lee had just weakened his line. He hoped to advance from his position west of the Weldon Railroad and then circle north to sever the Southside tracks into Petersburg. Gregg's cavalry started the attack with a reconnaissance on September 29. His 4,350 troopers rode south out of Globe Tavern about 6:30 A.M. on September 28. The 2nd Brigade under Charles H. Smith turned west at Wyatt's Crossing; Davies's 1st Brigade continued southward to Reams' Station before wheeling right.[3]

Butler was defending this area. He had pickets at the front, but his main force was still in camp. Dunovant's men were situated on the Boydton Plank Road, just below Burgess' Mill; Young's cavalry, under the temporary command of Lt. Col. J. Fred Waring, the Jeff Davis Legion, was along the Vaughan Road near Gravelly Run; and Gen. James Dearing's troopers, a small brigade, serving for the moment with Butler to replace Rosser's force, were posted in Fort Archer near Peebles' Farm. Dearing was ill, so his brigade was led by Col. Joel S. Griffin, who had gained his rank via political connections rather than experience.[4]

When his pickets reported that the Yankees were coming, Butler hurried his troopers to the front. Cobb's Legion met Davies just west of Reams' Station, and their mere presence was sufficient to send this wing of enemy riders back to the Weldon tracks, where they remained in place through the rest of the day.[5]

Smith, however, pressed forward, following the Vaughan Road all the way to Hatcher's Run. By now Butler was in position behind the stream with all his South Carolinians and most of Young's troopers. The Federals probed his line, but at any sign of resistance, they fell back. After Smith was satisfied that the Rebels were strongly posted (plus had infantry to the north), he retired to McDowell's Farm west of Arthur's Swamp. Couriers were rushed back to the Union army headquarters to report on Smith's reconnaissance.[6]

Hampton and Butler, not about to allow Smith to rest in peace, headed after the enemy to seek battle. About 5:00 P.M., Roger Pryor, a former general now serving as a scout, located the Union position, and reported his findings. "Advance the column," Butler said, with each word given deadly emphasis. "We will attack them."[7]

Matthew led the assault on horseback; his men trailed him on foot. After crossing a branch of Arthur's Swamp, the Rebels charged up the slope toward the Yankees' ranks. "Nothing could be heard," one recalled, "but the boom of cannon and the bark of musketry."[8] But the attack was repelled.

As Matthew reassembled his men for a second charge, he was informed

PETERSBURG BATTLE AREA

1864

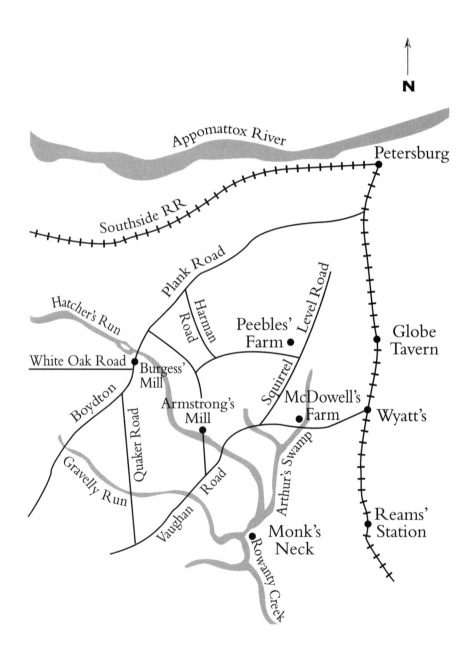

that Rooney Lee's division had come up to reinforce him. Butler waited while these troopers moved around him to assume a position on his right, then, just as the sun was setting, ordered an assault. The enemy was driven from their lines along Arthur's Swamp and back to the Wyatt farm, just west of the Weldon tracks.[9]

Satisfied with his day's work, Butler, under Hampton's orders, retired from the field. Pickets were posted west of Arthur's Swamp to keep watch on the enemy; the rest of the men rode back to their camps.[10]

The Yankees, too, were content to cease fighting. The men under Davies finally left Reams' Station and assumed the defense at the Wyatt farm; Smith's battered troopers moved eastward across the tracks to the Perkin's House, where they spent the night.[11]

The next day, September 30, belonged to the infantry. While the opposing cavalries rested, the foot soldiers began their portion of the battle. Warren's V Crops and John G. Parke's IX Corps, 20,000 Federals, supported by forty-two cannons, headed west out of Globe Tavern about 9:00 A.M. They marched in a single column along the only road that cut through the heavily wooded area. Their goal was to capture the outer Confederate works around Peebles' Farm, then wheel north to sever the Boydton Plank Road, the wagon trail lifeline into Petersburg. Progress was slow. The Union was not positioned for their attack until about 1:00 P.M. Warren's men made the initial charge, and easily drove Griffin out of Fort Archer. While the V Corps established a defensive line in the clearing, the IX Corps moved northward toward the Boydton Plank Road.[12]

Butler was exasperated by Griffin's feeble performance. None of his troopers was killed or even wounded, but fifty-six were taken prisoner. After the battle, Matthew pressed charges against the political colonel in hopes of dismissing him from command.[13]

The main Confederate force (A. P. Hill's corps, 20,000 men in the divisions led by Bushrod Johnson, Mahone, Wilcox, and Heth) was arrayed behind defensive works along the Boydton Plank Road. About 5:00 P.M., as the Federal IX Crops approached and began to form ranks for a charge, the Rebels moved out of their entrenchments to assault the disorganized Union troops. This sudden, unexpected sortie surprised the Yankees, who reeled in retreat toward Peebles' Farm. Hill's onslaught ended as darkness fell. The enemy still clung to the ground won earlier that day. Their casualties were more than 2,200, compared to about 600 for Lee's men.[14]

As the weary adversaries rested, black clouds billowed over their heads, and then a drenching rain started to fall. Brilliant lightning strobed the sky above, and thunder bellowed without pause. The dusty ground turned to mud. But the miserable conditions did not deter the Rebels. They had the

Yankees out of their trenches in the open, and Hill planned on renewing his assaults in the morning. He expected to annihilate the enemy's force.

Matthew was included in Hill's plans. His role was to protect the Rebel right flank, specifically the Vaughan Road running east to west below Peebles' Farm. Dunovant had picketed the area during the day, but that night he returned to his camp. He had done so without permission, and Butler was angry with him for disobeying orders. About 10:00 P.M., upon hearing of Dunovant's withdrawal, Butler sent the brigade back to Armstrong's Mill, where they would be in position at morning's first light.[15]

Dunovant was no doubt miffed at being ordered to leave the comforts of his camp, and this seemed to cloud his judgment. Instead of taking the safer route (west of Hatcher's Run) to Armstrong's Mill, he opted for a shorter path, fording the stream and following its eastern bank. And he rode at the head of his column, rather than using his skirmishers to lead the way. "There is no danger on this road," he proclaimed, "I will be the advance guard myself tonight."[16]

Just short of his objective, Dunovant was stopped by a challenge. "Halt!" an unseen sentry commanded. "Halt or we fire!" The speaker was Capt. E. S. Austin, 6th Ohio, a Yankee regiment serving under Davies. His brigade was there in strength, also hoping to assume a post near Armstrong's Mill.[17]

"Why in hell do you stop me?" the Rebel leader bellowed back with unseemly arrogance. He thought he was encountering one of Young's pickets. "This is General Dunovant."[18]

"I don't know you," came the answer. "Dismount, one of you, and advance and give the countersign."

"I tell you I am Dunovant. Let me pass!"

"Damn Dunovant! We don't know you . . . dismount and come up here [to] let us know who you are, [or] we will fire."

Back in the column, others knew that they had stumbled into the enemy. "We are up against Yanks," one whispered.

"How do you know?"

"That fellow talks through his nose."[19]

Dunovant, however, had not caught on to his peril. He turned to Andrew P. Butler, a young cousin of Matthew's, who was serving as an aide. "Get down," Dunovant ordered, "and give them the countersign."

Andrew tried to convince Dunovant that the challengers were Federals, but the general refused to believe him. "Are you afraid, Sir?" he sneered.

Andrew dismounted and started forward, knowing that he was headed for a Federal prison. "I am not afraid," he said over his shoulder to Dunovant, "but I am gone up."[20]

As Andrew approached the Union troopers, one called out, "Dismount!" He did not know that the man he was challenging was seven feet tall, and it seemed he was still astride his horse.

"Damn you, ain't I dismounted?" Andrew called back.

"He's a rebel!"

With that shout, the Yankees opened fire. Fortunately, Andrew had cleverly approached those challenging him from an angle, so although he was captured, the Union volley missed Dunovant's party. Their shots did, however, send the Rebels scurrying into rapid retreat. Dunovant led his men through the dark and still pouring rain in a circle around the enemy position and on to Armstrong's Mill. This roundabout route was unnecessary. The encounter had scared Davies as much as the Confederates, and he had wheeled about and hurried back to his original line.[21]

At dawn, A. P. Hill attacked from the north, hoping to roll up the Yankees right flank. Other infantry headed east, toward the Union left, with Butler on their right flank. He rode in column with Young's brigade leading, Dunovant's men trailing. Under cloudy skies (the rain had finally halted), the cavalry trotted down the muddy Vaughan Road, passed the Squirrel Level Road intersection, and arrived at McDowell's Farm without encountering significant opposition. The enemy to Butler's front had disappeared. But where had they gone: north to join the Federal infantry or eastward in retreat to the Weldon Railroad? Matthew decided to stop until he learned the location of his adversary. As Young's troopers dismounted (Dunovant's men were still in the rear), the heavens opened and it began to pour again.[22]

To the north Hill's attack had been stymied. Feeding his troops piecemeal against the Yankee breastworks (hastily dug during the night) along the Squirrel Level Road, he was unable to dislodge the enemy. One brigade after another was thrown back. After the battle was over, the Union remained firmly ensconced. Grant had succeeded in pushing his front westward, which further threatened Lee's lifeline for supply through Petersburg.[23]

The fighting, however, was not over. Upon learning of Butler's advance, Gregg (who had ridden north to aid the infantry) marshalled his cavalry and headed south to confront the Rebel troopers. They sat on the Yankee flank and had to be dislodged if the Union was to hold its hard-won position. Matthew had not anticipated an assault, so when the Northern horsemen charged his post at McDowell's Farm, he was caught napping and forced into retreat. Young's Brigade fled along the Vaughan Road to its intersection with the Squirrel Level Road, forded one of the branches of Arthur's Swamp, climbed the hill just west of the morass, and finally stopped on the peak, where they could look down into the bog.[24]

The Federals were in hot pursuit. They charged up the rise, were thrown back, but in turn repelled a counterattack from Young's men. The Rebel brigadier (returned to command) was incensed over his trooper's inability to drive the enemy from their post. "[Young] was cursing and storming in that stentorian voice of his," a watcher related, "which could be heard for half a mile."[25]

"Hold your ground down there, you damn scoundrels," he bellowed from the summit.[26] But his men gave way.

This pattern of battle, charge and countercharge, was repeated throughout the morning and into the afternoon. The rain continued to fall. And although Dunovant with his men had finally come up to join in the repeated charges, Matthew was unable to penetrate the Federal line. The fight evolved into a stalemate. Words replaced bullets.

"Good, fat beef over here," a Rebel would challenge to remind the Yankees of Hampton's successful cattle raid. The enemy answered with insults of their own.[27]

Butler, of course, was plotting to find a means to dislodge the Federals. He advised Hampton, who was with Rooney Lee in reserve to the north on the Harman Road, of his situation, and the two developed their strategy. Hampton would personally lead the two regiments (the 9th and 13th Virginia) south on the Squirrel Level Road to charge the Yankee right. When Butler heard the "Rebel Yell," he would attack from the front. Hampton reached the front about 3:00 P.M.[28]

Just as Hampton was about to order his men forward, he discovered that he was out of position. He had come too far west. The troops he was about to charge wore gray. He was poised to attack Butler's force.

Matthew had heard Hampton's coming, but he thought the threat came from Gregg. He had turned his line to front the Yankees. Riding at the fore, Butler spotted an approaching rider. He drew his pistol, took aim, and then holstered his revolver with disgust. He recognized the horseman, a close friend from Virginia. Hampton, too, quickly saw that he was facing comrades, and he held his fire.[29]

The two Confederate forces merged, and Butler and Hampton met to plan new tactics. A few of Butler's troopers had charged the enemy, whose pickets withdrew from the swamp to run for the main Union position atop an opposite hill. They could be seen crossing a narrow causeway through the bog.

Butler saw that the bridge represented a trap, a point of concentration, which the enemy could cover with artillery. He called Dunovant into the conference to ask if he thought he could flank the Union instead of exposing his men to this peril.

"Let me charge 'em," Dunovant replied. "We've got 'em going, and let's keep 'em going."

"I'm afraid I'll lose too many men," Butler protested.

"Oh, no we won't. My men are perfectly enthusiastic . . . an' we've got the Yankees demoralized. One more charge will finish 'em. Let me charge."

Butler, who had been conversing calmly, was upset with Dunovant's stubborn insistence on moving forward. "His face flushed," an observer noted, "[and] his eyes seemed to grow darker." In a quick fit of pique, Butler let his temper get the better of his judgment. "[Then] charge them, Sir," he snapped.[30]

Dunovant wheeled his horse and shouted to his troopers, "Forward!" No one moved. The dismounted brigade recognized the peril ahead. "Forward!" Dunovant repeated as he guided his horse toward the causeway. Matthew moved up beside him, and the men reluctantly formed both left and right of their mounted leaders. The line advanced slowly, then with a rush for the bridge. Dunovant led the way.[31]

Just as Dunovant entered the causeway, the enemy fired a volley, and he toppled to the ground. When Butler saw him fall, he called out, "Who is that shot?"

"General Dunovant!" came the reply.

"Is he killed?"

"Yes."

"Carry him back," Butler ordered, "[but] don't let the men know it." He was afraid that if the troopers learned of Dunovant's death, they would halt their assault. Most, however, were already retreating, unwilling to face the enemy's fire, concentrated on the only path through the swamp. The Rebels reformed along the western edge of the morass.[32]

Butler hurried back up the hill to where his guns were emplaced. Pointing out the location of the Union troops, he personally directed their fire against the enemy's position. The enemy artillery answered. A fragment from an exploding Yankee shell struck and killed Dr. John B. Fontaine, medical director for the cavalry corps, who had run to the front in hopes of tending to Dunovant.[33]

The two adversaries battled in place for several hours. The cold rain continued. "Fearfully bad weather for cavalry fighting," a Rebel prisoner muttered to Davies. "Yes," the Federal brigadier answered. "You people were not content in your camps, but must come out here for a fight, and I guess you got one."[34]

Butler wanted to advance, but he was waiting reinforcements from Rooney Lee. About dusk he saw through the mist a group of men falling away from the forward line. He rushed down the hill to order them back to their position. As they filed toward their post, Butler spotted an officer lying behind a tree. Once again, when faced with cowardice, Matthew lost his temper.

"What in hell are you doing there?" Butler yelled with fury. "Go to the front at once, sir!"

"I'll go if the men will," the officer stammered as he sprang to his feet.

"The men are already there, you damned coward," Butler snarled. He drew his pistol and leveled it at the quivering officer. "If you don't go to the front," he threatened, "I will blow your brains out myself. [And] if you ever lead my men off this way again, I'll kill you!"[35]

When it became obvious that reinforcements from Rooney Lee would not arrive before dark, Matthew ordered an assault on the Union position. His men crossed the mire, drove the enemy back to McDowell's Farm, then charged the main Federal line. "An ominous silence ensued for a moment," Union major Myron H. Beaumont remembered, "when suddenly the . . . woods in our front became alive with rebels, who came on at a double-quick . . . yelling like . . . fiends, firing as they advanced . . . the . . . buzz of bullets, the shriek of solid shot and shell, and the fierce tearing whirr of canister, were enough to terrify brave hearts and older heads."[36]

But, despite repeated attacks by Butler's Confederates, the Federal line held. Nightfall came. Gregg remained in control of the field. The battle was over, and the Union's flank was secure. Grant had successfully advanced closer to Lee's vital supply lines through Petersburg.[37]

CHAPTER 14

Burgess' Mill

AFTER THE CONTEST AT MCDOWELL'S FARM, BOTH ADVERSARIES RESTED in camp through the following weeks. Aiken took temporary command of the fallen Dunovant's brigade; Young was still in charge of his troopers. The men bivouacked west of Hatcher's Run, behind a line that extended from Armstrong's Mill south for two miles to Monck's Neck bridge.[1]

A number of subjects dominated the men's conversations. The war, of course, was discussed, with the main event being the battle of Cedar Creek. On October 19 Early had sent his army ahead in a surprise attack on the Union forces, who thought their prior conquests had ended the fighting in the Valley. The Federals were routed from their camps, but when Jubal's soldiers stopped to search for plunder, the Yankees regrouped under Sheridan to mount a fierce counterassault. The Rebels were driven into a frantic withdrawal. Although the enemy casualties were almost twice those for the Confederates (5,764 versus 3,100), the victory was decisive. Lee would later recall the residue of Early's force to Richmond; Jubal would lose his command.[2]

Another topic of avid interest to the Confederates was the impending presidential election in the North. Early had this in mind when he risked battle in the Valley. He hoped that a rout of the Yankees would swing votes from Lincoln to his Democratic challenger, the former commander of the Army of the Potomac, George McClellan, who was running on a peace platform. If he defeated Lincoln, the war would come to an end, won with ballots instead of bullets.[3]

Grant, too, was well aware of the impact that military action could have in deciding the election. "[He] will make desperate efforts [soon] to gain some success," Hampton predicted, "[and] unless he is successful, Mr. Lincoln will be defeated, and we should be safe."[4]

The Federals attacked on October 27. Grant launched a separate probe against each end of Lee's undermanned line. Above the James River, he sent the X and XVIII corps into White Oak Swamp, hoping to turn the Confederate left flank and then rush to Richmond. Longstreet was in command along this front. Although he had just come back to duty after being wounded in the Wilderness battles, "Old Pete" had not lost his touch. He quickly perceived the Federals' plan, and was in position, waiting to meet the enemy, when they emerged from the mire. Longstreet's troops opened fire; the Yankees fled.[5]

Three Federal corps attacked Lee to the south, outside of Petersburg. Grant's strategy here was to charge the Confederates' breastworks along the Globe Tavern line with Warren's V Corps and Parke's IX Corps. Their assault would hold A. P. Hill's infantry in place, allowing Hancock and his II Corps to swing southwest, go around the Rebel trenches, and then scurry north to sever the Southside Railroad, supplying Lee from the west. Gregg's cavalry would be posted below the infantry to guard Hancock's flank.[6]

Parke advanced at 3:00 A.M. When he reached the Rebel line, he found his adversary well protected by an "abatis of rails and slashed timber." He formed his troops as if planning to charge the strong works, but Parke had no intentions of taking the offense. He instead ordered his troops to entrench, to protect his position from an improbable attack by A. P. Hill. Parke remained in place throughout the day.[7]

Warren moved out at 4:00 A.M. His corps had just been heavily reinforced with conscripts, so a substantial portion of his force "were ignorant of the manual . . . [and] had never fired off a musket." He was further handicapped because the roads to his front ran north to south, while he was going west. His men had to hack their way through dense woods. And then it began to rain. "Parts of the command soon got mixed up," Warren ruefully recalled, "and connections between brigades were lost everywhere." He finally reached the Rebel line at 9:30 A.M., only to find it (as Parke had) impregnable.[8]

Meade and Grant came to Warren's field headquarters at 10:30 A.M. They brought news of Parke's impasse plus orders for Warren to send a division ahead on his left to join Hancock's advance from the south. Warren's force, however, was so scattered, it was 12:30 P.M. before he finally found and dispatched Crawford's two brigades. They had lost their way earlier, and were soon astray again. "The denseness of the woods . . . caused great delays in the movement," Warren stated, "causing breaks in the line and changes in direction. . . . His men were . . . lost in great numbers. . . . Whole regiments [had no] idea of where to find the rest of the division." The march was eventually called off that evening.[9]

Hancock had better luck. At 3:30 A.M., he headed down the Vaughan

Road, forded Hatcher's Run, then moved northwest up a narrow forest path by Dabney's Mill toward the Boydton Plank Road.

Butler was defending this area. His pickets contested the Yankee advance. "We were obliged to [mount]," one Rebel trooper recalled, "without attending to the niceties of the toilette or breakfast."[10] Matthew's skirmishers slowly fell back toward their comrades, stationed along the Quaker Road, west of the plank road. Upon finally arriving at their main line, they found that Butler had dismounted his men and was ready to greet the following enemy. It was 1:00 P.M.

Gregg, protecting the Yankees' left flank, came up the Quaker Road, and began skirmishing with Matthew's entrenched horsemen. It was probably here that an old woman in a nearby home emerged with her broom, which she shook at the enemy troopers.

"You can't kill anybody with that," a Rebel said with a laugh.

"I know I can't," she answered grimly, "but I can let them know what side I am on."[11]

To the right, Thomas W. Egan's infantry moved out from under the forest bordering Hatcher's Run, and found that the way west down the White Oak Road was open. There was a gap in the Rebel line. Hampton had sent word to A. P. Hill that he needed to send some soldiers south to fill the void, but Hill felt he could not spare the men. His messenger, riding to tell Hampton this news, had been captured by the Yankees. Since Hampton had not heard from Hill, he assumed that these reinforcements were in place.[12]

Egan moved down the White Oak Road into Hampton's rear, then halted under Hancock's orders. The Union commander had a strategy to take advantage of the breakthrough. He would send his other infantry division, led by Gershom Mott, after Egan. Mott would pass Egan to lead the column farther west, around the last of the Rebel entrenchments facing south, and head for the Southside Railroad. Gregg would trail Egan to protect the Union flank from Hampton from below.[13]

Just after Mott had started his men forward, Grant and Meade rode into Hancock's headquarters with word of Warren's supposedly oncoming brigades. They ordered Hancock to hold in place until Crawford arrived.[14]

The delay gave Hampton a much needed reprieve. Having finally learned of Egan's entry into his rear, he took steps to halt further progress by the Yankees. He ordered Butler to break off his engagement with Gregg and rush northwest to block the White Oak Road. Matthew moved quickly. And when in position, he joined Hampton to plan an attack on Hancock. Rooney Lee would hurry up the Boydton Plank and charge from the south; Heth's infantrymen would leave their trenches to assault

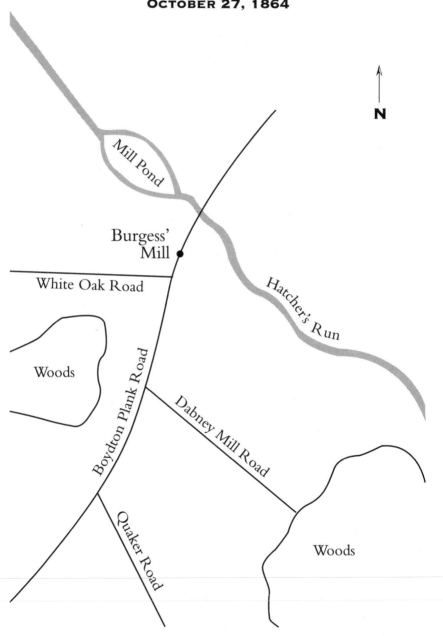

BURGESS' MILL
BATTLEFIELD

OCTOBER 27, 1864

N

Mill Pond

Burgess' Mill

White Oak Road

Hatcher's Run

Woods

Boydton Plank Road

Dabney Mill Road

Quaker Road

Woods

from the north; Butler's cavalry would fall on the Federals from the west. Everyone was in place by 4:00 P.M.[15]

Hampton's plans were perfect. Hancock heard Heth's infantry approaching, but he thought they were the Union force he was awaiting. He was totally surprised by the charge of the Rebel foot soldiers. As Hancock faced north to meet the threat from above, Rooney Lee's cavalry stormed up from the south. Butler attacked from the west. And as if the onset from the three Confederate wings were not enough to scatter the enemy, Mother Nature added her fury to the contest. The heavens opened and a pouring rain began to fall. Hancock's force started retreating toward the Dabney Mill Road to seek the haven of the nearby forest.[16]

As Butler's men advanced, he trailed on horseback. To his right, he suddenly noted several mounted officers moving with the forward line. One was his younger brother, Oliver (called "Nat"); another was Preston Hampton, the son of the commander. "[They] had no business in such a perilous position," Butler would say later. Worse yet the two aides were drawing the enemy's attention to themselves by waving their hats to encourage their comrades, charging on foot. Matthew signaled frantically to the two lads to fall back. Finally, they noticed his firm gestures. Nat peeled off to the left; Preston started to the right toward his father, riding a few hundred yards to the right and behind Matthew. All at once Preston staggered in the saddle, then fell to the ground.[17]

Another rider galloped up to where Preston lay, leaped off his horse, and rushed to help the stricken lad. Suddenly he, too, toppled. A Union musket ball had struck Hampton's older son, Wade Jr., in the back. Hampton soon reached the tragic site, and gathered Preston in his arms. "My son, my son," he sobbed. He saw that the lad had been shot in the groin, and from past experience, knew that his boy was dying. With the rain mixing with his tears, Hampton pressed Preston to his breast, kissed him as if he were yet a baby, then whispered a few encouraging words into his ear. Preston tried to reply, but could say nothing.[18]

When Butler rode onto the scene, Hampton looked up and said, "Poor Preston!"

"Is he dangerously wounded?" Butler asked.

"Yes, mortally."

Hampton then pointed to a wagon, parked under a nearby shed. "I wish you would have that . . . pulled around, and have his body moved out of the range of fire."[19]

Others were now at hand, and they took charge, lifting Preston into the wagon. Young Wade, not seriously hurt, was assisted onto his horse for the return to the rear. Butler remained at the front; Hampton rode alongside the cart, but soon came to a halt. "Too late!" he muttered. Turning his horse about, he hurried back to the action, where he assumed the direction of his artillery's fire on the retreating Federals.[20]

Darkness came early that day because of the storm, and Hampton had to end his assaults on Hancock, who had gathered his force in the woods east of the Boydton Plank Road. The Rebels did, however, plan on renewing battle at first light, so Hampton had his troopers hold in place through the night. Dawn came. The enemy was gone. Hancock and the other Union corps had retired in the hours before sunrise. But Hampton still sent his men after the Yankees to harass their retreat and assure they went back to their lines. Butler caught up with Hancock halfway between Dabney's and Armstrong's Mill, charged his rear guard, and put the Federals into a panicked flight. "I then withdrew my command," Hampton stated, "and the troops returned to camp."[21] He went back and buried his son.

Grant had lost the battle, but the defeat did not hurt Lincoln in the election. He easily won a second term on November 8.[22]

Butler must have realized that this meant that the war would be fought to its bitter end, which would see the South losing and the end of slavery. But he ignored this obvious outcome, and continued to deal with his blacks as if nothing would change. "Aaron has behaved badly," he said in a note, written on November 3, to his overseer. "I have made up my mind to sell him. What are boys like him bringing . . . six or seven thousand? Only one thing will save Aaron . . . that he marry Emilene as soon as practicable. . . . And if she does not look out, she, too, will go to the first speculator."[23]

Although Butler's dealings with his slaves seem harsh, he probably viewed himself as a father figure, who had to be involved in every aspect of their lives. He was responsible for their behavior as well as their well-being.

Another example of Butler's myopic racial views was an incident involving a captured black Yankee soldier. The man was brought to Matthew, who declared him a slave, belonging to the one who had taken him prisoner. "Captain Hogan gave me two nice . . . horses for him," the trooper said, "[and] sent the negro home and put him in a cotton patch."[24]

Hogan had made a foolish trade considering events that were taking place out West. Sherman had earlier divided his army, sending half to Nashville to face a coming assault by Hood's Army of Tennessee. The rest of the Federal force had returned to Atlanta. After setting the city afire on November 15, Sherman started marching southeast through Georgia toward the sea. The Rebels had no one in place to stop him.[25]

Georgians, of course, were mortified by this unopposed march across their state, and the 7th Georgia (serving under Young) applied for a release from their duty in Virginia to go south to defend their homes. The request was approved by Lee. In bidding farewell to the regiment, Butler displayed his aptness for politics. "Will you do me the kindness," he wrote Maj. Edward C. Anderson, the unit leader, "to assure your officers and men of my regard for them as soldiers, and of the deep interest . . . I will always feel [toward] their . . . welfare. I wish them every success."[26]

Winter had arrived in Virginia, but as the bitter cold settled over the land, Grant made one more foray to dislodge Lee from Richmond. Warren with three of his divisions plus one of Hancock's and Gregg's cavalry started south along the Jerusalem Plank Road at dawn on December 7. Their objective was to rip up the Weldon Railroad track below Stoney Creek Station and cut the flow of supplies to the Rebels in Petersburg. Rain fell all day, but the Yankee force managed to reach Sussex Court House that evening.[27]

Early the next morning, the Union headed for Jarratt's Station on the Weldon Railroad. They soon encountered Rebel cavalry (Matthew and Rooney Lee, sent by Hampton to disrupt the enemy's progress), but they had the advantage in numbers and were able to fend off the Confederates. The van of the Federal column reached Jarratt's about 2:00 P.M., but Warren elected to wait until his entire force arrived before starting his task of destruction. About 6:00 P.M., when all were at hand, he sent parties north to rip up the truck. By midnight, the workers had removed rails and burned ties all the way to the Nottoway River. After setting the trestle afire, the Yankees returned to Jarratt's to spend the night.[28]

After being rebuffed earlier that day, Butler had gone ten miles south to Belfield on the Meherrin River. The Confederates had erected forts along the southern banks of the stream to guard the tracks there. He would use them to offset his lack of numbers and halt the enemy's progress. His men took the place of local reserves, young boys called into service by the emergency. One was crying.

"What's the matter?" a militia officer demanded.

"I'm scared."

"You're crying like a baby," his superior scoffed.

"Yes," the lad sobbed, "I wish I was a baby, and a gal baby at that."[29]

On December 9 Warren headed south from Jarratt's to continue ripping up the railroad tracks. The Yankees met no opposition until about 3:00 P.M., when they neared Belfield and found Butler waiting for them. Each looked to the other to make the first move, but neither was willing to initiate battle. After 8:00 P.M., the rain resumed, turned to sleet, and then snow. Strong winds blew. The temperature dropped below freezing during the storm.[30]

WARREN'S RAID ON BELFIELD

DECEMBER 7–12, 1864

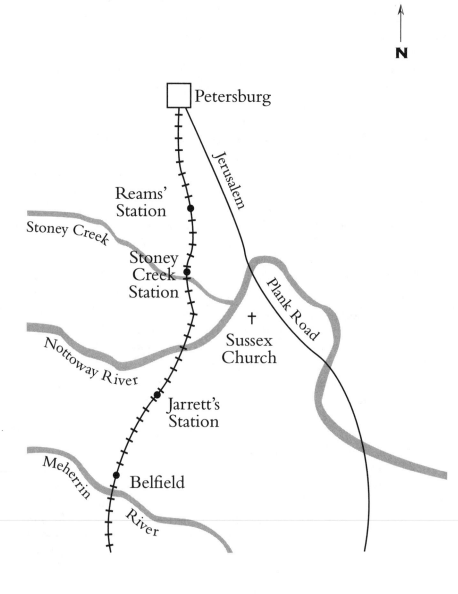

N

Petersburg

Jerusalem

Reams'
Station

Stoney Creek

Stoney
Creek
Station

Plank Road

† Sussex
Church

Nottoway River

Jarrett's
Station

Meherrin

Belfield

River

"Trees were blown down," a trooper recalled, "but not a man nor a horse was hurt. We were covered with snow . . . [but] I never slept better in my life."[31]

Butler spent the night in the open by a campfire. His aides told him then that earlier that day, one of his scouts had gone up to a farmhouse and told the pretty mistress he had come for brandy for Butler. "Why, of course, [he] shall have it," was her answer, and she rushed back inside to get a bottle from her stock. The lady evidently was a friend of Matthew's, one of his many female admirers. His staff knew the scout had kept the liquor for himself, so they attempted to provoke Butler by asking how he had enjoyed it.

"The scoundrel," Butler exclaimed with a smile, "he used my name, imposed on that young lady, and yet never gave me a drop. . . . If I could catch him, I'd make him pay for his villainy [*sic*]!"[32]

Everyone laughed. Taking advantage of the camaraderie, one of the troopers sitting by the fire noted, "You have the advantage of us, General."

"How?"

"You have but one foot to get cold and we have two."

The comment was cruel, and all held their breath, waiting for Matthew to fill the sudden silence with angry oaths. Butler said nothing. He did, however, offer a rueful smile, showing that he accepted the jibe as a token of friendship.[33]

About 3:00 A.M., Butler learned that Warren had chosen to use the darkness to retreat. He roused his troopers, and prepared to pursue the Federals. The winds still blew from the northwest, snow covered the men and their mounts, and it remained bitterly cold. "Well, boys," Matthew noted as the riders fell into line, "if we survive this weather . . . we need not fear the Yankees."[34]

The Rebels followed their adversary north. As Matthew brought up the rear, he and his staff were suddenly accosted by a horse trotting toward them from the opposite direction. Even though it was dark, they could tell that the rider was asleep, his head buried out of sight in his mount's mane.

"Wake up, Thompson," Butler barked.

The trooper snapped to an erect position, reddened with embarrassment, turned about, then galloped north to catch up with the column.

"How did you recognize that fellow, General," an amazed aide asked. "You couldn't see his face."

"I didn't recognize him," Butler replied, "(but) I knew his horse."[35]

Butler's ability to call each of his men by their name was known, but this incident revealed that he could identify each of their mounts, too. This personal touch was awesome, and was one of the many reasons why Matthew was held in such high esteem by his command.

Warren's men, trudging along the muddy road, pelted by the blowing snow, and badgered from the rear by the trailing Rebels, were exhausted by the time their van reached Sussex Court House. The Federals stopped there until morning, then resumed their retreat. Sharp ruts in the snow-covered road cut into the feet of the slow-moving soldiers. Butler, however, was no longer chasing after them. He had turned west to go back to his camp. Warren finally reached his bivouac on December 12.[36]

When Butler reached his camp, he found a new, uncommon task awaiting him. Warren's men had destroyed almost twenty miles of the Weldon Railroad. Matthew was put in charge of repairing the tracks. "A novel duty for a cavalry officer," one said, "but the general went at it with his usual vigor."[37]

Butler moved his headquarters to Belfield, and put his entire command of 940 men to work. Some went into the forest to cut wood for ties; others cleared the roadbed; the rest built fires, used to heat and straighten the rails that Warren's infantry had bent. Two weeks of effort restored only about six miles of track, a commendable record, but much too slow to suit the South's needs. Butler looked for a better solution, and found the answer in a railroader, living nearby. The experienced superintendent impressed three hundred slaves as his crew, and the blacks rebuilt about five miles of track for every one achieved by Butler's troops. Before year end, the task was completed.[38]

While the men were working, they no doubt followed the war in the west. Hood's attack on Nashville began at Franklin, where he foolishly charged a fixed Union position held by John Schofield's corps. The Rebels were thrown back with fearsome losses that included six general officers.[39] Hood should have abandoned his campaign, but when Schofield moved north into the Nashville works, Hood went after him. On December 15, George Thomas, in overall command of the Yankee forces, came out from behind his breastworks to assault the Confederates. His charge destroyed Hood's army. It was the most decisive Southern defeat of the Civil War.[40]

Closer to home, Sherman continued to advance unopposed across Georgia. On December 21, his forces took Savannah, where they rested on the coast through the end of that year. Suspecting that Sherman's next move would be to trudge north into South Carolina to move at will through this state, Hampton asked that his troopers be shipped south to defend their homeland. Union infantry "bummers" and Judson Kilpatrick's cavalry had mistreated the Georgia population, torched their houses, and stolen their valuables.[41] South Carolina could expect no less and probably worse. On January 15, 1865, Lee granted Hampton his wish.

"I . . . have concluded," he wrote to Jefferson Davis, "to detach Genl Butler's division of cavalry to S.C. for service there this winter."[42] The troopers would ride the railroad south, but leave their horses in Virginia. New mounts would be purchased upon arriving at Columbia. In a burst of optimism, Lee assumed that the Rebel forces converging from many points onto the scene would trounce Sherman, so he made his orders conditional: Matthew must return to Virginia in time for the spring campaign. Butler began the trek home on January 19.[43]

CHAPTER 15

South Carolina

ON THE SAME DAY THAT BUTLER AND HIS CAVALRY STARTED TO BOARD the trains leaving Virginia, Sherman left Savannah and began his invasion of South Carolina. The 60,000-man Union force moved in two wings: Oliver Howard commanded the right wing, the XV and XVII Corps, which sailed for Beaufort, where they disembarked and started marching up the coast toward Charleston; Henry Slocum was in charge of the left wing, the XIV and XX Corps, which was split in two, with half on each shore of the Savannah River as they headed northwest toward Augusta, Georgia. The Union cavalry, led by Judson Kilpatrick, accompanied Slocum.[1]

Union general William Tecumseh Sherman was born in Lancaster, Ohio, in 1820. When his father died in 1829, the lad was sent to live with a family friend, Sen. Thomas Ewing, who raised young "Cump" as if he were his son. After graduating from West Point in 1840, Sherman served thirteen unexceptional years in the army, then resigned his commission to embark on a series of failures: banking in California; law in Kansas; head of a military school in Louisiana. The war revived his languishing career. He fought well during First Manassas, but when Sherman was sent to Kentucky to take command of this Western front, he encountered problems. Stress brought on a nervous collapse. Grant, however, took him under his wing, and Sherman won prominence for his role in the Union victories at Shiloh, Vicksburg, and Chattanooga. When Grant came east to become general in chief, Sherman replaced him as head of the Western armies.[2]

Sherman had hoped to advance rapidly into South Carolina, but rain started to fall on January 21, and it continued to pour throughout the next two days. The Yankees bogged down in the mud. "[I am] stuck in the swamps," a Northern soldier wrote home, "in . . . sand knee deep, cold as a dog, [and] sick as the dickens on poor rations."[3] After two weeks of struggle, the enemy's progress was only fifty miles toward Augusta and Charleston.

SOUTHERN
SOUTH CAROLINA

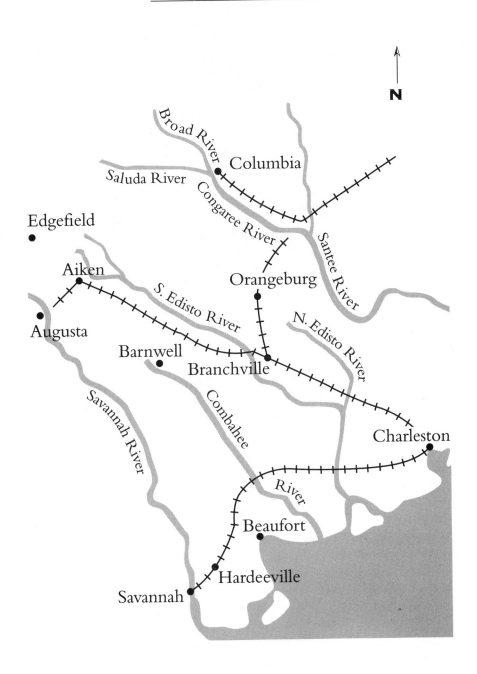

William Tecumseh Sherman. COURTESY LIBRARY OF CONGRESS

Beauregard, commanding the district, hurried to defend these two cities. He sent William J. Hardee with his 14,000 men out of Charleston, south to the Combahee River to block Howard's advance on the port. The three corps from the Army of Tennessee, led by Alexander P. Stewart, Carter L. Stevenson, and Frank Cheatham, were started east to check Slocum's threat to Augusta. Their ranks, however, were only roughly 2,000 each, due first to the casualties suffered in the disastrous Nashville Campaign, then subsequent straggling during their retreat. Joseph Wheeler's 3,000 cavalry would hold the city until their arrival.[4]

Butler and his men arrived by train in Columbia around February 1. After disembarking, some of the gray troopers mounted horses procured from the surrounding area and raced down Main Street. People cheered them as they rode by. "It was an inspiring sight," one Rebel wrote, "to see . . . old men congregating . . . and congratulating themselves that [the capital] was now safe."[5] The riders moved south below Columbia and camped on the western bank of the Congaree River. With Sherman's army slowed by the swamps in the low country, the authorities allowed the cavalry to make quick visits home to see their families.[7] Matthew went to Edgefield to see Maria and his boys.[8]

Thomas Muldrop Logan. COURTESY PHOTOGRAPHIC HISTORY OF THE CIVIL WAR

One week later when he returned to duty, Butler found changes in his command structure. Young had been sent south to Georgia to head a cavalry division located in that state. Col. Gilbert J. Wright, leader of Cobb's Legion, had been placed in charge of Young's brigade. Born in 1825 near the village of Lawrenceville, Georgia, Wright stood six feet four inches tall and was noted for "bulldog courage" and "a sentorian [*sic*] voice." After service as a private in the Mexican War, he had studied law, then started to practice in Albany, Georgia. He joined the Confederacy in 1861 as an officer of Cobb's Legion (the Albany Hussars), and became its commander in 1863. He had served under Hampton in Virginia throughout the war.[9]

Also new was Thomas Muldrop Logan, given permanent command of Butler's former brigade. Aiken, who had been acting as temporary leader, returned to his post as head of the 6th South Carolina. Born in 1840 in Charleston, South Carolina, Logan joined the Hampton Legion as an infantry officer about a year after his graduation from North Carolina College. He fought in all of the key battles in the East, then went west under Longstreet to Chickamauga and Knoxville. Upon his return to Virginia, Logan was promoted to colonel in charge of the Legion. He was severely wounded on June 13, 1864, during the battle of Riddle's Shop. Just now recovered, he was advanced in rank to brigadier general and sent south to defend his home state. Beauregard assigned him to Butler.[10]

Beauregard came to Columbia on February 7 for a meeting with Hampton. The South Carolinian argued that assuming defensive positions, dividing their army between Charleston and Augusta, could never stop

Joseph Wheeler. COURTESY PHOTOGRAPHIC HISTORY OF THE CIVIL WAR

Sherman's advance. The Rebels had to concentrate their numbers and take the offense. His recommendation was to make a stand at Branchville, a central rail depot between the two cities. A battle, even if stalemated, would deplete Sherman of supplies, and force him back to Savannah. His reasoning was good military strategy, and Beauregard agreed with Hampton. But he issued no orders for others to join Stevenson, the first of the Army of Tennessee corps to arrive, already stationed at Branchville.[11]

Four days later, Sherman's two wings suddenly converged on Branchville. The Northern advance on each flank had been a feint; the Yankees were moving on Columbia.[12] As Stevenson retreated, the Rebel defenders in Augusta and Charleston found that they were now in the rear of Sherman's force and hopelessly out of position to protect South Carolina. Beauregard was left with only one option: to start his divided infantry in a wide circle around both ends of the Union line toward Charlotte, North Carolina. He would consolidate his army there to battle Sherman. Wheeler was ordered to Columbia to join Butler. Their combined numbers, 4,500 troopers, were too few to stop the enemy, but they might slow his process, giving the Confederate foot soldiers time to get into position.[13]

Born in 1836 in Augusta, Georgia, Joe Wheeler attended West Point, and served in the cavalry after his 1859 graduation. He resigned in 1861 to join the South. He began the war in the artillery, was soon promoted to colonel in charge of the 19th Alabama infantry (who fought at Shiloh), and on October 30, 1862, rose to brigadier general of cavalry under Braxton Bragg. Wheeler had led all of the western horsemen ever since that date.[14]

Wheeler, only five feet five inches tall, was somewhat reluctant to come to Columbia. He was not afraid of the enemy; Joe did not want to serve under Hampton. His date of rank preceded the South Carolinian's, and he had expected to be in command if the cavalry was ever combined. Beauregard, however, wanted Hampton to head the horsemen, so he had sent a hurried appeal to Richmond to raise Hampton to lieutenant general. This promotion was granted on February 15.[15]

Hampton placed Wheeler's cavalry west of Columbia along the Saluda River; Butler's men assumed a position southeast of the capital on the Congaree River. Both looked for Sherman's arrival.

Matthew grew impatient with the waiting, so he decided to move south on February 15 to find the Federals. Riding through a cold rain, he soon met the Yankees' XV Corps at Congaree Creek, a favorable site for battle. The ground was swampy with only a narrow causeway winding through the mire. An earthen fort stood at Butler's end of the passage. After unlimbering the horse artillery he had brought to the front, Matthew formed his men and opened fire on his adversary. "I compelled Sherman's column to deploy," he related, "and disclose its strength."[16]

The Union numbers were vast, but Butler's position was impregnable, precluding a frontal assault. The Yankees were forced to resort to a flanking movement above and below the stream. As these men converged on the Confederates, Matthew started to retreat back toward the capital. He reached the Congaree River about dusk, where he prepared to demolish the covered bridge over the water. His riders poured highly inflammable rosin on the floor of the span, laid fat pine from end to end, then lit a fire that quickly consumed the structure.[17] To the west, Wheeler burned the bridge crossing the Saluda River.

Although these efforts would delay the Federal advance, nothing could be done that would prevent the enemy's capture of Columbia. Beauregard announced on February 16 that he would leave the city the next morning. Stevenson's infantry would lead the way, followed by the artillery, then Hampton and the cavalry.[18] The mayor, Dr. T. J. Goodwyn, would ride out to greet the enemy and surrender the capital. He would promise no resistance in exchange for their sparing the town from torching.

Goodwyn had a valid reason to worry about fires. When Sherman started his invasion, he had vowed to reap vengeance on South Carolina. "I almost tremble at her fate," he said, "but feel that she deserves all . . . in store for her."[19] Most of the small towns that his army had passed through (Hardeeville, Grahamville, McPhersonville, Barnwell, Midway, Blackville, Orangeburg, and Lexington) had already been burned.[20]

There was more to fear, however, than just fire. Sherman's soldiers had been sacking homes, stealing all kinds of personal belongings. "They [came] pouring into every door," Mrs. Alfred P. Aldrich of Barnwell said, "and without asking to have bureaus and wardrobes opened, broke with their bayonets every lock . . . hunting for gold, silver and jewels."[21]

An elderly lady in Lancaster was interrupted during her morning devotions. "Get up, old woman," a Yankee shouted as he burst into her house. "Praying will do you no good now." The soldier snatched the gold spectacles from her face, then emptied her pockets.[22]

What the Union soldiers could not take, they destroyed. One filled his canteen with sorghum from a heavy jug, then stuffed a tobacco plug into the crock. "Some feller'll come along and taste that sorghum," he said to the farmer's wife, "and think you've poisoned him. Then he'll burn your damned old house."[23]

Even more frightening was the abuse of women. Although not many whites were raped, the blacks seemed a special target for the Federals. "The poor negroes were victimized by their assailants, many of them . . . being left . . . a little short of death," an observer stated. "Regiments in successive relays subjected scores of these poor women to the tortures of their embraces."[24]

By midmorning of February 17, only Matthew's riders remained in Columbia. They were posted on Main Street, near the Capitol. "The stores were all closed," a trooper wrote, "but crowds of negroes and debased whites were breaking open the doors and helping themselves."[25] Butler stood in place until he spotted the enemy approaching only blocks away. He reluctantly gave the order, "Right about, march!" and moved his column north on the Winnsboro Road. They rode for eight miles, then halted at Killian's Mill, where they dismounted. "Exhausted by anxiety and [no] sleep for two days and nights before," Butler recalled, "we slept so soundly that we were not aware until . . . morning, at least I was not, that Columbia had been destroyed by fire."[26]

Matthew was embittered by the destruction of the state capital. He could not have prevented Sherman from capturing Columbia, but Butler thought he had the Union leader's word to spare the town if he left without firing a shot. "Columbia, fair . . . Columbia," he said later. "Let the charred remnants of this beautiful, disarmed and helpless city speak for the good faith and honorable conduct of the other side."[27]

Sherman claimed that Confederates had set afire the bales of cotton that lined the downtown streets, that they had created the conflagration. Butler's force, however, left at noon on February 17; the flames that gutted about forty square blocks of the capital did not begin until 8:00 P.M. The holocaust was centered along three main boulevards (Assembly, Main, and Sumter) north of the Capitol. Sherman and his army were responsible for this atrocity.[28]

The fall of Columbia isolated Charleston, so the South had to abandon that city, too. Hardee headed north with his 14,000 plus men on February 17, following the coast, rushing for North Carolina via Cheraw, South Carolina. His goal was to get in front of Sherman's army, to converge with the Army of Tennessee, marching parallel to his left on the west side of the Federal forces.[29]

The Union pursued Butler, and reached his position the next afternoon. He decided to make a stand. Although under orders to delay the enemy's advance, Matthew's tenacity was more likely based on his anger over the torching of Columbia and the many reports of outrages by the Yankees against his fellow people. "We deployed along the ridge in front of the railroad station," Matthew stated, "and kept fighting until dark."[30] He then headed for Winnsboro.

Withdrawing slowly northward, continuously skirmishing with the Yankees, Butler passed through Ridgeway on February 19. He reached Winnsboro by morning. "It became my painful duty, Butler noted, "to have destroyed Governor Aiken's fine old wine [sent from Charleston for safety] to prevent its tickling [the enemy's] thirsty palates."[31]

On February 21, Butler turned east off the main road and moved to Gladden's Grove, where he planned to forage his horses. The rest of the Confederate column (all three divisions of the Army of Tennessee, Wheeler's cavalry, and bands of refugees fleeing from the enemy) continued to plod north toward Charlotte, assumed to be the next objective for Sherman. Beauregard hoped to consolidate his meager forces and make a stand there.[32]

While Butler was at Gladden's Grove, the Yankees moved into Winnsboro, which isolated Matthew and his troopers from their compatriots. Hampton sent a message, ordering Butler to "rid myself of wheels by dispatching all my wagons northward," then rush [south] around Sherman's right flank, thru Columbia if possible, and up the Union left flank to "rejoin the troops moving toward Charlotte."[33]

Butler dispensed with his wagons, then started east on February 22. He soon encountered Union infantry, blocking his path. "After a sharp fight . . . continuing long enough to develop the strength of the enemy to my front," he recalled, "and finding that I could not overcome so strong a force, I moved [northeast]." He was still expecting to pass around the Federals. But

NORTHERN
SOUTH CAROLINA

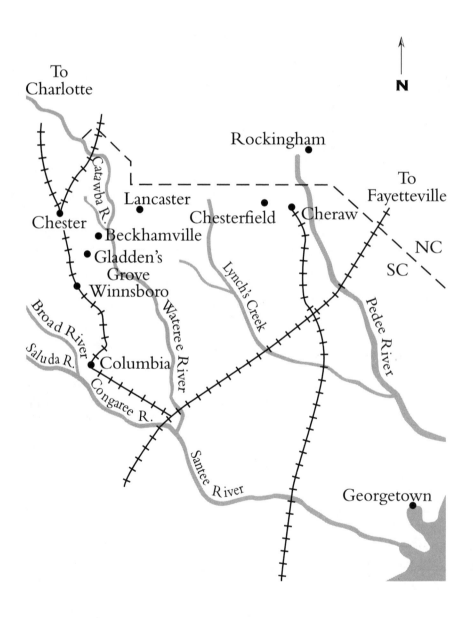

N

To
Charlotte

Rockingham

To
Fayetteville

Catawba R.

Lancaster

Chesterfield

Cheraw

Chester

Beckhamville

NC

SC

Gladden's
Grove

Lynch's Creek

Winnsboro

Broad River

Wateree River

Pedee River

Saluda R.

Columbia

Congaree R.

Santee River

Georgetown

the Yankees remained inexplicably in the way. The puzzle was solved late that same afternoon, when his men brought a recently captured prisoner into Butler's headquarters. This officer came from the XX Crops, who were part of Sherman's left wing. The enemy had turned perpendicular to the route to Charlotte, and were now hurrying east, probably for Cheraw, then Fayetteville, North Carolina. Butler sent word of his discovery to Beauregard and Hampton, then headed north for Beckhamville.[34]

Although Beauregard received Matthew's message, he did not act upon it. He was no longer in charge. Robert E. Lee was so alarmed by the deteriorating situation, as commander in chief of all Confederate armies, he asked his old friend, Joe Johnston, residing in Lincolnton, North Carolina, to return to duty and replace the Creole. Johnston went to Charlotte to confer with Beauregard, who gave up his post with a sigh of relief. He knew the cause was hopeless.[35]

Late that afternoon, as Butler rode up to a plantation mansion where he hoped to spend that night, he saw the owner sitting on the porch. "Here I am," the eighty-two-year-old Dr. Cloud cried, "and I ain't no Union man, either!" He obviously thought the riders were Yankees.

Butler and his staff dismounted, then joined Dr. Cloud on the veranda. Their host continued to assume that Matthew and his friends were Sherman's men, but after awhile, he began to have doubts.

"Who are you fellows?" he asked.

"General Butler's command," an aide answered.

"Which one of you is General Butler?"

Matthew, who wore no insignia, was pointed out.

"I knew your father well," Dr. Cloud said with a smile. "I used to see you as a small boy cutting capers . . . never expected to see you amount to anything."

Everyone laughed. Dr. Cloud then suggested to Matthew that he take his horses down to a corncrib to be fed. When the animals had had their fill, the Rebel officers returned to the house.

"Young man," Dr. Cloud asked Butler, "Would you like to have a drink?"

"Yes, Sir. After the fatigues and trials of the day, I think a little something wold be very acceptable."

As they sat sipping their drinks, Dr. Cloud pointed to a manure pile in an adjoining field. He told Butler that he had hidden his watch and other valuables underneath the dung. His silver was concealed on a nearby island.

"I don't want to discourage you," Butler said, "but the negroes on your plantation will conduct the Yankees straight to the island, and they will steal every article of value."

Dr. Cloud scoffed at the idea that his slaves would betray him. After an excellent meal, Butler and his men slept in the yard. They left the next morning.[36]

"I afterwards learned," Butler wrote, "that [Dr. Cloud] had been strung up by the neck twice by Sherman's troops (in an attempt) to coerce him into disclosing the whereabouts of his silver. . . . They failed, but his negroes [did] betray the places of concealment."[37]

On February 23 Butler continued to gallop northward, camping that night at Anderson's Mill. The next morning, he tried to turn east by fording the Catawba River at Gouche's Ferry. A hard rain had been falling since yesterday, so the stream was almost at flood stage. The current was so quick, when Butler tried to swim his horse across, they were swept down river. "The situation," Butler stated, "looked rather squally." Fortunately, he soon found a better crossing, and managed to move his force over the water. The men spent the night in the area, then pushed on the following morning into Lancaster.[38]

Matthew had expected to find some home guardsmen there, but most of the citizen soldiers had scattered, leaving only "old men, women, and children." The militia's weapons were stacked in the courthouse. Before he left the village, the guard commander, Gen. A. C. Garrington, had ordered them destroyed by burning the county building if the enemy showed up. "[The locals] implored me," Butler stated, "not to permit this, as it might lead to the destruction of the entire town. I therefore impressed two wagons and started the muskets and ammunition to Charlotte."[39]

By now Butler was east of the Federal army, whose van was southwest of his location and stymied by the overflowing banks of the Wateree River. Matthew started south, looking for a good site to greet the oncoming enemy. He halted that night just short of Cantey's plantation. Matthew had hoped to attack the Yankees, who were finally crosing the stream, at dawn, but that evening the continuing downpour exploded into a cruel storm. "The night was the darkest and the rain the hardest I have ever known," Butler related. "It made the attack at daylight impossible."[40]

On the morning of February 26 Butler and his riders reached Cantey's plantation, where they saw a group of enemy foragers helping themselves to the corn and hay in the barn. Matthew immediately ordered a charge, which sent the bummers running for their lives. The Rebels followed them south to Little Lynch's Creek, more a swamp than river. After crossing a span over the muddy current, Matthew's man started to wade through the surrounding marsh. "The water," Butler recalled, "[came] up to the saddle skirts." All at once, the Yankees they were pursuing appeared in their rear and opened fire. The Confederates turned on them and killed, captured, or wounded the entire party, seventeen in number."[41]

This was not the first instance where Matthew or other Rebels had shot the stragglers from Sherman's army whom they found looting homes. The Confederates were incensed by the atrocities inflicted by Union bummers on innocent civilians, and they never hesitated to deliver quick justice. Sherman took note of this in a message to Hampton. "Our foraging parties are murdered after capture," he wrote, citing a few instances. "I have ordered a similar number of prisoners in my hands to be disposed of in like manner. You cannot question my right to 'forage on the country.' It is a war right as old as history. . . . Give notice to your people . . . that every life taken by them simply results in the death of [a] . . . Confederate."[42]

Hamtpon replied with a threat of his own. "For every soldier of mine 'murdered' by you, I shall have executed at once two of yours, giving . . . preference to [Union] officers in my hands."

He went on to scorn Sherman's right to forage. "There is a right older, even, than this, and one more inalienable—the right . . . every man has to defend his home and to protect those who are dependent on him. . . . From my heart, I wish that every old man and boy in my country who can fire a gun will shoot . . . as he would a wild beast, the men who are desolating their land, burning their homes, and insulting their women."

"You have permitted, it not ordered, commissions of . . . offenses against humanity," Hampton insisted. "your line of march can be traced by the lurid light of burning houses. . . [leaving] an agony that is more bitter than death." He concluded by repeating this threat. "Whenever you have any of my men 'murdered' or 'disposed of,' . . . the terms appear to be synonymous with you, you will let me hear of it, that I may know what actions to take. . . . I hold fifty-six of your men as hostages for those whom you have ordered to be executed."[43]

Sherman was probably pleased to see that his "scorched earth" policy had infuriated Hampton. He knew, however, that the South Carolinian would not hesitate to retaliate if any Confederates were executed. The plans to "dispose of" Rebel prisoners were dropped.

After the affair near Cantey's plantation, Butler rode west, where he spotted a Federal wagon train, parked between two enemy infantry elements. The teamsters were just hitching their horses. He decided to attack. "The shrill blasts of our bugles sounding the charge," a trooper stated, "away we went shouting, shooting and hewing with sabre. It [took] but . . . a few seconds [to capture] 200 prisoners and nineteen splendid army wagons, each drawn by six fine mules, clad in harness as our Confederate teamsters had not seen for many a day."[44]

Butler hurried his prize eastward, crossed over Little Lynch's Creek, then Big Lynch's Creek, and set up camp along the far shore at Kellytown. The steady, three-day rain had finally stopped. The night was clear but cold. The Yankees following Butler halted on the western bank of the stream.

Hoping to delay Sherman's fording of the water, Butler sent pickets up and down the creek that evening. Their task was to alert him of any attempted crossing so he could mass his meager numbers at any threatened point. The 6th Carolina trotted south with their commander, Col. Hugh Aiken, in the lead. As the troopers plodded along the shore, their column easily seen in the bright moonlight, a shot rang out from the opposite bank. Aiken toppled from his saddle. He died instantly from the sniper's well-aimed bullet.[45]

The loss of one of Butler's best officers proved to be unnecessary. The Yankees had had no intention of attempting to cross Big Lynch's Creek that evening. They were holding in place until their columns closed. Matthew waited for two days, then after sunset on February 28, rode east. An enemy force followed close on his heels. Galloping throughout that night, Matthew arrived at Cheraw, where Hardee and his infantrymen were ensconced. The 14,000 Confederates who had left Charleston had dwindled through straggling to about 10,000.[46]

Butler quickly suggested that Hardee marshall his force to join him in attacking the Federal van (the XX Corps led by Francis P. Blair, Jr.). "He did not appear to think it advisable," Matthew wrote later, "and perhaps he was right."[47]

Hardee offered a different tactic. Butler should take his troopers northwest to Chesterfield, where he would be on the Yankee flank. Matthew left the next morning, March 2, and after "fighting at every point," assumed position. That night he received a hurried call to come in person back to Cheraw.

Upon reaching Hardee's headquarters, Matthew found the general conducting a council of war. "After your experience today," Hardee asked Butler, "what do you advise?"

"You should get your men across the Pedee [River, east of Cheraw] at the earliest possible moment," Butler replied.

"There is no occasion for haste," Lafayette McLaws, an infantry corps commander under Hardee, retorted.

"You asked my opinion," Matthew said with a shrug. He refused to argue with McLaws. "I have given it frankly, and heard nothing to induce me to change it."[48]

Hardee decided to follow Butler's advice, and he began to dictate orders to abandon Cheraw in the morning. "Change that to take effect at once," Butler interrupted. He noted that Cheraw was a depot for a huge store of supplies, and it would take time to load up all that the army could carry.[49]

The Rebels worked through the night, and by morning of March 3, Hardee's force had crossed the Pedee River, where they turned left to head for North Carolina. Butler waited in town for his troopers to return from Chesterfield to form a rear guard. "I had scarcely time," he stated, "before the enemy reached the outskirts of Cheraw. . . . I then deployed everything I had across the different streets and fell back to the bridge [under] a sharp fire, returning shot for shot. So close was the call . . . as my rear . . . passed out at the east end, the enemy was entering the west end."[50]

Butler knew he could not allow Sherman's men access to the span, so he ordered a charge on foot to push the Yankees backward. "We drove the enemy," he wrote, "and set fire to the piles of rosin deposited at intervals along the floor of the bridge. We soon had it in flames."[51]

Determined to keep the Federals from crossing over the river, Matthew formed his troopers along the far bank of the Pedee, where they "kept up a lively sharpshooting until ten o'clock" that night. Hardee took advantage of the time gained, and escaped into North Carolina.[52]

Butler, however, stayed in South Carolina. He refused to give up the defense of his state. "With [just] a handful of men," he noted, "we could get only an occasional blow at [the Union] detachments foraging and plundering helpless inhabitants."[53] His vengeance was relentless. For example, when his men came to Butler with five Federals they had just caught looting a farm home, he exploded with anger. "[Why] in . . . hell," Butler bellowed, "did you bring them to me?" He did not want prisoners. If his cavalry found Sherman's bummers pillaging, they should kill them on the spot.[54]

Hampton, however, soon called Butler to North Carolina. "Do not . . . delay Sherman's march," he wrote. "For God's sake let him get out of the country as soon as possible."[55] Following the same route that Hardee had taken, Matthew arrived in Rockingham on March 5.[56]

━━◆━━

Sherman considered his desolation of South Carolina as being humane, since it was intended to break the will of the Confederate people and thus hasten the end of the Civil War. The net result would be fewer casualties for both sides. "I am not a Boar," Sherman insisted. "War is war, and you can make nothing else of it."[57]

His strategy seemed to work; the fighting soon ended. But one can argue that the war has extended into perpetuity. Hatred for Yankees still flames brightly today, particularly in rural South Carolina.

CHAPTER 16

North Carolina

Sherman's target in North Carolina was Goldsborough, a city connected by rail to the ports of New Bern and Wilmington on the Atlantic Ocean. He would reprovision his force there, then continue north to join with Grant against Lee at Richmond.[1]

This strategy was dependent on the Yankees driving the Rebels from Wilmington, the last major Confederate-held port on the sea, and then clearing a path from this town and New Bern to Goldsborough. Steps to this end had already started prior to Sherman's departure from Savannah. On January 17 a combined Federal operation under Gen. Alfred H. Terry and Adm. David D. Porter had captured Fort Fisher. This bulwark, located on a barrier island near the inlet to the Cape Fear River, protected Wilmington.[2] John Schofield with his Army of the Ohio, the XXIII Corps, rushed east out of Tennessee to Washington, D.C., where they set sail south to finish the task of taking the city. Wilmington finally fell on February 22.[3]

The Yankees already held New Bern, located 100 miles up the coast, seized in March 1862, during Burnside's Roanoke Island Campaign.[4]

After taking Wilmington Schofield decided to drive inland only from New Bern. He needed to rebuild the railroad along the way, and the track from there to Goldsborough was not only in better condition but also held some usable cars and locomotives. Jacob B. Cox's division led the army westward on March 7. Schofield expected to reach Goldsborough by March 21.[5]

Sherman's force entered North Carolina on the same day that Schofield began his trek inland. The four corps headed northeast in parallel through the Cheraw area: Howard with his right wing, the XV and XVII Corps, marched to the south; Slocum and the left wing, the XIV and XX Corps, to the north. Kilpatrick's cavalry covered the Union flank from above the plodding columns.[6]

NORTH CAROLINA

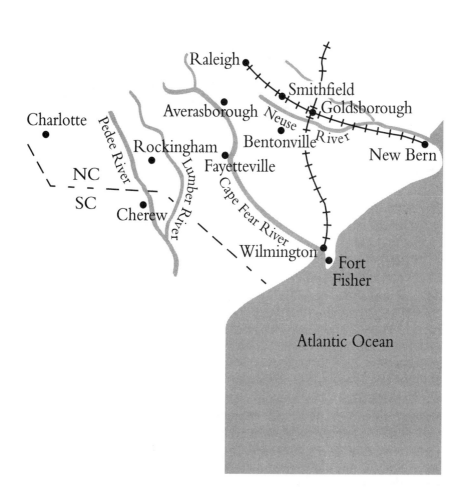

N

Raleigh

Smithfield
Averasborough
Goldsborough
Neuse River
Charlotte
Bentonville
Rockingham
New Bern
Pedee River
Fayetteville
NC
SC
Lumber River
Cherew
Cape Fear River
Wilmington
Fort
Fisher

Atlantic Ocean

Evander McIvor Law.   COURTESY PHOTOGRAPHIC HISTORY OF THE CIVIL WAR

Johnston's army was still scattered, unable to offer a challenge to the Union's progress. The three corps from the Army of Tennessee were at Smithfield; Hardee had turned at Rockingham and was rushing east toward Fayetteville; Butler, who had rejoined Hampton and Wheeler, was following Hardee; and Braxton Bragg, in command of Robert F. Hoke's division, recently added to Johnston's numbers, was at Goldsborough, directing the feeble effort to halt Schofield's advance.[7]

On March 3, while passing through Rockingham, Butler acquired yet another leader for his former brigade. Evander McIvor Law had been sent south by Richmond to join Johnston. Law reported to Bragg, who gave him to Hampton, who assigned him to Butler.[8] Born in 1836 in Darlington, South Carolina, Law graduated from the Citadel, taught in military schools in Alabama prior to the war, and then joined the Confederacy as an infantry officer. He fought with distinction in each of the early battles and was rewarded with a general's star and brigade command in October 1862. He served under John Bell Hood at Gettysburg and Chickamauga, then came east to combat Grant. Severely wounded at Cold Harbor, he was just now returning to duty.[9]

Law's date of rank entitled him to brigade command, so Butler moved Logan aside, making him the "supernumerary" assistant to Law.[10]

On March 7, as he trailed Hardee's infantry eastward out of Rockingham, Hampton split his force into two columns: Wheeler to the north; Butler to the south. Because he was closer to the enemy, Matthew was the first to encounter Kilpatrick and his riders, moving parallel to the Confederates while supposedly protecting Slocum's left wing. The Northern troopers were actually on a looting spree. Matthew ordered a charge.

"We recaptured some Catawba wine that [Kilpatrick] had . . . [stolen] from a citizen," Butler stated, "and took a number of prisoners."[11]

The local citizens were glad to see the Rebel horsemen passing through their town. "Our cavalry column was hailed with joy by the women and children," one of Butler's riders recalled. "They were quite liberal in supplying us with hot biscuits just from the oven."[12]

Heavy rain started to fall on March 8, and it poured throughout the day. Probably confused by the storm, Kilpatrick's column swerved north and inadvertently drove a wedge between Hardee and Hampton. When he discovered his mistake, the Northern cavalry chief decided to take advantage of his situation. He arrayed his troopers along the two main roads running west to east in an attempt to ambush Hampton.

Hampton, however, never appeared. He was moving along a third road to the north, progressing slowly because of the continuing rain.

As Kilpatrick wondered over the whereabouts of Hampton, he learned about the third path to the north. A brigade led by George E. Spencer was dispatched to block this road, too. About nightfall, Kilpatrick, his headquarters party, and his mistress, Marie Boozer, a teenage trollop from Columbia who had taken refuge with his entourage after the burning of the capital, headed north to join Spencer.[13]

Butler and his men, too, rode slowly north through the rainy, black night. Wright led the way with Law ringing up the rear. About 11:00 P.M., as the Rebel van came within a mile of Spencer's camp, they suddenly bumped into the end of Kilpatrick's column. The Union general was up ahead, about to enter his subordinate's bivouac; his escorts, the riders that Butler had encountered, were protecting the rear. The enemy horsemen halted when they heard the jingle of the Confederates' advance.

Butler thought that the cavalry crossing his path were Yankees. Turning to Capt. Mose Humphrey, in charge of the squadron at the head of Wright's strung-out columns, he whispered, "Do you have anybody on this road?"

"No, Sir."

"Stay here," Butler ordered. He rode forward alone to challenge the riders.

"Who comes there?" Matthew called out after he reached hailing distance.

"Fifth Kentucky," came the reply. They *were* Yankees!

"Ride up, Sir; I want to speak with you."[14]

A Federal lieutenant and his orderly trotted ahead and followed Butler as he wheeled, then rode back into the midst of his men. After quietly capturing the Yankee officer and his aide, Butler sent some troopers through the trees lining the road to surround the twenty-eight enemy riders, waiting for the return of their leader. They were quickly encircled and forced to surrender without a shot. "It was," a Confederate would gleefully recall, "the coolest thing that I ever witnessed."[15]

Butler notified Hampton that "the enemy's pickets have been taken without any alarm being given. . . . His camp [is] at our mercy." The cavalry commander brought Wheeler with him to the front, where they met with Matthew to plan "a morning call on Kilpatrick."[16]

Butler had sent scouts ahead and they had come back to report that the enemy was camped with a swamp to their front with woods on both sides. Kilpatrick was asleep in a house well to the rear of the bivouac. Hampton decided to attack at dawn: Butler would charge around the morass to the left; Wheeler would circle to the right. When Matthew briefed his men, he added one more element: the troopers were to drive through the ground all the way back to Kilpatrick's cottage. Their priority was to capture the Union leader.[17]

After spending the night resting with "a pine root for a pillow," Butler rose before dawn to form his men. He gave Wright the honor of attacking the enemy camp; he would follow close behind with Law's regiments. They waited in place as Wheeler's troopers trotted forward, then began filing to the right. Once Wheeler seemed in position for his advance, Matthew ordered the assault on Kilpatrick's camp.[18]

Following close behind Wright's hard-charging troopers, whose progress through the pines and brambles enveloped in a misty fog could only be tracked by gleeful shouting, Butler was astonished to see over a hundred Rebel soldiers coming back toward him. "Suspicion flashed through [my] mind," he recalled, "that [we] had been repulsed. It turned out these were Confederates, who [had been] prisoners, broke away and running for liberty. One poor fellow in a frenzy of delight seized my leg, embraced and kissed it."[19]

At first the enemy offered little resistance, choosing to flee in all directions. "Having vanquished the foe," one Rebel disclosed, "we now set about in a rather disorganized state to vanquish what was left on the field in the shape of everything good to eat or wear."[20]

The calm did not last long. Once the Federal troopers found safety in the bordering forests, they whirled about to open fire on Butler's men, who were exposed in the clearing while pillaging the Yankees' tents. "Pandemonium reigned in every direction," Matthew stated. He had ridden all the way to the rear, close by Kilpatrick's cabin. Most of the Union bullets now decimating his force came from the right, where Wheeler's men had failed to appear.[21]

As Butler wondered what happened to his compatriot, Wheeler suddenly rode up. He was accompanied by only two or three members of his staff. "Where's your command," the diminutive cavalryman shouted above the din of battle.

"Scattered [to] hell!" Butler bellowed back. "Where's yours?"

"I tried to attack from my side but encountered a bog," Wheeler lamely explained. "Couldn't get my command across." Butler had been fighting on his own.[22]

The key to the battle lay with the Federals' artillery, pitched near Butler's position. Yankee gunners had returned to their cannons and were unlimbering, preparing to fire into the Rebel ranks. In a desperate move, Butler gathered up a makeshift squadron to charge the pieces. They were met by a flurry of grapeshot. "Sixty-two men were killed in [just] a few minutes," Matthew ruefully recalled. He had no choice but order a retreat.[23]

Kilpatrick was not there to celebrate his victory. At the first sounds of battle, he had leaped out of bed to rush outside. Dressed only in his underwear, the Federal leader was shocked by the sight of Matthew's riders bearing down on him. A Rebel trooper reined his horse to a stop.

"Where's General Kilpatrick?" he demanded.

Thinking quickly, Kilpatrick pointed out a Yankee fleeing the area on a black horse. "There he goes!" he shouted.

As the Rebel chased after this quarry, Kilpatrick grabbed another horse, mounted bareback, and escaped from the camp.[24]

Marie followed Kilpatrick out of the house. She began "running about, wringing her hands, calling on the good Lord to save her."[25] A gallant Rebel took pity on Marie and led her to a nearby drainage gully, where she would be safe from the bullets whizzing overhead. Despite the best efforts of her savior, Marie "[kept] lifting her head from time to time [to peer] above the ditch to see what was going on."[26]

Kilpatrick claimed that his losses were only about 200 killed, wounded, or captured; Butler, however, noted that he took almost 500 Federal prisoners. Regardless of the numbers, Kilpatrick was embarrassed by the foray on his camp. Union infantrymen jokingly referred to the affair as "Kilpatrick's Shirt-Tail Skedaddle."[27]

After retreating from Kilpatrick's camp, Hampton swing around the Federal position and headed for Fayetteville. He arrived the evening of March 10. Hardee and his infantry were in town, and they brought him up-to-date. Johnston had sent the rest of the army to Kinston to join Bragg's forces in opposing Schofield's advance out of New Bern. The battle had raged for three days, but the Confederates were too few to hold the line. Bragg had withdrawn to Goldsborough.[28]

Matthew spent the evening in a private home in Fayetteville. Before retiring, he had handed all of his clothes to a black laundress for cleaning. Butler was lying naked in bed when soon after sunrise an excited aide rushed into his room and shouted, "The Yankees! The Yankees!"

Scrambling out of bed, Matthew donned the only garb at hand: his boots, hat, and overcoat. He hurried outside and mounted, then galloped away from the direction of gun shots. He could not being himself so illy clad to battle. Perhaps Matthew chuckled to himself when he recalled that Kilpatrick had faced a similar dilemma only a few days ago.[29]

Hampton was up and in the streets of Fayetteville when the Northern scouting party rode into town. Although he had only seven men with him, Hampton never hesitated. He led a charge that so surprised the Yankee riders, they wheeled and ran. Eleven of the enemy were killed, twelve were captured, and the rest, forty-five, escaped back to Union lines.[30]

The close presence of the enemy suggested that Sherman was moving on Raleigh. Hardee started his infantry north to protect the capital; Hampton and his cavalry stayed behind to guard the rear. After collecting his clothes, Butler and his riders crossed the Cape Fear River to set up their guns on the hills that overlooked the town. When Sherman's force appeared, they opened fire. At the same time, they set aflame the only bridge over the stream.[31]

These delaying tactics were unnecessary as the Yankees were only closing their columns. Sherman had planned on remaining in Fayetteville until his stragglers caught up with the rest of the army. While he rested in town, Hardee moved to Averasborough, Johnston took the rest of his infantry to Smithfield, and the cavalry was posted between these Confederate forces.[32]

During this brief peaceful interlude, one of Matthew's companies noted that their commissary, Old Nat, had become a health hazard. "By a vote in the saddle," one of the troopers recalled, "[we] decided that [Nat] should take a bath or else lose his rank."

"Now, men," poor Nat argued, "you know the Gineral has ordered us to stay in line."

"That doesn't apply to you," his comrades hooted, "you are a non-combatant."

"Well," Nat conceded, "if I must, I must."

Stripping, he waded into the waters of a nearby stream. "He lathered his face and neck," a compatriot stated, "and soon had soapsuds running down all over his body. He was in this condition when General Butler suddenly rode up."

"What in the devil is this?"

"Well," Nat explained, "I was dirty and the boys. . ."

"What command to you belong to?" Butler interrupted.

"Why, Gineral, I'm company commissary."

"Company commissary hell!" Butler exploded.

Although acting as if Nat's leaving his post was a serious offense, Matthew could hardly keep from laughing at the ludicrous sight of a man clad only in bubbles. "Butler was too sensible [an officer] to punish him," a soldier related, "so Nat got what we all needed, a good washing."[33]

Sherman left Fayetteville on March 15, with Howard's troops moving northeast toward Goldsborough. Slocum's force marched north as if advancing on Raleigh, the state capital. The latter arrived at Averasborough the next day, where they found Hardee entrenched, ready to make a stand.

The Rebels were posted along a narrow front bounded by the Cape Fear and Black Rivers. Hardee had chosen this site to offset his disparity in numbers: 8,000 Confederates versus 15,000 Yankees. He arrayed his men in five lines, front to stern, with the garrison soldiers from Charleston at the fore. He thought that these unproven troops would probably give way when attacked, but if he could withdraw by echelon, bringing his veterans into battle after the enemy's advance had been blunted, he might be able to halt Slocum's progress for a day or so. The delay would give Johnston time needed to gather his forces for a concentrated assault on Sherman's army.

The enemy charged Hardee's post at Averasborough three times on March 16. The Federal XIV Corps quickly dislodged the Rebels' first line in their 10:00 A.M. attack; the second rank reeled to the rear about 1:00 P.M.; but the Union's third assault at 4:30 P.M. was repelled by Hardee's veterans. A heavy rain that afternoon aided the Confederate effort. Hardee congratulated his men for "giving the enemy the first serious check he has received since . . . Atlanta."[34]

That night Hardee quietly abandoned the field to withdraw northward to await Slocum's next move. The Yankees did not follow. Instead they turned east to plod toward Goldsborough. Howard was following a parallel path to the south, but because he had not been encumbered by battle, the Yankee right wing was a day's march ahead of their counterpart.[35]

The Confederate cavalry kept track of the Federal advance. Wheeler's riders confronted Slocum's wing; Butler's men sparred with Howard's force.

Hampton coordinated these efforts from his headquarters, located near the Cole plantation a few miles south of Bentonville. When he learned from the reports by his horsemen that Sherman's wings were widely separated, Hampton sent a message to Johnston urging him to take advantage of the Union mistake. Slocum was approaching his position, which afforded an excellent ground for battle. If Johnston hurried his force south, Hampton would delay the enemy until the Confederates were in position to attack the isolated Union columns.[36]

Johnston received Hampton's note at dawn on March 18, and he readily agreed with his recommendations. Stewart and Bragg immediately started south from Smithfield; word was sent to Hardee to hurry to Bentonville, too.[37]

At the same time, Wheeler's cavalry (the riders led by George G. Dibrell) rode west to seek out Slocum's van. When they made contact, they started skirmishing, first fighting, then falling back, cleverly luring Slocum's force toward the position that Hampton had selected for the battle. Sherman, accompanying Slocum's wing, doubted that Johnston would ever risk a fight, but he decided to take no chances. Late that afternoon he ordered a halt to close his columns.[38]

Slocum was positioned exactly where Hampton wanted him: on the road to Goldsborough a few miles south of the village of Bentonville. The enemy faced a barren field, surrounded by dense woods; Hampton (Dibrell's cavalry) occupied a line atop the ridge running north to south, east of the Union camp.

Just after dark the troops from Smithfield started to arrive on the field. Hoke's division, still under Bragg's command, assumed Dibrell's post atop the ridge below the pike; Stewart's Army of Tennessee took up a position inside the forest above the road, west of Bragg, facing south. Hardee had been too far away to reach the front that night, but when he finally reached the scene, his men filled the gap between Bragg and Stewart.[39]

Johnston's battle plan called for Dibrell's cavalry to lure Slocum into attacking Bragg's line atop the ridge. When his volleys brought the enemy to a halt, Stewart and Hardee would charge out of the woods to hit the Union flank. Johnston expected the onslaught to force a Union retreat, which he would pursue vigorously. He would destroy Sherman's left wing. Butler, still fronting Howard, would have no role in the fight.[40]

When morning dawned on March 19 Sherman had no idea that he faced a battle, and he played into Johnston's hands. The Federal leader started south to join Howard, but before departing, he ordered Slocum to advance eastward. "There is nothing there but . . . cavalry," he noted. "Brush them out of the way."[41]

Johnston's plan worked perfectly. But at the critical moment of battle, Bragg lost his nerve and cried out for reinforcements. He thought that William P. Carlin's division from Slocum's XIV Corps, leading the Northern assault on his position, was about to break the Confederate line. Johnston sent over half of Hardee's force (McLaw's Division, just now reaching the field) from Stewart to Bragg. As they rushed into place about noon, the Union started to retreat.[42]

This change in plant not only delayed Stewart's assault on the Federal flank but also deprived that commander of the numbers he needed to devastate the Union's withdrawal. His men, augmented by Hardee's remaining division led by William P. Taliaferro, finally advanced at 2:45 P.M. Although they pressed the Yankees south of the pike and then westward, the shocked XIV Corps gained the safety of a line, built by comrades in the trailing XX Corps, and escaped annihilation. Had Bragg joined in the charge, per Johnston's battle plan, the Rebels might still have won a victory, but the timid general held his infantrymen in place. That night Johnston pulled his forces back to their original position.[43]

Johnston claimed a moral victory for the Rebels. "One important object was gained," he stated, "restoring the confidence of our troops, who had either lost it in the defeat at Wilmington or in . . . Tennessee. All were greatly elated by the event."[44]

Neither adversary took any offensive action March 20. The Rebels started to evacuate their wounded (1,694 out of a total 2,606 casualties, almost 1,000 more than the Federal losses); Slocum awaited reinforcements to come up form Sherman's right wing.[45]

Johnston expected the Federals to combine their forces, and he depended on Butler, posted to the southeast, to watch out for Howard's approach. Matthew, however, was no longer on duty. The effects of no sleep, little food, and exposure to the elements finally took a toll. He fell seriously ill, and turned over temporary command of his division to Evander M. Law. Logan resumed charge of Butler's former brigade.[46]

The campaign in North Carolina in March 1865 offered only lost opportunities to Butler and his Rebel compatriots. Hampton's "Morning Call" on Kilpatrick failed to capture the Northern cavalryman because Wheeler did not carry out his role. And Johnston's assault at Bentonville might have succeeded had not Bragg proved again that he was a poor leader.

These battles, however, were meaningless. The war was essentially over. The South had lost their bid for independence.

The only question remaining for Matthew was whether he would survive the war. Enemy bullets were not a threat; he was sick, so desperately ill that Hampton wold soon send a recommendation to Richmond that Law take over permanent command of Butler's cavalry division.[47] Once again Matthew's future lay in the hands of his doctors.

CHAPTER 17

The End of the War

On March 20, as Butler lay sick in bed, his troopers sparred with Sherman's right wing. Howard was hurrying west up the Goldsborough Road to unite with Slocum against Johnston. Matthew's cavalry were too few to halt the approaching Union; they could only hope to prevent Howard from cutting across the Rebel rear.

Johnston was well aware that enemy reinforcements were at hand, but he was encumbered with his wounded. And he had only one avenue for extricating his army, a solitary bridge over the high water of Mill Creek to his rear. He could not abandon the casualties from yesterday's battle, so Johnston elected to hold in place while a column of wagons toting the injured passed slowly through this bottleneck. He prepared for Howard's imminent arrival by aligning his force along an east to west line, facing south.[1]

Slocum, reinforced by troops from the tail of Howard's wing, confronted the Rebel line throughout that day, but the fighting was limited to skirmishing. Howard arrived on the field about 4:00 P.M. and took up a position to the right of Slocum, facing north. Butler's horsemen slipped into place on the far left of the Confederate line.[2]

Johnston was ready to withdraw by the morning of March 21. He knew, however, that he must not retreat. Doing so would let Sherman march unimpeded to Goldsborough, where he would merge his already superior force with Schofield's Army of the Ohio, advancing unopposed from the sea. This combination would assure the Federals of an overwhelming advantage in troops, resulting in certain defeat for Johnston and probably ending the war. So he remained in place, counting on a miracle. "We [hold] our ground," he wrote to Lee, "in the hope that [the Yankees'] greatly superior numbers [will] encourage him to attack."[3] Repelling an enemy charge might give Johnston a chance to counterassault and rout Sherman's army.

It rained on March 21, a cold drizzle throughout the morning, then a downpour all afternoon. The storm, however, would not prevent battle.[4]

Sherman, not expecting a fight, began to move his army east, starting Slocum behind Howard's entrenched troops. On the Union right flank, Joseph Mower grew impatient with the standoff and about noon, he led his division ahead to reconnoiter the Confederate left. He soon saw that Butler's two brigades stood in his way. One, however, the South Carolinians, possibly because Matthew was not there to steady them with his usual coolness, fled their post, opening a path for Mower's infantry to pour into the Rebel rear. After capturing Johnston's headquarters, they moved toward the span over Mill Creek, the only avenue for a Confederate retreat.[5]

The Rebels rallied to this threat. Hampton personally led Butler's 2nd Brigade as they charged the Yankees from the north; Hardee directed a cavalry and infantry assault from the west. Mower was forced into retreat. "That was Nip and Tuck," Hardee drawled to Hampton once the field was secured, "and for a time, I thought Tuck had it." He laughed at the time, but Hardee soon cried. His only son, Willie, just sixteen years old, had been killed in the fray.[6]

As the day ended it became obvious that Sherman would not risk another assault. Johnston had no choice but to retreat. He started to withdraw about 10:00 P.M., and by the morning of March 22, he had left the field. He retired to Smithfield. Sherman moved for Goldsborough, which Schofield had occupied on March 21. Slocum's force left Bentonville on the 22nd; Howard's wing headed east on March 23.[7]

When Sherman reached Goldsborough, he set up camp with the intention of resting his troops for several weeks before moving to unite with Grant against Lee. He planned to head northwest about April 10, fake an assault on Johnston, and force the Rebels to retreat to Raleigh. Sherman would then wheel north and follow the Weldon Railroad up to the Roanoke River, which runs along the boundary between North Carolina and Virginia. From there he would veer northwest to impost his force between the armies under Lee and Johnston and prevent any possible juncture. Events outside of Richmond soon changed his mind.[8]

Grant broke through the Confederate line at Five Forks on April 1 and severed the last remaining supply line into Richmond. Lee was left with two equally unpalatable alternatives: he could either surrender or abandon Richmond. Lee elected to flee, and on April 3, he started west, heading toward Amelia Court House. Lee planned to wheel south at this point to move into North Carolina, where he would hook up with Johnston.[9] Grant began a vigorous pursuit of Lee.

Sherman left Goldsborough April 10 as scheduled, but his plans were changed. He meant to attack Johnston, hoping to capture his army before Lee's arrival.[10]

Johnston and Lee had been discussing a strategy, where the Army of Northern Virginia would leave Richmond and hurry south to join against Sherman. After routing his army, the two would wheel north to take on Grant. So when he received word from President Davis on April 5, saying that Lee was "concentrating toward Amelia Court House," then adding "your knowledge of . . . Lee's plans will enable you to infer further movements," Johnston assumed that this scheme was in motion. He had no idea that Lee was in a desperate retreat; no one had informed him that the Army of Northern Virginia had been driven from their trenches at Richmond.[11]

After preparing his force to move northwest (including a reorganization of the army into three corps under Stewart, Hardee, and Stephen D. Lee), Johnston left Smithfield April 10, following the North Carolina Railroad, using the track to speed his retreat. Hampton's riders brought up the rear. Butler, although still weak from his recent illness, resumed command and accompanied his troopers.[12]

Fully expecting orders telling him where he must unite with Lee, Johnston was no doubt numbed by a wire from Davis, received late that night, which reported Lee's surrender to Grant at Appomattox Court House. The president asked Johnston to come to Greensborough to confer on future action.[13]

The two met in Greensborough on April 12. Others at this conference included Beauregard and three members of the president's cabinet: the secretary of state, Judah P. Benjamin, the postmaster general, John H. Reagan, and the secretary of the navy, Stephen R. Mallory. "I was fully sensible of the gravity of our position," Davis related, "[but] I did not think we should despair."[14] He offered a series of proposals for continuing to fight. When Johnston tried to note that their cause was futile, the president refused to listen. "Neither opinions nor information was asked," Johnston stated.[15] The meeting ended in an impasse.

John C. Breckinridge, the secretary of war, joined the band the next morning. He persuaded Davis to allow Johnston to ask Sherman for an armistice "to enable the civil authorities to agree upon terms of peace."[16] The president agreed only because he was sure that the Yankees would reject this petition. He then left for Charlotte, on his way west where he hoped to find a general who remained willing to continue the war. Johnston returned to his army, which after passing through Raleigh had reached the Hillsborough area. He then sent a letter to Sherman asking for a truce.

Sherman, thinking that Johnston was about to surrender, eagerly agreed to suspend hostilities. In his reply he not only outlined boundaries

NORTH CAROLINA

APRIL 1865

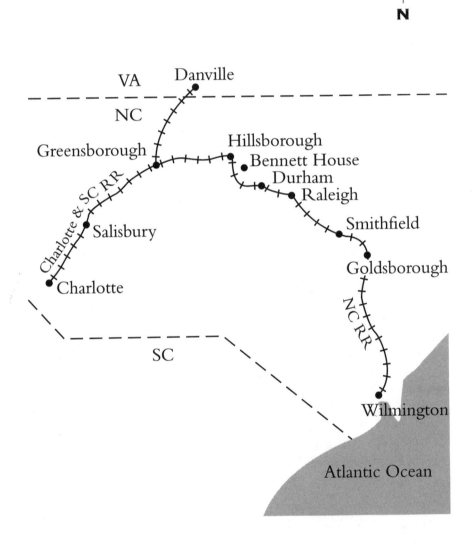

N

Danville

VA

NC

Greensborough

Hillsborough

Bennett House

Durham

Raleigh

Charlotte & SC RR

Salisbury

Smithfield

Charlotte

Goldsborough

NC RR

SC

Wilmington

Atlantic Ocean

for their two armies but also held out the same conditions for capitulation "as made by . . . Grant and Lee at Appomattox Court House."[17]

Johnston and Sherman met at the Bennett House, a small cabin north of the railroad, midway between Hillsborough and Raleigh, on April 17. Hampton, with a troop of cavalry, accompanied Johnston; Butler remained with the army. Sherman opened their discussion with the news that Lincoln had been assassinated the night of April 14. He told Johnston that "he could not oppose my army . . . Lee had surrendered, he could do the same with honor and propriety."[18]

Johnston had no problem with laying down his arms, but he had come to offer more. Assuming the role of a civilian, he proposed surrendering all Confederate armies, provided a satisfactory reentry into the Union for the Southern states was included in the pact. This was beyond Sherman's authority, so he requested time to consider Johnston's overture.[19]

When the two met again on April 18, Sherman accepted the terms suggested by Johnston. He doubted that Washington would support the agreement, but he was anxious to bring an end to the war. "I knew well that Johnston's army could not be caught," he noted. "The country was too wide open; and . . . his men could escape us, disperse, and assemble . . . at some [other] place. . . . [T]he war could be prolonged indefinitely."[20]

Both generals returned to their armies. The armistice would remain in effect until Sherman received a response to their proposed pact from Washington. Johnston had no similar worry. He had concluded that "only the military part of our Government had then any existence."[21]

Hampton, distraught with the idea of surrendering, continued to fight the war. On April 20 he sent a letter to his Federal counterpart, Kilpatrick, accusing him of violating the truce. After reviewing the line between the armies, he stated, "All of your men who cross it must do so at their own risk."[22]

About this same time Hampton wrote to President Davis and offered to form a cavalry command out west. "My mind is made up," he declared. "I shall fight as long as my government is in existence . . . I shall never take the 'oath of allegiance'. . . . No evil can equal that of a return to the Union."[23]

Just as Sherman had expected, Washington refused to accept the agreement that he and Johnston had fashioned. When Hampton learned of this, he knew that a surrender under the terms given to Lee was imminent. He decided to ask President Davis to withdraw his cavalry from Johnston's army so they would not be included in any capitulation. Hampton and Wheeler took the train to Charlotte; Butler stayed in camp in charge of all the horsemen.[24]

Johnston, accompanied this time by Butler, rode to the Bennett House on April 26 to meet with Sherman. The Union general offered only the conditions given Lee by Grant, and Johnston accepted them. A formal surrender would take place the following day.[25]

Hampton arrived back in camp that morning, coming soon after Butler had left for the Bennett House. Upon Matthew's return with news of Johnston's surrender, Hampton assembled Butler's division in regimental formation and asked for volunteers to join him in accompanying President Davis west to continue the war. "Our men," one related, "did not seem to take to [the proposal]."[26] Only thirty stepped forward.

Wheeler talked to his troopers, too, and about 600 volunteered to go with Davis. He and Hampton left camp late that night, riding separately but heading for the same destination: Washington, Georgia, where they would catch up with the president.[27]

Matthew stayed behind to prepare the list of names for surrendering the cavalry. The number was small, for many had already deserted or ridden with Hampton and Wheeler. "When my signature was attached to those rolls," he wrote, "I performed one of the most painful duties of my life. . . . I never recur to it without a feeling of sadness and gloom."[28]

Johnston had about $17,000.00 in silver in hand, and this was distributed among the men. Matthew's share was a paltry $1.75.[29]

"We separated . . . the first day of May, 1865," Butler recalled, "and marched to our homes with full consciousness of duty well performed."[30] He rode into Edgefield on May 5.[31]

"[I was just] twenty-nine years old," Butler summed up his status, "with one leg gone, a wife and three children to support, with seventy slaves emancipated, a debt of $15,000, and in [my] pocket, $1.75 in cash."[32] Four years ago he had anticipated a promising future; now the months ahead looked grim.

CHAPTER 18

Governor Orr

WHEN BUTLER ARRIVED BACK IN EDGEFIELD IN MAY 1865, HE FOUND THE state government no longer in power. The governor, A. J. McGrath, had been arrested, charged with treason, and imprisoned in Fort Pulaski, Georgia. The Union military had assumed control. They had divided South Carolina into nine districts, each garrisoned by troops whose prime duty was to keep the peace. Gen. Quincy A. Gillmore was in command.[1]

Gillmore had established the nation's first free black community on Hilton Head Island in 1862, and he was eager to extend this scheme throughout South Carolina. Congress had passed the Thirteenth Amendment back in January, but because the needed three-fourths of the states had not yet ratified it, the slaves in South Carolina, including the seventy that Butler owned, remained in servitude.[2]

Gillmore grew impatient with the delay, and in mid-May, he issued a proclamation that declared, "People of the black race are free citizens . . . it is the fixed intention of a wise and beneficent government to protect . . . their freedom."[3]

Many ignored the edict, but Francis Pickens, Matthew's father-in-law, immediately obeyed Gillmore's decree. On May 23, he gathered his slaves, told them they were free, and offered each generous wages if they would sign a contract to work on his plantation through the rest of that year.[4] His field hands all agreed to stay, but most domestics left.[5]

Butler quickly followed Pickens's example—no doubt with a similar result. The prospect of cooking and cleaning her own house must have upset Maria. It is unlikely, however, that she ever performed these tasks because Butler probably hired black girls as servants. Most had remained in the area, still working as domestics but doing so in different homes as a way of expressing newly found liberty. "I must go," one informed her former mistress, "if I stay here, I'll never know I am free."[6] Their effort, however, usually fell short of previous standards, which probably raised constant complains from Maria.[7]

In addition to farming Butler resumed his practice of law. He opened an office in the heart of Edgefield, east and south of the Saluda Hotel. He was surrounded by competing lawyers: W. W. Adams on the left; LeRoy Youmans to his right; and Stanmore Griffin and Henry Addison across the street. Eighteen other counselors vied with this group for the few clients able to pay for legal service.[8]

Matthew's practice consisted mostly of filing suit on behalf of clients who were owed money, usually $300 or less. Other work included writing wills, defending petty criminals, or attending to details regarding the sale of property. The fees from these cases were small, and Butler averaged only about eight clients per month. The chances for a lucrative income lay with corporate retainers, but in the tiny village of Edgefield, there were few such opportunities available.[9]

With so many contenders bidding for so little business, Matthew must have been unsure of his future. South Carolina also faced uncertain times. The state wanted to reenter the Union, but the process for doing so had not yet been defined. Pres. Andrew Johnson and the Congress were at loggerheads over who was in charge of Reconstruction.

Johnson argued that because secession was illegal, the Confederate states had not left the Union. Thus Congress did not have a role to play in their Reconstruction. The president felt that he alone had the duty of imposing terms to protect against future rebellion, terms that must be met before any state could resume its place.[10]

Congress, led by Charles Sumner, the abolitionist senator from Massachusetts, and Thaddeus Stevens, a Pennsylvania representative, also did not recognize secession. But they asserted that by their rebellion, the Confederate states had reverted to being "territories," which needed guidance and permission from Congress for readmission to the Union.[11]

Since Congress was not in session, Johnson was free to push his view, and he moved quickly to take advantage of the situation. He issued an edict on June 13 directing South Carolina to convene a convention to alter or amend the state constitution to "enable such loyal people . . . to restore . . . relations with the Federal Government."[12] The president noted three changes he deemed essential for reentry into the Union. Slavery must be abolished, the Ordinance of Secession had to be repealed, and the debt the state had assumed in order to wage war must be renounced. "It will not due," Johnson professed, "to levy and collect taxes . . . to pay debts . . . created in an effort to . . . subvert the . . . United States."[13]

Delegates to this convention would be qualified voters as of December 20, 1860, provided they had taken the amnesty oath, set forth in an earlier presidential decree. Johnson appointed Benjamin F. Perry, former state representative and senator, once a strong Union man, as provisional magistrate until a new governor was elected, preferably by direct vote.[14]

Matthew attended the meeting in Edgefield, held at the Odd Fellows and Mason Hall on August 7, to select its delegates to the constitutional convention. Although he was a key figure during the deliberations, Butler was not included among the six who would go to Columbia. He was unqualified. Former Confederate officers were not allowed to take the amnesty oath.[15]

The convention met at the Baptist Church, Plain Street, in Columbia on September 13. The caucus abolished slavery in South Carolina, repealed the Ordinance of Secession, set qualifications for voters (white males, neither a pauper nor a current member of the military, at least twenty-one years old and a resident for the last two years), decreed that the elections of both governor and lieutenant governor be transferred from the legislature to the people, set up a judicial system throughout the state, and abandoned the "parish" system for representation that in the past had provided the Low County (Charleston) with a disproportional number of seats. The delegation did not, however, repudiate the war debt, one of Johnson's requirements for readmittance into the federal Union. The president decided to overlook this omission, and he approved the new constitution. Elections were scheduled for October 18.[16]

Just prior to the convention, President Johnson had extended special pardons to 845 South Carolinians who had been denied taking the amnesty oath.[17] The former soldiers were now qualified to hold public office, and Butler was no doubt included in this number, because on October 4, he declared his candidacy for state representative from Edgefield. Ten men ran for six seats, with Matthew finishing first, with 132 votes. The other five elected were M. L. Bonham, B. M. Talbert, Luke Culbreath, John Landrum, and W. H. Moss.[18]

James L. Orr won the governorship. Born in 1822 in Anderson, South Carolina, he was a lawyer and publisher before entering politics. He served as a state representative for two years, then was elected to the U.S. Congress. His five terms in the house were crowned by his elevation to Speaker in 1857. Although he was opposed to secession, Orr accepted a commission in 1861 as colonel, commanding the 1st South Carolina Infantry. He left his post in 1862 upon being named by the state assembly as a senator in the Confederate Congress. He stayed in Richmond through the end of the war.[19]

The legislature met in a special session that began on October 25. The old capitol had been torched by Sherman's troops and the new (current) building was not yet completed, so the politicians assembled at South Car-

Gov. James L. Orr.
COURTESY UNIVERSITY OF NORTH CAROLINA PRESS

olina College. The representatives gathered in the chapel, the senators in the library.[20] They ratified the Thirteenth Amendment, selected John L. Manning and Perry as U.S. senators, and accepted a report for the regulation of blacks, prepared by Judge David L. Wardlaw and Armistead Burt. Butler returned to his home in Edgefield on November 13.[21]

The need for a "Black Code" arose from compassion that the landed gentry, from whose ranks the legislature had been formed, felt for their former servants, who composed almost 60 percent of the total population. They regarded blacks as children who needed guidance and protection in assuming their newfound role as free men. The plantation owners assumed from past experience that the former slaves would not work as hard as needed to support their families; they also knew that poor "white trash," 20 percent of the state's households, hated the blacks and would take advantage of any opportunity to cheat them. Matthew and his friends were not concerned with the small farmers, working plots of less than fifty acres, making up 15 percent of the community, and having neither the need for nor much interest in the blacks.[22]

Although the subject was not discussed, the codes also recognized the long-felt fear of the blacks. Slave uprising was no longer a factor, but revenge for past abuses was probably on many minds. Whites were safe only when the blacks were kept under control.

The legislature met again on November 27. After confirming the election of James Orr as governor, providing for a state militia, and passing those laws required for normal governmental operations, the politicians turned to the black question. Everyone seemed to have a point to consider, and most were covered in four bills that dealt with every aspect of the lives of the former slaves. The law considering domestic relations of people of color (anyone who had more than one-eighth Negro blood) alone had ninety-seven sections.[23]

As Butler watched this list grow and grow, he realized that the assembly was viewing blacks under the light of past experience, e.g., slavery. This was the only comfortable relationship that these onetime masters could accept. Butler disagreed with this approach to "protecting" the former servants from the harsh realities of freedom. "We should grant simple civil rights upon the Negro," he argued, "leaving to the future the settlement of his [social and] political status."[24]

Matthew had no illusions of equality between the races. "[Ours] is essentially a white man's government," he related often, "set up by white men . . . ever since controlled by white men, and will be to the end." Blacks could never fully participate because innate "discrimination is an impossible bar to [their] complete emancipation . . . . neither education, Christianity, nor any other civilizing and enlightening influence can remove it." The solution to this problem, as he saw it, was not to integrate the blacks within the white society but to give them their own community, preferably in Africa where they had originated, where they could have a fair chance for "social, political and industrial advancement."[25]

When the assembly finally voted on and passed the Black Codes, Matthew was one of only sixteen legislators who cast a ballot against their passage.[26]

The South Carolina legislature adjourned December 21. Butler returned to Edgefield, where he soon learned that the state was in trouble. Congress had assembled in Washington, D.C., and its members and their constituents were outraged by the Black Codes, enacted by not only South Carolina but also the other former Confederate states. Stevens and Sumner convinced their comrades that these laws proved the South unrepentant, that their senators and representatives should not be accepted until a Joint Committee had decided "whether the Southern states are entitled to be represented."[27] These deliberations would suspend implementation of Johnson's plan, clearing a way for Congress to take control of Reconstruction. South Carolina would not reenter the Union; the state would continue under Orr's leadership, but remain subject to the watchful eye of the military.

Almost 7,500 soldiers were posted throughout South Carolina, with a small band located in Edgefield. Several days after Christmas, a drunken white trooper accosted two local citizens. When they refused to listen to his insulting comments, he wrested one to the ground, drew a pistol, and fired a shot that just missed his victim's ear. A mob, including Butler, gathered. Most just watched the confrontation, but a young man, a former Confederate soldier, decided to intercede. He pulled out his revolver and killed the Union cavalryman.

The dead soldier's compatriots hurried to the scene and threatened vengeance on the townspeople. Butler assumed command of the situation.

Mrs. Jane Tweedy Perry Butler.
COURTESY THE PERRYS OF RHODE ISLAND

"If you do not [stop these] threats and march your company back to their quarters," he warned the sergeant leading the Yankee squad, "[you] must take the consequences. There are . . . six hundred ex-Confederates [here] who might no longer be restrained."[28]

The soldiers withdrew, but Adelbert Ames, Federal post commander in Columbia, was not about to let this incident go unpunished. He sent troops to Edgefield to take the killer and the abused citizen into custody. Both of them, however, had left town, so the Union soldiers arrested former Confederate general Martin Gray and several other men instead, charging them with "complicity" in the affair. Then, during the night, these prisoners were escorted back to the capital, where they were incarcerated with common criminals.

Matthew followed the party to Columbia that evening, and early the next morning contacted Ames to protest his treatment of the prisoners. The general agreed to place them in more comfortable quarters. A few days later they were sent to Charleston. Gary and his compatriots were eventually released without being charged or tried for the crime.[29]

About this same time, Butler's aged mother had trouble with the occupying Federal army, too. A soldier posted near her home in Greenville stole one of her horses. She rushed straight to military headquarters to lodge a protest.

"This is Jane Perry Butler," the adjutant said when he introduced her to his commander, "sister of the Hero of Lake Erie, Oliver Hazard Perry." He obviously assumed that this Northern connection would impress his colonel and induce him into assisting the seventy-four-year-old lady.

Mrs. Butler was offended by his implication. "I would much rather be known," Jane snapped, "as the mother of Calbraith Butler!"[30]

On January 1, 1866, Gen. Daniel E. Sickles formally replaced Gillmore as chief of the military command occupying South Carolina. Born October 20, 1819, in New York City, he attended New York University, where he studied law. Sickles soon entered politics, serving first as state senator, then in the U.S. House of Representatives from 1857 to 1861. The Civil War began, and he entered the military, taking charge of the Excelsior Brigade. Sickles fought in the East. Despite generally poor performance, usually because he refused to obey his orders, he was promoted to division, then corps command. Sickles lost his right leg at Gettysburg, and had just recently returned to duty.[31]

Sickles had the right to overrule any decisions by the state, and on his first day in office, he declared the Black Codes to be "null and void. . . . All laws," he said, "shall be applicable alike to all inhabitants."[32] This interposal was one of only a few inflicted by Sickles. He and Orr had been close friends for years, and he was reluctant to impinge on the governor's authority. The military, for the moment, was no longer a problem for Butler and the state.

The soldiers, however, were not the only Federals that occupied South Carolina. Agents for the Bureau of Refugees, Freedmen, and Abandoned Lands had been placed throughout the state.

The Freedmen's Bureau, as it was better known, was set up by a bill, passed by Congress in March 1865. The agency was charged with being involved in all matters that related to blacks. Oliver O. Howard was selected as commissioner on May 12. He then named state commanders, dubbed assistant commissioners, who in turn hired subagents, former military officers, to cover local communities. Gen. Rufus Saxton was placed in charge of South Carolina, Georgia, and Florida; his man covering Edgefield was Gen. Ralph Ely.[33]

When they created the Freedmen's Bureau, Congress felt that the need for such an agency would be brief. Its tenure would last only for one year after the end of the war. And although its authority was very broad, the actual effort was limited to just a few areas: helping blacks negotiate work contracts; protecting their rights; apportioning abandoned land, e.g., coastal plantations in South Carolina, occupied by the Union army during the war, to the ex-slaves; providing transportation for displaced blacks for their return to their homes and families; setting up hospitals; distributing food and clothing to the indigent; and providing ground and buildings for black schools.[34]

The whites of Edgefield (and probably Butler) expected the Freedmen's Bureau to be an imposition, nothing more than "a grand Yankee scheme to [assist] the designs of abolition speculators in [stealing] Southern lands, houses, libraries, pianos, jewelry, silver spoons."[35] Abuse of the system did occur, but Ely, a native of Michigan who started the war as a regimental captain, fought with the host that captured Hilton Head Island, then moved north to serve under Burnside at Antietam, Fredericksburg, Knoxville, and then in Grant's Virginia Campaign, proved a reasonable man. For example, he visited Edgefield in December 1865 to address the blacks. "Under no circumstances [will you] receive . . . [any] land from the Government," Ely advised. "[You] must work and have no hope of subsistence but in working."[36] He encouraged blacks to ask their former masters for employment, and he promised the land owners that he would require the ex-slaves to "keep their engagements faithfully and honestly."

Although South Carolinians had little to fear from the Federals in their midst, they had good reason to worry about those in Washington, D.C. Early in June 1866 the Congress passed the Fourteenth Amendment. Two of its four provisions, assuring equal rights to citizens and the voiding of debts incurred in support of the Rebellion, were tolerable to most Southerners, but the others were unpalatable. One provided that the white leaders of the South, Confederate politicians and their compatriots who had served in the military, could not hold a public office; the second decreed that if states denied blacks the vote, representation to Congress would be almost halved. This would ensure the Radicals an overwhelming majority to dictate further reprisals against the South.[37]

Although Butler was no doubt concerned and probably already thinking of ways to deal with this threat to his state and his own political future, he could not devote his fulltime to this problem. He had personal matters at hand. In July he formed a new law partnership with John E. Bacon and moved into roomy, more comfortable offices.[38] Butler also went to Augusta to purchase an artificial leg. "I should have liked to have gone up North where I would have had a larger number to select from," he noted, "but I do not feel that I can afford it."[39]

Maria was not at home to share these events. Pregnant with their fifth child, she had gone to Greenville to visit her twin sister, Eliza. "I hope you will write to me," Butler begged in a July letter, a repeat of the plea he made so many times during the war. "I will feel very miserable and lonely until you return."[40] Maria neither wrote nor did she come home. Matthew then took a drastic step. "I can stand it no longer," he declared on July 14. "I send Thomas for you and hope you will come tomorrow."[41] Maria came back to Edgefield for the last days of her confinement.

By August 1866 it was obvious that Johnson was the better friend of the South than Congress. For example, back in April, he used his powers to halt the military's rule in South Carolina. "The law can be sustained and enforced . . . by the proper civil authority," he declared in an order direct-ing soldiers to leave the state. The number of troops faded from 7,408 in January to 2,747 by yearend.[42]

It was equally apparent that Radical Republicans would continue to defy the president's program for Reconstruction. They were striving to win a sufficient majority in the fall Congressional election to override Johnson's vetoes. The South recognized that they had to counter this threat by sup-porting candidates, Democratic or Republican, throughout the country who would oppose the president's foes. They began their campaign favor-ing Johnson by attending a National Union convention held in Philadel-phia starting August 14.[43]

Although most of South Carolina was represented at the assembly, Edgefield, following Matthew's bidding, refused to send delegates. "Johnson has done nothing," he noted, "for which [we] should feel thankful."[44] He considered the president inept, and thought that an effort to defeat John-son's adversaries would be futile.

Governor Orr, however, was still willing to try. Knowing that opposi-tion to the "Black Code" had led many in the North to favor the Radicals, he sought to diffuse this issue by calling the legislature into a special session to modify "existing laws with reference to persons of color."[45] Other sub-jects covered in this September assembly included relief for debtors, con-struction of a new state prison, and providing corn for the needy.

Butler, of course, attended this gathering in Columbia. Showing a keen interest in debtors' problems, he noted that since the state had emancipated the blacks, thereby destroying the property they represented, the former owners, including himself, were entitled to relief. He proposed that "all contracts involving . . . the purchase of slaves . . . [anterior to the twenty-seventh day of September 1865] be null and void . . . and that all parties indebted . . . be declared not liable for such payment."[46] This try at escap-ing his indebtedness backfired; the legislature rejected his bill.

Matthew left the assembly early to rush back home. On September 23, 1866, he was with Maria when she gave birth to a baby girl. They named her Marie Calhoun Butler.[47]

When Butler returned to Columbia in November to attend the regular session of the legislature, he found its members dejected. The Republicans had swept the national elections that fall, capturing 75 percent of the House and 80 percent of the Senate. The Radicals held the balance of power in their battle with Johnson over whom would control Reconstruction.[48]

Butler had anticipated this result. It may have led to his becoming physically ill. He spent most of the time in bed in his hotel rooms.[49] He was present, however, when the House rejected the Fourteenth Amendment by a vote of ninety-five to one. The Senate's voice tally against ratification was unanimous.[50] After joining in the legislature's snub to the Republican Congress, Butler went back to Edgefield. He again moved his law offices because his partner, John Bacon, had accepted a judgeship. Matthew was practicing alone for the moment.[51] He was busy adapting to this change, but kept an eye northward, watching for a response from the Radicals in Washington.

His suspense was soon over. Congress passed its first Reconstruction Act in March 1867, which reestablished military rule. Ten of the Confederate states were organized into five military districts. Sickles took command over North and South Carolina, supervising the state governments until new constitutions had been drawn and approved by the voters: all males, white and black, twenty-one years or older, residents for one year, and not participants in the Rebellion. Electing the legislature would follow, and after the members ratified the Fourteenth Amendment, the state would reenter the Union. Johnson tried to block the measure, but his veto was overridden on March 2. He had lost the battle to control Reconstruction.[52]

A few weeks later a supplementary act was passed that ordered the registration of voters in the former Confederate states. They would elect delegates to a fall convention to draft a new constitution. Since blacks held the majority in South Carolina, they held the balance of power and became a target for the opposing sides.[53]

Butler had a chance to influence their vote. In early May he was appointed to the state Commission for the Poor, a body charged with assisting families (mostly black) who were without "means of support and who must perish without charitable aid."[54] Butler published a notice detailing the steps required to obtain relief, and on May 22, when a supply of corn and bacon reached Edgefield, he arranged for distribution through the county.[55]

Matthew also reached out to the blacks with a political appeal. He and others of the landed gentry throughout the state held meetings in an attempt to sway the former slaves into supporting the Democrats, who they stated would better protect the blacks' interests. These sessions started with fervent speeches citing the close bonds that had been formed between the races through the years. "Why should we not be friends?" Hampton argued. "Is this not your home as well as ours?"[56] Warnings of potential disaster if the blacks gave their support to the Republicans followed. And then Matthew and his friends offered a free barbecue.

The Radicals used a different strategy. Although many were truly interested in helping the blacks realize their newly found freedom, some leaders were intent on exploiting the vote of former slaves for personal gain. These included Northerners now living in the South (carpetbaggers), native citizens not from the plantation set (scalawags), and ambitious, often ignorant blacks. They helped establish "Loyal Leagues," secret societies that met at night to hold elaborate services and ceremonies, "carried out in darkness, with [the] clanking of chains and shuffling . . . of hooded figures." They required a fearful oath, binding the members to follow their instructions, e.g., vote Republican.[57]

As a result of both sides' efforts, most of the blacks in South Carolina signed up to vote in the fall. The whites laughed at the ignorance displayed by some of the ex-slaves who took part in the process. "Quite a number brought along bags . . . to put [their register] in," an observer wrote, "and in nearly every instance, there was a great rush for fear we would not have registration enough to go around."[58] Butler probably saw this absurd behavior in Edgefield, but he also realized that most blacks knew exactly what they were doing. Fearing a return to slavery, they were determined to employ their majority at the polls to protect their freedom. They would never entrust their future to former masters.

Although Butler was deeply involved with this campaign and concerned with its lack of success, he still had to earn his living as a lawyer. And he often found a need for help from friends. In a July letter to Benjamin Rutledge, former wartime subordinate, commander of the 4th South Carolina Cavalry, now practicing law in Charleston, Matthew noted, "I again find myself appealing to [your] chivalry . . . to have me marked as appearing for the defense in the case of Roundtree versus Jas. A. Talbert."

Rutledge must have been prosecuting this case, because Matthew then added, "The Yankees learned a great deal of the art and science of war from the South, and defeated us with our own accomplishments. I propose the same to you [regarding] the U.S. courts for I . . . confess that I am a novice."[59]

Sickles, too, was involved with the federal court, but in a different way. In August 1867 he refused to obey the order of a judge in North Carolina. Johnson was infuriated. "A conceited cuckold," he seethed, "is an abomination in the sight of God."[60] The president relieved Sickles from duty.

Gen. Edward R. S. Canby replaced Sickles. A native of Kentucky and a graduate of West Point, he had won fame in the Civil War first by routing the Confederates under Henry H. Silbey in New Mexico, then leading the expedition against Mobile toward the end of the conflict. Canby was noted for being an able administrator, and proved to be as good if not a better friend to South Carolina than the petulant Sickles.[61]

In September Butler formed a new law partnership with an old rival, LeRoy F. Youmans. Their office was located in the county courthouse.[62]

With Youmans handling the details of day-to-day practice, Matthew was freed for campaigning in the upcoming election. He participated in a series of meetings held in Edgefield, then Columbia, directed at "securing harmony of action among . . . white people throughout the state" in the upcoming election.[63] Such efforts, however, were too little, too late. Almost 65 percent of the registered voters were blacks, and 82 percent cast their ballot, most for holding the constitutional convention.[64]

The balloting had included names of candidates to make up the delegation. Blacks won seventy-six seats, two-thirds of these ex-slaves. Forty-eight whites were selected, half scalawags, half carpetbaggers.[65] Edgefield sent four blacks to the assembly (David Harris, Prince R. Rivers, John Bonum, and Robert E. Elliott, the latter pair actually residents of Charleston) and three whites (Frank Arnim, John Wooley, and George P. deMedicis.).[66]

The convention met in Charleston starting January 14. Dr. Albert G. Mackey was elected president. He and the rest of the whites dominated the proceedings because most of the blacks were too ignorant to take an active role. "They wore their best clothes," a reporter wrote, "and tried to be dignified."[67]

The session lasted for fifty-three days and in the end, produced a credible constitution, consistent with that found in most Northern states. The document was submitted by General Canby, who called for an April balloting to approve the measure.[68]

During the last weeks of the convention, the same body met as Republicans to select their candidates for the coming elections of state and national offices, also scheduled for that April. Robert K. Scott, a native of Ohio and successor to Saxton in charge of the South Carolina Freedmen's Bureau, was nominated for governor.[69]

Butler and his friends saw the need to compete, and on April 2, 1868, they met in Columbia to select their slate of candidates. They nominated William D. Porter, a Charleston judge, for governor. He refused to campaign, but it made no difference in light of the black majority. From April 14th through the 16th, they swarmed to the polls "like locusts in Egypt" and their votes not only gained approval for the new constitution but also handed the Republicans a decisive victory. They won all of the House of Representative seats in Washington. Scott and his entire ticket were elected to the state offices. Democrats gained only 6 of the 31 state senator seats and just 14 of 124 legislature posts. A third of the senators and almost two-thirds of the representatives were blacks.[70] "The white man's government in South Carolina is destroyed," the *Edgefield Advertiser* said. "The State, we fear, becomes a Santa Domingo."[71]

In Edgefield Republicans won every seat. Frank Arnim was elected state senator; the seven representatives to the House included John Wooley, Samuel J. lee, Prince R. Rivers, T. Root, David Harris, John Gardner, and Lorenz Cain.[72]

With local elections set for early June, there was yet a chance to stem the black tide. Johnson, however, would be no help. The president was in a personal fight for his own political life. Back in April he had been impeached by the House for violating the Tenure of Office Act, and he was being tried by the Senate. The members voted on May 16, and Johnson was acquitted by just one vote.[73]

Some Edgefield whites sought a new approach to winning the black vote in the upcoming local elections. They issued threats. "When our present contracts with . . . members of the Loyal League . . . expire," a plantation owner retorted, "let us cease to give them employment."[74] Butler, however, was committed to maintaining good relations with the ex-slaves. He joined Francis Pickens and other leaders in drawing up a resolution on June 1 that said, "We are willing to guarantee all just civil rights to the Negro." Matthew's speech backing this position was said to be "able and eloquent."[75]

Words alone, however, could not change the attitude of black voters. White Republicans were elected to all of the Edgefield positions: judge of the Probate Court, the clerk of courts, the three county commissioners, sheriff, coroner, and school commissioner. When reporting these results, the newspaper headline taunted, "Nary a Nigger," chiding the blacks, who had put carpetbaggers and scalawags into office.[76]

Political defeat caused Butler to rethink his position vis-à-vis blacks. Although he was opposed to their integration into politics, he would not attempt to take away their rights. He sought a way around their majority at the polls. Matthew and several friends founded the Immigration Society of Edgefield, a corporation set up to lure white laborers to South Carolina. They sold shares, twenty-five dollars each, using the money raised to entice recent arrivals from Europe to their area. They hoped over time to bring enough aliens into the state to build a white majority. "We must," Butler explained, "make ourselves independent of the Negro."[77]

The blacks, however, held the balance of power at that time, and Canby responded to their recent victory by calling for an assembly of South Carolina's newly elected officials in Columbia on July 6. Governor Scott took office on July 9. Several days later the legislature ratified the Fourteenth Amendment, opening the way for the seating by Congress of the state's representatives and senators. Canby ended his military rule on July

24, leaving South Carolina in the hands of the carpetbaggers, the scalawags, and the blacks.[78]

⚊⚬ ⚏⧫⚎ ⚬⚊

During early Reconstruction, Butler, following Wade Hampton's example, offered a friendship to the former slaves. He freed his servants before ratification of the Thirteenth Amendment, argued against the passage of the Black Codes, helped to plan and carry out a plan for feeding the poor, regardless of color, and he appealed to blacks as respected citizens for their votes in the '68 elections. His attempt to work within the system, however, was futile because Matthew's class, the educated and experienced whites, men of property whose money would pay for government, were excluded from its operation.

South Carolina sent a white committee to Washington to warn Congress that "they would never submit quietly to Negro rule." Thad Stevens found this amusing. "What the protest claimed as grievances," he laughed, "[I regard] as virtues."[79] With blacks providing his party a large majority throughout the South, he saw Republicans retaining control of political power perhaps forever.

Such avarice for omnipotence would cost the nation and blacks dearly. By miscalculating the determination of white people in the South to oppose rule by a then ignorant class, Stevens and his fellow Radicals assured racial strife, sometimes shadowy, often overt. The resulting scars have never healed. His intentions aside, Butler was drawn into this vortex.

CHAPTER 19

Governor Scott

ROBERT KINGSTON SCOTT WAS A TALL, BUSHY-HAIRED MAN WHO OOZED with self-confidence. The incoming governor had been born in 1826 in Pennsylvania but grew up in Ohio. He moved to California in 1849, where he became both a miner and a physician. Scott next prospected for gold in Mexico, and then in South America. He eventually returned to Ohio to begin a career as a merchant and realtor. When the Civil War began, he raised an infantry regiment, which took part in the siege at Vicksburg, then accompanied Sherman on his march through Georgia and the Carolinas. Scott was breveted major general at the end of the war. Instead of going home, he stayed in the South, serving as the chief of the Freedmen's Bureau for South Carolina, a position he held until elected governor.[1]

Scott's administration included Lemuel Boozer, a white native of Lexington, South Carolina, as lieutenant governor; Francis L. Cordozo, a freeborn mulatto from Charleston, as secretary of state; Niles G. Parker, a carpetbagger hailing from Massachusetts, who came south as an officer of a black regiment, as treasurer; Daniel Henry Chamberlain, also from Massachusetts, as attorney general; John L. Neagle, a scalawag from Rock Hill, South Carolina, comptroller; Franklin J. Moses, a Charleston scalawag, adjutant and inspector general; and Justus K. Jillson, yet another carpetbagger from Massachusetts, superintendent of education.[2] All would play crucial roles in state government throughout Reconstruction.

The South Carolina senate had thirty members, twenty of whom were white, ten of whom were black. This body included five carpetbaggers, fifteen scalawags, three ex-slaves, and seven freeborn blacks. David T. Corbin, a white native of Vermont who had come south with the Freedmen's Bureau, then practiced law in Charleston, was elected president pro tem.[3]

The house, 134 members, included 86 blacks, 54 of whom were ex-slaves, 32 were born free. About half were illiterate. Forty of the whites

Gov. Robert K. Scott. COURTESY
UNIVERSITY OF NORTH CAROLINA PRESS

were scalawags; the rest (8) were carpetbaggers. Franklin Moses, who also held the state post of adjutant and inspector general, was elected Speaker.[4]

Butler was, of course, concerned with what the state's newly elected officials and legislature were planning to do, but he was even more intrigued with the national scene. The Democratic party had met in New York that July, and adopted a platform whose planks included "the immediate restitution of all thirty-seven states, amnesty for all offenses during [the Rebellion], and regulation of the elective franchise by the several states."[5] Gov. Horatio Seymour of New York had been nominated for president, and a victory over Ulysses S. Grant, the Republican candidate, would being a quick end to Reconstruction.

Butler had not taken part in this national effort, but he was eager to join in the fray. He started by attending a local Edgefield meeting on August 3, 1868, to pick delegates to the upcoming Democratic convention in Columbia to select members to the electorial college. Matthew was named one of nine who would represent the village.[6]

He also immediately began campaigning for Seymour. On August 4 in a speech at Aiken, Butler attacked Grant. "He can no [more] well rule the country than a doctor can practice law or a lawyer can teach engineering," Matthew jeered. "But if the Radicals are victorious, we must gather up our personal treasures and bid farewell to the land that gave us birth . . . and seek some happier scene."[7]

One of the tactics that Butler and his friends used in their efforts to elect Seymour was to form local Democratic Clubs in every community. Each had two objectives: to make sure that all whites cast a ballot; and to bear arms in defense of their homes against probable (in their minds) black outrages. Based on his Civil War experience, Matthew was a logical choice and elected president of the Edgefield Club.[8]

This was a more measured response than that of another, more flamboyant band of whites, the Ku Klux Klan (KKK). They used terror, riding in the dark of night, disguised by robes and hoods, burning crosses in front of black homes to discourage the occupants from voting.[9]

The KKK was first formed in 1866 in Tennessee. Nathan Bedford Forrest took command of the organization, and as the Grand Wizard, directed its gradual expansion throughout the South.[10] The Klan arose in South Carolina in 1868. Matthew never joined (membership was usually limited to lower-class whites), but Edgefield had a chapter, described as being "so strong and well organized that it had everything its way."[11]

The outrages committed by South Carolina's Klan varied in severity. They stole ballots from the black commissioner in one hamlet.[12] "They asked me what ticket I was going to vote," a black in another village testified. "[When] I said 'Republican' . . . one of them beat me over the head with a pistol."[13] And three Klansmen murdered Rev. B. F. Randolph, the black senator from Orangeburg, by shooting him in daylight as he waited for a train at the station near Cokesbury.[14]

Blacks could not directly resist these assaults by the Klan, so they sought recompense in a similar, secretive way. After a visit by hooded horsemen, they would set out in the dead of night to put a match to white property.[15] And since they seldom knew the identity of their oppressors, they set aflame the most prominent targets, the gin mills, barns, and houses of the wealthy. Butler no doubt feared for his home.

Governor Scott took advantage of this turmoil by inducing the legislature to establish a state police for opposing the Klan. The act set up constables in each county. Extra deputies, paid three dollars a day, were hired where needed. Such a small force was ineffectual toward protecting blacks, but it served Scott's other, political objectives: to offer employment for blacks, and to give him an organization for imposing his will throughout the state.[16]

The money to fund the constable program as well as the state's other activities was raised through a bill authorizing the selling of $1 million in bonds. Scott, Chamberlain, and Parker were appointed to a Financial Board to administer the plan, which they soon exploited as a source for illegal income.[17]

The legislature also guaranteed $1 million in bonds to fund the completion of the Blue Ridge Railroad, a major link in the system that would cross the mountains to the west to join Charleston to Knoxville, Tennessee. The line had begun construction in Anderson in 1851, but to date extended only thirty-three miles to Walhalla. The initial funding had included state money. If the road was never completed, South Carolina would lose its investment. This project would soon become a "tar baby" of graft and corruption that would eventually ensnare Butler.[18]

Another major bill was the reorganization of the state judicial system (as called for in the new constitution) that set up separate circuit courts for civil and criminal cases. Judges would be named by the legislature, assuring a Radical bias. Butler and other lawyers were opposed to this change, calling it "repugnant to our customs and habits of thought."[19] Such fears were warranted. The system was soon in shambles due to the poor quality of the many new magistrates.

Throughout that fall, as Matthew dealt with challenges from the national election, the violence of the Klan and the equally brutal response from the blacks, and the actions of the state legislature, he returned every evening to an empty home. Maria, pregnant with their sixth child, was again visiting her twin sister. Butler missed her company. Hoping to lure her home, he offered to "fix up a room for . . . Eliza."[20] But Maria remained in Greenville.

Grant won the presidential race in November. His election ended the need to keep blacks from voting, so the cruel nightly visits by the Klan soon ceased.[21] Matthew, however, shifted his position opposing persecution of the blacks. He remained against violence, but with his leadership, the Democratic Club of Edgefield adopted a harsh resolution at their November meeting. "We will employ no person or keep him in employment," they said, "who will continue to vote the Radical ticket."[22] Supporting the Republicans would now cost a man, white or black, his job.

Francis Pickens, Maria's father, would not have agreed with so strict a measure, but he was no longer participating in community affairs. Both his health and his fortunes had rapidly declined since the end of the war, and he had become a recluse in his plantation home outside of Edgefield. Pickens died on January 25, 1869.[23]

Maria may have missed Pickens's funeral. She was never in robust health, and with her baby due at any moment, Maria was probably at home, resting in bed, on the day her father was buried. She gave birth to Susan Elise Butler, named for her aunt, on January 31, 1869.[24]

This addition to his family further strained Matthew's meager finances, and in late April, he took steps to augment his income. The state had established a Land Commission to buy property, which they would subdivide into plots for the ex-slaves to purchase and farm. Butler offered to sell 650 acres of his holdings at ten dollars each under the program. His former servants, eighteen in all, heads of families who were still working these fields, objected. Their labor over the years had built this estate; they filed a protest with the commission, asking that Matthew be required to sell only to them. But Butler needed cash. And since the blacks' demands called for "terms allowed in such cases," he would not trade with them.[25] The state officials countered by rejecting his application, but Matthew soon found a wealthy, white man, W. W. Spencer, who bought the tract.[26]

Others did sell property to the state, but the program did not benefit blacks. The Land Commission proved a farce, a way for stealing money. Governor Scott, for example, purchased several homesteads, which he resold to the commission at exorbitant prices. When the resulting costly plots were placed on the market, no one could afford them.[27]

Another devious ploy was to sell worthless land to the state. A parcel outside of Charleston dubbed the "Hell-Hole Swamp" was purchased for $38,400, but the acreage was under water and impossible to farm. "[Even] an alligator," Butler said, "can hardly live there."[28]

With the cash from his sale to Spencer, Butler managed to survive through the fall of 1869. He and Maria, however, were having marital problems. She continued to spend time with her sister in Greenville; Matthew resorted to seeking the companionship of other, more amiable women. "He spent many an evening in Aiken," a current relative related, "drinking and whoring."[29]

Maria knew about his relationships because Butler kept in touch with some of these ladies via the mail. She deemed their letters sinful; he was not impressed. "You would object to my writing to old sweethearts on a Sunday," he wrote perhaps bitterly in his March 27 note to Maria, once again visiting Eliza, "so I have denied myself the pleasure."[30]

In the spring of 1870 Matthew's attention returned to politics. Corruption was rampant in Scott's administration, and to pay for the monies being siphoned out of the state's treasury, the legislature had raised taxes to an unconscionable level. The rates on Butler's estate, for example, had been increased from five to seventeen mills and the assessed valuation of his properties had been upped from two to five dollars per acre.[31] The coming fall elections were critical to correcting these problems.

A few whites urged a campaign of violence, using force to prevent the black majority from voting. Butler, however, remained committed to integrating blacks into the political system, and on June 15, 1870, he met with others in Columbia to form the Union Reform Party. The delegates acknowledged in their platform that the changes brought by the war should be "regarded as verities having the force and obligation of law," pledging acceptance of the Fifteenth Amendment, which banned voting restrictions based on race.[32]

Circuit Judge Robert B. Carpenter, a Republican carpetbagger from Kentucky, was nominated as the party's candidate for governor. Butler was then proposed as lieutenant governor. Since he did not want to be present while his name was being discussed, Matthew left the hall. But before exiting, he noted that "I labor under political disabilities." As an ex-Confederate, he was disqualified by the Fourteenth Amendment from holding office.[33]

In light of Butler's revelation, William E. Marshall, a Charleston black, was also nominated as lieutenant governor. "I do not . . . possess the necessary qualifications," he quickly noted, "[and] decline an honor which I would be proud to own . . . I cheerfully transfer it to General M. C. Butler, whom it will be my pleasure to support."[34]

Two more blacks were presented; both also declined to oppose Butler. "Our colored friends present have taken this matter into their own hands," a friend of Matthew's related, ". . . and since they continue to press [for] the nomination of General Butler, I am satisfied to let it go . . . as the will of the Convention."[35] Matthew was placed on the ticket.

His "political disability" was quickly erased. Butler petitioned South Carolina senator Thomas J. Robertson to act in his behalf, and the latter introduced a bill (S.R. 1057) on July 13 to remove Matthew's Fourteenth Amendment exclusion from holding public office. Both houses immediately passed this act, and two days later, President Grant added his signature. Butler was now free to run for lieutenant governor.[36]

Seeing that the new party sought the support of blacks, Governor Scott activated the state militia, supposedly to protect the former slaves. His real motive was to install a force that could intimidate the blacks into voting Republican and reelecting him to office. Only blacks were allowed to enroll in the local companies. The chance to don "ribbons and plumes" and parade to the cadent beat of drums was irresistible. The ranks were rapidly filled and armed.[37]

In keeping with the times, one of the state's officers turned this situation to his advantage. Franklin Moses, the adjutant general, was placed in charge of obtaining weapons for the militia. He contracted for the 10,000 antique muskets owned by the state to be converted into breechloaders. His arrangements included a kickback of one dollar per weapon for his personal bank account.[38]

The troops proved a problem for the Union Reform Party. As he campaigned throughout the state, Butler was harried by the militia when he tried to document corruption in Scott's regime. "It was a regular understanding among them," Butler said later, "that I was not to be allowed to speak."[38]

The militiamen would come to the meetings, stack their arms, and then wait for the opportunity to disrupt Matthew's speech. If their presence was not enough to disperse those who had gathered to hear Butler's talk, the citizens soldiers would interrupt him with shouts. And when that did not discourage him, they would throw rocks. Butler, however, could not be intimidated. What a Charleston crowd threatened one of his black supporters, Matthew joined him on the stage and "stood by his side until he had said what he had to say."[40]

In another instance in Greenville, a militiaman in the audience made threats against Butler. "I got down, "Matthew related, "and went into the crowd and remonstrated with him. [The incident] was terminated without bloodshed."[41]

Butler's attempt to woo the blacks found disfavor with compatriots. "He says blacks and whites are common people," the *Sumter Watchman* complained. "[He] berates the Scott administration because they have not given the Negroes offices enough!"[42] Matthew, of course, knew that he had assumed an unpopular position, but he saw this as the only way for honest men to regain control of the state government.

The campaign to bully the blacks into voting for Scott and the rest of the Radicals continued through October 19, the day of the election. That morning in Edgefield, one of Matthew's black supporters entered the poll, cast his ballot for the Union Reform party, then went back outside. A militiaman, upon hearing that the former slave had supported the opposition, shot and killed him.[43]

Scott's strategy of oppression worked. The black vote was overwhelmingly Republican, and he was reelected, winning 85,071 out of 136,608 total ballots. Half (15) of the senate seats were contested. Four incumbents were returned, 11 new members joined the assembly. Twenty-four of the 30 senators were Radicals, 11 were blacks. Although only 51 of the representatives held their posts, the Republicans maintained their control of the house, capturing 113 of 134 seats. The number of blacks fell to 75, still a majority.[44]

C. W. Montgomery was elected president pro tem for the state senate, Moses retained his position as Speaker for the house, and Robertson returned to the U.S. Senate. Matthew was nominated for this post, and although the Radicals would never had named him, Robertson took no chances. Utilizing ill-gotten gains from his office, he purchased votes in the legislature, paying $500 to the rank and file and $2,000 to influential members of the assembly, spending about $40,000 total.[45]

Butler graciously accepted these election results, but some whites sought ways to continue the contest. "The solid black vote cast against the nominees of the Reform Party is a declaration of war," the Charleston *Daily News* editor professed. "It is . . . the duty of white men to organize and arm themselves."[46] His was a blatant call for reactivating the Klan.

Back in 1868 when the Klan first surfaced, their goal was to prevent the blacks from voting. The reappearance of the night riders in late 1870 had a different objective: to disarm the Negro militia. The citizen-soldiers continued on duty, and this menace of ex-slaves carrying muskets was too abhorrent to endure. A number of confrontations arose, most of which ended with orders from Scott for the blacks to surrender their weapons. Butler was never directly involved in these clashes, but he played a role. "A messenger came down [to say] the Negroes were out of line [in Laurens]," he testified at hearings on the Klan. "I advised some of the young men [from Edgefield] to go up there."[47]

Although Butler would not join in a general assault on the blacks, he was willing to take part in attempts to limit their status in society. He was mostly concerned with land. Blacks should work the soil but not share ownership. Butler helped found an Edgefield Agricultural and Police Club that November. The members agreed to neither sell nor rent their property to the former slaves. They also vowed not to hire blacks noted as "bad characters." If a white man refused to take part in this plan, he would be treated with silent contempt. "Let him get sick or even die," their pact read, "he will find . . . none to cheer [his] lonely hours or to bury the tainted remains but his nigger associates."[48]

In the midst of these bitter times, a family event offered respite. Maria gave birth to a third daughter, born December 29. She was named Jane Behethland, honoring the grandmother who had watched over Matthew during his teen years in South Carolina.[49]

The following months saw the violence of the Klan grow to unprecedented levels. What had started as a disciplined effort to disarm negro militia units exploded into personal vendettas. Blacks were whipped for seeking employment that was usually reserved for whites; James Henley, a black man living in Spartanburg County, was beaten because he accepted an appointment to a political office; and the night riders raided the house of Judge William Champion, a white man said to favor social equality between the races.[50] These brazen assaults were often preceded with a threat, published in the local newspapers. "Read the stern warning affixed," read a message sent to the *Edgefield Advertiser,* "and call upon the mountains to hide you."[51]

When the beatings escalated into murder, often a lynching by a masked mob, the national government took notice and action. Congress passed a series of laws, culminating with the Ku Klux Klan Act on April 20, 1871, giving the president the power to declare "any unlawful combination that menaced the public safety of a state [shall be deemed] a rebellion."[52] Federal troops were sent and dispersed throughout South Carolina to protect the blacks.

Although Matthew favored keeping blacks in their place, he was opposed to the violence, and he decided to take steps toward implementing a more peaceful approach to the problem. He put together a lottery plan to fund immigration into South Carolina, hoping to bring enough settlers to create a white majority. In order to give the scheme his full attention, he resigned his law practice on March 31, 1871.[53]

The plan called for the selling of tickets to a series of concerts to be held at the Academy of Music Hall, located in Charleston, commencing October 1, 1871. Attendees had a chance to win a prize, awarded via a drawing held after each performance. Butler hoped to sell a total of 150,000 seats at $5 each, generating $750,000. He would pay out two-thirds of this, half in cash, the Grand Prize being the Hall itself, valued at $250,000. This was probably the only way the owner, John Chadwick, could recoup an investment in what was in these hard times a "white elephant."[54]

With the remaining $250,000, Butler would buy "fertile land" in four corners of the state to resale "at low prices and long credit" to immigrants. He would establish recruiting posts in Europe and the North to entice an "intelligent, self-reliant, thrifty laboring population."[55] Matthew would gain personally, both through a salary for running the operation and the sale of some of his property to the newcomers.

The local newspaper supported his plan, but the editor worried about the class of people moving into the state. He urged Butler not to import "Paris Communists." Swedes, however, would be "just fine."[56]

Edgefield was obviously too small and too isolated for his operations, so in May, Butler left his home and moved to Columbia. Maria and the girls accompanied him; their three boys were sent to Greenville to spend the summer with grandmother Jane Perry Butler.[57]

Matthew may have had other reasons for abandoning Edgefield. His romantic involvement with three local ladies was creating problems. Martin Gary, his partner in the lottery, accused Butler of being "a cold-blooded seducer and abductor of the daughter of his friend and neighbor."[58] Mrs. Harris, a housewife and close friend, had recently borne a boy bearing a strong resemblance to Matthew;[59] and Mrs. Johnson, no doubt impregnated by Butler, had left town to give birth to her baby in Baltimore. He was paying her expenses. "I will provide you with a comfortable home," Matthew wrote, "if you consent to your child's going to a proper place which I will select to be educated."[60]

Mrs. Johnson was living in a boardinghouse, 380 Chase Street, run by Rosa Mills, whose husband, Thomas, earned his living as a plasterer. They had two children, a seven-year-old daughter, Leallia, and a thirteen-year-old son, William. Others renting rooms included John Mealcolm, a piano dealer, and the Jenkins, William, a cooper, his wife, Josephine, and their baby, George. Also living in this residence were Mrs. Hawkins, Rosa's mother, and Hester Graham, domestic servant.[61]

Butler sent Rosa money on a regular basis, not only to pay Mrs. Johnson's board but also perhaps as blackmail. "If you are basing your [demands] upon the lies that Dr. Warren tells you," he related, "you will always be disappointed. I have made no fortune and find it hard to support my family."[62]

Mrs. Mills, however, remained insistent. "Send thirty dollars immediately," she wrote shortly after receiving this letter from Butler. "I want it badly."[63]

Butler's trysts seem to connote lack of character, but they must be viewed within the standards of his day. "There was no legal proscription against fornication," historian Oliver Vernon Burton notes. "[This was] illustrative of the sexual . . . double standard in the plantation dominated state." Some wives (probably not Maria) actually took pride in their husband's philandering, since it offered proof of his being a "good catch," still attractive to other ladies. "The wife had her security," Burton relates, "the planter his freedom, and everyone else had religion."[64]

Butler needs no one to apologize for him or to explain why he had so many liaisons. His granddaughter, Ellen, however, offers us an interesting rationale. "He was a bit of a rounder," she allowed, "but that is the fate of a handsome man."[65]

Upon his arrival in Columbia, Matthew learned that the corruption and waste in Scott's administration continued unabated. The legislature, for example, spent that year over $150,000 for wines, cigars, and groceries for members. "The State has no right to be a State," Sen. C. P. Leslie said with tongue in cheek, "unless she can afford to take care of her statesmen."[66] The cost for chandeliers, sofas, and spittoons was approximately $40,000, but these bills were padded with bribes, bringing the total cost to about $90,000. And the public printing expenses (for a company owned by members of the assembly) were over $150,000, three times as much as in previous years.[67]

These examples of graft, however, were negligible when compared to the bond scandals. The state borrowed money for its operations by selling bonds or using them as collateral for loans. From the original authorization of $1 million in 1868, the official value issued had grown to over $8 million. The state's credit, however, was so poor, the bonds had sold at far under par, yielding only about $3.5 million.[68]

The corruption in this program took two forms: monies collected went to the pockets of the bond commission instead of the state's treasury;

and the selling agent in New York, H. H. Kimpton, Attorney General Chamberlain's college roommate, sold additional, unauthorized issues, perhaps as much as $6 million. It was impossible to calculate the total because Kimpton's books were hopelessly jumbled.[69]

Taxes on landowners such as Butler had soared in order to keep the state afloat. In May 1871 Matthew and other plantation owners met in Columbia to take action. The "Tax-Payer Convention" was called to investigate the "fearful and unnecessary increase of the public debt"; to find a way to halt the "wild, reckless and profligate" spending by the legislature; and to ask relief from paying two levies of tax that year.[70] Butler was named to a Committee of Eleven sent to discuss these matters with Scott.

After meeting with the governor, Butler returned to report to the convention. Scott had been most cordial and had responded favorably to their questions. He agreed with his visitors that "a large number of [the state] officials could be profitably dispensed with," and he promised to work with the legislature to "induce economic restrictions." He noted that the personal violence throughout the state had evolved from his "trouble in finding a proper class of men for Trial Justices," and he vowed to correct this problem. Other concessions from Scott included seeking minority representation in the assembly to "educate the majority," amending the law to provide open counting of election ballots, and suspending the collection of the second tax until March 1872.[71]

Most important, the governor showed Butler the printed statement of South Carolina's funded debt, $8,865,908, which was far below rumored numbers. This report was false, only about half the actual total, but Scott swore it was "substantially true."[72] Some historians have said that Butler knew the claim was wrong and that he accepted a bribe to lie in his report to the Taxpayers Convention.[73] Other evidence, however, disputes this accusation. J. L. Neagle noted later that his cohorts on the bond commission "laughed at [having] succeeded in deceiving the members" of Butler's Committee of Eleven.[74]

While in Columbia, Butler began contacting the various railroads in an attempt to induce them to extend their lines through Edgefield. He was acting as one of five, appointed by the village, to seek this advantage.[75] And this activity soon led to his involvement in yet another case of official corruption, the Railroad Ring.

The scheme to steal money through the state began back in early 1870. Attorney General Chamberlain originated this plan with a letter to Kimpton, in which he noted, "There is a mint of money in this, or I am a fool."[76] He was referring to a takeover of the Columbia & Greenville Railroad.

South Carolina owned stock in the C & G, an investment made prior to the war to aid its development. Chamberlain's idea was to steal these issues. An innocuous bill designed to "dispose of unproductive property" was passed in March by the legislature, and under its auspices, the shares of this railroad were acquired by state officials at one-tenth their value. The deal was then completed by buying up individual holdings with government funds. John J. Patterson was named vice president in charge of the line.[77]

Several months later, a second bill was enacted by the assembly in which the state lien on the company's bonds were transferred to a lesser mortgage. These securities, having no value when pledged first to South Carolina, were suddenly worth $1.5 million. Kimpton immediately started to sell them. The proceeds flowed into the pockets of the cabal.[78]

Further graft was blocked by state support for a rival line, the Blue Ridge Railroad, but this was easily resolved. In March 1871 the conspirators induced the assembly to approve a bill combining the two roads. Passage was achieved via bribes to the legislature. This act also included South Carolina's guarantee of $4 million in new bonds.[79]

The state held shares in the Blue Ridge, so before the merger could be completed, these had to be purchased: 13,100 at one dollar each. The funds were raised via private investors, one of whom was Matthew C. Butler. Contacting the railroads on behalf of Edgefield had exposed him to what seemed to be a legitimate business opportunity. When the new corporation was formed July 22, 1871, Col. James. S. Cothran was named president; Butler was elected to the board of directors.[80]

The conspirators had expected to profit by selling the bonds guaranteed by the state, but they soon discovered that South Carolina's credit was so bad, few buyers were willing to take the risk. Patterson and his friends developed a new tack. In January 1872 they proposed a plan to ask the legislature to approve the surrender of $4 million in bonds to the state in exchange for scrip (essentially cash) having a value of $1.8 million. Matthew, finally realizing that he was involved in a scam, resigned from the board.[81] He probably did not depart empty-handed. Having made money through his connection with Patterson and his cronies, Butler "wanted no investigation of his financial [interest] in the Blue Ridge Railroad."[82]

Others, including President Cothran, also left the company, so Patterson took charge. Using bribes totaling over $50,000, he secured passage of the exchange act. Opponents, however, secured an injunction blocking payment. The courts later declared the bill unconstitutional, and the chicanery eventually collapsed in bankruptcy.[83]

In June 1871, just as Butler was becoming entangled with the Railroad Ring, he was also assuming a new vocation. Tickets to the lottery were selling poorly (the project was doomed to failure), so he had to find another means of earning income. He and Gary were named general agents of South Carolina for the Universal Life Insurance Company. This was a mutual firm. The insured were stockholders, too, so they shared in all profits.[84] Matthew was less than enthusiastic with his new position. He referred to it as the "common refuge."[85]

As fall approached, the violence of the Klan continued. The 7th Cavalry, led by Maj. Lewis M. Merrill, occupying South Carolina, knew who was responsible, but they had made no arrests because they were convinced that the local courts were too intimidated to convict anyone. Grant finally made an effort to halt the outrages. He issued a proclamation on October 17 suspending the writ of habeas corpus and ordering the apprehension for federal trial of the whites who had violated the Ku Klux Klan Act. Merrill's troops rounded up several thousand over the next thirty days. Only a few were ever prosecuted, but the campaign succeeded in ending these nightly rides.[86]

Butler was not arrested, but he was questioned by the Select Committee of Congress regarding Klan activities. During this wide-ranging interview, which covered, among other topics, politics, the Land Commission, and race relations, Matthew denied intimate knowledge about the Ku Klux. "I have heard of them," he admitted. "I think there is [a den] in Edgefield. But if I ever saw [a member], I never knew him as such."[87]

This interrogation was grueling, and if Butler was not discouraged by the questioning, he soon had other reasons to be so. In November Scott reneged on his pledge to suspend the second tax collection of the year. Some accused Matthew of misrepresenting his discussion with the governor, and he was forced to defend himself with a letter to the newspaper. "The promise," he maintained, "was clear, reiterated, conclusive and unmistakable."[88]

The attacks continued. Shortly after spending a quiet Christmas with his family, Butler was dismayed by the U. S. Senate speech of George F. Edmunds of Vermont, naming him as being one of the South Carolina heads of the Klan. Matthew was so upset by these false charges, he dropped all activities and rushed to Washington to defend himself.[89]

Upon his return to Columbia, Matthew found that others shared in his discouragement. His party had embraced a policy of "Passivism" and opted not to compete in the upcoming state elections. "A Democrat might secure some petty office here and there," a spokesman said, "but no Democrat will . . . get any place worth having in South Carolina."[90] Butler had already proven this point in 1870, and was quite willing to step clear from the strife between the whites and their former slaves. "As long as [the blacks] don't touch my house," he proclaimed, "[both can] shoot and kill as many as [they] please."[91]

Butler was concerned about his home, a target for burning by blacks, because he had placed his Edgefield estate up for sale. The manor was located on fifty acres, half of which was virgin forests, the rest ground under cultivation. Also included was a "fine orchard, vineyard, well and spring convenient" to the house and outbuildings.[92]

In April 1872 Liberal Republicans led by Carl Schurz met in Cincinnati to form a national opposition party. They were upset with the corruption in Grant's administration and hoped to turn him out of office. Horace Greeley, the fiery editor of the *New York Tribune*, received their nomination for president. The Democrats, knowing they had no chance in a three-party race, also named Greeley as their candidate, a bitter pill to swallow because the newspaperman's views, especially on tariffs, were consistently opposed to theirs. Grant won renomination from the Republicans.[93]

Butler was standing aside, but in August while calling on his aged mother in Greenville, he was asked to comment on the upcoming race. Noting that Scott was angry with Grant because the president had dubbed him a thief, Matthew made a jocular quip about the campaign. "What will we Greeley men do should Scott declare for Old Horace," he stated. "What a combination! Whew!"[94]

Scott was really no factor because he was leaving politics. The constitution did not allow him a third term. The Republicans nominated Moses, Speaker of the House, as their candidate for governor.[95]

Moses was among the most corrupt men in the government, and some Republicans were afraid that both the state and the party would be destroyed under his administration. The dissidents, led by former governor Orr, now a scalawag, met in Columbia a few days after the Radical Convention to nominate an alternative ticket, headed by Reuben Tomlinson.[96] He was a Pennsylvania carpetbagger, first a missionary, then superintendent of education in the Freedmen's Bureau, and now the state's auditor. "The entire contest is a struggle between thieves and plunderers," the *Edgefield Advertiser* announced. "We have no preference between these [two] combatants. . . . Let us pray!"[97]

The Democrats, continuing their passivism strategy, declined to compete. Butler spoke for the party. "We deem it unwise to nominate a . . . ticket," he said. "We demand of the Republican Party [they] . . . fulfill their pledges and give the State an able, honest, and economical government. [And] we [condemn] the corruption and robbery which . . . pervade the executive and legislative departments of the state government."[98]

Grant was reelected; Moses won the governorship that November. Staying aloof from politics, Matthew concentrated on selling insurance, attending to details for the approaching lottery, and tending to personal activities in Columbia. He and Maria attended the South Carolina Club Ball, held November 9 at the Nickerson House. "The dress of the ladies and their beauty deserve more extended notice," the reporter for the *Edgefield Advertiser* related. "Among [the] particular noticeable were Mrs. General M.C. Butler."[99] Although the times were tough, the socially elite (as they did during the war) kept up appearances.

━━━ ⚜ ━━━

Governor Scott's four-year administration produced rampant corruption, funded by ever increasing taxes levied by a black-dominated legislature. The state's debt at the onset of his first term was bout $5.4 million. Four years later, it totaled $18.5 million, almost $6 million of this in unauthorized conversion bonds, most of which had found its way into the pockets of dishonest politicians.[100] The election of Moses promised a continuation if not a compounding of this corruption. Although his past course of pacifism had not worked, Matthew continued to reject violence as a solution to this problem. Its call, however, would eventually prove irresistible.

CHAPTER 20

Governor Moses

FRANKLIN J. MOSES, JR., WAS A SCALAWAG, BORN IN 1838 IN CHARLESTON, the son of a famous father. The elder Moses was a renowned lawyer, whose political career included posts as state senator, circuit judge, and currently chief justice of the South Carolina Supreme Court. Young Moses left college in 1855 after only one year of study, married into a leading Southern family in 1859, and was living at his parents' home when the Civil War began. His avid support of secession led to his first job, private secretary to the just-elected governor, Francis Pickens, Butler's father-in-law.[1]

Moses, a tall and handsome man, proud of his handlebar mustache, avoided military service during the war. He began a legal career in 1866, then moved to Sumter that same year to become editor of a conservative newspaper. Moses saw the coming of Reconstruction, and in 1867, started publishing a series of articles supporting the Radical view. He hoped to position himself to profit from imminent black rule.[2]

He was quickly dismissed by the owner of the newspaper, but Moses had already gained his objectives. He was elected both adjutant general and representative in 1868. And when Moses assumed his seat, the members of the state house named him Speaker. During his four years of holding that powerful office, he was most noted for flagrant corruption: accepting bribes, issuing fraudulent pay certificates, and embezzling state funds.[3]

The blacks continued to dominate the legislature, holding not only the majority of seats but also the foremost offices. S. A. Swails was elected president pro tem in the Senate; Samuel J. Lee was named Speaker for the House.[4]

In early December the assembly elected John J. Patterson to the national Senate. His campaign was run from a bar close to the Capitol, where Patterson slipped cash to legislative members in exchange for their vote. He spent almost $40,000 for the seat.[5]

No doubt disgusted by the political scene, Butler saw no reason for remaining in Columbia. The lottery, deferred for three months due to meager ticket sales, had finally been drawn in January. The proceeds were insufficient to fund his immigration scheme. And his sales of insurance had failed to produce a meaningful income. The time had come to return to Edgefield.

Butler began a series of visits to his home in January by attending a meeting of the local medical association. He was "looking well," a reporter wrote.[6] Although he was not quite ready to leave Columbia, Matthew prepared for the move by setting up a new law partnership while in town with S. B. Griffin.[7]

In another attempt to add to his income, Butler turned again to the railroads. Despite his bad experience with the Blue Ridge, he invested (probably borrowed) money in the recently resuscitated Columbia & Greenville line. He planned not only to personally profit but also to use his influence to run their tracks through Edgefield. In May Matthew was elected chairman of the board. "The road," the newspaper said, "will soon be put in first class condition."[8]

Butler also continued his efforts in behalf of the taxpayers. In July 1873 he filed a court suit, claiming that the issuance of conversion bonds, now totaling almost $7 million dollars, was both a "fraud and illegality." Matthew sought a stay to prevent the South Carolina fiscal officers from levying additional taxes toward paying any interest for these securities.[9]

Butler was well aware that this suit was only an indignant gesture. Most judges had been appointed by the Radical leaders, and the courts were not about to hinder their benefactors from using their offices for personal gain. The men tapping the state's till were so sure of their freedom from prosecution, many openly admitted their crimes. "Why," John Patterson laughed when warned to reform his fraudulent ways, "there are . . . five more years of good stealing in South Carolina!"[10]

That fall Butler took steps to assure the futures of his three sons. Frank left home for Spartanburg, South Carolina, to attend Wofford Fitting School, an academy for boys studying for college;[11] Willie and young "Cabby" were sent to the Carolina Military Institute, Charlotte North Carolina. It had just been opened by one of Butler's old friends, Col. J. P. Thomas. "Your [two] sons," he would soon write, "are . . . doing well."[12]

The boys, however, were disgruntled because Butler had already dictated their future professions: Frank would be a doctor, Willie a lawyer, and Cabby a soldier. Each had hoped to follow a different career. Frank wanted to enter politics, Willie had no interest in being a lawyer, and Cabby was not yet enamored with the military. Matthew was aware of his boys' discontent, but he was accustomed to command. He made decisions, issued orders, and then allowed no discussion.[13]

Francis Wilkinson Pickens Butler.
COURTESY ELLEN ADAMS GUTOW

William Wallace Butler.
COURTESY DECENNIAL RECORD OF THE CLASS
OF '83 OF PRINCETON COLLEGE, N.J.

Matthew C. "Cabby" Butler.
COURTESY ELLEN ADAMS GUTOW

That same month Butler accepted another responsibility. He agreed to be vice president for the South Carolina branch of the Southern Historical Society. He would coordinate an effort to "collect and classify all facts and incidents that would throw light on the causes and the conduct of the late War." Matthew appointed Dr. Maximilian Laborde as secretary to carry out the actual work.[14]

Butler gave another this task because that November he was too busy trying to make a living. The nation was in the grip of a financial depression, brought about by the sudden failure of Jay Cooke's New York banking house.[15] "Times are dull and hard," the Edgefield newspaper stated. "Trade, except on Saturdays, is but a sickly phantom."[16]

On November 6 Butler came to Edgefield to take part in the annual Sale Day.[17] This was a gala event, a meeting of old friends at a host of parties. During the height of the festivities, Matthew received word to rush back to Columbia. His daughter, Jane, was desperately ill. The child, not yet three years old, died on November 13, 1873.[18]

The tragedy brought Butler and Maria back together. A month or so later, she revealed that during this crisis, she had become pregnant again.

For Matthew, perhaps looking for a cause to help take his mind off this blow, Governor Moses offered a prominent target. His corruption in office was outlandish. The vain scalawag had disdained living in the official residence in favor of buying the most conspicuous home in the capital, the Preston Mansion. He paid $40,000 for the house, most of it coming from a bribe for his approving a fraudulent printing bill. "He sold everything connected with the Governor's duties which could be exchanged for money," a reporter said, "honors, emoluments, pardons . . . even empty military titles."[19]

Selling pardons was Moses's specialty. During his time as governor, he released 457 convicts from prison, forty-one in a single month.[20]

Taxes, too, continued to climb. The landowners held a second Taxpayers Convention in Columbia on February 17, 1874, to study and find solutions to the problem. Butler was one of those representing Edgefield. Committees met and offered a number of resolutions, the most important being that they were subjected to "taxation without representation," because only a few of those levying assessments, the members of the legislature, held taxable property. For those assemblymen holding land, its total value was less than the sum of their salaries.[21]

Citing the futility of looking for relief from the men who had created their problems, Butler suggested they bypass the state officials and send a committee of fifteen to Washington to present their complaints to both the president and Congress. This plan was accepted, and Matthew was included in the delegation.[22]

After presenting their case to both houses of Congress, which referred the matter to their judiciary committees, the group called on other key officials to "lay before them the pitiable plight of South Carolina."[23] Butler and his fellow landowners met first with Vice President Henry Wilson, then with most members of the president's cabinet. Each received the delegation with "much warmth" and took "the greatest interest" in their dilemma.[24]

Upon visiting Grant, however, Butler and the group saw that he was unalterably opposed to any federal intervention. "[Your] state has a complete sovereign existence," the president noted, "and must make its own laws." He then divulged the reason for this position. "A portion of my sympathy," he confessed, "has been abstracted by . . . a speech delivered during [your meeting] which contained . . . more villainous slander than I have ever experienced before."[25] He was alluding to comments made by Martin Gary, who had spoken out against the trip to Washington.

Grant's position held and the landowners failed to receive any help from the federal government. Their gathering did, however, produce one positive result. Each county set up a Tax Union, whose local members would make sure that all levies were not only fairly assessed and collected but also spent wisely.[26] Some relief was achieved, and this organization proved useful in future political campaigns.

Following his visit to Washington, Matthew returned to Columbia, but he only stayed there a short time. He soon moved his wife and family back to their former home in Edgefield. And on July 8, 1874, Maria gave birth to yet another daughter, whom they named Daisy Eugenia Ransom Butler. The baby was probably premature and sickly from the start. Only two months later, on September 5, she died. Daisy was buried in the village cemetery in the same grave holding the brother and sister who had preceded her in death.[27]

Butler's return to Edgefield found him facing an armed enemy, the local black militia. Ned Tennant, the leader for these troops, "was somewhat of a dashing character," according to an observer, "[who] adorned his hat with a long black ostrich plume. [He] was not a full-blooded negro . . . judging from the color of his skin."[28] Tennant, usually wearing his military uniform, owned a fine horse, which he rode through the town most days just to tease the residents with his menacing presence. Late at night after most whites were abed, he would call his troops to assemble for drill with the beat of African drums, a reminder of the presumed savage origins of his race. The constant repetition of this ploy was bound to bring a confrontation between Tennant and Butler.[29]

The first showdown came on July 4, 1874. A rifle club of whites, the Sweetwater Sabres, had assembled close by the black militia's usual drill site.

Both had gathered to celebrate the holiday. That evening, however, riders galloped up to Tennant's house and fired several shots through his front door. He waited until he was sure the aggressors were gone, then beat a "long roll" on his African drums to call his men to arms. While blacks rushed toward his house in answer to the summons, whites were rallying in Edgefield. The following morning, Col. Andrew P. Butler, a distant relative of Matthew's and the leader of the Sweetwater Sabres, ordered a pair of emissaries to confront Tennant.[30]

"What is the meaning of this unheard of and outrageous assemblage?" Rev. John P. Melling and Dr. H. A. Shaw demanded of Tennant. "[If we are] not assured at once of [your] willingness to disperse [your] negroes, we [will] attack."[31]

Tennant was cowed by the threat, and he meekly ordered his force to disband. He must have seethed inside, however, over being embarrassed in front of his troops, and no doubt plotted revenge.

The militia continued to drill, "growing more impudent and unbearable every day."[32] That September when Tennant's men once again answered the call of his drums, Butler led a force of whites to confront the blacks. The adversaries met at a plantation not far from town. When Tennant refused to disband his troops, Matthew, drawing on his Civil War experience, formed his followers into a battle line and prepared to charge. At that moment, Union troops, stationed at Edgefield, reached the scene. They succeeded in separating the two adversaries, thus avoiding bloodshed.[33]

That same month, the Republicans assembled in Columbia to nominate their candidate for governor in the coming election. They met under a cloud of protest lodged against the current incumbent, Moses. "[His] pledges," dissidents said, "have not been . . . redeemed. Sound policy has been discarded and reckless extravagance manifested." They further related displeasure from the National leaders. "[They] admonish us to . . . retrace our steps, and vindicate . . . the integrity of Republicanism."[34]

But although Moses was obviously unsuited for renomination, the Radicals were unwilling to surrender the graft and corruption that lined their pockets. They turned to Daniel H. Chamberlain, the carpetbagger from Massachusetts. During this term as attorney general from 1868 to 1872, Chamberlain had shared in many of the schemes to defraud the state: the Railroad Frauds, the Land Commission, and deceiving the Taxpayer Convention. He had left service in 1872 to open a legal practice in Columbia. His supporters assumed that he would condone the continued plunder of South Carolina.[35]

The dissidents, too, thought that electing Chamberlain would mean no change in corrupt practices. In October they met in Charleston to nominate John T. Green, a scalawag but an honest man now serving as a judge, as their splinter candidate.[36]

Butler and the Democrats knew they had no chance of defeating either candidate, but using the Tax Union organizations for naming a delegation, they still met in Columbia in early October and endorsed Green for governor.[37]

Matthew took an active role in supporting Green. Working with local leaders in Edgefield, he organized a panel of speakers to tour the surrounding area giving speeches favoring the dissidents' candidate. Butler spoke four times that October, first at Red Hill, then Pleasant Lane, Jno. Atkin's Place, and Edgefield.[38]

The election that November was closer than in the past. Chamberlain, however, won the race with 80,403 votes, 11,585 more than the total garnered by Green.[39]

Slipping again to the sidelines, Matthew returned home to his family, his farms, and his law practice. He no doubt anticipated a quiet winter. Ned Tennant, however, seething with hatred from the embarrassment he had endured during the confrontation between his militia and the whites led by Butler, soon changed this outlook. During the night of January 13, 1875, a cohort under Tennant's order crept up to Matthew's house and set it aflame. Butler, Maria, and their girls barely escaped the resulting inferno.[40]

The culprit was easily captured, and he confessed that Tennant had hired him to torch Matthew's house. Despite the urge to wreak revenge, Butler remained committed to working within the system. He asked for and was given a warrant for Tennant's arrest by a trial justice. An all-black posse assembled to bring the felon into custody. When they cornered the militia leader, however, they found Tennant accompanied by his band of armed blacks, ready to resist his capture. The constable in charge sent word to Butler for assistance.

Matthew quickly gathered his white neighbors, and they galloped to the confrontation. As they approached, Tennant's troops opened fire at the oncoming riders. Butler and his company dismounted. Their answering rounds sent the militia scrambling into the nearby woods.[41]

Butler by now was wild with rage and he was determined to put an end to the threats of an armed black militia. The next morning, he assembled almost a thousand whites to comb the countryside to capture the black troops and relieve them of their rifles. Tennant and his panic-stricken men managed to evade the searchers by wriggling through the brambles and brush toward Edgefield. Three days later they reached the town and surrendered their weapons to Lawrence Cain, a local black leader, who locked all the muskets in the court house. When Butler and his riders learned of Tennant's action, they raced to the village, stormed the building, and took charge of the arms.[42]

Cain was badly frightened, and he sent word to Chamberlain that "an outbreak [is] inevitable. . . . The colored people of the village will be attacked."[43]

Butler had no such plan, but was probably surprised by Chamberlain's reply. The governor refused to intrude in the affair. Instead, he issued orders to all militia and rifle clubs in the state to disband.[44] Chamberlain was proving to be nothing like the man his party thought they had elected.

CHAPTER 21

The Red Shirts

MASSACHUSETTS NATIVE DANIEL HENRY CHAMBERLAIN WAS BORN IN 1833 to a rich family, financially able to send their son to Phillips Academy, Amherst, Yale, where he earned his college degree, and Harvard Law school. He entered the Federal army in 1864 as a lieutenant, serving with a black regiment. "I carried my sword south," he said later, "and when the war was over, remained there."[1]

He began his life in South Carolina as a cotton farmer. Soon failing as a planter, Chamberlain turned his efforts to politics, and was elected attorney general in 1868. He was less dishonest than his Radical peers, but although Chamberlain did not especially profit while in office, he was in a position to and did help others to steal. His participation in the widespread graft evidently weighed on his conscience, because in 1872, he retired from government service to start a law practice in Columbia.[2]

Chamberlain was a small, spare man whose cold demeanor was enhanced by chiseled features, dark mustache, and a bald pate, surrounded by a fringe of graying hair. He was quiet, determined, and disposed to "speeches and writings that were models of style and diction." This observer goes on to say, "He toiled diligently to [compose] elegant addresses, admirably suited to cultivated audiences, but delivered to people who . . . enjoyed and understood only rant, shrieks, arm waving, foot stomps and funny stories about hogs . . . and hound dogs."[3]

Like his predecessors, Chamberlain faced a legislature composed of a few unprincipled whites influencing a majority of blacks, many of whom were illiterate. The Radicals held 91 of 124 House seats, with two-thirds of their number being black. Robert B. Elliot, graduate of Eton College, England, one of the most corrupt representatives, was elected Speaker—the second black to hold that post.[4]

Republicans dominated the Senate, holding twenty-six of the thirty-three seats. Sixteen of the members were black, including Swails, reelected president pro tem.[5]

Gov. Daniel H. Chamberlain.
COURTESY UNIVERSITY OF NORTH CAROLINA PRESS

Chamberlain, like Scott and Moses, had promised reform. But unlike the previous governors, whose pledges were tongue-in-cheek, he was serious. Chamberlain had shocked the Radicals in his December opening address, in which he criticized the unfair tax system, asked for a reduction of state spending, and demanded reform of the public schools, the election procedure, and the judiciary. "The evils that surround us," he stated to those who had created them, "are deplorable but . . . transitory. . . . If we who are here today shall fail in our duty, others more honest . . . will be called to our places."[6]

The legislature no doubt thought these words were only for show, but Chamberlain soon proved them wrong. He vetoed a number of funding bills that included provisions maintaining the flow of graft. Despite their majority, the Radicals were not able to surmount Chamberlain's opposition. He was a hero to long-suffering conservatives. "To have a governor honest in his purpose, and inflexible in his determination to put down fraud," the *Charleston News and Courier* related, ". . . is more than South Carolina ever expected to have under Republican rule."[7]

Butler was not among those acclaiming Chamberlain. He was no longer interested in compromise, and was committed to driving all Republicans from office. He would devote every energy to this course, but only after finding a new home for his family.

The house he purchased that spring lay just outside of Edgefield. The manor, "East Hill," built in 1849, was about one hundred feet in length. A tall columned porch shaded a pair of heavy double doors, which opened to an exceptionally wide hall. Five rooms filled the front: the central aisle, two drawing rooms, the dining area, and a guest bedroom. In the rear, there were three bedrooms, a small screened porch, and a stairs leading to a half-

East Hill. PHOTO BY THE AUTHOR

story attic. All the windows rose from the floor up to the twelve-foot, plas-tered ceiling to allow maximum light.[8]

Maria's bedroom was on the far left rear. Butler slept in quarters to the far right rear. He made some interesting modifications to his room. Mat-thew bricked the windows and added a door, three feet off the ground with no steps to the entry, on the east side. This arrangement, he claimed, made it easy for him to "slide" onto his horse, tethered outside, thus avoid-ing strain to his amputated foot. This also gave him (Maria would soon dis-cover) a chance to sneak women into his bedroom and "entertain" them in total privacy.[9]

Butler spent much of this period traveling to and from Greenville to visit his aged mother. She was no longer living alone. Matthew's younger sister Elise and her husband, Charles A. Carson, had brought the ailing, eighty-four-year-old woman into their home. Jane Butler died on July 11.[10] Matthew was deeply saddened by her death.

About this same time, events were unfolding in faraway Mississippi that would have a profound effect on both Butler and South Carolina. Under the leadership of Sen. Lucuis Q. C. Lamar, whites devised a scheme to retrieve their state from carpetbagger-scalawag-black rule. They started by nominating a full slate of Democratic candidates for the coming election, and then implemented the actions that would bring them success. "It was not a campaign," one historian wrote, "it was a revolution!"

Like South Carolina the blacks had been organized and armed as state militia. The whites countered with their own military "clubs" of rifle-carrying men, many former Confederate soldiers. They came en masse to Republican rallies to taunt the speakers and disrupt the assembly (despite the presence of black troops). Their objective was to demonstrate to the ex-slaves that the current government lacked the capability to protect them and their rights as citizens. They meant to intimidate those blacks supporting the Radicals, to elevate their fear to the point they would become too afraid to cast a Republican ballot.

On a more positive note, the Democrats, too, held meetings. "Immense crowds came in orderly procession with bands and banners," an observer stated, "pausing at every hilltop [along the way] to fire a cannon." This pageantry, followed by fervid speeches and free barbecues, was designed to sway the watching, wide-eyed blacks into giving them their vote.

Adelbert Ames, a former Union general and now governor, panicked and appealed to Grant for federal troops to bolster the Republican cause. Lamar, however, had anticipated this request, and he had strictly forbidden violence, which would have brought intervention from the army. The president had no choice but to refuse Ames's plea. The Democrats won every post in the November election, and Mississippi was returned to white rule.[11]

The Radicals, of course, still held the power in South Carolina. And they continued their effort to tap the public till. The assembly (bribed, no doubt) picked two scoundrels for circuit judges that December: former governor Moses and William J. Whipper, a black from Pennsylvania, described as being "utterly without character." Chamberlain was appalled with the legislature's choices. "The election of these two men to judicial office," he wrote, "sends a thrill of horror through the state."[12] He refused to sign their commissions. Moses opted not to contest the governor's decision; Whipper filed suit, but the courts sustained Chamberlain.

Conservatives from the Low Country were delighted, and showered Chamberlain with their praise. The *Charleston News and Courier,* for example, printed a detailed summary of the governor's accomplishments: a reduction in the public debt, significant economies in government operations, no abuse of granting pardons, a marked improvement in the qualifications of appointees, and reform of the tax system. Chamberlain's presence at coastal social, literary, and political gatherings was eagerly solicited.[13]

Butler went to Columbia in January 1876, to chair the meeting of the Democratic State Central Committee. Although this group decided to "revive" their party for the November elections, they could not agree on the approach. Charleston "Cooperationists" promoted a coalition with Chamberlain, in which they would support him for governor but run

Democratic candidates for the legislature; Butler and his friends proposed a straight-out campaign, à la Mississippi, competing for every office in the state "from governor to coroner." Finding they could not settle their differences, the body issued a compromise manifesto. "In the [coming] contest . . . we must win," they stated. "The security of property as well as the safety of person [depend on it]."[14]

Each county was assigned a leader to set up Democratic clubs in every voting ward. The objective was to enroll all white men (not already Republican) in the state. Edgefield was organized by March, and under Butler's guidance, declared, "We are sternly opposed to any fusion, coalition, or compromise even with professedly honest Republicans."[15] They would not budge from the position Matthew had taken back in January.

On May 4 Butler changed law partners again, joining in practice with his younger brother Oliver.[16] Both had lost limbs during the war (one his foot, the other an arm just before Appomattox), so they made a tragic pair. That same day Matthew left for Columbia to attend a state meeting of Democrats. The main reason for gathering was to elect delegates to the national convention, to be held in June in St. Louis. Butler was named an alternate.[17]

After settling this issue, the members turned to state matters. A committee on resolutions offered a mild proposal that urged using "the utmost vigor and zeal in perfecting a thorough and compact organization" for conducting the coming political campaign.[18]

Martin Gary responded with a counterplea, asking that the party "put a straight-out ticket in the field," i.e., take the Mississippi approach to restoring whites to power. His appeal evoked considerable debate. The delegates representing the Low Country argued that backing Chamberlain offered the Democrats their best chance of winning a majority in the legislature; Matthew and his supporters insisted that only total defeat of the Radicals would restore white rule. When the roll was tallied, the Charleston view was accepted by a vote of 70 to 42.[19]

Upon returning home, Butler took a brief hiatus from politics to serve as the defense attorney in the case of *Earle v. Bailey,* a libel suit against the *Greenville Enterprise.* His arguments were judged by an onlooker "more brilliant, more logical, more eloquent, more learned, more conclusive." Even the opposition was won over by Matthew's address. "That was the most powerful specimen of forensic eloquence that I ever heard," W. D. Simpson said in a note to Butler. "I congratulate you."[20]

About a month later, Butler learned that the delegates named to represent South Carolina at the national Democratic convention in St. Louis, John Bratton and W. D. Porter, had both decided not to attend the June gathering. He agreed to go in their stead. Matthew campaigned for Sen. James A. Bayard of Delaware, but in the end, joined with the majority in supporting Samuel J. Tilden as the party's candidate for president.[21]

On July 7 during an evening meeting with clients at the Edgefield Courthouse, Butler received a note asking him to come to Hamburg, a South Carolina hamlet just across the Savannah River from Augusta, Georgia. The village was populated mostly by blacks, and was well known as an area where whites could expect insolence and harassment.[22]

Such an incident took place there July 4. Two young men, brothers-in-law Henry Getzen and Thomas Butler (neither related to Matthew), were driving a wagon, heading home from a visit to Augusta. Upon entering Hamburg, they found black militia (Company A, 9th Regiment) drilling in the middle of the road and blocking their route. There was room enough to drive around the troops, but the whites were not about to yield the right of way. They insisted that the blacks step aside. Doc Adams, the head of the uniformed men, refused to move. An angry exchange of curses followed. Just when violence seemed inevitable, the impasse was checked by a sudden rainstorm. Adams and his men scattered for cover; Getzen and Butler, soaked by the downpour, continued their westward trek toward home.[23]

Robert Butler, Thomas's father and a "lucrative" client of Matthew's, pressed charges against Adams for blocking the thoroughfare. Prince Rivers, the local justice, well known as an obstinate black, also a state representative and militia general, set July 6 as a trial date. At the onset of the proceedings Adams cursed the judge. Rivers immediately ruled the defendant in contempt, and postponed the hearings until July 8.[24] Robert Butler thought this delay was just a ruse to allow Adams and the militia to escape censure, so he sent Matthew a note, asking him to come to Hamburg to assure that the case was prosecuted.

By now the whole countryside knew about this incident, especially the threats that Adams had made against the two white boys both during and after the confrontation. So as Matthew, armed only with a law book, trotted toward Hamburg the morning of July 8, Col. A. P. Butler was calling his Sweetwater Sabres to muster. He was responding to an urgent note from Matthew (most likely sent before he left Edgefield) to bring his force to Hamburg, to attend Adams's trial, and help to see that justice was served. Their appearance was expected to be symbolic, since the men were "expressly ordered to leave our rifles and carbines (behind)." They rode armed with "only pistols and sabers."[25]

Butler reached Hamburg about noon, where he and Robert Butler met with Henry Sparnick, the lawyer for Adams and the militia, at Mr. Damm's store. They discussed the case, and agreed that if the blacks made an apology, the charges would be forgotten. Sparnick went to consult with Adams; Butler walked over to the court to see Prince Rivers.[26]

Matthew's first questions was whether Adams and his men were to be tried as civilians or as militia. Rivers treated this inquiry as a joke. "Depends on the facts," he sneered. Butler then asked if the blacks were planning to show up for their trial. "Don't know," Prince said with a grin. "I'll have them called."[27]

A constable was sent to bring Adams to court. He soon returned to report that the militia had gathered up the street and seemed in a defiant mood. "This . . . has gone on long enough," Butler stormed, "and it is about time to put a stop [to it]. Those negroes must give up their arms at once."[28]

Rivers protested, saying the village would not be safe without its guard. Knowing that the Sweetwater Sabres would soon reach town, Butler assured Prince that he could supply protection. He no doubt now rued his order to the whites to leave their muskets back at Edgefield. His sudden decision to disarm the militia would initiate a fight. Adams and his men would surely resist surrendering their weapons.[29]

Butler's rash resolution to bring the blacks to battle was atypical, a reaction unlike the cool judgment he usually displayed. He failed to take into account the repercussion bound to follow. There would no doubt be casualties, and as the leader of the whites, Matthew would be held responsible. He was putting his political future at risk.

The judge agreed to meet with Adams and attempt to persuade him to hand over his weapons. While waiting for Rivers to return, Butler was accosted by Sam Spencer, sent from Adams (probably at Sparnick's suggestion) to arrange a parley away from Prince's office. Matthew and Spencer strolled over to the Council Chamber, but found only Gardner, the town mayor, there. Butler repeated his demand that the militia give up their arms, but the black intendant claimed that his authority did not extend to the troops.[30]

Disgusted with all the delays, Butler left for Augusta to call on another client about an unrelated matter. He met some young men along the way, and when asked about the situation in Hamburg, noted, "We want those guns and we're bound to have them. . . . I may need your services . . . this afternoon."[31]

Upon his return to Hamburg, Butler was greeted by four blacks (Pixley, Edwards, Sims, and Spencer), all looking for a peaceful solution to what was growing into an ominous confrontation. While Matthew was visiting Augusta, A. P. Butler and his Sweetwater Sabres had ridden into town. The whites were obviously itching to take on the black militia. Butler accompanied the mediators to Spencer's office to meet Adams, but after waiting for twenty minutes with no appearance from the militia leader, Matthew went to Rivers's chambers, where he found Prince no longer grinning, and painfully aware that the whites were intent on using force to disarm the blacks. Although he had failed in his first attempt, Rivers proposed making one last try at convincing Adams to give up his arms. "If they will not yield," he noted, "they must take the consequences."[32]

Rivers rushed to Adams, who had barricaded about forty-five of his troops in their drill room, the second story of the Sibley building, a brick warehouse located alongside the bridge to Augusta. The blacks refused Rivers's plea to turn over their weapons. Prince returned, gave Matthew the news, and then left town because "he did not consider it to be altogether healthy for him to remain."[33]

It was now about 7:00 P.M. Matthew conferred with the leaders of the Sweetwater Sabres and those representing a few supporters who had come over from Augusta, and the decision was made to send the blacks an ultimatum: give us your arms within the next half an hour or we will attack. The whites, about seventy in all, deployed in front of the brick Sibley warehouse. Five, including McKie Meriwether, the young son of a local patriarch, advanced as skirmishers. All waited a response from Adams. None came. About 7:30 P.M., Butler's men opened fire.[34]

The militia shot back. The exchange was both sporadic and ineffectual, since the whites had mostly pistols to fire and the blacks had only two rounds per man in their arsenal. Suddenly, about sunset, Meriwether collapsed, hit and killed by a bullet to his head.[35]

"If the white men were determined when they began that business," one participant related, "this sad and unexpected death added ten-fold fury to their feelings."[36]

A few left the firing line to try a different strategy. They pushed a framed shanty toward the armory, using it as a shield, planning to lodge it against the front door, set it aflame, and smoke the blacks from their stronghold.[37]

When Matthew saw what they were attempting, he stepped forward and ordered a halt to their efforts. He had a better idea. Butler recalled seeing an old cannon in Augusta, and he sent a squad across the river to fetch that weapon to the front. They returned, bringing not only the piece but also about a hundred more whites to join the fray. The gun was loaded with stones, nails, and other loose impediments, and fired four times.[38]

The missiles bounded harmlessly off the brick building, but the noise itself was enough to unnerve the blacks inside the armory. They started clambering one after another down a ladder, propped against a rear window, to scatter into the now dark night. The whites, of course, spotted the shadowy figures in flight, and opened fire. Jim Cook, a black town marshall but not a militia member, was shot and killed.[39]

Shortly thereafter, another black fleeing the area was dropped by a single round, fired by one of the Clinch Riflemen, an Augusta club. His aim was aided by the moon, which had broken through clouds to shine brightly on the scene below.[40]

Many blacks surrendered. John Parker, a corporal with the militia, was herded to the area where the prisoners were being assembled. Matthew was there, and he asked, "Are you one of the damned rascals?" Parker replied, "Yes." Just as he spoke, someone shot him in the back. Parker was wounded, but not killed.[41] Butler was appalled, and "condemned [this malicious act] in the severest terms."[42]

The search for blacks and their rifles continued until about 2:00 A.M. Twenty-nine were arrested, most found under the floorboards or in the cellars of nearby buildings. Doc Adams was among the few who had escaped capture. The Sweetwater Sabres were guarding the prisoners; all of the white men from Augusta had by now gone home. After ordering a detachment of South Carolinians to take the captives to Aiken for jailing, Butler set out for Edgefield.[43]

Those remaining with the blacks were disgruntled. "It was not a dear piece of work for us," one noted, "losing one of our best men and having only two negroes dead and another wounded." The group agreed "we could not have a story like that go out as a record of the night's work."[44]

Turning to Henry Getzen, one of the whites accosted by Adams on July 4, and the only man there who could identify the militia officers, they asked him to "designate those of the meanest character and most deserving for death." Getzen pointed to A. T. Attaway, who was pulled from the ranks and shot. David Phillips was the next to be killed, then Albert Minyard, Moses Parks, and Hampton Stevens, each a leader in the militia.[45]

When Pompey Curry was called, he bolted and fled. The whites fired, one bullet clipping him in the thigh. He fell as if dead. The whites assumed they had killed Pompey, but when they turned their attention to the remaining prisoners, the wounded black crawled into some high grass, and escaped execution.[46]

After having killed the militia's officers, the whites told the remaining blacks to run. They scattered, dodging a hailstorm of lead. Three of the twenty-three were wounded, but no more died.[47]

While the massacre was taking place, other whites were wreaking vengeance on the town. Stores were robbed, Rivers's house was ransacked, fences were town down, and the village wells ruined.[48]

Unaware that his orders to march the captives to Aiken had not been obeyed, Matthew rode home to Edgefield. He was still distraught, atypically unsettled by the confrontation. "He talked till late at night," his son, Frank, stated, "and the family was spellbound [by] his graphic discourse on the subject."[49]

Butler learned of the massacre the next morning at his law offices. Appalled, finally recognizing the folly of his actions, Matthew immediately took steps to avoid blame for the killings. "The collision was a sort of spontaneous combustion," he wrote in a letter to the *Augusta Chronicle and Sentinel*. "I was not the leader of this body of infuriated men, and I left [as] the crowd [was] arresting the negroes."[50] His statement was, of course, untrue.

Although Butler was trying to escape censure, Martin Gary was attempting to credit him for the massacre. "You've very effectively and handsomely demonstrated," he praised, "what could be done and must be done."[51]

Gary was right. Immediately after the incident, white opinion, which had been divided, joined in favor of a direct challenge to carpetbagger-scalawag-black rule. Most whites condemned the Hamburg killings, but they could not live with Chamberlain's response. He had been standing with one foot inside both the Democratic and Republican camps. Now he had to choose a side. He condemned Butler. Denouncing the Hamburg incident for "atrocity and barbarism, the triviality of the causes, and the inhuman spirit [marking] . . . its stages," the governor appealed to Grant to send troops to protect the blacks in South Carolina.[52]

Taking advantage of the coalescence of white hostility toward Chamberlain and his federal soldiers, Butler and Gary convinced the Democratic party to convene on August 15 in Columbia. Gary prepared for this meeting by conferring with Col. Sam Ferguson, who had come east from Mississippi to share his campaign experience with South Carolina. They developed a detailed, thirty-three step guide for winning the upcoming election, a plan to intimidate the blacks and expel the carpetbagger. Although most of the points were obvious things to do (e.g., offer old and helpless voters transportation to the polls), others were chilling in their demand for violence. "Never threaten a man individually," Gary stated, ". . . the necessities of the times require that he should die. A dead Radical is very harmless. . . . A threatened Radical [can be] often very troublesome, sometimes dangerous, always vindictive."[53]

No plan, however, could succeed without a viable candidate for governor. Wade Hampton was the obvious choice, but the former Confederate leader, spending the summer vacationing in the mountains near Cashiers, North Carolina, had said he would not run. Butler took on the task of wheedling his wartime commander to accept the call to campaign. Realizing that Hampton would never condone the violence called for in Gary's plan, Matthew deliberately omitted these details in a letter he composed to the potential nominee. He showed the note to Gary just before the two set out on a fox hunt.

"Goddamn!" his associate exclaimed, "that is a winning card!"[54]

Hampton, unaware that he was committing to an infamous plot, accepted the call. About this same time, a scheme was developing in Edgefield to assassinate Butler. Dick Lundy, the leader of the blacks who had planned the killing, openly bragged about their designs. When Butler's friends learned of his boasting, they quickly seized Lundy and tossed him in jail. He confessed, and the threat collapsed.[55]

Four days later, August 12, Chamberlain, accompanied by Robert Smalls, an illiterate black Congressman from Beaufort, and Judge Thomas J. Mackey, came to Edgefield to talk to the former slaves. But when he mounted the platform, the governor found his audience of 2,100 included 600 whites. Gary and Butler were present, and asked for equal time to speak. Chamberlain, naively thinking that an honest debate would ensue, acquiesced.[56]

The plan was to destroy the blacks' confidence in Chamberlain with insults to his face. So when the governor rose to speak, he was greeted with hoots and hollers, so many he could not complete his address. But when Butler started his speech, the crowd grew silent. He began by castigating the governor for his record in office. Matthew then pointed to Smalls. "There is the man," he bellowed, "who has [said I was] a leader of the Ku Klux. I dare him to open his lips on this stand today!" The whites roared. "Kill the damned son of a bitch!" one cried. "Kill the damn nigger!" another voice demanded.[57]

Judge Mackey calmed the crowd with humor by making fun of the attacks on Chamberlain and Smalls. Gary soon brought back the tensions. He berated Chamberlain with vicious personal assaults for twenty minutes, then turned to the mob to ask, "Must I hit him again?" "Yes!" came the answer. "You damn bald-headed renegade," Gary sneered, whirling around to face his quarry. "[You were] a bummer of Sherman's army."[58]

At this point Butler left the dais, supposedly to get a drink of water. His departure was the signal to a man, hiding behind the podium, to pull the props out from under the scaffold. Gary jumped clear as the stage collapsed, hurling the governor, Smalls, and Mackey to the ground. Thoroughly frightened, the Republican trio hurriedly left for Columbia, their humiliation duly noted by the host of startled and intimidated blacks.[59]

Encouraged by their successful assault on the governor, Butler and Gary hurried to Columbia on August 16 to attend the state Democratic convention. Matthew nominated Hampton as the straight-outs' candidate for governor. The number who favored an accommodation with Chamberlain had so ebbed, they were unable to mount an opposition. The former Confederate general won by acclamation.[60]

Hampton, having finally learned of Gary's plan, hoped to renounce violence toward the blacks during his acceptance speech. He found it impossible. "I intended to take issue with . . . the Edgefield Resolutions," he stated later, "but the convention sat down so hard on [them], there was no use saying a word."[61] He instead concentrated on offering his view of the task ahead. "My sole effort," he shouted, competing with tumultuous cheers, "shall be to restore . . . State government to decency, to honesty, to economy, and to integrity."[62]

And so the Red Shirt Campaign began. Butler's plan to deceive Hampton into following an antiblack approach toward winning the governorship had worked. But the ruse cost him the friendship of his former commander. Hampton would never forgive Matthew for his perfidy. "I was careful not to say one word of praise . . . for Butler," he wrote after the contest ended. "I certainly did not commend [him] for the campaign of '76."[63]

Chamberlain moved immediately to thwart the Democratic threat to his reelection. Grant had approved his appeal for federal troops, so on August 25, the governor ordered two companies of the 18th Infantry into Edgefield. He had assumed they would put a halt to the harassment that he had personally suffered during his visit earlier that month, but he never anticipated Butler's tactical response.

Matthew led an exultant welcome of white men and women, who met the soldiers with cheers as they entered town. They shouted heartfelt thanks for coming to protect *them* from unwarranted assaults from their exslaves. The black leaders, at first dumfounded by this reception, attempted to get the troops' attention, shouting that *they* were the ones in need of safekeeping, but were "unnoticed and elbowed aside."[64]

The Federal force had expected to be greeted by sullen rebels, who would resent their coming, so they, too, were at first astonished by the greeting. The soldiers quickly saw through Butler's strategy, however, and "grinned broadly" in "keen appreciation of a good joke."[65] The whites continued to court the infantrymen with friendship through the following weeks, causing one Republican to glumly write, "Sending troops does no good. They like troops. The more . . . they get the better they are pleased."[66] Chamberlain's plans to use military force to assure his reelection had failed.

The Red Shirt, the symbol for overthrowing carpetbagger-scalawag-black rule for South Carolina, was first used on September 5. An all black Hamburg grand jury had met and indicted seventy-eight whites, including

Butler, for the July 8 murders. The defendants, accompanied by about a thousand mounted men, rode to Aiken to surrender for the trial. Many wore red (bloody) shirts as a sign of defiance. Judge Pierce L. Wiggin, no doubt intimidated by this hostile mob, postponed the hearings until after the election. Bail was set and paid. Matthew and his accomplices returned home in triumph.[67]

Hampton visited every county throughout the state, and each meeting followed a similar pattern. Riders wearing red shirts would greet the candidate at the outskirts of town to accompany him to the speakers' platform. As he trotted into the village, Hampton was saluted by bands, who had "learned to play with some success a single tune—two or three others with less." Whites and blacks from miles around had massed for the occasion, and when Hampton started to force his path through the crowds toward the dais, the air was filled with clamorous cheering. The stands were smothered with flowers, draped in bunting, and adorned by a beautiful girl, wearing a costume representing Liberty. Prominent locals opened the affair with speeches, and then Hampton gave his talk, which included assurances to the blacks in the audience they would not suffer when he was governor. His words no doubt rang hollow, given the mounted Red Shirts who surrounded the gathering. A free barbecue followed.[68]

Butler attended only six political meetings (Lexington, Greenville, two at Edgefield, Winnsboro, and Marion).[69] His lack of a more leading role was no doubt due to his falling-out with Hampton. Alexander C. Haskell, the party chairman, made the complete tour, attending to the details for all of Hampton's appearances.

The speaking and pageantry were not the principal goal of the gatherings. As one attendee related, "The demonstration of the men on horseback, to impress the negro, was the real object. . . . The Red Shirts and the Rebel yells were . . . arguments (they) understood."[70]

Intimidation of the blacks was central to Gary's plans. He was racist, and given free rein, would most likely have committed some travesty that would have ruined the campaign. But he was held in check by Butler, who with usual "coolness and deliberation, acted as the governing wheel."[71] In July, for example, Francis W. Dawson, the editor of the *Charleston News and Courier*, rebuked Gary for his bigoted views. Gary challenged the newspaper man to a duel. Butler quickly intervened, and calmed both parties.[72]

On September 16 the Republicans convened and nominated Chamberlain as their candidate for governor. His was an unpopular choice to party dissidents. Elliott, the corrupt, black Speaker of the House, led a group that was peeved over being hindered from reaping graft. They held up proceedings for fourteen hours before allowing a vote. Chamberlain took 70 percent of the ballots, but the victory was marred by the inclusion of Elliott and carpetbagger Thomas C. Dunn, both bitter enemies of his, on the state ticket.[73]

The governor continued the campaigning, started before his nomination, and in most instances, met the same problems (Gary's plan) first encountered at Edgefield. A local Democratic leader would accost him prior to a meeting and demand equal time in addressing the audience. Chamberlain would agree. As he stepped up to the podium, however, the governor was greeted by "companies of mounted white men [wearing red shirts], marching in martial order, and under the command of officers . . . who gave orders and were obeyed."[74] As he tried to speak, Chamberlain was interrupted with jeers and queries about Hamburg. "I will tell you about Hamburg," he angrily snapped back at Abbeville, "whereupon I heard distinctly the click of a considerable number of pistols."[75] He opted not to continue with his comments.

Finally fed up with the intimidation, Chamberlain sent out a decree on October 7 forbidding "the existence of all . . . organizations . . . known as Rifle Clubs."[76] Butler and his friends had no intentions of obeying the order, but complied in a comical fashion. They simply changed the names of the groups, switching to ludicrous titles such as "The Allendale Mounted Baseball Club, the Baptist Church Sewing Circle, or Mother's Little Helpers."[77]

On October 14 Chamberlain returned to Edgefield for another attempt at swaying blacks into voting the Republican ticket. The meeting was held in Academy Grove, a field outside the village near an abandoned schoolhouse. Few whites were present at the start. Shortly thereafter, Butler rode up to request that his men be allowed to attend the session. Colonel Low, commander of the federal troops protecting the participants, agreed, but only if Matthew bore the responsibility for their actions.

"In a few moments," an observer recalled, "the cavalry commenced filing down the hill . . . fifteen hundred riding four abreast . . . [to] make a complete circle right around the meeting. . . . The [podium] was in the center, and they . . . surrounded it . . . they all wore red shirts, [and had] no arms except for pistols, strapped . . . [inside] a belt."[78] Following Matthew's orders, no one disrupted the speakers. The blacks, however, could not help but fear for their lives and the Republican cause.

Some blacks, particularly in the Low Country, were not intimidated by the Red Shirts' bullying. They battled back. Examples include the September 6 Charleston riot, where a mob of angry blacks wounded about fifty whites; a September 15 confrontation near Ellinton, where blacks fought a two-day battle with whites, resulting in forty-one total casualties; and on

Edgefield County Courthouse. PHOTO BY THE AUTHOR

October 15 at Cainhoy, located thirty miles inland and upriver from Charleston, where black militia disrupted a joint political rally. Six whites were killed and sixteen were wounded.[79]

Taking note of the escalating violence, Chamberlain requested more Federal troops, and on October 17 Grant sent "all available forces" in the Atlantic military division into South Carolina. The troops were dispersed throughout the state.[80]

The election took place on November 7. In Edgefield Butler arrived at the courthouse (one of two polling places) about 6:30 A.M. He found a scene that was probably typical throughout South Carolina. Red Shirts were posted on horseback in the courthouse square. "They would gallop from box to box . . . yelling and brandishing their pistols . . . to prevent Republicans from voting," a local black, Paris Simpkins, recalled. "I [knew] that if I voted the Republican ticket, I would be murdered." He then claimed that many of the whites cast multiple ballots. "There were 3,000 votes polled over and above what we [in Edgefield] were legally entitled to by the census, which was recently taken."[81]

The U.S. troops were, of course, on hand, but the plan to win their friendship had paid off. Most sympathized with the whites, so as long as Matthew's men remained nonviolent, they allowed interference with black voters to continue.[82]

The ballot count was revealed on November 17, and to no one's surprise, both parties declared a victory. Hampton received 92,261 votes against

Chamberlain's 91,127. Samuel J. Tilden, the Democratic candidate, won the race for U.S. president. The Board of Canvassers, however, all Republicans, citing fraud in three upstate counties, threw out their votes, giving Chamberlain the governorship and Rutherford B. Hayes the state's electoral college votes.[83]

The official tally would be determined by the combined assembly, where confusion also reigned. The Democrats had a majority in the House, 64 of the 124 seats; the Republicans dominated the Senate, 18 of the 33 posts. Hampton had a one-vote advantage, which assured him the governorship. But the opposition again cited fraud, and by withholding accreditation to five Democrats elected from Edgefield County and three from nearby Laurens, the Republicans hoped to control the assembly and elect Chamberlain as governor. The legislative battle began on November 28.[84]

CHAPTER 22

Redemption Day

Although Butler had not run or been elected to a state office, he went to Columbia to attend the opening session of the legislature. He served as an aide to Hampton. The two would be forever estranged over Matthew's less than truthful letter inducing his former commander to run for governor as a straight-out candidate, but they had made a chilly peace.

The legislature met November 28, 1876. All of the senators were allowed to enter the capitol, but the U.S. troops posted at the doors, installed by Chamberlain to keep order, refused to permit the "fraudulently elected" representatives from Edgefield and Laurens counties to set foot in the house chambers. All sixty-four Democratic assemblymen then walked to nearby Carolina Hall, formally convened, and elected William H. Wallace as their Speaker. The fifty-nine Republican representatives stayed in the capitol, where they organized, then selected E. W. M. Mackey as their Speaker.[1]

When word of the snub to the Edgefield representatives reached the village, Butler's peers were infuriated, and began preparing to march to Columbia to confront the soldiers denying their spokesmen their seats. Matthew heard of their intentions, and he sent a note urging caution. "Be quiet . . . stay away from Columbia," he related. "We [don't] intend to fight the U.S. troops . . . the majority . . . are still with us."[2]

Two days later, early in the morning before the troops had assumed their post, the Democratic representatives moved into the house chamber. The Republicans arrived about noon. Both claimed they were the rightful occupants, and both proceeded to carry out the state's business, speakers shouting to be heard above each other's din. Afraid of losing their position, everyone remained inside of the capitol for four days. "The negroes sang, danced and kept up their wild junketing," one participant recalled. "[Our] meals came through windows from friends outside."[3] The obstinate representatives slept on the floor at night.

Chamberlain appealed to General T. H. Ruger, commander of the federal soldiers, to evict the "illegal" members from Edgefield and Laurens, but he refused, noting that his only authority was to keep the peace. The governor then sought a more violent solution. He summoned a black militia company from Charleston, the Hunkidori Club, 100 men, to the capital to forcibly oust the Democrats. When Hampton heard of the scheme, he called his Red Shirts to Columbia. Almost 6,000 reached the city within twenty-four hours. An armed conflict was imminent.[4]

Butler took command of the incoming whites. "He keeps a watchful . . . and a loving eye upon them," one reporter said. "A word from him, they become like sucking doves."[5]

But not for long. The Red Shirts decided on their own to storm the capitol to evict the Republicans. But when the mob reached the building, they found Hampton blocking their path. "Go home quietly," he implored. "You've made me your Governor, and by . . . God, I will be your Governor! Trust me!" Wallace and his followers then voluntarily left the capitol, and returned to Carolina Hall. The crowd dispersed.[6]

On December 5 the Senate and the Republican members of the house met in joint session and proclaimed Chamberlain governor. He was installed on December 7. The Democrats, both senators and representatives, assembled shortly thereafter, and proclaimed Hampton governor. He was inaugurated on December 14.[7]

South Carolina thus had two governments. The decision as to which was legitimate was left to the courts. On December 6 the state supreme court ruled that Chamberlain's election was invalid, saying that the Board of Canvassers had no right to reject ballots; they further noted that the Republican house lacked a quorum and thus had no authority.[8]

Subsequent decisions also supported Hampton. Both, acting as governor, pardoned convicts. The courts upheld Hampton's amnesty in two instances (Amzi Rosborough and Tilda Norris), thus recognizing his authority; they ruled that Chamberlain "had no rights" to reprieve Peter Smith.[9]

More important, the Democrats found a way of using the courts to cut off funding for Chamberlain. They obtained an injunction, prohibiting the banks from honoring withdrawals by the Republicans. Hampton, too, was barred from obtaining the state's money, but he appealed to taxpayers to give him one-tenth of their annual bill. Almost $120,000 poured into the Democratic coffers.[10]

On December 20 the Democratic assembly met to elect a U.S. senator to succeed Thomas Robertson. Butler and Samuel McGowan were nominated, and Matthew was selected on the first ballot, winning 64 of the 79 votes. The Republicans elected David Corbin, former state senator and chief prosecutor during the Ku Klux Klan trials, to the same post. Following the usual Radical fraudulent practice, the latter spent $20,000 in bribes to influence the balloting.[11]

Both legislatures adjourned December 22. Both governors continued their rule. Despite Hampton's success in the courts and obtaining funds to run the state, Chamberlain remained adamant on holding his position. The only element in his favor was the military, which continued to keep the Democrats from occupying either the chief executive's office or the capitol. Removal of the federal soldiers was the key to returning South Carolina to white supremacy.

The president would make this decision, but the office was essentially vacant. Grant was leaving; his replacement was in doubt. Tilden had probably won, but his majority in Florida, Louisiana, and South Carolina was disputed. If all three states' electoral votes were unjustly passed to Hayes, he would gain the presidency.

John B. Gordon, the former Confederate general and now a senator from Georgia, saw an opportunity to take advantage of this situation and strike a deal. He approached Hampton, meeting with the would-be governor, Matthew, and other state leaders in Abbeville, South Carolina. Their conference, so secret that none of those participating would ever admit attending, was held at the Noble mansion, the same house that Jefferson Davis had used for the last caucus of his cabinet. Gordon proposed a bargain: South Carolina would give Hayes their electorial vote in exchange for his withdrawing federal troops from the state. Hampton, Butler, and their comrades accepted the pact.[12]

Gordon took this deal to Hayes, and he, too, agreed to the trade.[13] All that remained was for Congress to meet and tally the electoral ballots.

The legislature had established a procedure to resolve which of the two ballots (one favoring Tilden, the other for Hayes) submitted by three Southern states would be accepted. They set up a commission, composed of five justices from the Supreme Court (two Democrats, two Republicans, and one independent), five Senators (two Democrats and three Republicans), and five Representatives, (three Democrats and two Republicans), to make this decision.[14]

Tilden had an advantage with this arrangement, but the Republicans found a means to tip the scales their way. They elected David Davis, the nonpartisan court justice probably favoring Tilden, to the Senate. His seat on the commission was assigned to Justice Joseph P. Bradley, one of Hayes's advocates.[15] Congress met February 1 to start the tally.

Two days later the disputed return from Florida arose, and was submitted to the Republican-biased commission. They ruled in Hayes's favor. The count proceeded slowly. On February 16, Louisiana's contested votes went to Hayes. Only South Carolina's ballots remained under question, and there was no doubt they would be awarded to Hayes. The trade that Gordon had negotiated was no longer necessary. The Federal troops might well remain in South Carolina.[16]

Gordon, however, forced Hayes into keeping his bargain. He threatened to start a filibuster that would extend beyond March 4, the day that Grant's term expired. The election would stay undecided, the nation would not have a president. But if the Republicans promised to withdraw U.S. troops from the South, Gordon would step aside and allow Hayes's inauguration. They agreed. And on March 2, Hayes took the oath as president.[17]

Butler immediately headed for Washington to attend the Special Session of the Senate, called for the purpose of inaugurating Hayes. He planned to present his credentials as South Carolina's senator, and to assume his office. Corbin, too, went to the capital, expecting the Republican majority to seat him. The deal that gave the presidency to Hayes had not included representation in the nation's upper house.

When Butler reached Washington, he took up quarters in a two-room, ground floor flat, located on "F" Street between Thirteenth and Fourteenth Streets. He soon discovered that his notoriety for liking ladies had proceeded him. Corbin's cronies planned to entrap him in a compromising stance with a woman of the demi-monde, catch him in the act, and destroy both his reputation and any chance of his winning the South Carolina senate seat.

Fortunately for Butler, he learned about the plot, and proceeded to set a snare of his own. He enlisted the aid of an old friend, former Confederate Naval officer James M. Morgan. On the night scheduled for the harlot's call, Matthew hid in the bedroom; Morgan waited in the parlor.

"A heavily veiled woman [soon] boldly entered [without a knock]," Morgan recalled, "and seemed considerably excited when she found me alone in the room."

"Where is General Butler?" she demanded.

"He knows all about this conspiracy. Take a seat, and you'll probably see some fun when your friends arrive."

She decided to flee instead, and started for the front door. Morgan intercepted her path, and guided the woman out through the back so she would not encounter and tip off the conspirators, no doubt close behind.

Butler and Morgan quickly exchanged places. And a few moments later, five "carpetbaggers" burst into the room.

"What do you mean by this intrusion?" Butler exclaimed as he struggled to rise. His stump was bothering him, so he was not wearing his artificial limb and was using crutches.

His intruders were so flushed with hilarity, they took no note of Matthew's indignation. Two sped across the floor, threw open the door to the bedroom, and then fell back with astonishment at seeing Morgan, alone, reclining on a settee. He jumped up, lifted a chair, and began brandishing it as a weapon.

"Butler," Morgan remembered, "was hopping about on one crutch while making menacing flourishes in the air with the other. He [used] a most highly sulphurated vocabulary when his angry passions were aroused, and was [employing] it with unstinted prodigality."

The flustered interlopers thought now only of escaping the room. "They did not stand on any order of their going," Morgan wrote, "but struggled among themselves for the honor of . . . first to reach the street. Thus ended the adventure of the veiled lady."[18]

On March 4, the Special Session of the Senate met to induct their newly elected members. Twenty-one were seated, but neither Butler nor Corbin were installed. The decision as to which was entitled to represent South Carolina was delayed until after the Committee on Privileges and Elections had reviewed the credentials and made their recommendation. And they would not meet until the fall.[19]

Butler returned to Edgefield, but he was soon en route back to Washington. He accompanied Hampton, summoned to the capital by the president. Their trip was like a triumphant procession, crowds greeting them with ovations at every stop along the way. They met with Hayes on March 28. Chamberlain, too, saw the president. "My opponent," he stated, "is fully prepared . . . to overthrow the government . . . I represent." Hayes, however, was not impressed, not even sympathetic. He had made a deal with South Carolina, and kept his word. On April 2 he ordered the federal troops to leave the state. And upon Hampton's return to Columbia, he found the offices of the governor vacant, except for a clerk, who gave him the state seal. It was Redemption Day. Reconstruction had finally ended.[20]

Since he could do nothing politically until the Senate met in November, Butler returned home to resume his practice of law. He found himself a hero, as evidenced by an ad run by a local haberdasher. "M. C. Butler . . . hats for sale," the copy read, "gotten up in the latest and handsomest style of the season . . . straw with a wide brim."[21]

Butler also resumed his role as a planter, and in that capacity, continued to perform as president of the Edgefield Agricultural Society. He appointed twenty-one local men to attend a statewide meeting in Anderson that August. "We're not a very lively body," he noted, "but still have vitality enough to be recognized."[22]

Upon his return to Washington that fall, Butler rented the same rooms at 1219 F Street that he had used last March. Frank, his nineteen-year-old son, accompanied him to act as his secretary. The lad had successfully completed two years at Wofford College, and given his interest in politics, was probably rewarded for his effort with a short stint in the capital.[23]

The committee on Privileges and Elections had returned to Washington that October, but after five weeks of meetings and discussions, they had yet to take up the case of *Butler v. Corbin*. There was no question who had won; the problem was a reluctance by the Republican majority to add more Democrats to their opposition.

Butler quickly took charge of the campaign to seat himself as a senator from South Carolina. Although not allowed on the Senate floor, he set up headquarters in an adjoining cloakroom, where he managed the effort of supporters.[24] His main advocate was the carpetbagger from South Carolina, the state's other senator, Republican "Honest John" Patterson.

Under ordinary circumstances, Patterson would not have been in Butler's camp. He had been given, however, a powerful incentive. If Patterson led the battle to seat Matthew, he would not be prosecuted (and no doubt convicted) in South Carolina for corruption.[25]

Patterson had other reasons for supporting Butler. He knew that his political life in South Carolina was over, and that his future lay in returning to Pennsylvania, where the Cameron family held control. When Simon Cameron was senator in the 1840's, Andrew Butler, Matthew's uncle, had stood by him during a difficulty, a debt of honor that had never been repaid. Cameron's son was now senator, and he was bound to fulfill his family's obligation to the Butlers. He used his influence to pressure Patterson into endorsing Matthew.[26]

The game began on November 20, 1877, with a motion from Allen G. Thurman, Democratic senator from Ohio, to discharge the Committee on Privileges and Election from consideration of Butler's qualifications. "There has been more time given [them] for committee work than I ever knew," he noted, "yet . . . [they have] adjourned day after day after sitting half an hour to an hour and a half . . . and gone . . . enjoying themselves in this beautiful weather . . . to the theater at night . . . and to the horse-races."[27] He asked that the whole Senate vote on whether to seat Matthew.

The chairman of the committee, Republican senator Bainbridge Wadleigh of New Hampshire, offered a vigorous defense of his group's delay. "I say to the Senator from Ohio," he bristled, ". . . my Committee . . . has not been remiss in the performance of its duty."[28]

The debate over Thurman's motion dragged on for days. And Patterson took advantage of this chance to speak by offering his reasons for supporting Butler. "I would sooner lose my right arm than do anything [that decreased] the supremacy of the Republican party," he announced, "but I am voting to carry out the will . . . of the people, whom I have the honor to represent. . . . They believe [Butler] was elected. The courts have decided that the Legislature which elected him is legal . . . and I am bound by their mandate."[29]

George F. Edmunds of Vermont, one of the radical Republicans, sneered at Patterson's virtuous stance. "Statements in the public press [say]," he bellowed, "that he should go to the penitentiary unless he should vote to admit a certain claimant."[30]

Gordon rose to defend Patterson. "I wish to place the Senator upon notice," he coldly addressed Edmunds. "If corruption is to be charged by insinuation and innuendo . . . upon like evidence I could convict Republican Senators of . . . seeking to change the very sanctuary of justice into an altar of sacrifice for a Senator who dared to break through the lines of party and vote according to . . . his conscience."[31]

"I am very glad," Edmunds replied, "that my friend has put that little speech into the midst of mine. . . . [But] it is not well for the Senators to put on night gowns of morality and draw it over the top of their heads and say, 'Don't look at me.' It might be too scant in the skirts for that."[32]

Following this insulting exchange, the Senate finally acted on Thurman's motion to dismiss Wadleigh's committee so the full body could consider Butler's credentials. The proposal passed on November 26 by two votes.[33]

In the debates that followed, Sen. Aaron A. Sargent of California led the assault on Butler by using the Hamburg massacre to discredit his character.[34] Similar charges had recently appeared in newspapers. "He is a man of low origin and habits," the *Chicago Times* had written back in May, "as of the overseer and slave dealer class . . . conspicuous for his brutality to negroes, an importer of Russian bloodhounds to hunt down runaway slaves."[35]

Butler had anticipated Sargent's assaults, and through Gordon, introduced a statement from Edgefield blacks attesting to his benefic character. "We, the undersigned colored people . . . state that most of us have known General M. C. Butler from the days of his boyhood," they averred. "He was one of the first to recognize . . . our freedom from slavery, and again and again has defended our race in the courts . . . without pay. . . . We know nothing [about] the Hamburg difficulty, but from intimate knowledge of General Butler's character, know that he is not capable of counseling or aiding in such riots."[36]

On November 30 Thurman ended the hearings by moving that "M. C. Butler of South Carolina be sworn in as Senator." The assembly was polled; Matthew was confirmed by one vote. Cameron knew that Butler would win, so despite the pressures he had placed on Patterson, the Pennsylvanian protected his Republican image by casting a negative ballot.[37]

Butler took his seat (the worst in the chamber, placed farthest from the dais) on November 30, 1877. He received appointment to only one committee (Military Affairs), which emphasized the inferior role the Republican majority saw for him.[38]

The Senate probably expected Butler to sit quietly and take no part in the debates that followed. If so, they were mistaken. Matthew would not hesitate to rise to refute any challenge to himself or his state. "I never seek controversies of any kind," he wrote in a note to Edward Wells, "but when others *insist* on forcing one on me, I shall not decline it."[39]

Soon after taking his seat, Butler introduced a resolution demanding formal Senate investigation of the assertions by Edmunds that Matthew had obtained support from Patterson in exchange for not filing charges of personal graft against the carpetbagger. Others stepped into the breach.

"A debate . . . is not business," James G. Blaine declared. "If the Senate adopts this resolution, nothing [else can] be done. . . . The Senator from South Carolina has gained all . . . he could gain . . . by showing his willingness . . . for the investigation. . . . The matter should stop . . . here."

"I have invited the investigation," Butler stated. "I have not urged it."[40] His resolution was accepted, but discussion postponed. The Senate adjourned that same day, and the issue was never raised again.

CHAPTER 23

U.S. Senator

Upon his return to Washington, in early January 1878, to take up his duties as a senator, Butler rented a house at 1219 F. Street, NW.[1] Maria and the girls accompanied him to the capital; all the boys were away at school, Frank in his third year at Wofford College, Willie and Cabby at the Carolina Military Institute.

Butler found his job overwhelming, his office besieged with letters from constituents. Some sought federal employment, others asked him to petition the Senate to fund local projects or to solve their personal problems (receive a pension, obtain amnesty from the Fourteenth Amendment, recover property confiscated during the war), and many simply wanted his advice on a profusion of subjects. "I shall not be surprised," Matthew said to George B. Lorning, "if I receive an enquiry as to the best method of adjusting a baby's diaper."[2]

Obtaining legislative favors for his constituents from South Carolina was difficult for Matthew since he had little sway with the Senate. He was both a member of the minority party and worse yet, a newcomer with no "chits" to cash from prior associations. And he suffered from a personal stigma. Butler's reputation was stained by the Red Shirt Campaign in general and the Hamburg massacre in particular. He soon realized that his attempts to gain individual's patronage would be frustrated. "I wrote you that you had been nominated and would be confirmed a Supervisor of the Census," he notified one office seeker, "[but] yesterday, this miserable creature [Hayes] in the White House withdrew your name. Why I cannot comprehend. . . . I cannot express my disgust."[3]

Butler did, however, find success in directing federal money to his state's coffers. During this second session of the Forty-fifth Congress, he obtained $5,000 to improve the navigation of the Pee Dee River; $20,000 for constructing a lighthouse on Paris Island; $1,500 in tariff reductions, imposed on bells for St. Michael's church in Charleston; and $200,000 for

Sen. Matthew Calbraith Butler. COURTESY LIBRARY OF CONGRESS

clearing Charleston harbor. "[He has achieved] more," the *Edgefield Avertiser* wrote, "than has been accomplished for the State in the past fifty years."[4]

The Charleston project provides an interesting example of Butler's political skills. The port was blocked by sands that had shifted into the main channel. The available draw at low tide was barely thirteen feet. Although the Corps of Engineers had received approval to resolve the problem, the 1878 federal budget provided only $5,000, not enough to even design a solution, much less clear the passage. Most would have raised a vocal complaint in Congress, but Matthew chose a more subtle approach. "I found emollients more effective in overcoming opposition," he stated, "than firecrackers and invective."

When Captain Eads, an engineer responsible for solving a similar problem on the Mississippi River, came to Washington to report his success, Butler took him aside and talked Eads into accompanying him to Charleston to look at the harbor. This visit ired the local project manager, Gen. Quincy Gillmore, who was upset over the inference he was incapable to opening a path through the channel. He appealed to his superior in Washington, who "found" $40,000 to fund a design of underwater jetties to clear the sand. Gillmore's ideas were sent to the Army Board of Engineers, who obtained approval by the War Department. Sec. George W. McCray recommended the plan to Congress. With the impetus for the project coming from Republican sources, Butler's enemies had no reason for objecting to the resulting $200,000 amendment (attached to an annual Rivers and Harbor bill), which passed with little opposition.

Later, when his influence had improved, Butler managed to put this port project on a continuing appropriation plan, which eliminated year-to-year debates for funding approvals. Almost $2 million was eventually spent to clear a twenty-six-foot low tide channel, making Charleston one of the world's busiest harbors.[5]

Matthew fit well into Washington's social scene. Tall, handsome, armed with Southern gentility and blessed with an attractive wife, he was a frequent guest at the many capital parties. "I have met Senator Butler . . . at some dinners," one observer wrote, "[He] is a great favorite in society here."[6]

Maria enjoyed the attention given her husband, and she played her role as the grande dame. She joined exclusive St. John's Episcopal Church, but in an unusual burst of economy, purchased only one seat in a front pew. While she sat through the sermons, her girls stood in the back of the sanctuary.[7]

Although Butler was fully occupied with Washington, he kept up with the political scene in South Carolina. Hampton was running for reelection in the fall, and Matthew was upset with rumors that the governor might accept a fusion with the Radicals. "If . . . steps should be taken by anybody to change or subvert the policy by which we carried the state [in] the last election," he said in an April 3 note to Martin Gary, "[then] he [should] be eternally damned by the people of the state."[8]

Congress adjourned on June 20. Matthew hurried back to South Carolina to assist in securing Hampton's reelection as governor. He found the contest already over. The Republicans offered no opposition. Butler took his entire family on a vacation to West Virginia (White Sulphur Springs) that August,[9] then came home to campaign. His talk at a rally in Edgefield on October 31 was met with such prolonged applause, it "almost precluded the possibility of his saying aught in acknowledgment. . . . He warned his hearers against over-confidence," a reporter continued, "and impressed all with the necessity of working with as much zeal as they displayed two years ago. . . . The 'amens' were numerous and hearty. . . . Any independent candidate . . . in this county will have cause to congratulate himself if he escapes a coat of tar and feathers."[10]

Hampton was elected November 6 by a tally of 169,550 to 213. But the next day, while hunting deer, he was thrown off the mule he was riding, and suffered a broken leg. The wound festered. As Hampton lay presumably dying, his duties were assumed by the lieutenant governor, William D. Simpson. December 10, the day that Hampton's leg was amputated, the legislature met and named him U.S. senator, replacing the carpetbagger, John J. Patterson, whose term was ending that month.[11]

Gary had expected that place for himself, a reward for past efforts in behalf of the party. He was already at odds with Hampton's benevolent attitude with blacks, and found this latest slight his rationale to offer open opposition to the regular Democratic leadership, including his old friend and neighbor, Matthew.[12]

When Butler returned to Washington in December for the third session of the Forty-fifth Congress, Maria remained in Edgefield. The Democrats had won control of both the House and the Senate in the elections last fall, and the lame-duck Republican legislature was expected to sit for only a month or so. Matthew took rooms in the Metropolitan Hotel.[13]

At the start of the session, Butler was appointed to a select committee to investigate new transportation routes to the seaboard.[14] He no doubt relished the assignment, since it opened the opportunity for him to influence the railroads into running track through South Carolina, an interest that he had been pursuing for years. Matthew had only started on this effort when his attention was diverted to an explosive, partisan issue.

On December 16 James G. Blaine of Maine presented a resolution to assemble a committee to look into charges that in the Southern states, the "rights of suffrage for [black] citizens . . . were denied by [the] violence or threats of armed [white] men." His motion was based on an 1871 law, banning the presence of men bearing weapons at the polls.

Butler immediately challenged Blaine by introducing an amendment to his resolution demanding that "the committee be instructed to sit with open doors."

"One of the troubles in the whole investigation of the Southern question," Blaine objected, "has been that the very men who were intimidated at the polls were still more intimidated on the witness stand."

"[Blaine's allegation] . . . is entirely without any proof to sustain it," Butler countered. "If [the Senator] desires . . . a free, full, complete, thorough . . . investigation . . . I cannot see why he should object to my amendment."

"I have had as many as two hundred letters . . . giving details of great outrages upon the right of suffrage."

"The Senator [noted] the other day . . . that he based his statements upon the newspapers of the country. . . . If he based his statements upon the . . . press alone, he and I should have been hung and quartered long ago."

The Senate exploded with laughter over Butler's clever riposte, but he was not smiling. "I could go into his state with a corps of detectives," he threatened, "and . . . make his state a stench in the nostrils of the civilized world."

"Do it," Blaine replied.

"I could do that," Butler answered, "but [it is] wrong . . . for any committee . . . to sit and take testimony with closed doors upon any subject which affects the people."[15]

In a partisan vote, Butler's attempt to amend Blaine's resolution was defeated. A committee was formed to investigate election fraud in the South. Matthew, however, gained the chance to counter this group. He was named as head of a committee to investigate similar practices in the North. In a series of meetings in Providence, Rhode Island, Butler was able to prove widespread abuse. "They say they have never seen an election since 1860 where money was not used," a reporter wrote. "The Greenback candidate for governor in the last election testified . . . that he [was paid] ten dollars for his vote. . . . When asked if [accepting a bribe was] wrong, he said, no, that everybody did it."[16] Matthew's findings were sure to offset the effects of misdeeds that Blaine would no doubt uncover below the Mason-Dixon line.

Congress adjourned March 3, 1879, then reconvened just two weeks later to start the Forty-sixth Session. Since his party was in power, Butler gained considerable stature. He was assigned a new seat (no. 22) in the second row, left of and close to the dais, and made chairman of the important Civil Service and Retrenchment Committee. Matthew was also placed in two other committees, the District of Columbia and Territories. Hampton, still in South Carolina, recuperating from his amputation, took Butler's spot on Military Affairs.[17]

The highlight of the session was the continuing debate over the Southern use of force to thwart blacks from casting a ballot in election. Butler was not about to concede anything to the Republicans, and he rose to challenge claims by Iowa senator William B. Allison.

"I would be obliged," he responded to one of Allison's allegations, "if he would state where there was any force of armed men at the polls in 1878 in South Carolina."

"Certainly . . ." Allison replied, only to be interrupted by one of his advocates, Henry M. Teller of Colorado.

"The reference," Teller noted, "is to an occurrence in Louisiana, not South Carolina."

"I do not," Allison admitted, "impute to South Carolina what did not occur there."

"Then I have nothing to say," Butler replied.

Teller then alleged that in South Carolina, the number of polling places had been cut back to make it difficult for blacks to vote. Butler again leaped to his feet.

"There is ample opportunity," he professed, "for every voter . . . to cast a ballot without the slightest molestation."

"Is it not a fact," Teller countered, "that there were less voting places . . . now than . . . twenty years ago?"

"No, Sir; that is not a fact."

"The testimony [before our committee] so shows. . . ."

"That is not a fact."

The next day, Butler took on Blaine. The senator from Maine introduced evidence that black voters had been refused the right to cast a ballot in Sumter County, South Carolina. "'[An armed man] said to me'" Blaine quoted a black witness as saying, "'get away. . . . What business you got here?'"

"Within the last three days," Butler was quick to note, "an acquittal has been ordered in the United States court at Charleston on just testimony as that."

"Owing to a technical defect in the indictment," Blaine claimed.

"No, Sir."

"I think so entirely."

"The senator is entirely mistaken."[18]

These exchanges probably did not lessen the effects of evidence of voter abuse in South Carolina that Blaine introduced. They did reveal, however, that Butler was not about to be intimidated, and that he had become one of the leading spokesmen for the South.

The first session of the Forty-sixth Congress ended on July 1, 1879, and Matthew returned to Edgefield to celebrate Frank's graduation from Wofford College. The lad had ended his schooling on an uneven note. He scored 80 or higher for Latin, English, and History, but only in the 60s for Greek, Literature, and Rhetoric.[19] Frank left home again that fall to attend the Medical College of Charleston, where he began his training to be a doctor. Willie, too, left Edgefield to study law at Princeton University.[20]

In December, Butler, Maria, and the two girls went back to Washington for the Second Session of the Forty-sixth Congress. They rented a place at 210 North Capital.[21]

Matthew now assumed a more positive role in the Senate. As a member of the District of Columbia Committee, he introduced three bills: providing money for conducting local government's affairs, legalizing the health ordinances for the capital, and regulating the use and preventing the waste of water from the Potomac River.[22] He represented the Committee on Territories by proposing an act to reapportion the legislatures for Montana, Idaho, and Wyoming, which was passed by the Senate.[23] And he continued his efforts on behalf of his constituents. Matthew obtained government approval for the transfer of arsenal property in Charleston to Holy Communion Church, funding for the design and raising of a statue at Spartanburg to honor the Revolutionary War hero, Gen. Daniel Morgan, and consideration of a new courthouse and post office in Greenville.[24]

Congress adjourned on June 1, 1880, and Butler hurried home to start the fall political campaign. He began by giving advice to John Dargan, a Democratic dignitary, on a way to counter Gary's attempts to take over the party. "If [we] postpone [our nominations] until about six weeks before the election," he related, "the opposition will not have time to organize."[25] Dargan and the other leaders ignored Butler's suggestion, but it made no difference. Gary could not raise support for his schemes.

Butler then traveled to Cincinnati, Ohio, to attend the Democratic National Convention. On June 23 he joined the rest of the delegation in nominating Winfield Scott Hancocok, a prominent Union general, as their candidate for president.[26] His opponent, James Abram Garfield, also a Northern general, but one who had gained little fame during the Civil War, had been named earlier as the Republican runner at their convention in Chicago.[27]

Hancock was an outstanding orator, and might well have won the presidency. But he considered it unseemly to openly campaign for office, so he remained at home, serving in the army, while Garfield stumped the country. The election that fall was a toss-up. If Hancock had captured New York, then he would have succeeded Hayes. Garfield, however, prevailed by 12,000 votes in that state, and it gave him the office.[28]

Butler, like Hancock, did not campaign. The South was sure to go Democratic, so there was no need for him to speak out against Garfield. And Johnson Hagood, representing the "Bourbons," Matthew's peers, was unopposed for the governorship.[29] That December, Matthew, Maria, and their daughters returned north to 210 North Capital for the final meeting of the Forty-sixth Congress.

Like most lame-duck sessions, the legislators did not produce much of importance. Butler introduced a bill asking for the punishment of tramps in the District; and he submitted the usual number of resolutions in behalf of his people back home. One called for the restoration of silverware, stolen by Sherman's troops from Isabella McRae; another, requested by the Sons of Temperance, asked for a constitutional amendment to ban the manufacture and sale of alcoholic beverages.[30] Matthew, who liked his liquor, must have entered this appeal with tongue in cheek.

Butler also continued standing up for the South. When Sen. Roscoe Conkling of New York began pouring insults on his state, Matthew rose to blast the Republican for having "swaggering insolence." Conkling answered in kind, and some said that "his setting down on Senator Butler was unusually heavy." Matthew could care less. South Carolinians admired his display of courage. "He did just what had to be done," the *Edgefield Advertiser* stated, "and is patriotic enough to do it every time."[31]

In another instance, when the state was accused by the census superintendent of committing fraud, Butler introduced a resolution asking for an official report by the secretary of the interior that documented the charge. "Senator Butler is always alive to the interests of South Carolina," the local newspaper reported.[32]

Congress adjourned on March 3, 1881, but Butler stayed in Washington for the inauguration of President Garfield and to attend the special session of the Forty-seventh Congress, gathered to organize for their regular December meeting. He was shocked to learn that although the Democrats held a two-vote majority in the Senate, the Republicans were again back in power. There was a traitor in the ranks.

Virginia had elected a Democratic senator in 1880, but the party was divided over paying the state debt. The upper class, Butler's counterparts, favored reducing expenses and raising taxes to fund the payment of old obligations. Those representing the masses urged readjustment, repudiating the prewar share for West Virginia and the borrowing by carpetbaggers during Reconstruction; and claiming credit for the destruction caused by the Federal army during the Civil War.[33]

Three parties competed for the Virginia legislature in 1880: Republicans, Democratic Funders, and Democratic Readjusters. The latter won, and elected their leader, William Mahone, the former Confederate general, senator. Although a Democrat, he sided with the opposition in the Forty-seventh Congress. This produced a tie, which was broken in favor of the Republicans by Vice Pres. Chester A. Arthur's vote.[34]

Mahone was no doubt influenced by the promise of chairmanship of the Agriculture Committee and patronage positions for three of his cronies. Butler and the Democrats were infuriated, and Matthew led their accusation of "a disgraceful bargain."

"I say there has been no bargain," Ambrose E. Burnside, former Union general and a member of the Republican caucus that had approached Mahone, declared.

"The Senator from Rhode Island," Butler responded, "may characterize it as false as much as he pleases."

"I say it is false, false, false, in every word, every letter!"

"I shall not be betrayed by any excitement."

"I am not the least bit excited."

"I congratulate the Senator . . . for being cool."

"I am perfectly cool."

"If I do not demonstrate [the bargain] by irrefragable testimony," Butler then announced, "I will resign my seat in the Senate."

The gallery, thrilled with Butler's overture, exploded with applause. Burnside was obliged to match his opponent's offer. "I will [resign] my [Chairmanship of the Foreign Relations] committee right off," he countered, "and I will say you have a majority on that side of the Chamber."[35]

Over the next few days, Matthew presented his case for a "disgraceful bargain," but his effort had no impact on the Republicans. They would not give up their gains. Burnside was fearful this might induce Butler to carry out his threat to resign. He arose. "If every member . . . were to assert . . . that the Senator from South Carolina had failed in producing irrefragable proof," he declared, "I . . . say for one, let him remain in his seat; we do not desire him to give it up."

Butler, a good friend of Burnside's, had the last word. "If . . . I have succeeded," he stated, "permit me to say that I shall not ask him to give up his committee."[36] His gesture of goodwill was met with laughter.

Despite this display of camaraderie, the Senate was at an impasse. The members could not elect officers or appoint committees. The special session adjourned May 2, its business postponed until October.[37]

At the height of the debate, Butler received the shocking news that Martin Gary had died April 9. Matthew could not attend the funeral, but later at a memorial service, he delivered a moving eulogy to his old friend. It was a prime example of Butler's eloquence. "I crave the poor privilege of stepping out of the ranks long enough to drop a tear upon the grave of M. W. Gary," he declared sadly, "and then move on as best I may to join the great army which has crossed . . . the river of death and is being marshalled on the plains of the endless hereafter."[38]

Matthew was in great demand as a speaker, not only for the poetry of his words but also for the power of his voice. "Though we sat in a carriage more than a hundred yards from the stand [with] a surging crowd massed between," a reporter wrote about Butler's talk at the unveiling of a Confederate monument in Charleston's Magnolia Cemetery, "we [could hear] every syllable of this beautiful speech as distinctly as if we stood at his elbow."[39]

When Butler returned to Edgefield in June, he set up a law partnership with his nephew, C. I. Woodward, then headed north to visit his once rival in the Confederate ranks, Tom Rosser.[40] The former cavalry commander was now living in Winnipeg, serving as the chief engineer for the Canadian Pacific Railroad.[41] Taking advantage of his post with the Transportation Routes to the Seaboard Subcommittee, Matthew visited Rosser to seek his counsel toward convincing a rail company to build a line that connected South Carolina with the West. The trip was probably a government-paid vacation, but Butler did hold an avid interest in railroads. On his return from Canada, he came home through Kentucky and Tennessee, looking for the best way through the mountains. Matthew documented his findings, and submitted a report to George H. Pendleton, chairman of the Senate's Railroad Committee.[42]

On July 2, with Butler still in Canada, Garfield was shot in Pennsylvania Station by a disgruntled office seeker. The president had been waiting for a train to take him to a college class reunion. His assailant, Charles J. Guiteau, a Radical Republican, thought he had been denied a government job because of his politics. Murdering Garfield, in his unsound mind, would "unite the . . . party and save the Republic."[43]

Garfield clung to life, but it was clear that he would not survive his wounds. One bullet had hit his arm, another had lodged next to his spinal cord. He suffered from internal hemorrhaging. Doctors told the president they could not operate. Death was near. "I am glad to know my condition," the courageous Garfield replied. "I can bear it."[44]

The president, however, lingered for weeks. Hopes for his survival arose. But when his wounds showed signs of infection, it was obvious he could not last. Garfield died the night of September 19, 1881.[45]

Chester A. Arthur took over the presidency on the next day. He was born October 5, 1829 in Vermont, graduated from Union College, and was a New York lawyer up to the start of the Civil War. Arthur joined the state militia, served as a quartermaster with the rank of brigadier general until 1863, then resigned to resume practicing law. He became a Radical Republican, and in 1871, his politics brought him the lucrative post as collector for the Port of New York. His misuse of patronage led Hayes to relieve him in 1878. Arthur went to the 1880 Republican Convention as manager of the campaign to reelect Grant to a third term. Although failing in this endeavor, Arthur was given the nomination for vice president as a gesture toward reuniting the party.[46]

Throughout the crisis of Garfield's dying, Matthew was busy tending to matters of personal interest. He attended a State Agriculture Society meeting in Greenville that August, visited the Atlanta Cotton Exposition in September, and gave a stirring speech at the Grand Parade of the South Carolina Battalions at Yorktown in October.[47]

Butler, Maria, and the girls went back to Washington in October. All three boys were busily pursuing the careers their father had selected for them. Frank, after his graduation from the Medical College of Charleston, had begun his internship at that city's Roper Hospital; Willie was studying law at Princeton; Cabby had hoped to enter West Point, but had done so poorly at the Charlotte Institute, his grades precluded appointment to the Academy. He planned to correct this deficiency by attending classes at Union College in Schenectady, New York.[48]

The Butlers moved into new quarters at 514 13th Street NW.[49] The second Special Session of the Forty-Seventh Congress met from October 10th through the 29th, and the impasse was finally resolved. The Republi-

cans took control, electing their officers and gaining charge of the committees. Butler kept all of his previous posts, but was no longer chairman of
the Civil Service and Retrenchment Committee.[50]

The First Session of the Forty-Seventh Congress met on December 5,
1881, and remained seated for eight months. Not much was accomplished.
Butler attended to details relating to his committee work, submitting
reports on gambling in the capital, the need to establish a home in Washington for destitute colored women, and ideas for setting up civil rule in
Alaska. And he continued his service to the people back in South Carolina.
Matthew presented their many petitions, and started efforts toward estab-
lishing a naval station at Port Royal outside of Beaufort.[51]

While in Washington, Butler received word that his son, Cabby, had
done well at Union College. He was now qualified for West Point, and
George D. Tillman, who represented Edgefield in the House, had given
him an appointment.[52] All three boys were now embarked on the careers
Matthew had determined for them.

Butler returned to Edgefield that fall to campaign for his party and his
own future. If the Democrats continued to hold the South Carolina legislature, he would return to the Senate. It was no contest. Democrat Hugh S.
Thompson swept the governor's race. The party captured both the House
and the Senate.[53]

Matthew and his peers celebrated at the South Carolina Club Grand
Ball, held in Columbia at the Hall of Representatives on November 23.
Two weeks later he was elected to another six year term in office.[54]

CHAPTER 24

Second Term

Upon returning to the Senate in December 1882, Butler was among the first to enter the chamber. He was compulsively punctual and was rewarded for this trait today by special mention in the chaplain's opening prayer. No other Democrat was there; only four Republicans had also bothered to show up on time. Matthew looked more in sorrow than anger toward what he called a "beggarly account of empty benches."[1]

Butler was in need of prayer. Not only did he face an uphill fight for his programs (being in the minority because of Mahone's treachery), but also he was financially embarrassed. The costs of his position plus family expenses (especially his boys' college tuitions) had drained his resources. He was forced to approach his old friends and ask them for a loan. Pierce Young, his wartime subordinate, had borrowed $100 back in July, and Butler not only requested payment but also an additional sum to "tide him over."[2]

Putting personal difficulties aside, Butler plunged into his Senate duties. He first spoke out in favor of a bill to reform civil service, a measure calling for the hiring of lower-level clerks based on a competitive examination. Garfield's assassination had shown a pressing need for reducing the pressure of office seekers following elections. The Republicans, being in power, had little interest in losing the patronage accruing to the victors, and they sought to defeat the measure by introducing a host of amendments. Butler was disgusted by their efforts.

"[You] come in . . . at the eleventh hour, changing . . . every feature of the bill," he accused William B. Allison of Iowa. "[You] say you favor civil service reform. . . . I do not understand such friendship."

"I adopt the precise language of the Committee on Civil Service and Retrenchment," Allison replied, "[which] has met the approval of some distinguished gentlemen without respect to party."

"The Senate has been moving amendment after amendment," Butler shot back, "which practically . . . substitute for the original proposition."

Others joined Allison to defend the Republican strategy for killing the measure. One said that Butler was being too sensitive over the matter.

"I have a right to be sensitive," Butler noted, "when I have been making an effort to do what I believe . . . my duty to this country outside of party."[3]

In the end the Republicans prevailed. Reform of civil service was defeated. But the confrontations between Butler and his adversaries did not end. An exchange with George F. Hoar of Massachusetts soon followed.

Discussing a bill to prohibit giving money for corrupt political purposes, Butler asked Hoar for an example. "Buying shotguns to shoot negroes," was the reply.

"Or to buy votes and disenfranchise 136,000 people, as is . . . done in Massachusetts," Butler angrily responded.

"What does the Senator mean?"

"I mean . . . that they have disenfranchised 136,000 men in the state of Massachusetts," Butler repeated. "I propounded a polite inquiry to the Senator . . . [but] when he injects into his reply a piece of venom, I propose to answer . . . in similar manner."[4]

The *Edgefield Advertiser* applauded Butler. "His retort was apt and pertinent," the editor concluded. He then noted that our "Senator never tolerates this sort of innuendo."[5]

In late January Butler and George Edmunds of Vermont were involved in an exchange of insults. The latter, defending the nomination of Emory Speer as U.S. district attorney for Georgia, said that the assignee had been verbally abused by Leroy Youmans, Matthew's former law partner, during a recent trial. Butler disputed the allegation.

"You have been misinformed and misled," he related. "I was present . . . and can give evidence rebuking [your] charge."

"Judge Bond," Edmunds stated, "[says] the newspaper reports . . . were substantially correct."

"Then the Judge convicts himself," Butler scoffed. "If any such thing had occurred, it would have been [his] . . . duty to protect the counsel."[6]

One might assume that because Butler was so frequently involved in confrontations, he was cantankerous, a man never happy with any situation. Matthew, however, was not a boor. He simply would not tolerate such behavior from others. The British poet, Matthew Arnold, then traveling in the United States, noted that he had "met a number of public men in Washington, and that Senator Butler of South Carolina impressed him as being a specimen of the class of cultivated men quite common in public affairs in England."[7]

The Senate adjourned on March 3, and Butler returned to South Carolina where he could "look after his fences—not political but agricultural."

He told a local reporter "the sight of my old Edgefield home . . . has a tonic effect on me."[8]

Maria, however, remained in Washington. Both the girls, Marie, age seventeen and Elise, age fourteen, were in school, and their mother did not want to disrupt their classes. The boys were scattered, too. Frank had finished his internship, and was now taking postgraduate courses at the prestigious New York Polyclinic; Willie was completing his final term at Princeton; Cabby was about to enter West Point. Butler spent the spring and summer at home alone.[9]

The Forty-eighth Session of Congress began on December 3, 1883. Matthew, Maria, and the girls took up rooms at the Metropolitan Hotel.[10] Willie, too, came to Washington. He had graduated from Princeton in June, but could not practice law in South Carolina until authorized by the state supreme court. Until receiving this approval, he would serve as his father's secretary.[11]

The Republicans controlled the Senate, and as a result, Butler found his role reduced. He was appointed to only two committees: Naval Affairs and Territories.[12] Matthew, however, was not rendered idle by this move. He looked for and found issues that kept him busy. For example, in late January, he introduced a bill that would entitle each senator to a clerk, whose $1,000 per year salary would be paid from the contingent fund. This measure was easily passed, and Butler promptly hired Capt. George B. Lake as his assistant.[13]

In early February Matthew became involved with a bill regarding the national interest in fertilizer, imported from the Guano Islands. Congress had seen the need to keep this resource exclusive for the United States, and had enacted an ordinance in 1872 that both prohibited its export and fixed the resale price for bird droppings. Those in the business (many from South Carolina, who mixed the guano with locally mined phosphates) preferred selling overseas, where they could charge higher prices and make more money. The Republicans were willing to grant their wish by suspending implementation of the law.

Butler, of course, supported legislation that indulged his constituents, but since the Republicans were raising the issue, he remained silent. This roused suspicions from his adversaries. They were by now well aware of how cleverly he used them to achieve his goals.

"I [note] how adroitly my free trade friend from South Carolina works the provisions of this bill," Sen. Omar D. Conger of Michigan said. "He is ingenious, shrewd, quiet."

"I have not opened my mouth about this bill."

"I know it," Conger replied, "but it was to draw an expression from [you] that I was making these suggestions."

Despite continuing gibes from Conger, Butler would not take a position. Suspension of the earlier bill was finally brought to a vote, and passed. Matthew was among the majority casting a favorable ballot, and no doubt chuckled as he revealed his support for the measure.[14]

About a week later, Butler arose to offer a resolution calling for a report on an experimental tea farm that he had induced the Department of Agriculture to start in South Carolina, another example of his serving his state. The Senate gave its unanimous consent to his request.[15]

More serious matters came to the fore in late February. The navy was asking for money to make significant changes to the fleet, to replace their old wooden ships with ironclads. The Senate was not disposed to grant these funds, so Matthew devised a strategy to divert his cohorts' attention. Speaking for the Committee on Naval Affairs, which had drawn up a bill supporting the navy's request, he introduced an interview he had held with Adm. David Porter.

Butler: How long would it take to get a navy the size you have indicated?

Porter: I think five years will do the whole of it.

Butler: Do [foreign] governments build them themselves or do they let them out by contract?

Porter: Almost all their ships are built [by] private establishments.

Butler: Is there a navy-yard in the United States that could build a ship out and out now?

Porter: There is. I had one built . . . once, and when I got through with her, I weighed forty pounds less than I did when I started.

Butler: Whose fault was that?

Porter: She cost $400,000 . . . at a navy-yard; she could have been built by an outside [contractor] for $200,000 with no trouble at all.

Butler: What do you attribute the difference . . . to?

Porter: Politics. . . . The navy-yards are very much used for political purposes. . . . If I was a politician, [and] could get my friends into the navy-yard, I would do [it] . . . but if I was in charge, I would do all I could to stop it.[16]

By opening this side of patronage, Butler deftly diverted Republican attention from funding new ships to protecting their interests in providing jobs in the navy yards. "Every step in building these ships," Sen. Eugene Hale of Main proffered, "shall be under the advice of the advisory board."[17]

Others joined in the defense of the federal navy yards, and were no doubt influenced to support the funding bill due to their views on patronage. But in the end, the program's funding remained the key question. Matthew summed up with a dramatic speech. He started with a list of the

U.S. cities exposed to shelling by a European navy. Included were those along the Atlantic coast, plus the Great Lakes ports, vulnerable through the opening of the St. Lawrence River.

Butler then detailed the strength of political enemies. "England," he stated, "can throw a fleet of thirteen armour-clad on our coast, and in four weeks, ten more. . . . Germany . . . can today mobilize her whole force in eight days. . . . In three weeks, [she] could have a fleet of six powerful armor-clads off the port of New York. . . . Italy, with her . . . swift cruisers would be very formidable."

"Our old wooden vessels are rapidly going to decay," he said in conclusion. "Why not retire them from service . . . replace them with improved naval ships, built after the latest models. . . . . I hope . . . that the bill reported from the committee . . . will be passed by the Senate."[18]

His speech was impassioned, but Butler failed to rouse his colleagues. The vote on funding the navy bill was postponed.

In late March Matthew once again was forced to defend his state. The Senate was considering a bill for allocating federal funds to educate the blacks of the South. Those in favor assumed that the children of the ex-slaves were denied a place in the public schools. Butler, opposed to national interference with South Carolina's educational system, tried to refute this claim.

"There are . . . about 280,000 children of school age within the limits of the State," he stated. "There is an annual attendance of about 173,000 upon the common schools, leaving about 108,000 . . . not [attending]. . . . But . . . private schools absorb quite a number of children that age."

"In the whole country, Henry W. Blair of New Hampshire contended, "there are only 500,000 attending private schools of every description . . . the larger proportion . . . in the Northern states."

"[Our] common school system," Butler countered, "is as good as is to be found in any state." After noting that the two races used separate facilities, he submitted a testimonial from H. P. Montgomery, the black principal of the Normal Institute for Colored Teachers. "What an overwhelming reply that is," Matthew exclaimed "to the intimation . . . made on the floor of the Senate." He concluded his argument by stating, that "We have taxed ourselves . . . and 95 per cent of the money raised for school purpose is paid by the white people, the property owners, and the colored people get their full share of it."[19]

Matthew was no doubt sincere, but he failed to mention possible differences in the quality of education between the black and white schools. No one brought up this point, but if they had, Butler would probably have attributed this discrepancy to the inherent diversity between the races.

In April Matthew and his family returned to Edgefield. The Senate was still in session, but perhaps Maria could not wait any longer to go home. Butler stayed in town for only a few days, then went back to Washington.[20] His leaving may have been influenced by the village's recent vote to ban the sales of alcohol. "[Our] hearts and homes [will] never again be clouded with the dark shadow that rests where liquor has full sway," Woman's Christian Temperance Union (WCTU) spokeswoman, Mrs. W. C. Sibley, avowed. "All honor to the colored people who voted for Prohibition!"[21]

The more probable cause for Maria and the girls' early return to Edgefield was because Matthew was out of money and could no longer afford to rent the house in Washington. He tried to raise cash in June by asking an old friend, John C. Haskell, to factor a debt, owed him by South Carolina judge Thomas J. Mackey. "It ought to be good," he stated. "Won't you speculate a little and give me 50 cents on the dollar?" His conscience must have bothered him, because Butler added in a footnote to his letter, "I think Mackey stuck Governor Hampton for $400."[22]

The Senate adjourned July 7, 1884; Butler immediately headed for Chicago to attend the Democratic National Convention. He probably eagerly anticipated the session, because on June 3, the Republican Party had nominated former senator James G. Blaine as their candidate for president. This choice was unexpected because Blaine had political problems. He had taken bribes from railroad interests; he was out of touch with the time, a "bloody shirt" waver; and Blaine was a staunch supporter of the spoils system. Most thought him vulnerable to defeat because of these issues. For the first time since the Civil War, the Democrats envisioned electing one of their own as president.[23]

The favorite for the Democratic nomination was Stephen Grover Cleveland. A preacher's son, he was born on March 18, 1837, in Caldwell, New Jersey, but at the age of four, moved to Fayetteville, New York (close to Syracuse), where he grew up. His family was too poor to send him off to college, so at age seventeen, Cleveland went to Buffalo to prepare for a legal career under the tutelage of attorneys Sherman Rogers, Henry W. Rogers, and Dennis Bowen.

Cleveland was admitted to the bar in 1859. Although a resolute Union man, he avoided military service in the Civil War by hiring a substitute to assume his place in the draft. He built a successful legal practice, then began a political career that soon rocketed. Cleveland was elected mayor of Buffalo in 1882, governor of New York in 1883, then Democratic nominee for president in 1884.[24]

"Cleveland is stout," a reporter described him, "has a well-fed look, is indeed a good liver. . . . He is getting bald; he is getting gray. . . . He dresses well, carries himself well, talks well upon any subject with which he is familiar . . . upon subjects with which he is not familiar, he does not venture to talk at all."[25] Butler would find him independent, a man who put principle above party.

Following Cleveland's nomination, Butler returned home to congratulate Willie for gaining approval from the state's supreme court to practice law. The lad had not only opened an office in Edgefield on June 12, but also assumed charge of the family properties, the life that Matthew had planned for him.[26] Frank, too, was following his father's longheld dreams. He was working as a physician in Columbia.[27] Only Cabby presented a problem. Although still at West Point, he had failed mathematics in his first year, and was in danger of being dismissed.[28]

Butler began traveling throughout the state that fall to campaign for both Cleveland and Hugh S. Thompson, running for reelection as governor. His old wound, however, became inflamed, and Matthew was forced into returning to Edgefield to recuperate.[29] He followed the election returns from his home, and saw Cleveland gain the presidency by the narrowest of margins.

In early December Matthew went back to Washington for the last meeting of the Forty-eighth Congress. Knowing they would be living in the capital through the coming year (the Forty-ninth Congress would gather immediately following this assembly for President Cleveland's inauguration, then remain seated into 1886), Butler and Maria rented a spacious apartment at 1822 I Street NW.[30]

When he went to his Senate office, Butler found a note form an old flame, Clara Dargan, a girl he had squired while in Edgefield recuperating from his amputation. She had wed Joseph A. Maclean in 1872, had gained fame as a musician and poet, then separated from her husband. Clara wrote Matthew asking for help in finding a government job.[31]

Butler was thrilled that she still remembered him, and seemingly looked forward to renewing their longago romance. "Shall we not meet again," he replied, "to review the memories of those early days, and live for awhile at least in the halo they throw around us? I'm sure I would rejoice, and I trust you would, too."[32]

Clara, however, had no interest in reviving their love affair, and in her response to his letter, said bluntly that she was looking for employment, nothing else. Matthew must have been chagrined, and answered formally in May, "if I can oblige you, I will be most happy to do so."[33] He made "two or three ineffectual efforts" in her behalf, but was unable to find an opening for Clara. She continued to write him to ask his help, each note colder than the one prior. By 1888 their correspondence had ended.

The most controversial legislation to arise during the second session of the Forty-eighth Congress dealt with a ban on the importation of foreign laborers at low wages. There seemed to be wide support for the bill, but the Republicans, secretly opposed, sought to gut the measure by imposing only mild penalties for violation of its provisions. Butler was determined to thwart their efforts, and he offered an amendment calling for stiff fines against the workers themselves, shipowners who brought the foreigners into the country, and the businesses that employed the aliens.

"This bill pretends to do something," Butler explained when introducing his amendment, "[but] does nothing except . . . pat the American laborer on the head . . . giving him a bill which amounts to nothing."

Henry W. Blair defended the bill by attacking Butler's motives. "The Senator from South Carolina will pardon me if in listening to his somewhat unaccustomed role of . . . special friend of American labor I feel reminded of the proverb that it is well to beware of . . . Greeks . . . bearing gifts," he noted. "I have examined his amendment with a suspicion . . . [it] might not be from the very bottom of his soul."[34]

The generalities of Blair's attack against Butler failed to sway the senators. The foreign labor bill, including the amendment added by Matthew, was passed by a vote of fifty to nine on February 18, 1885, and became law.[35]

Although Butler succeeded in this contest with the Republicans, he failed when dealing with the Democratic President. Cleveland was determined to reform patronage by using business principles in filling public offices. He would select only the best men for each job, and refused to personally meet with applicants. Butler tried to circumvent this policy, but was rebuffed. He was forced to take an endorsement for a friend to the Interior Department. "I have ascertained," he said lamely, "this is the place to file."[36]

The Forty-ninth Congress opened its special session on March 3, 1885, and remained seated throughout the year. But Butler played only a minor role. Personal problems came to the fore, and in May, he returned to Edgefield to straighten out the lives of his three sons. Frank was probably a good doctor, but he was a poor businessman, unwilling to charge a reasonable fee for his services. He was in financial difficulty.[37] Cabby had been held back a class at West Point in January, and faced expulsion if he did not show a marked improvement in his grades;[38] Willie, however, presented the biggest dilemma. He had suddenly closed his law office and left the family plantation to go to Liverpool, England, to work as a consular clerk. He soon gained promotion to attaché in Bordeaux, France.[39]

Butler was furious with Willie. "Some become attached to the government pap by testing it," he warned. "[You will be] irrevocably wedded to the 'government trough,' and hopelessly dependent upon it for existence."[40]

"I have taken a great interest . . . in consular service," Willie countered, "and think I have mastered it sufficiently to [earn] rank. . . . I can't conceive of anything more natural than I should continue to obtain promotion or that you would be willing to lend me all the reasonable aid you can."[41]

Instead of using his influence as a senator to promote his son's new career, Butler took drastic steps to bring him home. He arranged an overseas excursion for Maria and the two girls to visit Willie to pressure him into returning to Edgefield. Although Butler was (as always) strapped for money, he could afford their sojourn; it would cost no more for his family to dwell in Europe than in Washington.[42] He would economize by moving to cheaper quarters, first at 730 Seventeenth Street NW, later to 1835 K Street NW, in the capital.[43]

The tour would also address another problem. Butler's youngest girl, Elise, had recently converted to the Catholic faith and wanted to become a nun. The sixteen-year-old was Matthew's favorite, and he was willing to allow her anything she desired. Her mother, however, was adamantly opposed to Elise joining an order. Butler no doubt hoped the diversion of a European trip would induce his daughter to give up her religious ambitions and end the dissension between Maria and Elise.[44]

Butler returned to Washington that summer, and as a result missed the August meeting of the State Agricultural and Mechanical Society. Had he attended, he would have heard a dynamic speech by a neighbor, one of the participants in the Hamburg Massacre, Benjamin Ryan Tillman. Only thirty-eight years old, a rustic, one-eyed farmer, Tillman combined oaths with literary eloquence in assailing the politicians for ignoring those making their living from the soil. "[You] have been hoodwinked," he howled to his audience, "by demagogues and lawyers in the pay of finance."[45] His ardent speech was the first of many that would in time bring Tillman to power in South Carolina and end Butler's career as a politician.

In early December the Senate opened discussion toward making the Dakota Territory a state. The Republicans saw an opportunity to bring four new senators to their side of the chamber, so they presented a plan to divide the area in two, and admit only South Dakota at this time. Butler spoke for the Democrats in opposing the scheme.

Noting that South Dakota had already held a convention to write their constitution, elected both state officers and a legislature, and named two senators, Butler declared that these actions were illegal because Congress had yet to pass an enabling bill. "[They had no right]," he argued, "to set up a [regime] in conflict with the government maintained by the National Government in the Territory."

"The tentative State organization on Dakota," Benjamin Harrison of

Indiana quickly remonstrated "[is] breathing the most thorough submission to the authority of the General government."

"The Senator is working himself into a passion."

"I am not in a passion. The Senator has never seen me in a passion or he would be able to discriminate."

"They have divided the Territory by an arbitrary line," Butler then charged, "which they themselves drew without the consent of Congress, settling for themselves the boundary . . . of the state."

"Michigan was just such a case," Harrison countered.

"The controversy was between the States of Ohio . . . Michigan . . . and Indiana as to the boundary lines," Butler replied hotly. "Congress had something to say about that."[46]

The argument droned on without resolution. A few days later Butler changed tactics by introducing a bill enabling the entire Dakota Territory to form a state government. He spoke at length when presenting his motion, noting that "the matter of making a State is a very serious business . . . it is not a game of chance between political parties, a plaything with which demagogues and reckless men may gratify their unsavory ambition."

After exposing the real political issue for the debate, Butler went on to declare, "If the Territory were as largely Democratic as it appears now to be Republican in politics, I [would still] feel constrained to oppose [Dakota] becoming a State."[47]

John Logan of Illinois, the former Union general, took umbrage with Butler's remarks. "He is opposed to the admission of Dakota," he asserted, "[because] it if comes in now it will have representation in the Congress . . . of a different political complexion from the Administration."[48]

"Not at all, Sir," Butler replied. He then introduced further grounds for rejecting South Dakota's application for statehood. "There is a wide gap between the census and the vote [for the constitution]," he quoted a leading Republican newspaper from Dakota, "and none are more conscious of that fact or more discreetly silent regarding it than the band of hungry office-seekers now posing in Washington as political martyrs for Dakota's sake."[49]

Both Logan and Harrison rose to draw comparison to the recent election in South Carolina, where only the whites had exercised the right to vote. "That," Matthew scoffed, "has about as much to do with this question as . . . the vote in Kamtchatka [sic] has."[50]

When the vote on Harrison's bill to bring South Dakota into the Union was taken in February, Matthew must have been surprised to see the measure defeated. His spirited opposition had been rewarded.

In April debate opened on admitting another territory, Montana, to statehood. Butler favored this proposition, but as with South Dakota, insisted that Congress first pass an enabling act. And this bill, he stated, should originate in the Committee on Territories, not from the Senate floor.

Harrison claimed that Butler's argument was only a subterfuge, that he would have opposed any enabling act brought before the committee. "That would be the place," he stated, "[to] call our attention . . . to our duty."

"I occupy," Matthew protested, "the position of one of a very feeble minority on that committee."

"A very strong minority," Harrison corrected.

"Very feeble in numbers, and perhaps in intellect, when compared with the Senator and his colleagues."

"A very strong minority," Harrison repeated firmly.

"Perhaps if you did not feel some guilt, you would not be so sensitive."

"I assure you that your own conscience, your own sense of right or guilt will give you full occupation without taking care of mine."[51]

Others, both Democrats and Republicans, opposed giving Montana statehood because her application had been submitted as an amendment to the bill proposing admission of the Washington Territory. Uniting two states in one statute was too reminiscent of the unhappy time when a balance between free and slave was a prerequisite for entry to the Union. Butler joined this group in defeating the amendment.

One week later, when the bill for admitting Washington Territory to statehood arose, Butler spoke out on a most unusual issue. The territory had given women the vote, and some Senators were demanding this be dropped before they would consider Washington's claim. "I do not wish to be understood as being in favor of woman's suffrage," Butler said April 9, "but the people of that Territory have the power to regulate those matters . . . themselves . . . it is their affair, not mine."[52]

"There are intelligent women, plenty . . . in every state," James B. Beck of Kentucky acknowledged, "but Congress cannot allow the most intelligent woman . . . to vote without allowing the most ignorant negro woman . . . in the South to vote. . . . That settles it for me."[53]

Other senators noted that the Washington electorate included aliens, many from Canada, and that they, too, should be barred from casting ballots. These voting issues brought about the defeat of the bill to admit Washington as a state.

Butler joined in one more debate before the end of the first session of the Forty-ninth Congress. He opposed passing a bill that defined butter and taxed competing products such as oleomargarine. The dairy farmers had induced introduction of this legislation.

Instead of speaking out against the bill, Butler tried a diversionary tactic. He offered an amendment that defined "pure" wine and taxed mixtures, which he dubbed, "compounded liquors." He knew this proposal was ridiculous, but thought a comparison between wine and butter would expose the folly of government "using its taxing power . . . to destroy a legitimate, *bona fide,* honest industry."[54]

"I shall vote for this amendment," he announced, "with the understanding that if [it is] adopted, I shall then vote against the bill. . . . This whole system of legislation is not only unconstitutional, but vicious in the extreme."[55]

The senators who supported the bill were so shocked by Butler's strategy, they deferred sure passage and agreed to debate the issue. In the end, however, they prevailed. The bill, without Matthew's amendment, was enacted.[56]

The verbal thrust and parry with his Congressional foemen must have been difficult for Matthew, particularly since his thoughts were focused more toward Europe than on Senate affairs. Maria and the girls had set sail in December 1885 to meet Willie at Bordeaux, France. Butler no doubt looked forward to their letters, which brought word of the family's conspiracies: Maria pressing Willie to give up his foreign service ambitions; he urging his mother to let sister Elise join the convent. "I have almost worked Ma to the point of allowing Elise to go for . . . a few months," Willie reported to Butler.[57] His optimism, however, soon sagged. Maria would never consent to Elise becoming a nun.

Willie also advised his father that despite being overseas for only a few weeks, Maria had spent most of the money Matthew had provided. "She would be glad if you will . . . forward a checque," he wrote. "She has only enough [left] . . . to last through the coming week."[58] Matthew had obviously misjudged Maria's ability to ration her resources. Luckily, he had just received $500 from *Century Illustrated Monthly Magazine* for writing an article, "The Cavalry Fight at Trevilian Station," so Butler could afford her request for cash.[59]

After a two-week stay at Bordeaux, Maria and the girls went to Tours; Willie remained at his offices, which he described as having "a plainess that would certainly conform to the tastes of a Jacksonian Democrat. They are barely out of the category of the shoddy genteel."[60]

Despite his mother's pleas, Willie was still intent on pursuing his career in the diplomatic service. His boss had decided to retire in a few months. "I trust," Willie wrote his father, "I may succeed him. Seems to me you can lend me a helping hand."[61]

Butler finally surrendered to Willie's ambition and interceded on his behalf. The position, however, was given to another. "Men who have from the cradle up been deeply died Republicans can [scarcely] afford

Marie Calhoun Butler.
COURTESY ELLEN ADAMS GUTOW

material assistance to one . . . exactly . . . opposite [in] training and instinct," the downhearted lad concluded. "The high authorities . . . left my fate in the hands of such men, which is unjust and inexcusable."[62] He later admitted that obtaining the post was "a question of pride to me, and the wound . . . is deeper because the inference is that I was . . . not deserving of promotion."[63]

Willie resigned from the foreign service that June and went to Paris to join Maria and his sisters, who had finally left Tours. He procured "comfortable and pleasant quarters" for all at a cost of $220 per month for room and board, "the lowest . . . that can be had for respectable living."[64] Willie then added, "I found that Ma . . . owed bills at Tours exceeding the 2,500 francs you gave me."[65]

The four spent three weeks sightseeing. "A person may make a tour of the globe," Willie wrote to Matthew, "and yet he will not have seen the world until he has visited Paris." The lad noted the "indescribable magnificence of the palaces . . . the uncomparable solidity and beauty of the public buildings . . . the elegance attained [by] the cultivation of all the fine arts. . . . [They] tell . . . of a grandeur, an advanced stage of civilization hardly approached [elsewhere] in the history of the world."[66]

In his next letter, Willie once again pleaded for more money. "I know it will seem to you . . . we are living extravagantly," he wrote, "but such is certainly not the case. We have been twice only to the Theatre . . . Ma amuses herself [by] painting and sketching."[67]

In July the Butlers continued their jaunt by traveling via a second-class train to Lucerne, Switzerland. They took rooms in the Swan Hotel, high atop a mountain overlooking a quiescent lake, "the most beautiful view I have ever seen in my life," Elise wrote her father. "[They have] the most

Susan Elise Butler.
COURTESY ELLEN ADAMS GUTOW

delightful honey and bread and butter," she added. "I expect to get tremen-
dous before I leave." Her objective in writing Butler was to ask him to let
both she and her sister, Marie, remain in Europe through the fall. "Do let
us stay," she begged, playing on his favoritism for her, "it would be the best
thing for me."[68]

Willie had written Butler about this same time telling him that their
cost for rooms and board in Lucerne would total $5.58 each day.[69] The
expense must have been acceptable to Butler, because when the Senate
adjourned in August, he went to New York, boarded a ship, and set sail for
Europe, where he joined his family. He visited Germany, Belgium, England, and France. "I went with my eyes and ears open," he stated sarcasti-
cally in a later Senate speech, "expecting to [note] among all of the classes
of laborers . . . squalor, degradation, poverty, and ignorance . . . [but] have
never seen . . . a more contented set of people."[70] He was teasing the
Republicans for citing cheap European labor as a reason for high tariffs.

The Butlers returned to the United States in late fall. The year had
brought marked changes to their family, all for the better. Frank's medical
career was failing in Columbia, but he had received an appointment with
the army to serve in the West as an assistant surgeon. Too old for an officer's commission, he would work as a civilian.[71] Cabby, repeating his
sophomore year at West Point, passed all of his courses that spring;[72] Willie
had resumed both his legal career and the management of his father's plantation. He even joined the local militia, who elected him a captain. "I presume . . . my Yankee friends," he joshed in an alumni update letter to
Princeton, "would construe [us as being] Midnight Raiders or Ku Klux
Klan."[73]

Butler returned to Washington in December 1886. He rented an apartment at 1738 I Street NW, then headed for the Senate Chamber to attend
the second session of the Forty-ninth Congress.[74]

The first issue to grab his attention was a measure to grant each state $15,000 for their agricultural colleges. "I shall vote for the bill," he noted, "because [it] puts . . . this matter under the control of the colleges. . . . We have the . . . constitutional power to make this appropriation . . . [just] as we have to [disburse] $100,000 to buy seeds." He was referring to a pet peeve, a previously passed boon now used as "pork" to solicit votes. "I sent some of the seeds assigned to me to one of my constituents, I believe purporting to be cabbage seeds," he reported, "and the result was . . . tobacco."

"[My] flowers," another chimed, "came up radishes."[75]

The Senate had a good laugh, then passed the grants to the state agricultural colleges.

In late January Butler opposed a measure to establish the Yellowstone National Park. "Powers are conferred on the commissioner," he argued, "which I think he ought not to have."[76] The measure prohibited hunting of game, giving the park's executive the authority to arrest, try, convict, and punish poachers.

"I haven't much faith in the preservation of game," he added. "The classes . . . that frequent the park are migratory, and once they cross the designated line, I do not know that there is anything to prevent . . . Senator Edmunds . . . from taking a shot at one of them."[77]

"He alludes to game," Edmunds said with a grin, "as he always alludes to me . . . as being about the only wild man left in the Senate. . . . I wish he had been to [Yellowstone] . . . then he would feel differently about this business."[78]

Matthew found himself in a very small minority on this matter. The bill passed on January 29 by a vote of forty-nine to eight.[79]

On February 15 Matthew tried to introduce a bill to allow the Washington Territory to call a legislative session to repeal their gross earnings act, a measure that excluded the Northern Pacific Railroad from property taxes. "[It is] common justice," he noted, "that this railroad company . . . be required to pay their proportionate share."[80]

The Republicans, probably receiving campaign cash from the railroad, were opposed to Butler's bill, and they used a parliamentary procedure to block a vote on this issue. The Northern Pacific continued to enjoy tax-free status on their 12 million acres.

Several days later Matthew took an unpopular position when he would not support a bill that banned polygamy in the Utah Territory. "I should be very glad to vote for any measure which would result in exterminating [this] . . . crime," he related, "but . . . the provisions of this measure clearly [violate] . . . principles of the Constitution regarding private and personal right of religious opinion. . . . I would prefer . . . the Territorial government . . . be abolished, root and branch, and that we should govern it as we are governing the District of Columbia."[81] As was so often the case, his stand was to no avail, and his suggestion ignored.

Butler's last duel of this session came on February 24, 1887. The Senate was considering a bill to set up a federal agency, the U.S. Cattle Commission, to carry out a plan protecting citizens from the danger of pleuropneumonia in beef. He viewed the act as infringing on states' rights, and assaulted it from two directions. First, to confuse the issue, he suggested an amendment to include maladies affecting other farm animals. "It might be just as important," he said, "to [add] provision for the extermination of . . . hog cholera . . . [and] glanders among the horses." Butler then argued that there was no need for a bill, that the states and territories already had procedures in place to deal with the cattle problem. "I submit," he stated, "the power is ample and abundant and complete to . . . destroy every vestige of this disease in this country . . . without doing violence to the Constitution." After pausing for effect, he noted, "I . . . am old fogy enough to profess some respect for that instrument."[82]

The Republican majority, per usual, had their way. The commission was established and given broad powers of search, which Butler described as "beyond any point ever claimed before in this . . . country."[83]

No doubt weary from fighting political battles in Washington, Butler returned to Edgefield in March 1887 to face more of the same in South Carolina. The scene at home, however, was much less glum. State support for "Pitchfork" Ben Tillman, the leader of the farmers' movement and adamant foe of conservative Democrats such as Matthew, was on the wane.

After mounting the political stage with a fiery speech to the 1885 State Agricultural and Mechanical Society, Tillman continued to inhabit the limelight by writing "position" letters, published by Charleston's News and Courier. "Every one of the 'aids' to agriculture," he listed, "is permeated, saturated, [even] . . . rotten with politics."[84]

His fellow soil tillers loved these assaults on the establishment, and they flocked to the Farmers' Convention he assembled on April 29, 1886. Tillman introduced six resolutions: to meet annually, to repeal the lien law, to lobby the legislature on farm issues, to establish an agriculture college, to set up an industrial college for girls, and to abolish the Citadel, all of which were adopted by the gathering.[85]

Tillman then organized an effort to elect delegates to the Democratic nominating convention, to be held in Columbia in early August. He succeeded in gaining almost a majority, who supported John C. Sheppard, a boyhood friend of Tillman, for governor. On the eve of the conclave, however, Sheppard renounced the key point in the farmer's platform, estab-

Chief Dennis Wolf Bushyhead
COURTESY THE PERRYS OF RHODE ISLAND

lishing a separate agricultural college, and Tillman's momentum collapsed. Only a handful attended the November 1886 assembly of the Farmer's Convention.[86]

So when Butler came back to Edgefield in March 1887, he found that Tillman had "retired" from politics. But only days after Matthew's return, Thomas G. Clemson, wealthy son-in-law of John C. Calhoun, died. He left both his Fort Hill estate and a cash endowment of $80,000 to establish a separate agricultural college for South Carolina.[87] Tillman saw Clemson's bequest as his ticket to power, and he immediately renewed his agitation for reforms.

Butler ignored Tillman's loud protestations. Although certainly concerned by the farmers' opposition to the ruling class in South Carolina, his interest at this time was more centered on West Point, where Cabby was once again in academic trouble. He had failed two subjects: chemical physics and mineralogy and geology. If he did not make up these deficiencies by September 1, Cabby would be forced to leave the Academy. Through hard study that summer (probably under the stern admonitions of his father), he scored high enough on his tests to remain with his class at West Point.[88]

In December 1887 Butler went back to the capital for the First Session of the Fiftieth Congress. He leased rooms for himself and Maria at 1751 P Street NW.[89]

The Republicans controlled the Senate, and gave Butler the same committee assignments that he had held in the prior session: Naval Affairs, Territories, and Routes to the Seaboard. A few days later, he gained an additional assignment as chairman for a new committee, charged to investigate and report on the government relations with the Civilized Indian Tribes.[90] This

Butler law office, Edgefield, South Carolina. PHOTO BY THE AUTHOR

post was of special interest to Matthew due to his relationship by marriage to the current treasurer for the Cherokee Nation, Dennis Wolf Bushyhead. Bushyhead had married Eloise Butler, daughter of James L. Butler, an older brother of Matthew, and Fannie Taylor, a Cherokee princess. He went west to California seeking gold in 1849, and worked the mines until 1865. He came back east to the Indian Territory when the Civil War ended, and ran a general store. Dennis had been chosen Cherokee Treasurer in 1882. He would later (1890) be elected chief of his nation.[91] He and Butler would enjoy a close association throughout the following years.

On January 28, 1888, Matthew took time from his Senate schedule to wrap up a deal in Edgefield. He paid $500 for a tiny building, located at 301 Buncombe, a block from the county courthouse, for Willie to use as his law office. The structure still stands today, serving as a headquarters for longtime South Carolina Senator, Strom Thurmond.[92]

Butler did not take an active role on the Senate floor during the early months of this session. His first comments came in April 1888, when he once more opposed dividing the Dakota Territory into two separate states. "The peoples of the Territory [claim] an inherent right to be admitted into the Union," he noted. "If this proposition is correct, what would prevent [a similar number of] socialists, anarchists, nihilists, communists taking refuge in a corner of [another] territory . . . and demanding the [same] right?"[93] His riposte helped to further delay South Dakota's bid for statehood.

Although Congress remained in session, both of the two political parties met in June to nominate their presidential candidates for the upcoming fall election. The Republicans gathered in Chicago, where they chose Benjamin

Harrison from Indiana to head up their slate; the Democrats assembled in St. Louis, and gave Grover Cleveland his chance for a second term.[94]

Butler probably went to St. Louis, then headed for New York to attend Cabby's graduation from West Point. The trip was no doubt bittersweet. His son received a commission as a second lieutenant, but ranked last in his class, a permanent blot on his military record.[95] Probably disgusted with Cabby's poor performance at the Academy, Butler took his son aside after the ceremonies to give him some fatherly advice. "Don't be a rocking chair soldier," Butler reproved.[96] Further embarrassment, Cabby knew, would not be tolerated. He was given a temporary assignment with the 14th Infantry, but was soon transferred west to the 9th Infantry, based at Vancouver Barracks in the Washington Territory.[97]

Upon returning to Congress in July, Butler carried out the threat he had first mentioned in a May letter to Francis W. Dawson, fiery editor for the *Charleston News and Courier*. "The Republicans," Matthew predicted, "[plan] to force a debate to create a diversion from the Tariff. . . . I will neither admit nor deny anything, but [shall] attack."[98]

Butler's chance arose when New Hampshire senator Henry Blair castigated the president for rejecting the Civil War pension bill that he had sponsored. "[Cleveland]," he sneered, "at least might send [us] his vetoes like a gentleman."

"We would be infinitely better off," Matthew countered, "if [the Senator] would fatigue us less with the measures he brings to this body for our consideration."

"Specify what measures," Blair insisted. He must have been astonished by Butler's sudden assault.

"[That] would be absolutely impossible."

"I think it would [be possible]."

"He says the President at least might send . . . vetoes in like a gentleman," Butler countered, ignoring Blair's demand for details. "What a terrible calamity it would be to this country if the standard of a gentleman had to be established by the Senator from New Hampshire. . . . It would undermine, it would destroy every rule [concerning] the subject recognized among civilized people."[99] Just as he did during the Civil War, Matthew gave no quarter when assailing an enemy.

Butler returned to South Carolina in August 1888 for the state's office nominating convention. Tillman was there actively promoting Joseph H. Earle for governor. Matthew's friends supported the incumbent, John P. Richardson, who was seeking a second term. Once again, Tillman's man stepped aside at the last minute, and Richardson won his bid to lead the Democratic ticket.[100]

Tillman was devastated. He re-retired to his farm outside of Edgefield.

Only seventy-five of his supporters came to the annual meeting of the Farmer's Association, far fewer than those attending the Farmer's Alliance, a rival organization. With Butler's cohorts firmly in power, Matthew could look forward to December and his election by the legislature to a third term as senator from South Carolina.

Butler, however, took no chances. When he resumed his seat in the Senate, Matthew took the lead in championing one of the farmers' major issues, the establishment of a Department of Agriculture. He joined in the debate on a key point—transfer of the Signal Service (weather forecasting) from the army to the newly proposed department, replacing its inexperienced officers with accomplished scientists.

"We ought to pause," Michigan senator Thomas W. Palmer cautioned, "before we take so radical a step."

"[Do you] really believe that [anyone] engaged in agriculture would object to the transfer?" Butler asked.

"I think at first blush—"

"Does the Senator," Butler interrupted Palmer, "believe that there is a single, scientific man in this country . . . who would not advocate the transfer?"

"[This service] should be thoroughly organized and put in perfect working order, so that it could be worked when it was transferred."

"This whole matter was discussed in the last Congress," Butler noted. "A long, elaborate discussion took place, and the very same argument . . . was offered then, that we ought to postpone the transfer . . . in order that the Military Committee might incubate upon it. Well, sir, we have been incubating over this thing from that time to now."[101]

Butler's arguments helped pass the bill, introduced in Congress by Missouri representative William H. Hatch, creating the Department of Agriculture.[102] Matthew no doubt felt that his efforts would be viewed favorably by South Carolina farmers, and help offset opposition from Tillman.

Congress adjourned in late October. Matthew went back to Edgefield, where he campaigned for both Cleveland and the state ticket. Richardson and his slate easily won, but despite gaining a popular majority, the president lost the race for electoral votes. The Republican, Harrison, would assume his place in the White House.[103]

In December 1888 the South Carolina assembly met and elected Butler to a third term as U.S. senator. His victory was tenuous. Tillman's supporters held a ten-vote majority in the House, and lacked only two votes from controlling the Senate. With Tillman sulking in Edgefield, however, no one stood in effective opposition to Matthew. He looked forward to another six years in Washington.[104]

CHAPTER 25

Third Term

THE PRIME ISSUE FOR THE 1888 PRESIDENTIAL CAMPAIGN WAS THE TARIFF. The Democrats favored an across-the-board slash in rates; the Republicans were willing to reduce the taxes on commodities, but wanted to retain or even increase duties for manufactured products. Back in July 1888, the House had enacted a bill, introduced by Texas representative Roger Q. Mills, which espoused the Democratic position. The Republican Senate began their deliberations in December.[1]

When Butler and Maria came north to Washington for the Second Session of the Fiftieth Congress, they settled into a flat located at 815 Seventeenth Street NW.[2] While she attended to making their quarters comfortable, he went to the Capitol to take part in the tariff debates. He listened to Republican arguments against Mills's Bill, one of which was advanced by Sen. Frank Hiscock from New York. "I know of no one," he related, "who does not concede that tariffs . . . [stimulate] production, increasing the product to the world's consumers, [producing] the abnormally low prices which we have to-day."

"I should be glad to understand," Butler replied, "how it is that with high protective tariffs, the price of a commodity in this country is reduced."

"France and German gave high protection . . . upon sugar," Hiscock explained. "The result was the development of their sugar beet industry . . . the world's product has been increased . . . [forcing] sugar down to its present low price."

"If that be true, may I ask if the protection given to . . . sugar in France and German has enhanced the value of the wages in those countries?"

"I have . . . no doubt about it."

"Your argument is not worth the time it takes to utter it," Matthew exclaimed, revealing the snare that he had laid for Hiscock. "The controlling reason that I have heard for a high protective tariff is . . . to protect

American labor from the pauper labor of Europe . . . now you prove that there is no pauper labor [overseas]."

"Oh no!"

"One word more. I have never believed in the doctrine that . . . taxation, high or low, has anything to do with wages. [That is] the most flagrant, the most untenable position . . . any intelligent people ever got into their minds."[3] Matthew, per usual, left no doubts in the wake of his views. He was, however, unable to sway the Senate into approving Mills's Bill.

About a month later Butler was strangely quiet regarding an issue on which earlier he had held a strong opinion. Senate Bill 185 was introduced, proposing statehood for Montana, both North and South Dakota, and Washington. Few made comment; Butler had nothing to say. The bill passed on February 21, 1889; Cleveland, in one of his last acts while in office, penned his signature the next day.[4] Eight new senators, probably Republicans, would soon join the legislature.

Congress adjourned March 2, 1889. Butler, however, decided not to return to Edgefield, and remained in Washington through that summer. He worked on his various committee assignments, gave an occasional speech, and spent leisure time with Maria and the two girls. In late May, for example, he took his family to Annapolis, where the four of them enjoyed a picnic.[5]

Matthew had another reason for remaining in Washington. He was touring the city, shopping for a house. He and Maria had been renting rooms for about thirteen years, but now he felt sufficiently secure in his political future to purchase quarters in the capital. He bought a modest home, situated at 1434 North Street NW.[6]

While waiting to occupy his new home, Butler kept tabs on his three sons. Cabby had transferred to the 5th Cavalry in February 1889.[7] Upon his arrival at Fort Supply in the Indian Territory, he probably met with Frank, working nearby as an assistant surgeon for the army.[8] Willie was still in Edgefield, where he practiced law and managed Butler's plantation properties.

Butler attended the opening session of the Fifty-first Congress that December, and found the Republicans in control of both houses and the presidency. They were in no mood to grant a South Carolina Democrat any plums of power. Matthew was given the same committee assignments (Naval Affairs and Territories) that he had held in the past.[9]

In January, however, when Matthew first addressed this Senate, the topic he raised had no relation to his committee work. He asked the federal government to fund a program to send blacks back to Africa. "The race question," he pointed out, "is a burning, vital issue, [which does not relate] to the negro . . . alone. . . . What is to become of the . . . Indians [or] Chinamen in our midst? Are they . . . to be made citizens, too, and allowed to vote?" Congress, he knew, would never follow this course. They had already forced the Indian on to reservations, and expelled the Chinese. Matthew was insisting on similar treatment for the blacks.

Warming to his subject, Butler went on to note that in the North, despite being given "every advantage of education and enlightenment," the black was still "branded with [a] mark of inferiority and excluded from . . . enjoying his . . . right of various callings." He documented this claim with a long list of occupations, not one of which was available to blacks. "Why?" Butler asked. "If some philanthropist who loves the negro from a distance would answer this question, I would be obliged. Is it race prejudice? Of course it is. . . . An unrelenting, unforgiving, incurable race prejudice." There was, he was arguing, no place for blacks to succeed in America.

"The bill," he concluded, "contemplates the gradual, orderly, and voluntary movement of the colored people out of the Southern states, and provides Governmental aid to enable them to . . . [go back] to the Free State of Congo or Liberia . . . the public lands of the West, or to the abandoned farm lands of Vermont or Massachusetts." The latter destination was a sarcastic reference to the origin of abolition.

Sen. George F. Hoar of Massachusetts rose to answer Butler. "The proposition," he declared, "is one of the most astonishing ever heard in the . . . Senate or in the legislative history of any free, civilized, and prosperous people . . . [deporting] millions of our laborers, born upon our soil, every one of them entitled . . . to [the rights] which the proudest or most fortunate possesses . . . to . . . that black and dismal cavern [of Africa], which the . . . white man has scarcely penetrated."

"We have no right," Hoar went on, "to ask the negro to turn his back on America until . . . a generation of negro children [have been] educated . . . and have failed in their duties . . . of citizenship, and [shown] they can not live in equality and in peace and in justice with . . . white fellow citizens."

"I really believe . . . that the race problem exists in the excited imaginations and in the ineradicable prejudices of a few white men," Senator Blair stated. "Instead of exporting . . . 8,000,000 colored people, [if] we should [send] to Africa 10,000 judiciously-selected [whites], and keep them there . . . the whole difficulty would be settled."[10]

If Blair expected Matthew to rise with indignation, he was disappointed. Butler was too cool to take the bait. He knew (probably from the start) that this bill had no chance of passing, and dropped his drastic approach to solving what he correctly perceived as a nationwide race problem.

The debate over his deportation plan exhausted Matthew. "I have been under the weather for ten days," he admitted in a March letter to Harry Hammond, "and do not appear to rally here. I [plan] to go home . . . and lay off for a week or so."[11]

In this same note, Butler revealed his deep-seated prejudice for blacks. He felt they were only capable of manual labor. Blacks who attended college would lead an idle life. "Once a fellow has learned to wear a clean shirt," he wrote, "he is not going [back] into the cotton patch."

Upon Butler's return to the Senate in April, he became involved in the bill to set up a government for the Oklahoma Territory, lands the Federal government planned to purchase from the Cherokee. Both houses had already approved the act; the question lay in the compromise recommended by the joint legislative committee.

Matthew, probably because of his relationship to Chief Bushyhead, had voted against this bill, and he continued his opposition with an attack on the committee's proposal. "We yielded then and we are yielding now," he exclaimed, "to the . . . unreasonable clamor . . . made by [those] who are anxious to get these public lands. . . . [This act] proposes to extend Territorial courts over the Cherokee country [with] provisions which cannot be enforced [because] of contradictions in this bill."

Others agreed with Matthew. "The district courts have unlimited civil jurisdiction over $100," George G. Vest, the Missouri senator said, "then there is a provision that the county courts have this same jurisdiction, and then there is a provision that there shall be no county courts."

"This will all be remedied after the Territorial Legislature meets," Illinois senator Shelby M. Cullom assured.

"Does the Senator hold," Butler asked, "that the Territorial Legislature [can] change an act of Congress?"

"No, Sir. I do not."

"It must change this act if it corrects this matter."

Butler had made a strong point, but this effort was in vain. Only four other senators joined him in voting against the compromise bill.[12]

A few months later the questions of statehood rose for the territories of Idaho and Wyoming. If Butler had any objections to their entering the Union, he raised them in the privacy of the Territorial Committee, because he had no comment when the vote came to the Senate floor. Two separate bills were presented and quickly passed. President Harrison signed both on July 9, 1890.[13]

Butler became involved in yet another debate in August, this time on the McKinley Tariff Bill. He raised objections to an increase in the duty for cotton-ties (used in binding bales) from 35 percent to 103.71 percent. "Before I get through," he proclaimed, "I shall [document] that this is nothing more than a deliberate, wanton piece of robbery [by] Congress . . . taking money out of the pockets from one set of people and putting it in the pockets of another."

Nelson W. Aldrich of Rhode Island was guiding the bill through the Senate, and Matthew questioned him. "Has there been any demand from any source . . . for this increase," he demanded, "and if so, from whom?"

"There has been a protest from all the people . . . engaged in [this] production."

"It has [not] been asked for by anybody," Arkansas senator James K. Jones protested.

"I know of one instance," Sen. Frank Hiscock of New York offered. "[An American] undertook to supply the market with cotton-ties, and the instant . . . he made a contract, the English [lowered the] price and he was unable to get another order."

"This American [tried] to make a corner on cotton-ties," Butler concluded, "but the [English] were a little too smart for him."

"His only purpose [was] in getting these orders was to make goods," Hiscock insisted.

"Patriotism!" Butler scoffed.

"Certainly. He is indeed a very patriotic gentleman."

"A gentleman acting entirely on patriotic motives . . . who has demanded . . . this duty be put up from 35 percent to 103.71 percent . . . imposing an enormous burden upon [Southern] people who are already overburdened and overtaxed . . . is inequitable, unfair, unjust, and can not be sustained . . . [under] any principle whatever known to honest, fair legislation."[14]

Butler's exposure of the plot to grant an advantage to one Northern manufacturer at the expense of all Southern cotton planters was to no avail. The Republican-controlled Senate retained the increase in duty on cotton-ties in their version of the McKinley Bill, which passed that October and raised tariffs to their highest point in history.[15]

Defeated in the Senate, Butler went home to South Carolina that fall to find that he had lost the political battle in his state as well. He was nor surprised. In March Tillman had renounced his vow to never seek political office by offering himself as a candidate for governor. "If you ask me to fight for it," he proclaimed to his farmer supporters, "I will fight as long as I have a dollar left and the health with which to fight . . . the [conservative] ring."[16]

Matthew's friends put up a spirited battle to deny the nomination to Tillman. They backed Joseph H. Earle as their candidate, and took part in summer debates, held throughout the state. Butler was asked to participate, but he declined to get involved.[17] His Senate duty provided a valid excuse, but his real reason for remaining aloof was probably because he recognized that Tillman could not be stopped. He wanted to avoid an association with a losing cause, thereby keeping his personal positioning vis-à-vis Tillman open.

Tillman defeated Earle at the September nominating convention, and despite the last-gasp candidacy of Alexander C. Haskell, a "bolting" Democratic and one of Matthew's cohorts, won election in November. And in December the reform-dominated legislature named John L. M. Irby, a representative and Tillman's campaign chief, to replace Wade Hampton in the Senate. Butler made a plea to Tillman to retain his old commander in office, but the new governor was bent on revenge. "[He] can attribute his defeat," he noted, referring to Hampton's support of Haskell, "to his own acts."[18]

When the Second Session of the Fifty-first Congress assembled in December 1890, Butler took his seat with a clear view of his own future. Tillman would no doubt win reelection as governor in 1892, but because the state constitution wold not allow him a third term in 1893, he would then try to assume Matthew's place in the Senate. Through the coming four years, Butler would take drastic steps to prevent this from happening.

The first major issue considered by the Senate was the "Force" Bill, a measure introduced in the House by Massachusetts representative Henry Cabot Lodge, calling for federal supervision of national elections to prevent the states from excluding black male voters. Butler was named as the prime example of abuse. "I went down and gave them tickets," Hoar quoted Butler, "and said that . . . they had a right to vote Republican . . . but if they exercised that right [imposing] taxes on me which destroyed my property . . . I [would] see that they left my plantation."[19]

"I brand that statement," Matthew retorted, "false and untrue."

"Anybody who is familiar with the incisive style of the Senator from South Carolina," Hoar answered, "would think . . . that it bristled . . . with the earmarks of his mode of speech."

"If any Senator upon this floor [says] I . . . intimidated any colored voters on my plantation . . . he stated what was untrue."

Hoar's accusations infuriated Matthew, and he prepared a detailed assault on both the Force Bill and its Republican sponsors, which he delivered on December 17, 1891.

> If the bills should become law, it will establish . . . here in Washington, an imperial, central power [which is] wholly irresponsible to the people, a political junta firmly rooted in the administration of our public affairs. . . .
>
> This measure, [which takes] elections out of the hands of the States and . . . the people, was inaugurated, formulated, and

is being pressed [for] passage by a few New England men . . . who do not believe in popular government. . . . A minority of the majority of this body . . . attempting to cram this bill down the throats of an unwilling people [should] be regarded . . . as shameless and brazen . . . a revolutionary purpose making them fit for popular impeachment.

Butler then turned and attacked the senator from Maine, William P. Frye. "The evidence that [he] produced the other day in his tirade," Matthew averred, "gave conclusive proof that this bill is not demanded."

"It was a speech," Frye protested, "not a tirade."

"It was a tirade . . . he would . . . bayonet [the South] into his way of thinking and voting. . . . I [should not] suppose for a moment that he would carry bayonets to my State. . . . He did not do so some twenty-five years ago, when [they] were plentiful and in daily use, with transportation furnished, [so] I am therefore safe in assuming he would not perpetuate that folly now."

Butler next detailed the expense involved. "The supervisors, the marshals, deputy marshals, canvassers, returning boards, clerks, etc. will constitute an army, organized and equipped, armed no doubt, to carry out the behests . . . of this oligarchy. . . . The pay of this army, the quarters for them . . . stationary, mileage, etc. . . . What will it cost the people[?] . . . Who can calculate it?"

After citing the corruption that evolved in South Carolina from giving blacks the vote, Butler ended his talk with a direct appeal to the senators from the West. "[You asked] our assistance in the Chinese question," he noted, reminding them of Southern support for the 1882 Chinese Exclusion Act. "We did not stop [then] to taunt you with . . . outrages you had perpetuated on this . . . race. We did not thrust our opinions offensively on you in regard to a question which you . . . [had] a more accurate knowledge than ourselves. Is it asking too much when we invoke similar treatment from your hands?"[20]

Matthew's speech, as well as similar protests by others from the South, proved decisive. Although Lodge's Force Bill had easily passed in the House, this measure never even came to a vote in the Senate. Civil rights for blacks would not become a reality for another seventy-five years.

Late that January Butler became involved in a comical exchange. Mississippi Senator James Z. George was disputing a proposal for apportioning representatives to the House, a filibuster against a measure that penalized states for denying blacks their right to vote. When Butler rose to ask if he could insert a point, George agreed to step aside for the moment.

"I object," Senator Aldrich of Rhode Island cried.

"The Mississippi Senator," Hoar of Massachusetts added, "has not yielded the floor."

"[Have you] yielded the floor?" Aldrich inquired.

"Oh, no, Sir. I have the floor. . . . I have been so much in the habit of having the floor of late that I may not know how to yield it."

"I have the floor," Butler insisted.

"[Senator George] cannot yield it to anybody," Edmunds of Maine noted.

"The Chair recognized me," Butler replied.

"What is the situation," the puzzled George asked.

"The Senator from Mississippi," Vice President Levi P. Morton ruled, "is entitled to the floor."

"Will the Senator from Mississippi permit me to read a few sections from the Revised Statutes?" Butler asked.

"If it is agreeable to the gentlemen of the Senate. I do not want to be guilty of anything like treason."

"I object," Hoar repeated.

"It is the duty of [Senator Butler] to take his seat," John Sherman of Ohio said as he joined the debate.

"It is quite unnecessary," Butler snapped back, "to administer that lecture to me."

"I insist," Sherman growled, "on [enforcing] the rule."

"The Senator from Mississippi," Morton reiterated, "is entitled to the floor."

George continued with his speech. He had been talking for about forty-five minutes when Aldrich rose from his seat to inquire, "[Will you] yield the floor?"

"I object!" Butler cried.

"Oh, no; do not object," George pleaded. "I am pretty nearly worn out."[21]

The Republicans eventually forced the filibuster to an end, but they could not pass their bill. The South was able to once again avoid federal interference in local elections.

Just before Congress adjourned, Butler took note of an attempt to locate the new Government Printing Office on land held by friends of the Republicans. The owners were asking $243,000 for what was now a neighborhood baseball field. He rose to object.

"I can say without fear of contradiction," he declared, "there are some badges of fraud about this transaction which the Congress . . . owes itself to have explained." Butler went on to note that in advertising for bids, limits were imposed "in such a way that [the government] could procure no other land but the baseball lot."

Nebraska's Senator, Charles F. Manderson, defended the deal. "Is it not true," he asked Butler, that "the commission" was not required to advertise [for bids]?"

"They were not bound to advertise, but they did."

"Is it not true that they could by private negotiation . . . have bought the property [in preference] to any other lot in the city of Washington?"

"So much the worse if that is true."[22]

John C. Spooner, a former businessman who had lived by the dictum that corruption was inevitable, if not proper, entered the debate.[23] "Were they not charged," the Wisconsin senator asked, "not only with the duty but with the power of selecting a site?"

"I suppose they were."

"I am astonished by the speech of the Senator of South Carolina," Joseph R. Hawlet of Connecticut announced. "This transaction is spotless. . . . I do not care anything about the [land] owner. . . . He is nobody to me; he is minus, worse than zero."[24]

Butler continued to argue, but it was an unfair battle. The Republican majority was bound to carry out the deal, and in the end, they succeeded.

Congress adjourned in March. Butler went back to Edgefield, where he found the state in far better condition than he had probably anticipated. Tillman had failed to produce the revolution pledged during his campaign. "[His] impolitic conduct," his biographer wrote, "had accentuated the hatred of enemies, antagonized friends . . . needlessly sacrificed many of the promised fruits of Tillmanism."[25]

Butler enjoyed a nonpolitical summer at home. That fall, however, he attended a reunion for former Confederates, held "under the oaks at Lanham's" just outside Edgefield. As Matthew rose to introduce the main speaker for the occasion, Gen. Ellison Capers, a reporter noted, "he looked like a magnificent soldier."[26]

Matthew's appearance probably hid his worried thoughts, focused on North Carolina. Elise, always delicate, was sick with a fever, and had gone to a resort near Highlands to recover in the fresh mountain air. She died on September 21, 1891. When writing her obituary, the newspaper correspondent remembered Elise as being "graceful as a lily. . . . [whose] eyes of unsurpassing beauty caught their expression from the deepest blue of the noonday heavens." She was Catholic, but was buried next to her two infant sisters and brother in the family plot next to the First Baptist Church.[27]

Butler and Maria were devastated by Elise's death. Two months later word arrived from Augusta that Willie, who had been attending an exposition at the Arlington Hotel, had suddenly died from an attack of uremia, the retention in the blood of elements usually extracted with urine.[28] Willie's demise on November 29 must have taken the heart out of Matthew.

"You, dear Calbraith," a friend wrote, "have been made to drink . . . bitter waters of affliction. The blows have come in quick succession."[29]

When Frank learned of his brother's death, he arranged to resign from the army and return home to assume control of Butler's property.[30] He would be delayed for almost a year, but Frank's presence was unnecessary because Willie had been a figurehead. The lands were really managed by a loyal black, a former slave purchased when he was a seven-year-old boy.[31]

Putting aside their sorrow, Butler and Maria went back to Washington in December 1891, where he attended the First Session of the Fifty-second Congress. Reaction to the high prices resulting from the McKinley Tariff had led to a Democratic sweep in the last fall's national elections, and Matthew found his party holding control. He was named to two standing committees, Naval Affairs and Foreign Relations, and to three select committees: to establish the University of the United States, to procure additional accommodations for the Library of Congress, and to lead a group (a continuing role) in charge of the Senate's relations with the Five Civilized Tribes of Indians.[32]

Despite having added duties, Matthew did not take part in the Senate debates until March 22, 1892. And when he did speak, his subject bore no relation to his committee assignments. He complained about the quality of air in the Senate chamber and its various offices.

"I think every Senator will agree with me," he groused, "there is something wrong about the ventilation . . . there must be something wrong about the structure." He suggested that the Senate hire an architect to study the problem.

"The air tubes . . . into this chamber," Joseph C. S. Blackburn contended, "are as well devised and as efficient and as good as is possible." The Kentucky senator was a member of the Rules Committee, who managed the Senate wing, and he was no doubt defending his group's performance.

"Do I understand," Butler queried, "my friend to apply his remarks to all of the committee rooms?"

"To every one of them."

"There must have been wonderful progress . . . since I was there."

"I allude to every one that is occupied today."

"Ah! There are [at least] forty that are not occupied because they can't be. That is . . . what I am talking about."

"It was known when they were [built] that [they] would not and never could be occupied."

"[The] architect ought to be arraigned and tried . . . for [spending] so much money [on] rooms which cannot be occupied by anybody."

"The architect is dead."

Blackburn continued to argue against passing Matthew's proposal, but the ventilation problem was so severe, most of the senators sided with Butler. His resolution won a quick approval.[33]

Earlier during this session, both the House and the Senate passed a ten-year extension of the Scott Act, an 1888 decree that required all Chinese immigrants to register or face deportation. Butler was appointed to the joint committee that would draw up a compromise draft of this legislation. When the group met that April, his views were deemed unacceptable by his peers, so he took his case to the Senate floor.

"There is a solemn treaty between [our] Government and the Chinese," he began. "I believe that the act of 1888 abrogated that treaty, and that the passage of that act . . . was a disgrace to the Congress of the United States."

"I understand the Senator is giving his support to the proposed amendment," a surprised John H. Mitchell, a senator from Oregon, noted. He certainly recalled Matthew's appeal to the Far West for tit for tat in rejecting the Force Bill, and had not anticipated opposition from the South on racial matters.

"[Now] that the Senator has called my attention to it," Butler replied, "I think I shall vote against [it]." He explained, "Here we are, inviting the Chinese people to engage in commercial intercourse with us by every possible means . . . yet in response to a demand from a very limited area of this country, the Pacific Coast, we . . . throw insult into the face of these people and . . . violate every treaty stipulation which we have ever made with them."

Although Butler was correct in his views, he was inconsistent. He had also advised in 1888 that the bill violated existing treaties between the United States and China, but had added, "I am willing to go as far as any other Senator in excluding the Chinese, and will vote for the bill."

When reminded of his remarks, Matthew replied, "I have regretted a dozen times [my voting] for . . . the Scott act, but I am not going to perpetuate the same folly [again]."

Butler's position was perhaps noble, but not political. The Exclusion Bill passed despite his objections, and he was not doubt looked upon as a traitor by the Far West.[34]

One month later Matthew spoke out in support of naval appropriations. Referring to "recent difficulties" in Chile (two sailors had been killed by an angry mob while on shore in Valparaiso; an indignant United States threatened war, but Chile settled the issue by agreeing to pay the victims' families an indemnity), he stated, "If Chile succeeded in getting . . . the vessel she was building in France . . . and got it around on the Pacific coast, she would have walked right in to the harbor of San Francisco without . . . opposition."

"We have warships," Missouri senator George G. Vest retorted, "able to compete with any now afloat."

"The Senator has been misinformed. . . . [Our cruisers] . . . are not armoured at all. . . . The only possible chance . . . would be to ram an enemy and sink the ship."

"Then it [is] necessary to have . . . first class armoured vessels in . . . every port in order to protect it. There would be more necessity for land defenses and torpedo systems. . . . We could more safely rely on them than . . . vessels."

"No nation in the world," Eugene Hale from Maine noted, "could hold its sway for one hour if it told its people that it was resorting to [only] . . . torpedoes to protect its great cities."

"The best way . . . to invite a naval war," Vest continued, "is to construct a great navy."

"Does the Senator know," Hale asked, introducing a new twist to the argument, "that the immense development in this country . . . for manufacturing every form of steel . . . [arose because] of the naval appropriations which he is condemning?"

"When Mr. Cleveland was President, I voted for liberal appropriations," Vest answered. "We had then . . . an overflowing Treasury . . . [now] we are staring in the face of a deficit."

"[This] naval appropriation bill is smaller than [that] of last year," Butler protested. "The real cause of our deficiency [is] in the enormous appropriations made for [Civil War] pensions. . . . But it is not part of my business. . . . Coming from the section of the country that I do, to even make a suggestion [here] . . . would be misconstrued and perverted."

"I have been led . . . to [believe]," Vest said, returning to his original point, "we now have war vessels . . . capable of meeting those of any other nationality."

"We have the finest vessels of their type afloat," Butler agreed, "but they are not armored war ships." Referring to a chart that had been distributed to all of the senators, he pointed out that since 1882, the United States had produced forty-two ironclads, i.e., two rams, seven gunboats, two torpedo boats, five monitors, three battleships, twenty cruisers, one dispatch boat, one training vessel, and one coastal defense ship. None had heavy armor. "I . . . voted cheerfully for every one," he recounted, "and if I had to economize [on the budget] . . . I should put the knife in somewhere else."[35]

The Senate agreed with him. Despite the opposition of Vest and other Republicans, the appropriation for more ships for the navy was passed.

The Senate continued in session throughout that summer, but many legislators left Washington to attend their party's 1892 national convention.

The Republicans assembled in Minneapolis on June 10, and renominated Benjamin Harrison for president. Two weeks later, gathering in Chicago, the Democrats named Grover Cleveland as their candidate. Later that summer both the Prohibition and Populist parties joined in the race with entrants.[36]

In South Carolina Tillman not only ran for his second term but also moved to strengthen the means toward achieving his platform for reform. "Kill off the race of fence straddlers," he urged voters. "Elect new men to take the place of the driftwood legislature."[37]

The conservative Democratic slate opposing Tillman and his ticket was headed by John C. Sheppard, a former governor of South Carolina. Butler's comrades probably expected his active support, but once again, he stood aloof from the campaign. "He [would] not lift a finger or utter a word," one of his cohorts complained.[38] Matthew was well aware that in 1894 he would need votes from Tillman legislators to retain his Senate seat, and he was not about to alienate anyone who might preside over his future.

The state campaign was tumultuous. "Instead of a calm discussion of differences of opinion," Tillman's biographer, Francis B. Simkins, wrote, "there was a resort to personalities, groundless accusations, and private revelations [that] were unseeming in candidates for . . . public office." He went on to note that "The crowds . . . spent most of their time yelling."[39]

Tillman's tactics succeeded. He was reelected, and in the legislature, only 8 of the 36 senators and 22 of the 124 representatives opposed the governor. And among the 102 assemblymen who supported Tillman, only 27 were holdovers from the previous house.[40]

On the national scene Cleveland failed to capture the popular majority, but he won the presidential election. The Populist candidate, James B. Weaver, received more than one million votes, many of which might have gone to Harrison and given him a second term.[42]

When the Fifty-second Congress reconvened in December, Butler spoke out against a bill that authorized the purchase of Cherokee land for white settlement. First he complained about forcing the Indians to pay "intruders" (squatters) for improvements they had made to their homesteads; then he objected to Government inaction in removing the squatters from Cherokee property that would not be sold.[42] His fellow senators probably wondered what he had in mind by raising these seemingly petty issues.

On February 3, 1893, Matthew finally revealed his true objective. Having drawn the Senate's attention to two types of inequities in the bill, he raised a third issue by introducing an amendment that allowed an Indian who had developed property the government was about to confiscate to buy that plot and stay in the territory. "I don't know," he claimed, "how many there are . . . perhaps not more than two or three."

When asked for an example, Butler acknowledged that he could verify just one, "a man who has opened a rock quarry." Connecticut's Orville H. Platt immediately saw through Butler's subterfuge. "If the Senator will put in by name . . . Chief Bushy Head [*sic*]," he offered, "I shall not object to it." "I [will modify] my amendment."[43] Matthew continued to argue (probably for show), but he had taken care of his cousin by marriage, and was willing to back down at the proper moment. He withdrew his opposition to the bill when the roll was called, and it easily passed.

A few days later, toward the end of the session, Butler joined a debate over an act to mandate automatic coupling of railroad cars. All carriers would be required to use a compatible system, to be selected by a commission appointed by companies controlling 75 percent of rail traffic.

Butler predicted that the stronger railroads would opt for a single design, too expensive for the weaker lines. "A young man in my own State," he further stated, "has secured a patent for . . . . automatic coupling of air brakes, which he . . . believes will revolutionize [railroad] transportation. . . . If we restrict the railroads to any particular device . . . it will stop all inventions and improvements."

Butler thought this bill granted too much power to the larger lines. He suggested that a committee composed of independent experts be named to recommend a compatible system, and that the time limits for implementing this new design be extended from 1895 to 1898. The Senate agreed and included this amendment when passing the bill.[44]

The Senate adjourned on March 3, 1893, then quickly reconvened in a special session to inaugurate Grover Cleveland as president. The standing committee responsibilities were also assigned, and Butler reaped the benefits for having his party holding the majority in the Fifty-third Congress. He not only retained his seat on both Naval Affairs and Foreign Relations, but was also named as chairman of the Interstate Commerce Committee. The Special Session ended in April, and Matthew returned Edgefield for the summer.[45]

When he arrived home, Butler was greeted by his son, Frank, who had finally been released from the army. The lad had not only taken charge of the family properties but also established a partnership with the town's leading physician, Dr. J. W. Hill.[46] Cabby, too, had come east to take a post as assistant riding instructor at West Point.[47]

Life was good for the Butlers. The rest of the nation, however, faced a turbulent time. Labor unrest dominated the scene. Thousands of workers were on strike, seeking higher wages and shorter hours. Management responded with violence and replacement employees to halt these walkouts and break up the unions, as illustrated by the riots at the Homestead Mill.[48]

In February 1893 the first signs of coming recession had arisen. The Philadelphia & Reading Railroad confessed that they would not meet the interest payment on their $125 million debt, and the company filed for bankruptcy. A crash in stock prices on Wall Street followed, and soon the banks began to shut their doors. The farmers were confronted with foreclosure of their mortgages. This economic debacle, the Panic of '93, was in the main attributed to an 1890 Congressional mistake, the Sherman Silver Purchase Act.[49]

Sherman's bill called for the purchase of 4.5 million ounces of silver every month by the treasury. They issued notes as payment, redeemable in silver or gold. The notes were then recirculated, open to additional redemptions. This led to a run on gold. The nation's reserves, over $700 million in 1890, had receded to less than $100 million. If the flow was not stemmed, the United States would have no choice but adopt a single metal (silver) standard, resulting in the devaluing of its currency throughout the world. The economy, already feeble, was likely to collapse. Cleveland summoned Congress into special session in August to repeal the Sherman Silver Purchase Act.[50]

This issue was sponsored by the Democrats and strongly supported by the business community, both of whom were major components of Butler's political base. His cohorts assumed he was on their side. He had, for example, repeatedly filed resolutions from the Charleston Chamber of Commerce against the remonetization of silver. And the president was so sure of his allegiance, he had assigned Butler control of patronage in South Carolina. But this was a question that did not follow party lines, and Matthew opted to join those against rescinding the bill. "When the people complain," he said in explaining his position, "the people are always right."[51]

What Matthew was really saying was that the farmers in South Carolina (and Tillman) were opposed to a repeal of the Sherman Silver Purchase Act, and Butler was certain to lose his chance for reelection to the Senate if he stood with his usual constituency and President Cleveland.

The strategy used to block repeal of Sherman's Silver Purchase Act was to filibuster. Matthew arose in October to add his voice to the clamor. "The Senate," he noted in defending his right for debate, "is a great deliberative body, intended by the framers of the [Constitution] to put a veto upon hasty, unwise, and improper legislation. It's the last refuge for minorities. . . . No despotism [is] so oppressive as [that] of a majority unrestrained." Butler was quoting John C. Calhoun.

"Compromise is the solution," he went on. "I will not vote for repeal unless it is accompanied by a proposition to continue the coinage of silver . . . making it a permanent part of the financial policy of the Government."

Butler wanted more cash in circulation. "There is not enough currency," he said, "for the transaction of legitimate business." He went on to note that the nation's money was unevenly distributed. "Of the one hundred and sixty-odd million dollars appropriated [each year] for pensions, nine-tenths of it is disbursed in the North. . . . It is," he quickly added, "the result of the fortunes of war, and I abide it."

Having stated his position, Matthew turned to attacking the claims of the opposition. "The credit of the Government is as good or better than any in the civilized world today," he noted, "collecting its revenue with relentless regularity [and] paying its obligations everywhere without default . . . in the very money . . . being derided on the floor of the Senate."

Why the panic over silver? "The only complaint that I have heard," Butler declared, "comes from men who are owners and holders of large investments, who know nothing and care less about the . . . people of this country. They [are] selfish and sordid . . . unsafe advisors [for] great questions of legislation."

"Investors," he explained, "discovered that industrial and corporate enterprises were . . . very largely overstocked . . . far beyond their earning capacity, and . . . began to put their concerns into the hands of receivers. . . . Another cause is . . . bankers in the great financial centers had loaned the money of their depositors far beyond the bounds and limits of prudence. When the flurry started and the depositors demanded their money, the banks could not respond. . . . They found themselves hampered by their own imprudence . . . and jumped on the Sherman Act."[52]

His arguments seemed to fall upon deaf ears. Two days later Matthew offered another compromise: to eliminate the 10 percent federal tax on notes issued by state banks. As a result of this levy, local currency, once common, had disappeared from circulation. "The only question," he averred, "is . . . will the banks take such steps [to] secure the men who hold its circulation . . . will the banks provide sufficient reserve to secure the depositors? That [I think] is about all there is in successful banking."

When reminded of previous problems of many state banks, Butler answered with a shrug. "Banks will fail," he pointed out, "as long as men are dishonest. Banks fail today; they have failed by the hundreds in the last three months, carrying down with them the destruction of millions of property."

Butler concluded his argument with a quote from Andrew Jackson. "One of the serious evils of our present system of banking," the former president related, "is that it enables one class of society by its control over the currency to act injuriously upon the interests of all the others, and to exercise more than just a proportion of influence in political affairs."

"That was a solemn truth," Butler declared, "and it is as true today as it was then." He would not vote to rescind the Sherman Silver Purchase Act until Congress addressed itself to rectifying the currency problem.[53]

The pressure brought to bear by Butler and his cohorts produced a compromise plan: The Sherman Silver Purchase Act would be repealed as of July 1, 1894; the Treasury's stock of silver bullion would all be coined; and paper money that was backed by specie would be only issued in dominations of ten dollars or higher. Victory was at hand. But the president would not yield. Cleveland would only accept a simple repeal.[54]

The vote was taken on October 30. Butler and thirty-seven others cast their ballots against unconditional repeal of the Sherman Silver Purchase Act, but forty-eight favored the bill. It passed. The Senate adjourned. Matthew headed for Edgefield to start the last campaign of his political career.

CHAPTER 26

Defeat

UPON HIS RETURN TO SOUTH CAROLINA, BUTLER LEARNED THAT HIS VOTE against repeal of Sherman's Silver Purchase Act had so antagonized his conservative base, many of them would no longer associate with him. "At the unveiling of the Confederate monument in Orangeburg, there were generals, colonels, majors and captains galore," the *Edgefield Advertiser* noted. "But General M. C. Butler was not there, nor was he invited."[1]

A few, however, tried to support Butler. Wade Hampton forgot his pique over Red Shirt strategy and proposed a plan for former Confederates to endorse Matthew by raising rival Democratic clubs to counter Tillman's political organization in South Carolina. "Unscrupulous demigods [offering] false promises have misled . . . our most honest men, [bringing] shame upon our proud state," he stated. "I still have an abiding faith in the men who followed the Starry Cross through trial and carnage, who bore with the heroism of martyrs [all] the suffering of the Reconstruction era, and who with a devotion and pluck never surpassed, rescued the State in '76."[2]

Hampton never said it, but his plan included using the black majority against Tillman by allowing them to take part in the fall election. Matthew, however, would not risk losing white rule. "We cannot disguise the fact that there are two factions in our party," he declared. "It only needs patience and tolerance and forbearance to bring [us] together. We cannot do this with the ballot degraded . . . by an appeal to the negro vote."[3]

Butler failed to recognize that Hampton's proposal was his only means for reelection to the Senate. He had assumed that the conservatives had no option, that since they would never vote for Tillman, they would have to cast their ballot for him. But the legislature would choose the next senator, and Butler needed candidates who supported his cause running against Tillman's aspirants to the assembly. The animosity of the conservatives toward Butler was so great, however, in most of the counties they never even bothered to nominate a slate. "Butler," Tillman's biographer stated, "was defeated before the canvas of 1894 began."[4]

274

Facing an impossible battle, Butler nevertheless began a speaking tour across the state in early December, first at Williamsburg, then at Bennettsville. "He came too late," a local newspaper recounted. "The Marlboro County people have already killed the senatorial calf for [Tillman]."[5] Following his address at Spartanburg, another reporter said, "When Butler says he is going to be elected, he becomes funny. He stands no more chance than a feline in Hades."[6]

No doubt discouraged, Butler returned to Washington in mid-December to assume his seat in the Senate. The issue at hand was the Hawaiian Islands. American sugar interests in this tropical paradise had led a successful coup against the native ruler, Queen Liliuokalani, in January 1893. They created a new government, then applied for annexation to the United States. Correspondence between these insurgents and the White House had been both frequent and secret. Republicans wanted these letters read in the open to the Senate.[7]

"Would it not be just as well to have these . . . printed?" Butler advised. "Why delay and waste the time of the Senate in reading them?"

"I know," Sen. William E. Chandler of New Hampshire quickly replied, "these [are] communications the Senate will wish to hear."

Butler was well aware that the Republicans were hoping to embarrass President Cleveland, and he moved to block this scheme. "I . . . object to the further reading of the letters," he said, "and [move] to refer the message . . . to the Committee on Foreign Relations, and that they be printed."

"No good is to be accomplished," Chandler insisted, "in opposing the reading."

"The country will survive whether these papers are read or not."

Each knowing the other was only playing politics, both Butler and Chandler reverted to repartee, which was rewarded with laughter from their fellow senators.

"I think the Senator from South Carolina is unwarranted in singling me out for denunication on the ground that I was seeking some partisan advantage of the President," Chandler protested with a smile, "whom I so constantly and so loyally supported on the silver question." Matthew, of course, had opposed Cleveland on this issue.

"If the Senator imagines . . . that what I said was . . . denunciation, I desire now to apologize . . . in the most unqualified manner. . . . The announcement of his nonpartisan patriotism has . . . sunk very deeply into my heart."

"I am so gland that I have been able to teach [the Senator from South Carolina] a lesson."

"I apologize."

"Hereafter we shall be sure he deals with questions of foreign affairs without [any] partisan spirit. . . . We all know that in the height of his statesmanship, [the Senator will] deal with every public question without the slightest regard for political parties."[8]

Butler accepted Chandler's jibes with good spirit, and allowed the letters to be read. Cleveland, however, was not deterred, and successfully blocked the annexation of Hawaii.[9]

Early that March, while the Senate remained in session, Butler left for South Carolina to speak at a citizen meeting in Edgefield. He found that even his neighbors were complacent about his candidacy for reelection. "As a demonstration of popular outpouring," the *Edgefield Advertiser* wrote, "his speech proved Dead Sea apples—dust and ashes."[10]

Matthew returned to Washington later that month, where he urged that monies paid to the Cherokee for their land be saved in the federal sub-treasury.[11] Once the Senate passed this resolution, serving the interests of his Indian cousin, Chief Bushyhead, Butler hurried back to Edgefield. "[He] is having his home . . . repainted inside and out," the local newspaper stated, "preparatory to [its] occupancy by himself and family."[12]

On March 29, just as Matthew was moving his wife and daughter back into their Edgefield home, a riot broke out in Darlington, which gave Butler the opportunity to exploit an inflammatory issue against Tillman. Local resistance to the dispensary had led to bloodshed.

The consumption of alcohol was a problem that had been faced throughout the ages. Drunkenness was abhorred by all, yet prohibition was impractical. The solution that Tillman conceived was state control of the sale of liquor.

Tillman prompted the legislature to pass a bill, which took effect on July 1, 1893, that provided that liquor could only be sold in state-run stores called "dispensaries." He reasoned that the "drys" would be pleased because all of the saloons would be closed; "wets" would be glad because they could still buy whiskey. Other benefits included control of the quality for the product, restriction on sales to minors and drunkards, and added profits to the state, "a consideration," Tillman noted, "not to be despised."

Opponents to the new law (both wets and drys) bemoaned the loss of personal liberty, and in many communities, local officials refused to shut down the saloons. Tillman fought back by offering spies a cash bonus for informing dispensary constables where illegal operations were taking place. The matter came to a head in Darlington.

Tillman sent twenty-two constables to that village to search for illegal saloons or "blind tigers" as they were popularly called. Angry citizens responded by seizing arms from the local militia and confronting Tillman's force. The result was a stalemate, and the state's men started for the railway depot and a return to Columbia. The locals followed them. As both approached the station, they met Paul Rogers, displaying a bloodied head and claiming that Chief Constable John B. McLendon was responsible for his lesions. McLendon panicked, drew a revolver, and opened fire, killing Frank E. Norment, an innocent bystander. A flurry of shots exploded on the scene, and when the smoke cleared, two more were dead and another two wounded. The constables fled into the open countryside, and were pursued but not caught by the inflamed townsmen.

Assuming that a statewide conspiracy had been started against the dispensary, Tillman opted to move decisively, to bring an immediate halt to any such action. He ordered the Columbia militia to Darlington to rescue his constables, who were hiding in the woods outside the village. All three of the companies refused his command. He then called a brigade of militia from Charleston to the scene, but they said that they would not "lend [themselves] to forment civil war among our brethren." Tillman finally appealed to farmers, asking them to volunteer for the mission. Edgefield responded with three companies, two of which went to Darlington, the other to Columbia to stand guard over the governor.[13]

Butler, too, went to Darlington to study the scene and to reap political gain. He reported there had been "not the slightest resistance to . . . enforcement of the dispensary law; on the contrary, the people of Darlington cooperated." Then he tore into Tillman. "There has not been the least excuse or justification for ordering the military to these points," he noted. "[Tillman] has done so at an enormous expense to the taxpayers of this State, and, of course, he will have to look out for that. . . . I need not . . . express my opinion in regard to the dispensary law, but . . . the Governor is attempting to enforce it in a harsh . . . and ill-advised manner. He must not imagine that . . . people . . . will quietly submit to invasion of their rights."[14]

Tillman was stung by Matthew's remarks, but was unable to refute the charges. The governor replied by complaining. "I have been at my post of duty," he groused, "while he has been away . . . galloping around the country letting off political screeds."[15]

Butler was quick to respond. "It is very natural that Governor Tillman should not want me in the State," he noted, "[because] I puncture the bubbles he blows up. . . . Besides, I can be absent two-thirds of my time, and do more good to the people than he could by being on duty all the time."[16]

Continuing to campaign, Matthew addressed the citizens of Allendale in late April, and he was greatly encouraged by their response. "His speech . . . [received] the deepest interest and undivided attention," the local newspaper noted. "A gentleman by instinct, a scholar, a soldier and a statesman are advantages that he will hold. . . . Today the universal verdict is that he is the right man in the right place."[17]

Returning to Washington in early May, Butler took part in a debate over raising tariffs on saltpeter. The proposal to protect local gunpowder manufacturers was based in part on Republican fears of a second rebellion by the South. The though appeared ludicrous to Butler, and he arose to refute the contention. "We shall be with you in the next war," he assured.

"I certainly hope that [you] will give us a duty which will protect the manufacture of saltpeter," Senator Chandler of New Hampshire responded, "so that if we are plunged into war by the impetuosity of the Senator from South Carolina . . . who came so near defeating us in the last war, we shall not find ourselves . . . destitute of saltpeter, and [forced] to resort to all of the extraordinary methods to which the South resorted for the manufacture of gunpowder." He droned on at length, imputing that the former Confederates in the Senate were trying "to strike down the manufacture of saltpeter and . . . cripple [production] of gunpowder."

Chandler had recently embarrassed Matthew with a witty repartee on silver. On this subject, however, he was not so knowledgeable, and Butler leaped to his feet to take advantage of the chance to gain revenge. "I should like to inform the Senator from New Hampshire," he stated, "that saltpeter is not required in the manufacture of smokeless gunpowder . . . the powder of the future. So his eloquence is lost."

Chandler must have sat red-faced with embarrassment because the Senate exploded with laughter over Butler's expose of his ignorance. When the ballots to increase the duty on saltpeter were called, the amendment was soundly defeated.[18]

Butler soon left the Senate, which remained in session, and returned to South Carolina to resume campaigning for reelection. He finally realized that his former conservative cohorts would not run a slate for the legislature to support his return to Washington. Tillman's men would dominate the assembly and no doubt place the governor in his seat. Faced with certain defeat, Matthew contrived a desperate strategy. He asked that those voting in the August primary be provided with two ballots, one for selecting legislators, the second for the people to elect their next senator. Butler also invited Tillman to join him in a series of debates, to be held throughout the state. Butler aspired to influence both the governor's candidates to the assembly and the local citizens, either of whom might decide his future fate.[19]

Tillman refused to agree to a direct election of South Carolina's senator, but he did accept Butler's challenge for debate. The two planned a schedule of thirty-five meetings, beginning in Rock Hill on June 18, ending in Abbeville on August 8.[20]

The Farmers Alliance had earlier asked both candidates to respond to a series of questions, and Tillman had replied that "too many issues will only confuse and divide us." He opted to concentrate on just three points: the abolition of national banks, the free coinage of silver, and an increase in the circulation of cash money. Butler had been given the same queries, and looking to appeal to Tillman's supporters, had provided the same answer. Their concurrence was "so remarkable," the *Charleston News and Courier* said, "they might have been written after a consultation between . . . respective writers."[21] If these debates were to be confined to issues, they promised to be dull. Butler had no intention of allowing that to happen.

Tillman began his Rock Hill speech by aligning himself with the farmers, who made up most of the audience. "I want to get down to the level with you boys that plow," he cried. "You expect a discussion of national issues. . . . I [will] take a bird's eye view of them, [but] I can't sweat and puff and cover them all today. If I tried, I [would] be like a piney woods pond, only knee deep." Tillman then repeated his promises to the Farmers Alliance.[22]

"I'm mighty glad to see you," Butler said when he took the stand. He made a plea for the people to elect the next South Carolina senator, then seemingly turned to address the silver problem. "If the Governor will lend me a dollar," he related, "I'll show you (smiling) that he is better off than me." The crowd laughed and cheered as Tillman came forward to handover a silver coin. "I'll give it back," Matthew promised the Governor, "or play crack-loo [a game, whose winner tosses a coin, which falls nearest to a crack in the floor] for it." Holding the dollar high in the air, Butler noted that, "The Governor says greenbacks whipped us, but I was thar. It was muskets and bayonets which whipped us, or we just tired of whipping Yankees."[23] He was reminding the audience of both his service and the fact that Tillman had avoided the war.

Butler then displayed a large yellow envelope. "I have plenty of ammunition [in] here," he averred, "and I want the Governor to understand that when I tackle the State administration, I [will] do so frankly. . . . He must take it like a . . . man. He must take his punishment. I shall take mine. I am used to it."[24] Matthew was making it clear that he intended to campaign on personalities, not issues.

Tillman, of course, was up to that task. The next day at Chester, talking to reporters prior to giving his speech, the Governor alleged that Matthew was attempting to buy the election with a "corruption fund" donated by the Wall Street bankers.

Butler was livid upon hearing of Tillman's accusations, and when it was his turn on the dais, he whirled on the governor and snarled, "[You are] an infamous liar!"

"The crowd was dumbfounded," a reporter wrote. "Everything was as quiet as the calmest sea." Butler's words were clearly meant to invite a duel. Tillman, however, remained seated, and coldly glowered with his one eye at Matthew. He refused to respond, he would not rise to Butler's challenge. As the tension died and the audience started to breathe once more, Matthew turned away and returned to the podium.

"Governor Tillman may go to the Senate," he proclaimed loudly, "but he will not go there by slandering me . . . by villifying, lampooning and misrepresenting [those] better than he is." Matthew then listed a series of charges against the governor: he had avoided military service during the Civil War, had accepted free passes from the railroads, and stolen money from the dispensary.

Tillman continued his silence throughout this diatribe. Perhaps he was afraid; more likely he was shocked. "It was the first time," one reporter wrote, "Tillman had ever been caught by the collar, so to speak, and shaken up."[25]

In the days that followed Chester, Butler persisted in his attacks on Tillman's character. The governor complained at Lancaster of Matthew's charges, "fouler and blacker than had [ever] been made against any man," and denounced Butler for his romantic liaisons, "happenings in my opponent's private life that are notoriously current." This was his only outburst. In the debates that followed, Tillman avoided any discussion of personalities. He only addressed the main issues, then asked for a raising of hands of those in favor of his candidacy. The vast majority waved their support. Seeing that taking the offense was ineffective, Butler switched tactics and totally ignored the Governor. "This canvas [has become] so one-sided," Tillman groused, "it is almost devoid of interest." The rivals became friendly, and even shared a buggy on the trek from Marion to Conway.[26]

This trucelike atmosphere ended on Charleston on July 12. Although the conservatives would not support Butler's candidacy, they had no qualms about assaulting Tillman, and he was roundly insulted by the crowd. "[You] are behind the times," he shouted angrily, "because [your] street cars are run by mules instead of electricity." He then turned toward Butler and accused him of denying his role at Hamburg in order to win acceptance by the Senate. "I was there!" Tillman declared proudly.[27]

"Maybe he was," Butler replied when it was his turn to speak, "but I did not see Tillman, and I have been told that when the shooting began he could not be found."[28]

The argument over who deserved more credit for killing the blacks at Hamburg peaked at Edgefield, the hometown for both candidates. The crowd that assembled at Academy Grove was surly, one reporter observed, "with eyes glistening like tigers, with hands on pistols, and with open . . . knives ready for deadly execution. . . . One overt act, only one blow [would] have participated a battle."

The governor spoke first. He reminded the audience of their prior support, summarized the contributions of his administration, and attacked President Cleveland for opposing the free coinage of silver. He then whirled to face Butler. "Unless you withdraw your accusation that I ran at Hamburg," he cried, "I am prepared to prove that the men who make that charge are liars." With that he sat down.

Butler arose to face the crowd. He was wearing an old straw hat and in his right hand, he held a long walking cane given him by friends. "I am glad," he opened his talk, "to see so many of the fair daughters of Edgefield here." After polite applause, Butler tore into Tillman. "How much sugar has he put in your gourd," he asked the audience.

"How much have you put in there during [your] eighteen years in the Senate?" a voice from the crowd answered.

"Just keep quiet now," Butler snapped back. "I know I am hitting you in sore places, but you must take it." As he continued to reproach the governor, "yells and applause for Tillman . . . drowned Butler's voice. The noise was terrific."

"Wasn't your house burned by negroes," one man shouted above the din, "because you took part in the riot?"

"Yes."

"But you denied it in Washington."

"Butler turned like a panther," a reporter wrote, "and quick as lightning said: 'That is an infernal lie.' Had he stopped at this, there might not have been any trouble, but he repeated [his charge] two or three times."

The crowd turned ugly, and those in front clambered up on the platform. Tillman was quickly surrounded by his bodyguards; Butler stood firm in the eye of the turmoil, "working masterfully to check the riot. . . . It was a squally time," the newspaper reported. "Pistols were changing from one pocket to another to be convenient for quick use."

The danger, however, passed. Those who had climbed up on the platform resumed their place in the audience; Butler continued with his address. "He gradually got salty again," an eyewitness remembered, "and there was another outbreak of cheering for Tillman." Butler was infuriated. "Any common jackass can bray," he bellowed, "but I [will not] be stopped in free speech. . . . I can not be frightened. I have seen too much real danger to be intimidated."

The meeting finally ended. "It may have been Butler's magnificent courage on the stand, or [perhaps] the old love, re-welling up in their hearts for their old, battle-scarred hero," the *Edgefield Advertiser* stated, "but there were many wild-ramrackers [cheering] for Butler, not enough, perhaps, to elect, but enough to take the sting out of defeat, and show him that Edgefield remembers."[29]

The candidates debated on through Lexington, Winnsboro, Orangeburg, Columbia, Newberry, and Laurens. The "truce" in personal attacks had ended at Charleston, and now with each succeeding stop, their assertions became more passionate and outrageous. Tillman's speech at Union on July 31 particularly enraged Butler. "He does not pay his debts," the governor contended. "[He] allows his mouth to be used as a sewer pipe, through which other people discharge their filth at [me]."

When Matthew arose to defend himself, the mob began to yell, and his voice could barely be heard above the din. He grew red in the face, and departing from his planned speech, threw out a challenge for Tillman. "I do not intend to wash our dirty linen in public," he said. "If he has a personal grievance against me, there is another way to settle it. He knows where to find me, and he can get all the satisfaction he wants."[30]

The crowd continued its screams, but Butler refused to retire. "I understand this is a put up job to howl me down, but you can't do it," he cried. "I'll take you blackguards one at a time, and give you all you want."

When the meeting ended, Matthew rushed to the depot to board the train to Spartanburg and the next debate. Tillman was seated toward the rear in a Pullman car, and upon learning that the governor was close by, Butler and his entourage started down the aisle to seek a confrontation. A horde of newspaper reporters followed them.

"You put these hoodlums up to howling at me . . . you have perpetuated a fraud and a lie," Butler raged when he finally found Tillman. "These matters must be settled personally . . . I'll meet you anywhere."

"You are old, infirm and one-legged," Tillman answered the challenge to a duel. "I won't fight you."

"And you're one-eyed."

"That don't hurt my physical power. I'm not afraid of you."

"Never mind my infirmities. When you want to fight . . . just say so."

Those crowding into the car with Butler were caught up in the confrontation, and Cal Caughman, a friend of Matthew, drew his revolver. Train conductor Dawkins quickly grabbed Caughman, hustled him back into the aisle, then returned to bring the encounter to a halt. "Be quiet," he urged. "I'll lose my job if I allow such things in my car."

Butler reluctantly returned to his seat. As the train pulled to a stop in Spartanburg, the reporters raced for the telegraph office to file their stories about the face-off.

The meetings that followed were anticlimatic, and the debates ended at Abbeville on August 8. On that same day Butler learned that in his hometown, the Democratic County Convention had gathered and endorsed Tillman for the Senate. Matthew knew that his campaign had failed. If he could not win in Edgefield, he had no chance in the rest of the state.[31]

Still Butler would not quit. First he followed through on an earlier threat to file suit with the court asking for an injunction that restrained the South Carolina comptroller or treasurer from paying the salary of any registrar on the grounds that the recently passed voting laws, complex measures designed to prevent blacks from casting a ballot, were unconstitutional. If he could prevent an election, Matthew would hold onto his Senate seat.[32]

A few days later Butler withdrew his candidacy in the upcoming primaries, preferring, he said, to take his chances with the legislature. He claimed in his letter that he had filed for the Senate seat on the assumption that the primary would include a separate ballot box for this office. Since this was not to be, he was not bound by his earlier application. His real reason was that all candidates were required to "pledge to abide with the result of the primary, and support all nominees of the party."[33] He knew he would lose the election; he could not keep his promise to endorse a "Democratic organization . . . controlled by a handful of selfish, corrupt ringsters."[34]

Despite Butler's lawsuit the primary was held August 30, and Tillman's candidates won a huge majority. Matthew now tried to influence the probable legislators. "I am not after reelection to the Senate," he wrote in a letter to the newspapers, "I am after the corrupt ring now disgracing the politics of the State. . . . I am in for the War."[35]

The general election was held in early November. John Gary Evans won the governorship; other Tillman men garnered the rest of the key state offices; and the new legislature was decidedly pro-Tillman. They met in Columbia on December 11. Disregarding Butler's arguments throughout the prior months, they named Tillman U.S. Senator.[36]

Butler returned to Washington later that month for the final assembly of the Fifty-third Congress. When he entered the chamber, "one or two who first saw him . . . rose [to meet] him, and in a moment, practically all the Senators from both sides . . . left their seats and flocked around him, expressing their sorrow for his defeat . . . he numbers his friends by his acquaintances."[37]

"A politician has to meet defeat as well as to enjoy a victory," he said to the well-wishers. "No man could expect to be at the top of the ladder all the time."[38]

Butler resumed his duties, and although he was a "lame duck," contin-

ued to take an active role in the Senate. When Henry Cabot Lodge of
Massachusetts demanded an explanation in January for the secretary of the
navy's withdrawal of the warships from the Hawaiian Islands, Matthew was
quick to note, "This [was] a very feeble and impotent attempt . . . to make
political capital" of the issue, and he demanded that this resolution be
referred to his committee on Foreign Relations. The Senate agreed with
him.[39]

Perhaps emboldened by this success, Butler made a last grasp at holding
his seat. On January 30 he introduced a petition that asked the Senate to
investigate the "numerous frauds, perpetuated in the late election in [South
Carolina] . . . under the directions of B. R. Tillman."[40] He hoped that his
fellow Senators could find a way to prevent Tillman from assuming office.
Probably with great sorrow, party leaders noted that Tillman was acceptable
to them, and Butler should step aside. Only then did he finally concede.[41]

Matthew became involved in one more controversy during this session
(adding to the power of the Interstate Commerce Commission so this
agency could control pooling by the railroads), but his heart was no longer
in the fight. The issue remained unresolved when the Senate adjourned
March 3, 1895.[42] Butler's political career was over.

--- ⚔ ---

During his three terms in the U.S. Senate, Butler took a leading role in the
floor debates that related to national issues. He served on a number of
major committees (Foreign Relations, Territories, Military Affairs, Naval
Affairs, and Interstate Commerce), and took personal credit for the many
visible accomplishments stemming from their efforts. Behind closed doors,
however, Matthew was equally effective, especially in obtaining federal
funding for local projects. "Two thousand dollars would cover the [contri-
bution paid toward] his salary by the people of South Carolina," an
observer related, "[but] by virtue of his efforts . . . ten million dollars have
accrued to the State."

Three-fourths of the money was invested in the state's waterways
(improvements to Charleston Harbor; river surveys of the Pee Dee, Wacca-
maw, Lynches, Wateree, Santee, Clark's, Edisto, Savannah, Congaree, and
Broad; digging the Mosquito Creek Canal, which linked the Santee to
Winyah Bay Bar near Georgetown; and constructing a coaling station and
dry dock at Parris Island).

Butler introduced and passed appropriation bills for a public building in
Charleston, the restoration of the custom house in that city, and the con-
struction of a United States courthouse/post office in Greenville.

Through his intercession, the state recovered $200,000 assessed under the Direct Tax Act of 1862. Coastal property holders in the counties of Charleston, Georgetown, Beaufort, and Colleton were paid $500,000 for lands confiscated during the Civil War. And many could credit Matthew for resolving their personal problems with the Federal Government. He had been a good Senator for South Carolina.[43]

CHAPTER 27

Major General

Butler was a poor loser. Incensed over losing his bid for a fourth term as a U.S. senator, he blamed his defeat on a betrayal by the South Carolina voters, particularly those from Edgefield County. Matthew vowed that he would never go home again.[1]

Committed to living in Washington, D.C., Butler formed a law partnership with C. M. Shelly and J. H. G. Martin. They established their offices in the Kellogg Building at 1416 F Street, NW in rooms 55, 56, and 57.[2]

Butler's pledge never to return to Edgefield was shortlived. In May 1895 he and Maria were forced to hurry back to South Carolina because of the illness of her twin, Eliza, who died in Greenville on May 16.[3] Her death was grievous to Maria, who had often sought her sister's home as a haven during the more difficult times of her marriage to Matthew.

Maria decided to spend the summer in Edgefield. Marie stayed with her, as did Cabby, who had taken leave from West Point to go to his aunt's funeral.[4] He was not due back at the Academy until September. Butler, however, was committed to his law practice in Washington, D.C. He returned to the capital at the end of the month, taking a roundabout way through Chicago to attend an unveiling of a Confederate monument. "He occupied a prominent place," a reporter related, "in the fraternization ceremonies."[5]

Although Butler was open to performing all the mundane duties of a lawyer, most of his time was spent as a lobbyist for special interests. His most important client was Chief Bushyhead and the Cherokee Indians. When Congress attempted in late 1895 to set up a special commission for supervising the tribes, giving this governmental committee the authority to "invalidate acts passed by [local] councils, fine, imprison, decide who is Indian, allot lands, et al," Matthew came to the tribe's rescue. Through the following months, he made repeated visits to the Capitol, calling on the senators and representatives, noting that since the Cherokee had signed a treaty with the United States, Congress could not pass legislation that violated this pact. The bill, attached to a nonrelated appropriation act, was withdrawn in 1896.[6]

Later that spring both political parties began making their plans for the presidential election. The Republicans met in St. Louis that June and nominated William McKinley as their candidate.[7]

The Democrats assembled in Chicago in early July. The populists (including Tillman) were in power, so Butler found no reason to attend. Free silver was still the party's key issue, a goal so improbable, the *New York Times* dubbed their proceedings "a party led by fools."[8] No candidate had come to the fore until Nebraska's William Jennings Bryan took the podium. "You shall not press down upon the brow of labor a crown of thorns," he roared. "You shall not crucify mankind upon a cross of gold." Bedlam followed his powerful speech, and an hour later, Bryan was nominated by acclamation.[9]

At the same time the Democrats were meeting in Chicago, the former Confederates were gathering in Richmond for their annual convention.[10] Butler was not there. Perhaps he was too busy with his legal practice in Washington. More likely he was preparing for Frank's wedding in Edgefield. His son was engaged to a patrician belle from Rock Hill, South Carolina.

Lilian Jones was the daughter of Capt. Iredell Jones, who had served with the infantry of the Hampton Legion. Her mother was the former Ellen Adams, daughter of the onetime governor of South Carolina, James H. Adams. Lilian was very pretty and very active in the Rock Hill social scene. Many balls were held, and she was always there, always dressed in finery. She wore "black silk with net lace outer skirt" at one, "white faille silk" at another dance held the following month, and "a dainty costume of pink silk en train, chiffon trimming" at yet another outing that same season. Her ornaments were usually diamonds.[11]

She and Frank were married in the Church of Our Savior, Rock Hill, on October 28, 1896. They then traveled south to Edgefield, where their reception was held at Butler's manor, East Hill. "The house . . . was a mass of beautiful chrysanthemums, roses and greens," a reporter described, "artistically arranged wherever flowers could find lodgement. . . . Two gifted pianists and a brilliant cornetist filled the hours [8:30 to 12:30] with music. The bride, a tall, slender brunette, has the most unsurpassing, beautiful teeth ever seen."[12]

Butler was certainly happy with the match, but at that time, may have been somewhat distracted by the events taking place in Cuba, matters that would lead to yet another significant change in his life.

On April 10, 1895, on a dark, stormy night, six men had embarked on a rowboat from the German ship *Nostrand* off the eastern coast of Cuba.

Maximo Gomez, seventy-two-years-old, was returning to his homeland to lead the revolution to free his people from Spanish rule. The small force that he found there was conducting guerrilla warfare against his adversary.[13]

Gomez soon realized that hit-and-run tactics would not bring independence, so he changed the strategy, reverting to a "scorched earth" plan: burning the sugar fields that provided the Spanish their profits, their impetus for occupying Cuba. "Blessed be the torch," he proclaimed.[14]

Spain countered by sending Gen. Valeriano Weyler to Cuba in February 1896. "The guerrilla is the fish," he declared, "the people are the water in which he swims." This was his rationale for implementing a "reconcentration" of all rural people to the cities, where they could no longer abet Gomez. The peasants were placed in squalid camps where they found little food or shelter. They died by the thousands.[15]

Americans watched with growing horror. Two newspapers, the *New York World* and the *New York Journal*, saw the opportunity for profit in Cuba's misery. Each printed daily stories that detailed accounts of atrocities. Their reports were mostly true, but when new disclosures were not available, they made up their tales of woe. The nation became aroused; the "yellow press" made money.[16]

President Cleveland, following prior U.S. policy, kept clear of the Cuban affair. William McKinley, easily elected in November 1896, hoped to repeat this example. Others in his administration, however (especially Theodore Roosevelt, assistant secretary of the navy), urged intervention. Given the passions of the American people, roused by the newspaper reports, McKinley found it impossible to ignore the problem. In September 1897 he instructed Stewart L. Woodford, his minister to Spain, to invoke a quick resolution. Otherwise, the U.S. government would "take steps as [it] deemed necessary to procure . . . tranquility."[17]

Spain tried to meet McKinley's demands. Weyler was recalled and replaced by Ramon Blanco, charged with setting up political autonomy for Cuba. This plan, however, backfired. Spanish loyalists saw the move as an abject surrender to the rebels, and on January 12, 1898, they started a riot in the streets of Havana. Concerned over American interests in the city, McKinley sent the battleship *Maine* to the scene. The ship reached port on January 25. Three weeks later, while at anchor, the *Maine* was rocked by a violent explosion, and quickly sank in the harbor. A total of 268 American sailors lost their lives.[18]

A court of inquiry was immediately convened by the U.S. Navy to determine if this disaster was an accident (a result of spontaneous combustion in a coal bunker igniting the magazine) or deliberate sabotage. They concluded on March 28 that the *Maine* had been blown up by a submarine mine, detonated by electrical wire from an onshore position.[19]

When he sent the report to Congress on April 11, the president did not emphasize the loss of the *Maine*. He asked for the power and authorization to "secure a full and final termination of hostilities between . . . Spain and the people of Cuba . . . [using our] military and naval forces . . . as may be necessary for these purposes."[20]

Congress was not so timid. After eight days of debate they passed a joint resolution that not only recognized Cuba as an independent nation but also directed the president to "use the land and naval forces of the United States to carry these resolutions into effect."[21]

Spain was left with no choice. She declared war April 21, 1898. America geared for battle. McKinley appealed for 125,000 volunteers. A million men stepped forward.[22]

McKinley planned on using the volunteers to expand the regular army, 28,000 men assigned to thirty-five regiments, scattered across the country. The states, however, raised a vehement protest. They demanded an independent role for the national guards. A compromise was reached. The militia would go on active duty as regiments, under their current officers; all brigade, division, and corps commanders would be designated by the federal government.[23]

Matthew watched this drama unfolding with apparent disinterest, but on April 26, when McKinley named both Joseph Wheeler and Fitz Lee to division major generalships (a move designed to arouse Southern support for the war), Butler saw his chance for glory. He held little admiration for either former Confederate. He had been a better soldier; he should have a commission, too.

Contacting a host of his friends, Butler asked them to write the president on his behalf. Many responded. Charles H. Simonton, a U.S. circuit judge, sent a recommendation to McKinley on May 3. "I endorse [him] in the strongest manner," Hampton wrote on May 5. "No better appointment can be made." That same day, C. E. W. Smith declared in his note, "[Butler is] in the prime of his life. . . . He is in every way equipped for the position." And fifteen renowned men signed a May 8 letter, saying, "Permit [us] to most respectively petition [the] appointment of General M. C. Butler to . . . Major General of Volunteers of the U.S. Army."[24]

The president eagerly yielded to the pressure. On May 22, he offered Butler the commission. Matthew went to the White House on May 31 to sign his Oath of Office. During his visit, he was surprised by the return of his binoculars, lost in the last days of the Civil War. A Mrs. Kemper from Virginia had found and kept them, and when she heard that he was reentering service, she surrendered her souvenir. "The last time I used these field glasses," Matthew noted, "I was a Confederate officer. Now I'm a Yankee."[25]

OATH OF OFFICE.

One to accompany the acceptance of every commissioned officer appointed or commissioned by the President in the Army of the United States.

I, *Matthew C. Butler*, having been appointed a *Major General, U.S. Vols* in the military service of the United States, do solemnly swear (or affirm) that I will support and defend the Constitution of the United States against all enemies, foreign and domestic; that I will bear true faith and allegiance to the same; that I take this obligation freely, without any mental reservation or purpose of evasion; and that I will well and faithfully discharge the duties of the office on which I am about to enter: So help me God.

M. C. Butler

Major General

Sworn to and subscribed before me, at _____ this ___31___ day of ___May___, 189__.

Butler requested and received permission to go back to Edgefield to tend to his personal affairs before he reported for duty at Camp Alger, located fourteen miles west of Washington, D.C., near Falls Church, Virginia. Matthew spent one week at home, then drove to Augusta on June 6 to take the train north to the capital. Despite his sixty-two years and bald-

Maj. Gen. Matthew Calbraith Butler. COURTESY NATIONAL ARCHIVES

ness, Butler was still an imposing figure. "He appears vigorous and hearty," a reporter wrote, "and [will be] equal to anything that the service may require of him."[26]

When he reported for duty, Butler was informed that he would command the 1st Division of the II Corps of U.S. Volunteers, headed by Maj. Gen. William M. Graham. His troops (ten regiments, 18,000 men) were organized into three brigades, with Col. Edward A. Campbell in command of the 1st, Brig. Gen. George A. Garretson the 2nd, and Brig. Gen. John P. S. Gobin the 3rd.[27] Matthew set up headquarters in an elegant mansion, Chittenden Farm, near the soldiers' camps.[28]

Butler's troops had been in training for about a month, and had already established an excellent reputation. Just a few weeks prior to his assuming command, they had passed in review in front of President McKinley, and had been "highly complimented on their appearance."[29] Their diligent efforts seemed in vain, however, because the war was already sprinting toward its climax.

Three arenas had been targeted: the Philippines, Cuba, and Puerto Rico. America hoped to subdue the enemy's forces in each, and if that did not bring Spain to her knees, they would then attack her homeland.

Only days after the start of the war, the U.S. Asiatic Squadron led by Adm. George Dewey was ordered to "proceed at once to Philippine Islands. Commence operations particularly against the Spanish fleet." Dewey immediately steamed south from his post off the China coast, and reached Manila Bay about dawn on May 1. He cautiously approached Adm. Patricio Montojo's eleven vessels, anchored along the shore in a half-moon formation, until he came within a mile of his adversary. He then turned to his flagship captain and said quietly, "You may fire when ready, Gridley."[30]

The battle was both brief and devastating. After only two hours, during which the U.S. fleet made five thundering passes by the anchored Spanish vessels, Dewey called a halt to assess the situation. None of his warships had taken any significant damage; eight U.S. sailors and one officer had been wounded. Three of Montojo's armada had been destroyed, however, and he was about to scuttle the rest, each of them crippled by Dewey's bombardment. The Spanish casualties included 161 killed, 210 wounded.[31]

Although the fight for the Philippines had essentially ended with Manila Bay, there was still the question of occupying the territory. On May 12, the task was assigned to Gen. Wesley Merritt, a Federal cavalry officer during the Civil War. His command included about 12,000 Western volunteers, training close to San Francisco, plus several regular army units. The first contingent (about 2,500 men) started west on May 25.[32] All of this took place before Matthew reported for duty.

Turning to Cuba, immediately following the declaration of war, the Atlantic Squadron (twenty-one warships commanded by Adm. William T. Sampson) steamed south to blockade Havana. The fleet arrived about 3:00 P.M. on April 22.[33]

Seven days later a Spanish armada left the Cape Verde Islands and started west for the Caribbean. Adm. Pascual Cervera y Topete led the seven-vessel fleet. Denied access to neutral ports, stymied by the U.S. blockade of Havana, he had no choice but to anchor at Santiago, almost 500 miles east of the Cuban capital, on May 19.[34]

When the United States learned of his landing, they ordered the Flying Squadron, seven warships under the overall command of Comdr. Winfield Scott Schley, to Santiago to trap the enemy's fleet in the harbor. He blundered badly. Confused by his instructions, he wandered for days throughout the Caribbean. Cervera, however, failed to seize the opportunity for escape, and he remained in port. Schley finally assumed position on May 29.[35]

The U.S. war strategists hoped to demolish the Spanish armada without resorting to a bloody naval battle, so on the same day that Commodore Schley took up his post outside Santiago, they ordered Maj. Gen. William R. Shafter and his V Army Corps, composed mostly of army Regulars, to Cuba. This force of over 19,000 men would land on the coast, drive inland, lay siege to Santiago, and finally capture both the port and Cervera's fleet. Shafter and his army set sail from Tampa on June 8, two days after Matthew had reported for duty.[36]

Having allocated ground troops to both the Philippines and Cuba, the War Department began planning for Puerto Rico, the third key theater of war. The I Corps, training in Georgia at Camp Thomas, located close to where the battle of Chickamauga had been fought, was assigned this responsibility. Butler must have realized that this decision meant that he would probably not see action.[37]

As Butler no doubt wondered what role he would play in the conflict, he had reason to recall a recent conversation held with Sec. of War Russell A. Alger. They had faced each other during the Civil War, and on the day that Butler received his commission, the two had discussed earlier, less friendly times.

"You rode a white horse," Alger noted, "which made you a mark for many of [my] Michigan riflemen."

"I'll go into [this] war," Butler promised, "on a less conspicuous horse."[38]

Their remarks were reported in the newspapers, and the Empire State Chapter for the Sons of the American Revolution responded by presenting Butler with a new mount, a Kentucky stallion called Admiral Dewey. Rich brown in color with two white legs, the horse was described at the July Fourth ceremony as "a famous walker, [who] trots, canters, gallops, and has style enough [for] a dozen campaigns." Matthew also received superb accouterments: a saddle, bridle, holsters, and saddlebags of the richest leather. "The saddle cloth," an observer detailed, "[is] gilt-laced . . . and has an embroidered gold eagle with two stars in the corner."[39]

Butler, however, needed more than just a horse to go to war. He had to assemble a trained staff. And the man he wanted most at his side was his son, Cabby. In November 1896 the young first lieutenant had left his riding post at West Point to rejoin the 7th Cavalry, stationed at Fort Huachuca, Arizona. Upon his father's request, Cabby was relieved from this duty, promoted to major of volunteers, and assigned to Camp Alger to serve Butler as his chief ordnance officer. He reported on July 19, 1898.[40]

Cabby arrived about the same time that Butler received reinforcements, a provisional brigade that included just two regiments, the 1st Connecticut and the 7th Virginia. The latter had been in camp only a short time when they got into trouble. One of their men started a fistfight with a black teamster. When it became obvious that the white soldier was losing the battle, his comrades charged into the fray. The black driver ran, the Virginians chased him, and in the process, bolted past a forbidden line. A sentry reported this incident to Butler.[41]

The rash volunteers may have been drunk, but they were probably not sodden with "Two Step," a local moonshine. The home brew was so powerful, it was said that after one drink, one could not take two steps without falling down.[42]

Infuriated by the breach of discipline, Butler decided to make an example of the Virginians. He confined the regiment to their quarters, and placed the 1st Connecticut as guards in thirty-foot intervals.

The Virginia state officials were appalled by Butler's harsh punishment, and they formed a committee that rushed to Camp Alger to demand an end to the confinement of their men. The found Butler seated on the front porch of his luxurious headquarters, where he was calmly smoking a cigar. Matthew listened to their frenzied entreaties, but refused to change his mind. "The Virginians needed a spanking," he announced, "and they got it. That is all!"[43]

While Butler was fighting the Virginians, the American V Army was battling the Spanish in Cuba. They landed on June 22, and by July 1, were in position to initiate an attack on Santiago. They charged at dawn from the east, but despite an overwhelming advantage in numbers, were not able to rout their enemy from his periphery positions at El Caney and San Juan Heights until later in the day. The port, however, was finally under siege.[44]

On July 3, about 9:30 A.M., the Spanish fleet made a dash to escape Santiago harbor. Sailing in single file, six of Adm. Cervera's warships left the port and headed west. All seven of Schley's blockading squadron concentrated their fire as each of the enemy's vessels steamed within range of their guns. By 11:15 A.M. five had been sunk. The last of the armada sailed through the noose, but the Americans gave chase, and caught up about 1:15 P.M. Rather than surrendering, the Spanish captain scuttled his ship.[45]

Santiago capitulated on July 14. Six days later an American force led by Maj. Gen. Nelson A. Miles started for Puerto Rico. Most of the men came from the I Corps, but one of Butler's three brigades, the 2nd under General Garretson, was included among the 15,000 troops that landed at Guánica on the southern coast of the island. Matthew was left at Camp Alger with no prospects for action.[46]

Miles took about two weeks to consolidate his position. Then, on August 6, he began a four-pronged march northward to confront the Spanish, who had concentrated most of their 8,000-man army at San Juan. As the Americans advanced they met very little resistance. The Puerto Ricans greeted them as saviors.[47]

All the while negotiations were underway toward ending the war. The first overture was made by the Spanish on July 18: independence for Cuba. America accepted that, but demanded three additional indemnities: cession to the United States of both Puerto Rico and Guam, plus holding onto "the city, bay and harbor of Manila" pending the conclusion of a treaty for peace. Faced with the probability of an eventual attack on their homeland, the Spanish agreed to these terms. The pact was signed on August 12, 1898.[48]

Butler had no regrets about missing out on combat. "I would have preferred to have gone to Santiago and joined the fight," he said, "[but] no old soldier is going to tear off his clothes [to get] into a battle. He knows [too well] what it means."[49]

With peace at hand, Butler probably anticipated his being discharged from the army. On August 19, however, this expectation vanished with the receipt of new orders that relieved him of duty with the II Corps and assigned him to a commission to arrange for "the evacuation of the Island of Cuba by the Spanish troops." He would serve with two other offices, Maj. Gen. James F. Wade and Adm. William T. Sampson. His immediate staff, which did not include Cabby, would accompany Butler to Havana.[50]

Prior to heading for Cuba, Butler hurried home to tend to personal matters, the most important being to arrange for the shipping of his fall cotton crop. He stayed in Augusta at the Planters Hotel. When he signed the register, Matthew, dressed in civilian clothes, did not include his rank when he wrote his name. "Lieutenants and newly made captains may do such things," the local newspaper reported, "but men who have been generals in two wars are . . . more modest."[51]

Matthew took the train to New York, where on September 5, he boarded a ship bound for Cuba. "Our voyage was most delightful," he said in a letter to Frank. "The sea was as smooth as a lake the greatest part of the way."[52]

The first of the commissioners to reach Havana, Butler had hoped to utilize the ship for his residence, but he soon found this impractical. "The water in the harbor is . . . foul from the city sewage," he noted, "[and has] a very offensive odor. . . . I [will] take my chances ashore."[53]

Butler moved into the Salon Trotcha, a luxurious hotel in Vedado, a coastal suburb, three miles west of Havana. He selected these quarters in hopes that they would be free of the disease that he feared, yellow fever.

"The sensation of being in the neighborhood of an invisible enemy, constantly in ambush, ready to attack you, is not . . . pleasant," he wrote in a note to Frank's wife, Lilian. "Charging the batteries at San Juan and El Caney in front of Santiago [would be] fun compared to it."[54]

Every morning Butler returned to the harbor to confer with the Spanish officials regarding the evacuation of their troops from Cuba. The two parties soon agreed on a plan to amass all the soldiers at Cienfuegos, a port on the southern coast. Contingents would start to depart for Spain on October 7. "There are 115,000 of them," Butler noted. "It'll take a good while to get them all out of the Island."[55]

Although there was agreement regarding this evacuation, Matthew soon found another issue to argue. The Cuban people were starving, and through his intercession, Butler had procured a million rations, sent from the United States to alleviate the suffering. When the ship arrived at Havana, however, local Spanish officials would not allow it to unload its cargo until a duty of $60,000 was paid. Butler solved this problem by diverting the vessel to Matanzas, a port sixty miles west of the capital, where the much-needed supplies were brought free ashore and distribution begun to the needy. "They will be a God-send to many poor creatures," Butler noted, "whose destitution is appalling, all brought on by the rapacity and cruelty of the devilish Spaniards."[56]

Butler's concern for the Cuban people went beyond just feeding them. Gomez's revolutionary army was still in place and still armed. "I am afraid that they'll become bandits," Matthew wrote in a September 26 letter to Secretary of War Alger. "My policy would be to . . . employ them as a constabulary force." Another alternative suggested by Matthew was to "advance [partisans] supplies and farming implements for one year, to be paid for form the proceeds of their first crop."[57]

The people of Cuba were well aware of Butler's efforts on their behalf. A number of influential citizens wrote President McKinley with the following request: "We venture to approach you . . . on a subject of vital interest . . . to all of the inhabitants of the Island. With a full and profound appreciation of the dangers that threaten us . . . to [help] us in solving the weighty problems of our social, religious, political and industrial future, we beg . . . to suggest the name of General Matthew C. Butler for the office of Military and Civil Governor of [Cuba]. . . . This distinguished gentleman [has] all the qualities . . . for this high position . . . and we feel safe in saying his appointment would be [most] acceptable to our people."[58] McKinley did not honor this appeal (the post was given in December to Gen. John R. Brooke), but the president must have been impressed by the local passion generated on Butler's behalf.

Butler, too, had a request. He wrote the adjutant general shortly after he arrived in Cuba to ask that his son be added to his staff. Cabby had been sent to Camp Meade, Pennsylvania, following Butler's appointment to Havana. The lad received the transfer, but army red tape delayed his orders until November. He finally reported for duty on the sixteenth.[59]

Cabby reached Cuba just when Butler was departing. He had applied for leave on November 5, saying that he needed to come home for a short time to take care of important business (which he did not identify).[60] Adj. Gen. Henry C. Corbin denied his request. "The President," he answered November 15, "does not think it advisable for you to leave at the present."[61]

Matthew had played this game before. On November 19, he repeated his plea, this time stating that he had "several matters that [I] would like to talk to the Secretary of War and the President about."[62] Again, Butler did not state any details.

"Proceed to Washington," Corbin wired back on November 21, "and report in person to the Secretary of War."[63]

Butler left Cuba on November 26, met with both President McKinley and Secretary of War Alger in Washington, took care of personal affairs in South Carolina, and returned to Havana by mid-December.

Nothing, of course, had changed during Matthew's brief absence, including his opinions about what needed to be done in Cuba. He had no doubt expressed his ideas in Washington, and upon returning to Havana, Butler resubmitted in writing his plan to arm the Cubans as a constabulary. He would personally organize a division made up of "one-half mounted and one-half infantry, 10,000 in all." Matthew was now less interested in creating employment for guerrillas; he was more concerned for the health of the U.S. soldiers stationed in Cuba. Once a local force was recruited, armed, and trained, he explained, "it would be safe to withdraw . . . our troops . . . [before] the sickly season sets in."[64]

Obviously, yellow fever and the unsanitary environment in Cuba, which he probably thought caused the disease, still scared Butler. "I never conceived," he wrote in an earlier memorandum to Surgeon General Walter Wyman, "that any people [who claim] to be civilized could survive so much filth and dirt."[65]

Butler's proposal, however, was rejected. And because the Spanish evacuation was just about complete and the peace treaty had been signed on December 10, 1898, he had little to do in Cuba. Matthew kept active through the end of the year with mundane projects: he submitted an application for the release from imprisonment of three Cuban insurgents; and he obtained and sent the plans of Havana's fortifications to Secretary of State

John M. Hay. Finally, January 20, 1899, Butler received orders to come back to the United States.[66]

When he reached Washington, Butler found that his duty was still not over. He was appointed to a panel considering court-martial for the army's chief of commissary, Brig. Gen. Charles P. Eagan.[67]

Hoping to win public favor for a run at the presidency, General Miles had accused Eagan of supplying tainted beef to the troops in Cuba. These "scraps and tailings," according to Miles, had been laced with secret chemicals to mask their foul odor. He asserted that not only had thousands of men been sickened by this meat, but also that Eagan had received kickbacks from the suppliers.

The chief of commissary was distraught by Miles's false allegations, and he demanded a trial to clear his name. "He lies," Eagan shouted from the witness stand, "in his throat, in his heart, in every hair on his head."

The trail dragged on until April, when Matthew and his compatriots finally rendered a decision. They ruled against both men. Miles was censured for waiting until the war was over before making his accusations; Eagan, although cleared of all charges, was criticized for making a "colossal error" in buying not tainted by essentially inedible beef.[68]

On April 15, 1899, the army decreed that since "his services [were] no longer required," Butler was eligible for an honorable discharge. He signed the release, donned civilian clothes, and headed for South Carolina and a long rest.

＊＋　≡◆≡　＋＊

Butler joined the army too late to enjoy an active role in the Spanish-American War, but this might have been to his benefit. He had become less flexible in his old age, aloof from his men, immune to their human weaknesses. Although he was known as a strict disciplinarian during the Civil War, Matthew never meted out punishment then as severe as that he inflicted upon the Virginia Volunteers. Leading these same troops into battle might have proved impossible.

But despite being rigid in command, Butler seemed more capable of compassion. His attempts while in Havana to help the Cuban people went far beyond the norm. They thought he had come, like most other foreigners, to exploit them; they found, however, that he was a friend, and they voiced their appreciation.

Probably the most important outcome of Butler's taking part in the war was his recapture of honor. During the past four years, he had been living under a cloud, a man stained with political defeat. Every trip to the Capitol to lobby his former compatriots must have been embarrassing. Now, suddenly an army general, Matthew had regained his lost stature. The stigma of being trampled by Tillman was wiped away. He could look forward to his remaining years with his head held high.

CHAPTER 28

The Final Days

BUTLER SPENT THE FALL IN SOUTH CAROLINA. "HE DOES NOT LOOK A DAY older than . . . fifteen years ago," a Charleston reporter noted, "and seems in fit physical condition to enter any contest that he desires. His progress about the streets was rendered very slow by the innumerable hand-shakings and stops for the exchange of . . . pleasant words. It looked as if every man in the city was a personal friend."[1]

After spending Christmas in Edgefield, Butler returned to Washington to arrange the wedding of his daughter, Marie. She married Lt. Robert Whitehead McNeely, a graduate of the Naval Academy, whose family's history in America dated back to the Revolutionary War. The ceremony was held at St. John's Episcopal Church in the capital on February 15, 1900. Rev. Ernest Paddock conducted the exchange of vows. All the male attendants were in uniform. The bride wore a dress made of white satin and an Italian veil, both of which had been passed down in her family through three generations. After their honeymoon, the couple lived at Indian Head, the site of the naval proving grounds, located on the Potomac River opposite Mount Vernon.[2]

Butler then resumed his legal career. He watched from Washington in July as the Democratics, meeting in Kansas City, again named William Jennings Bryan their candidate for president in the fall elections. He would oppose McKinley, whom the Republicans had nominated for a second term during their convention in Philadelphia in June. Theodore Roosevelt was his running mate.[3]

Butler not only avoided the Democratic convention: he refused to support his party's candidate. McKinley had made him a major general, and Matthew was not about to turn on a benefactor. "I think Mr. McKinley has made a most excellent president," he said. "He is thoroughly conscientious . . . and has the best interests of the country, both north and south, at heart." Matthew also attacked Bryan and Tillman. Their populistic ideas, he

Mrs. Maria Pickens Butler.
COURTESY ELLEN ADAMS GUTOW

asserted, "would . . . be rebuked by people south of the Mason and Dixon line," if not for their continuing need to vote as a white bloc to offset the potential of the black ballot.[4]

The Democrats, stunned by Butler's comments, hurriedly declared him a traitor. He in turn accused his attackers of spreading "vicious falsehoods and slander" about him.[5] The controversy, however, soon ended because of Matthew's family problems.

To avoid the late summer heat in Washington, Maria had gone by herself to a stylish resort at Old Point Comfort on the Virginia coast. The trip proved tiresome, and upon her arrival on August 23, she immediately went to bed. Local doctors were called, but they did not consider her condition serious. Butler was not told that she was sick. Four days later Maria died from severe neuramia. She was sixty-eight years old.

Butler, Marie, and Lieutenant McNeely went to Fortress Monroe, collected Maria's body, and proceeded south by train to Edgefield. They were met by Frank, his wife Lilian, and Cabby, who had come east from Fort Oglethorpe, his new berth after leaving Cuba in May. Her remains were put on view at Frank's home, then taken to the tiny Episcopal church, where Rev. R. W. Anderson conducted the solemn funeral service. Maria was buried in the village cemetery (Willowbrook), next to the graves of five of her children.

"She belonged to the high and queenly type of Southern woman that prevailed before the Confederate war," the papers reported, "a type gone . . . not possible except in those great days. Maria was . . . brilliant in society, where she reigned a queen, an accomplished musician, skillful painter, lover of literature . . . faithful wife and devoted mother. . . . She died in the confidence of a holy and steadfast hope."[6]

Matthew, of course, grieved over his loss, but he soon faced another family crisis. The Treaty of Paris ending the Spanish-American War gave the Philippine Islands to the United States (for which they paid $20 million dollars). The Filipinos wanted independence, however, not another foreign ruler, so in February 1899 they arose in rebellion.[7] Efforts to put down this insurrection were still in progress in the fall of 1900 when Lieutenant McNeely received orders to board the *Kentucky* and head for the Islands. Marie was pregnant, and was left behind, alone and no doubt afraid.

The problem was resolved by sending Marie back to Edgefield, probably to live at East Hall, Butler's mansion. The black maids who took care of the house could watch over her; Frank and Lilian would be nearby if needed.[8]

Butler continued to practice law in Washington, but on June 19, 1901, when word arrived that Marie had given birth, he hurried home to greet his first grandchild, Marie Butler McNeely. His daughter stayed in Edgefield through the fall, then in November, she and the baby headed for the Orient to join her husband, now stationed in China.[9]

The move was a mistake. On August 25, 1902, the child died of dysentery. "She was so bright," Marie said sadly. "Her beauty was faultless. . . . I was so proud of her."[10]

The baby's death seemed to crush Marie. She grew cold, "just like her mother," a current relative states. Although Marie and her husband remained devoted to each other, there were no more offspring. They lived in Washington in an apartment in the Chevy Chase Club after their China tour. When McNeely retired from the navy, he bought a peach orchard located outside of Columbia, but Marie refused to live in the "shack" that he built in the hinterland. The two eventually settled in Key West, Florida.[11]

Just prior to Marie's departure for China, the country was stunned by the assassination of McKinley. The president was attending the Pan-American Exposition in Buffalo, where on September 6, 1901, while greeting constituents at a noisy and confused reception, held at the Temple of Music, he was shot in the stomach by a rabid anarchist, Leon Czolgosz. "I didn't believe one man should have so much," he explained, "and another . . . should have none." McKinley lingered in pain for eight days before dying on September 14. Roosevelt's inauguration took place that same day.[12]

A few months later, in March 1902, Butler took great pleasure in calling upon the new president. This visit was made on behalf of his state to apologize for the insufferable behavior of her senior senator, Benjamin R. Tillman. During a debate in the chamber, he took exception to remarks by John L. McLaurin, and physically attacked South Carolina's junior senator. McLaurin battled back, and before onlookers could separate the two contenders, he bloodied Tillman's nose.[13]

Roosevelt was so incensed by Tillman's precipitating a fistfight, he sent him a personal note that withdrew an invitation to attend a White House dinner. Matthew was asked by South Carolina officials to meet the president and assure him that "the people in our state do not approve of the senator's acts. We hope this will not interfere with your plan to visit Charleston."[14]

"It will have no effect upon my course," the president assured, but he did not make the trip.

Shortly after his meeting with Roosevelt, while in New York City, Butler fell ill. His amputated limb had suddenly become inflamed. "I don't know . . . what the matter is, and I scarcely think the doctors do," he said in a note to Lilian. "One thing I do know . . . for three weeks I have suffered more intense pain than in all my life."[15]

Weeks later he was still in bed. "It's bad to be sick anywhere," Butler moaned, "but at a hotel it is very cheerless and discouraging."[16]

Hampton, beset with a valvular heart disorder, died on April 11. Butler, who was still confined, could not go to the funeral. "I suppose some of us will soon follow in his . . . wake," he mused, "as we so often did during his illustrious career on earth."[17]

Butler's physician, Dr. Gill Wylie, moved him from the hotel into a local hospital. He stayed in New York all through the summer, and did not return to Washington until early September. "I am gradually recovering," he wrote in a letter to Lilian, "but provokingly so."[18]

It was important for Butler to regain his strength, because he was about to start on the most important legal case of his career, *United States v. Cherokee Nation*. Chief Bushyhead had died in 1898, but Matthew was still retained as the Indians' attorney. And he, along with a band of other lawyers, was suing on their behalf for a monumental sum of money.

The basis for the suit lay in an 1891 agreement by the Indians to sell land that they owned in the Indian Territory, the Cherokee Outlet, to the U.S. government. The pact provided not only payment for the property but also a review of past claims never settled. The latter issue was still open due to a confusion over authority, which Congress settled in an act, passed in July 1902, which assigned the problem to the U.S. Court of Claims.[19]

Matthew filed three suits with this court: asking payment still owed for lands the Cherokee Nation had sold under prior treaties; the return of money improperly charged the Indians for the expense of going west in 1838 (the Trail of Tears); and interest on all unpaid funds. Any awards would go to individuals, not the Cherokee Nation.[20]

Butler was confident he would win this case. "I shall rejoice in a good comfortable fee," he predicted in a letter to his niece. Then he added a cautious note. "Never count [your] chickens until they are well out of the shell."[21]

The court found that the U.S. Government had made most payments due under earlier treaties, and although some money was still owed, this amount was small, about $25,000. They also ruled, however, that charging the Cherokee the cost of moving them from the east to the Indian Territory was improper. The government should have absorbed this expense. The Indians were entitled to not only a refund of $1,111,284.70 but also interest payments at 5 percent on this amount from 1838 to the present. This raised the total award to about $5.0 million.[22]

The Government asked the Supreme Court to overrule the opinion, but on April 30, 1905, they reaffirmed the Court of Claims decision. Over 30,000 Cherokee shared in the award, each receiving approximately $160.[23] The lawyers' fee was $250,000; Butler got $25,000.

"I've earned it," he declared. "I have been working on this case for five years."[24]

About the time that Matthew initially started his case for the Cherokee, Lilian became pregnant. She had a difficult term, and when the baby arrived, January 12, 1903, it was stillborn. She and Frank were so grieved, they could not bring themselves to even name the child.[25]

Frank had never prospered in his practice in Edgefield, and perhaps the baby's death was the grounds for his seeking greener pastures in Columbia, South Carolina. He moved his family there in 1903, where they shared a home at 1206 1/2 Main Street. He opened a medical office at 1213 Pickens Street.[26]

The times remained financially bleak for Frank, but he and Lilian did succeed in starting their family. Ellen Iredell Butler was born October 6, 1906; Maria Pickens Butler came along on November 20, 1908.[27]

In order to make ends meet, Frank and his wife took in borders. Their rent payments helped pay bills, but the real impetus was more likely stature. In those days it was considered "fashionable" for prominent families to house paying guests, both men and women, attending the nearby University of South Carolina. One young lady, for example, who boarded at the Butlers, married Patrick Nelson, founder of the most prestigious law firm in the state.[28]

Frank was a competent doctor (he published a number of papers on fever, the preeminent illness in those times), but he continued to struggle with collecting fees. Cash was always a problem. In January 1906, in hopes of improving his lot, he gave up his practice to become a traveling representative for a wholesale drug company. The commissions proved inadequate, however, and Frank abhorred being away from home. Only six months later, he applied for and won an appointment as physician for the state penitentiary. This position paid a steady wage, and the family finally lived in relative comfort.[29]

Frank's move to Columbia in 1903 did not bring Matthew to Edgefield to manage his plantation. Nor did he remain in Washington. He and three other partners (John K. Cowan, Admiral Schley, and Gen. Frank C. Armstrong) traveled south to the Arroyo Rico district in Chihuahua, Mexico, to investigate the potential for several mines. Both the "Ascension" near Monterey and the "Arozo Rico" sixty miles northwest of Parral looked promising, so in January 1904, Butler and his associates formed the Hidalgo Placer Mining and Milling Company to exploit both resources. Matthew was named president of the firm.[30]

After his April 1903 trip to Mexico, Butler returned to Washington to continue his work on the *Cherokee* case. He found time, however, for other endeavors, such as serving as president of the Southern History Association.[31]

Later that same year, Butler headed home for Edgefield. He was still bitter because the people there had snubbed him in the 1894 campaign with Tillman, and he was determined to break his ties to the village. Matthew had made up his mind to sell East Hill. His mood was not improved along the way. As the train was passing through Alexandria, a ruffian threw a half-brick through the window of his car. It bounced off Butler's head, cutting his scalp and almost severing an ear.[32]

Butler not only sold his home to Benjamin E. Nicholson on February 13, 1904, he included the rugs, all of the furniture, even the bric-a-brac that he and Maria had collected through the years.[33] When the children heard of his plan to part with everything, they asked his permission to retrieve items of special interest to them. He refused. They found, however, a means to their end. The black maids who managed the mansion secretly passed treasures to the children behind Matthew's back. Lilian, for example, received two antique Oriental vases, presented to Butler when he was a senator by the Japanese ambassador.[34]

A few months after Matthew returned to Washington, the Democrats convened in St. Louis, and selected Judge Alton B. Parker as their presidential candidate. Butler remained at home. He favored the incumbent, Roosevelt, nominated by the Republicans at their June convention in Chicago, but had no desire to state his position. Doing so would only result in another fruitless squabble with his Decmoractic friends. Matthew opted to stay aloof from the campaign.[35]

He was, however, in good humor, glad to be rid of Edgefield. His talk in October to the New York Southern Society reflected his revived spirit.

Butler opened his address by comparing his audience with the Northerners who had come South after the war to make their fortune at the expense of local people. They had gone North for the same purpose. "You are certainly the most thrifty, the most prosperous-looking carpetbaggers I have ever seen," he teased.[36]

Butler had other grounds for being happy. Although he was now almost seventy years old, Matthew had fallen in love again. The lady was a widow, Nancy deSaussure Bostick Whitman, who was pretty, charming, rich, and only forty-six, the same age as Frank. The couple has first met only months after Maria's death in 1900. She had lost her eldest son that same year, and the shared sorrow probably contributed to their romance.[37]

Nannie, as she was called, came from a prominent South Carolina family. Her grandfather, Benjamin Bostick, owned a huge plantation (Ingleside), 19,000 acres located along the Savannah River in St. Peter's Parish, upper Beaufort County. In 1850 his 215 slaves harvested more corn and cotton than any other farm in the area. Other significant crops raised included rice, peas and beans, and sweet potatoes. Bostick also possessed large herds of livestock: 126 milk cows, 250 beef cattle, 350 hogs, and 95 sheep. His annual income was estimated at close to $28,000.[38]

Bostick and his spouse, Jane Aseneth Maren, had twelve progeny. Their fourth child and second son, John Edward (Nannie's father) married Sallie Maria Martin. The couple made their home at Ingleside.[39]

When the Civil War began, Edward, despite his high rank in society, joined the Allendale Mounted Guard as a private.[40] His unit was soon converted into infantry (the 26th South Carolina), and posted at Charleston. In April 1864 the regiment went first to Wilmington, North Carolina, then to Richmond.[41] They served with Stephen Elliott's brigade, Bushrod R. Johnson's Division, Richard H. Anderson's corps.[42]

Edward, now a captain, made the wretched retreat to Appomattox, where he was the last soldier to be killed in Lee's army. Just when the negotiations to surrender were nearing completion, he opened fired at a line of Union pickets. They shot back, and Edward was mortally wounded.[43]

His family remained at Ingleside, but in 1866, after a former slave set fire to their house, Sallie Bostick and her four offspring fled north. They settled in Washington, D.C. In 1876 when she was only seventeen, Nannie married Charles Sidney Whitman, her brother Edward's classmate at the Naval Academy. They had four children: Edna, Charles, Nancy, and Edward. Whitman died in 1896.[46]

Matthew and Nannie dated quietly for five years before deciding to wed. They married in New York City in the Grace Church chantry on January 14, 1905. She wore "a costume of gray chiffon velvet, trimmed with Irish lace; her hat was a gray velvet . . . with white feather trimmings."[45] Sallie Bostick gave her daughter away; Cabby hurried east to serve as his father's best man; Rev. Winthrop McKin, son-in-law of the bride, conducted the noon ceremony.[46]

Two of Nannie's three surviving children were there to see their mother married, but both Frank and Marie failed to show. He approved of the match, but was not able to obtain leave from his position at the state penitentiary. Butler's oldest son and his family grew close with Nannie. She went to Paris each April to buy new clothes, then gave her "hand-me-downs" to Lilian and her girls, "which delighted them."[47]

Marie, however, was furious with her father, first for defiling her mother's memory by remarrying, then for taking a bride who was young enough to be his daughter. She vowed never to speak to Nannie, and remained estranged from Butler until his dying day.[48]

Butler and Nannie honeymooned in South Carolina at the estate he had purchased in North Augusta. This became their permanent home. Six months later they trekked to Nashville to attend Cabby's marriage to Margaret Harding Howell. She was a pretty girl, very petite, attended by six equally beautiful bridesmaids. The groomsmen, "all in uniform, wore cavalry yellow."[49] Frank was the best man. The decoration on the altar of the First Baptist Church included palm trees that were draped with American flags.

After the ceremony Cabby and his bride headed for the Philippines, where he had been assigned duty. They remained there until the spring of 1907, when he returned to the United States to serve as chief of commissary for Fort Riley, Kansas.[50] A son, Matthew Calbraith Butler III, was born June 30, 1907.[51]

Butler enjoyed his retirement at North Augusta. He began corresponding with Civil War comrades, providing Ulysses Brooks, for example, with details of old campaigns. His former aide was writing a book about Butler's cavalry. The toll of old age, however, often made Matthew ill. Frank made frequent trips from Columbia to treat his father.[52]

In January 1909 Butler's amputated limb swelled, and he began to suffer considerable pain. Frank was called, and he insisted that his father be taken to Knowlton's Hospital in Columbia. Butler's affliction was diagnosed as inflammatory rheumatism. Though the following months, attempts to treat his condition failed. And his bedridden condition had an adverse effect on the kidneys. The end was drawing near.[53]

Butler called a priest to his bedside on March 8, 1909. He was not asking for last rites; Matthew wanted to convert to Catholicism. Elise had found peace with that faith, but he had a different reason for changing beliefs. "The Little Sisters of the Poor first drew my attention," Butler stated to Fr. B. W. Fleming. "Their humble, holy lives, leaving their home and hearth to minister to the outcast . . . the aged, the forgotten of the world is my inspiration."[54]

Despite growing weaker each day, Butler remained cheerful, "showing the courage which had carried him through many a hard fought battle on the field of arms." He knew of his critical condition, yet he refused to die, kept alive by his supreme willpower. Cabby obtained leave from Fort Riley to be at his father's side. His time off expired while Matthew still clung to life, so the young captain had no choice but to sadly return to his post.[55]

A Southern veteran visited Butler late in March. When their discussion turned to the effort to raise a monument to honor the women of the Confederacy, the General immediately called for his checkbook. He donated ten dollars. "My comrades all and their sons," he noted, "[must] give according to their means."[56]

The morning of April 14, Butler was alert. He smiled and talked clearly with the few gathered by his side. The entourage included Father Fleming, Nannie, Frank, Maj. Harold W. Richardson, a scout for Butler during the war, and Marie. She had come south from Washington to finally relent and forgive her father (but not his wife) for his second marriage.[57]

About 4:00 P.M., Matthew slipped into a coma. He slept into the night with Father Fleming holding his hand. No one was aware of his death at 11:40 P.M. until the devoted priest reached out and raised Matthew's own hand to shut his eyes. He was seventy-three years old.[58]

South Carolina was ready. Within an hour of Matthew's death, a sentinel from the Richland Rifles, the local militia company, stood on guard outside the hospital door. Tocsins rang for one hour in most of the towns and villages throughout the state the following morning. The body was prepared for the funeral on April 16 at St. Peter's Catholic Church in Columbia.[59]

When Butler's remains were moved from Knowlton's Hospital to St. Peter's Church, they were escorted by twenty-four members of the Richmond Rifles and a contingent of Confederate veterans. The casket, placed in front of the altar, was covered with flowers: immortelles, roses, lilies, and blue violets. Bishop Henry P. Northrup from Charleston, assisted by Fathers Fleming, T. J. Hagarty, and J. J. Hughes, conducted the requiem mass. Father Fleming gave the eulogy.[60]

> The body that held his mortal soul . . . we will soon lay to rest, but his spirit, his soul, shall go marching on . . . into the ages, growing brighter with years and mellowing with time.
>
> I am not going to dwell to any length on the character of our great one dead. . . . I pass over the young soldier lending his

Matthew C. Butler's gravestone, Willowbrook Cemetery, Edgefield, South Carolina.
PHOTO BY THE AUTHOR

princely presence to war's rude tent, how this great son of Carolina drew his sword to shield her honor, and bled that hal-
lowed be her name. I leave to other hands the privilege of
[certifying] his record in the halls of legislation . . . to put South
Carolina in her right place before the world without compromise of honor [or] sacrifice of principle.

Death is a sad thing. It's the penalty of life. And whether
this felt-footed visitor comes to the cradle chamber or beckons
with bony finger to the chimney corner and tells the life trem-
bling like a leaf to follow, the visitor leaves in his path bowed
heads and broken hearts.

We grieve today because he whose death we mourn represented that type of civilization that is fast passing . . . that beautiful chivalrous life that flourished in the days of the dear old

South. It is dear with all its feudal faults, with all its vigorous virtue. [As] one of its last types, he has left to us Carolinians an example, to history a hero.

He had his failings, human nature claims us all . . . the violet and the oak [might] feel the same storm, but the high branches of the oak bear a blast and blow that the . . . hidden violet will never know.

In the midst of my tears, I . . . see faintly in the dawning day Lee, Stuart, Hampton, and Butler joining forces upon the other shore, never to part again.[61]

Following the mass, the casket was opened for hundreds filing past to view. The next morning, at 7:00 A.M., it was put on a train headed for Edgefield and burial. The stores in town were closed, and the merchants joined the crowds who gathered to meet the funeral car. Matthew was laid to rest in the Willowbrook family plot, beside Maria, Elise, Willie, and the three babies who had all gone before him. Thomas M. Lightfoot played taps; the Richland Rifles (who accompanied the body) fired a salute.[62] It was over.

Cabby was the first of Butler's remaining offspring to die. He was shot and killed (unjustly) by a jealous husband in Alpine, Texas, July 20, 1916. Frank died in Columbia on September 27, 1924. Marie passed away December 8, 1938, in Washington, D.C. Nannie outlived them all. She was eighty-three years old when she died in New York City on March 13, 1942.

ENDNOTES

PROLOGUE

1. U. R. Brooks, *Butler and His Cavalry in the War of Secession, 1861–1865* (Germantown, Tenn: Guild Bindery, 1994), 152.
2. Ibid., 153.
3. Ibid.
4. *War of the Rebellion: A Compilation of the Official Records of the Union and Confederate Armies* (Washington, D.C.: Government Printing Office, 1880–1900), series I, vol. 27, part 2, 744 (hereafter cited as *O.R.*).
5. Brooks, *Butler and His Cavalry,* 154.
6. Ibid., 155.
7. Ibid.
8. Mrs. A. I. Robertson, "Gen. M. C. Butler as a Confederate," *Confederate Veteran* 8, no. 3 (March 1900): 110.

CHAPTER 1: BOYHOOD

1. *South Carolina Genealogies* (Spartanburg, S.C.: Reprint, 1983), 238.
2. Ibid., 233.
3. Ibid., 234.
4. Ibid.
5. Ibid., 235.
6. Ibid., 237.
7. Samuel Eliot Morison, *"Old Bruin": Commodore Matthew C. Perry, 1794–1858* (Boston: Little, Brown, 1967), 4–5.
8. Ibid., 5.
9. Ibid., 7.
10. Ibid., 8–9.
11. Ibid., 10.
12. Ibid., 11.

13. Ibid.
14. Ibid.
15. Ibid., 234.
16. Oliver Vernon Burton, *In My Father's House Are Many Mansions* (Chapel Hill: University of North Carolina Press, 1985), 105.
17. John Grimball Wilkins, "Gen. Matthew Calbraith Butler, C.S.A.," *Confederate Veteran* 33, no. 3 (March 1927): 89.
18. Burton, *In My Father's House,* 115.
19. Ibid.
20. Matthew C. Butler to Lill B. Stowe, December 27, 1905, Matthew C. Butler Papers, South Caroliniana Library, University of South Carolina (hereafter cited as M. C. Butler Papers).
21. Burton, *In My Father's House,* 106.
22. James Henry Hammond, *Secret and Sacred: The Diaries of James Henry Hammond, a Southern Slaveholder,* ed. Carol Bleser (New York: Oxford University Press, 1988), 311.
23. Brooks, *Butler and His Cavalry,* 52.
24. *South Carolina Genealogies,* 238.
25. Robertson, "Gen. M. C. Butler as a Confederate," 110.

CHAPTER 2: MANHOOD

1. Brooks, *Butler and His Cavalry,* 53.
2. Burton, *In My Father's House,* 116.
3. Photograph, Matthew Calbraith Butler, Library of Congress.
4. *South Carolina Genealogies,* 243.
5. Brooks, *Butler and His Cavalry,* 52.
6. Burton, *In My Father's House,* 7.
7. Newspaper clippings (unidentified), M. C. Butler Papers.
8. Robertson, "Gen. M. C. Butler as a Confederate," 110.
9. Newspaper clipping (unidentified), Butler Family Scrapbook, South Caroliniana Library, University of South Carolina.
10. Edward B. Rosa to Matthew C. Butler, April 9, 1885, Harry L. and Mary K. Dalton Collection, Special Collections Library, Duke University, Durham, North Carolina (hereafter cited as Dalton Collection).
11. Newspaper clipping (unidentified), M. C. Butler Papers.
12. Robert W. Johannsen, *Stephen A. Douglas* (New York: Oxford University Press, 1973), 406.
13. David Donald, *Charles Sumner and the Coming of the Civil War* (New York: Knopf, 1961), 285.
14. Ibid., 286.
15. Jack Kenny Williams, "The Code of Honor in Ante-Bellum South Carolina," *South Carolina Historical Magazine* 54, no. 3 (July 1953): 115.

16. Ibid., 125.
17. George Fort Milton, *The Eve of Conflict: Stephen A. Douglas and the Needless War* (Boston: Houghton Mifflin, 1934), 235.
18. Ibid., 236.
19. Stewart Sifakis, *Who Was Who in the Confederacy: A Biographical Encyclopedia of More than 1000 Confederate Participants* (New York: Facts on File, 1988), 36.
20. *Edgefield Advertiser,* December 2, 1857, 2.
21. John B. Edmunds Jr., *Francis W. Pickens and the Politics of Destruction* (Chapel Hill: University of North Carolina Press, 1986), 139.
22. Newspaper clipping (unidentified), Butler Family Scrapbook.
23. Edmunds, *Francis W. Pickens,* 139.
24. Ibid., 138.
25. Hammond, *Secret and Sacred,* 270.
26. *Edgefield Marriage Records,* ed. by Carlee T. McClendon (Columbia, S.C.: R. L. Bryan, 1970), 27.
27. Burton, *In My Father's House,* 48.
28. James B. Griffin, *A Gentleman and an Officer: A Military and Social History of James B. Griffin's Civil War,* ed. Judith N. McArthur and Orville Vernon Burton (New York: Oxford University Press, 1996), 33.
29. Butler Family Bible, South Caroliniana Library, University of South Carolina.
30. *Edgefield Advertiser,* August 8, 1859, 2.
31. Ibid., September 9, 1859, 2.
32. Ibid.
33. Douglas Southall Freeman, *R. E. Lee: A Biography* (New York: Charles Scribner's Sons, 1934), 1: 402.
34. Steven A. Channing, "Crisis of Fear: Secession in South Carolina" (Ph.D. diss., University of North Carolina, 1868), 11.
35. Ibid., 56.
36. Ibid., 17.
37. *Edgefield Advertiser,* April 4, 1860, 2.
38. M. C. Butler to Maria Butler, August 7, 1860, Dalton Collection.
39. Ibid., July 23, 1860.
40. Ibid., August 7, 1860.
41. Ibid., August 30, 1860.
42. Butler Family Bible.
43. *Biographical Directory of the South Carolina House of Representatives,* ed. Walter B. Edger (Columbia: University of South Carolina Press, 1974), 382.
44. Henry D. Capers, *The Life and Times of C. G. Memminger* (Richmond: Everett Waddey, 1893), 285.

45. Channing, "Crisis of Fear," 315.

46. Benjamin P. Thomas, *Abraham Lincoln: A Biography* (New York: Knopf, 1952), 180.

47. Glyndon G. Van Deusen, *William Henry Seward, Lincoln's Secretary of State: The Negotiator of the Alaska Purchase* (New York: Oxford University Press, 1867), 193.

48. Channing, "Crisis of Fear," 321.

49. Griffin, *A Gentleman and an Officer,* 44.

50. Burton, *My Father's House,* 130.

51. Edmunds, *Francis W. Pickens,* 151.

52. Ibid., 153.

53. Channing, "Crisis of Fear," 350.

54. *Edgefield Advertiser,* January 23, 1861, 2.

55. Steven E. Woodworth, *Jefferson Davis and His Generals* (Lawrence: University Press of Kansas, 1990), 13.

56. Robert Selph Henry, *The Story of the Confederacy* (Indianapolis: Bobbs-Merrill, 1931), 26.

57. Milton, *Eve of Conflict,* 526.

58. W. A. Swanberg, *First Blood: The Story of Fort Sumter* (New York: Charles Scribner's Sons, 1957), 319.

59. Frank E. Vandiver, *Their Tattered Flags: The Epic of the Confederacy* (New York: Harper's Magazine, 1970), 54.

60. M. C. Butler to Maria Butler, June 9, 1861. Dalton Collection.

61. Milledge Luke Bonham, "Around 1865," *Edgefield Adversiter,* centennial edition, December 16, 1936.

62. *Edgefield Advertiser,* April 24, 1861, 2.

63. Manly Wade Wellman, *Giant in Gray: A Biography of Wade Hampton of South Carolina* (New York: Charles Scribner's Sons, 1949), 50.

64. Ibid., 34–35.

65. *Edgefield Advertiser,* May 29, 1861, 2.

66. Ibid., June 19, 1861, 1.

67. Brooks, *Butler and His Cavalry,* 62.

68. *Edgefield Advertiser,* June 12, 1861, 2.

CHAPTER 3: EARLY DAYS

1. Brooks, *Butler and His Cavalry,* 69.

2. M. C. Butler to Daniel R. Durisoe, November 3, 1864, M. C. Butler Papers.

3. Matthew C. Butler, Personal File, RG 94, National Archives (hereafter cited as M. C. Butler Personal File).

4. Hortense Woodson, *Companies from Edgefield in Confederate Service* (Edgefield: *Edgefield Advertiser,* 1960), 34.

5. Wellman, *Giant in Gray*, 51.
6. Mrs. C. E. Robinson, "Seth Thorton Prior," in *Recollections and Reminiscences, 1861–1865 through World War I* (Columbia: South Carolina Division, Daughters of the Confederacy, 1991), 1: 437.
7. Wellman, *Giant in Gray*, 51.
8. Herman Hattaway, *General Stephen D. Lee* (Jackson: University of Mississippi Press, 1976), 28.
9. John Coxe, "The Battle of First Manassas," *Confederate Veteran* 23, no. 1 (January 1915): 24.
10. Wellman, *Giant in Gray*, 52.
11. Walbrook Davis Swank, *The Battle of Trevilian Station: The Civil War's Greatest and Bloodiest of All Cavalry Battles* (Shippensburg, Pa.: Burd Street, 1994), 43.
12. Wellman, *Giant in Gray*, 52.
13. Coxe, "The Battle of First Manassas," 24.
14. *Edgefield Advertiser*, July 3, 1861, 2.
15. Edward Pollard, *The Early Life, Campaigns, and Public Services of Robert E. Lee: With a Record of the Campaigns and Heroic Deeds of His Companions in Arms, "Names the World Will Not Willingly Let Die"* (New York: E. B. Treat, 1871), 739.
16. Douglas Southall Freeman, *Lee's Lieutenants: A Study in Command* (New York: Charles Scribner's Sons, 1942), 1: 94.
17. M. C. Butler to Maria Butler, July 11, 1861, Dalton Collection.
18. *O.R.*, ser. I, vol. 2, 981.
19. Coxe, "The Battle of First Manassas," 24.
20. William C. Davis, *Battle at Bull Run: A History of the First Major Campaign of the Civil War* (New York: Doubleday, 1977).
21. M. C. Butler to Maria Butler, July 27, 1861, Dalton Collection.
22. Wellman, *Giant in Gray*, 66.
23. M. C. Butler Personal File.
24. Bradley T. Johnson, *A Memoir of the Life and Public Service of Joseph E. Johnston* (Baltimore: R. H. Woodward, 1891).
25. Samuel J. Martin, *The Road to Glory: The Life of Confederate General Richard S. Ewell* (Indianapolis: Guild Press of Indiana, 1991), 29.
26. M. C. Butler to Maria Butler, August 15, 1861, Dalton Collection.
27. Ibid.
28. Ibid., August 24, 1861.
29. Griffin, *A Gentleman and an Officer*, 55.
30. M. N. Tillman Collection, Magnolia Dale, Edgefield Historical Society, Edgefield, South Carolina.

31. M. C. Butler to Maria Butler, October 14, 1861, Dalton Collection.
32. John T. Gaston, *Confederate War Diary of John Thomas Gaston*, ed. Alifaire G. Walden (Columbia: Vogue, 1960), 3–4.
33. Stephen W. Sears, *George B. McClellan: The Young Napoleon* (New York: Ticknor & Fields, 1988).
34. James. M. McPherson, *Battle Cry of Freedom: The Civil War Era* (New York: Oxford University Press, 1988), 349.
35. Griffin, *A Gentleman and an Officer*, 129.
36. Wellman, *Giant in Gray*, 67–68.
37. M. C. Butler to Maria Butler, September 16, 1861, Dalton Collection.
38. Ibid., December 12, 1861.
39. James Conner, *Letters of General James Conner, C.S.A.*, ed. Mary Conner Moffett (Columbia: R. L. Bryan, 1950), 72.
40. Ibid., 72.
41. Ibid., 73.
42. E. B. Long and Barbara Long, *The Civil War Day by Day: An Almanac, 1861–1865* (Garden City: Doubleday, 1971), 160.
43. James Hamilton, *The Battle of Fort Donelson* (New York: Thomas Yoseloff, 1968).
44. William Marvel, *Burnside* (Chapel Hill: University of North Carolina Press, 1991).
45. William L. Shea and Earl J. Hess, *Pea Ridge: Civil War Campaign in the West* (Chapel Hill: University of North Carolina Press, 1992).
46. Joseph E. Johnston, *Narrative of Military Operations: Directed during the Late War between the States* (New York: D. Appleton, 1874), 102.
47. Wellman, *Giant in Gray*, 70.
48. M. C. Butler to Maria Butler, March 23, 1862, Dalton Collection.
49. William C. Davis, *Duel between the First Ironclads* (Garden City: Doubleday, 1975).
50. Clifford Dowdey, *The Seven Days: The Emergence of Lee* (Boston: Little, Brown, 1964), 43–44.
51. George B. McClellan, *McClellan's Own Story: The War for the Union: The Soldiers Who Fought It; The Civilians Who Directed It; and His Relations to It and Them* (New York: Charles L. Webster, 1887), 272.
52. Mary Chestnut, *Mary Chestnut's Civil War*, ed. C. Vann Woodward (New Haven: Yale University Press, 1981), 401.
53. *O.R.*, ser. I, vol. 11, part 2, 420.
54. Gilbert E. Govan and James W. Livingood, *A Different Valor: The Story of Joseph E. Johnston, C.S.A.* (Indianapolis: Bobbs-Merrill, 1956), 108.
55. Wiley Sword, *Shiloh: Bloody April* (New York: William Morrow, 1974).

CHAPTER 4: THE PENINSULA CAMPAIGN

1. McClellan, *McClellan's Own Story,* 286.
2. Stephen W. Sears, *To The Gates of Richmond: The Peninsula Campaign* (New York: Ticknor & Fields, 1992), 379–85.
3. Johnston, *Narrative of Military Operations,* 110.
4. Ibid., 116.
5. Brooks, *Butler and His Cavalry,* 72.
6. Ibid.
7. Ibid.
8. Ibid., 71.
9. Ibid., 74.
10. Ibid.
11. Ibid., 75.
12. Ibid., 76.
13. Ibid.
14. Ibid.
15. Gaston, *Confederate War Diary,* 7.
16. *O.R.,* ser. I, vol. 11, part 1, 443.
17. Ibid., 445.
18. Ibid., 569.
19. Dowdey, *The Seven Days,* 63.
20. Edward Porter Alexander, *Fighting for the Confederacy: The Personal Recollections of General Edward Porter Alexander,* ed. Gary W. Gallagher (Chapel Hill: University of North Carolina Press, 1989), 79.
21. Sears, *To the Gates of Richmond,* 75.
22. Jubal A. Early, *Autobiographical Sketch and Narrative of the War between the States* (Philadelphia: J. B. Lippincott, 1912), 70–72.
23. Brooks, *Butler and His Cavalry,* 58–59.
24. Long and Long, *The Civil War Day By Day,* 208.
25. Sears, *To The Gates of Richmond,* 92.
26. M. C. Butler to Maria Butler, May 14, 1862, Dalton Collection.
27. Ibid., May 24, 1862.
28. Ibid., July 19, 1862.
29. Ibid., May 11, 1862.
30. Ibid., April 30, 1862.
31. Ibid., May 24, 1862.
32. Dowdey, *The Seven Days,* 69.
33. McClellan, *McClellan's Own Story,* 358–59.
34. Warren W. Hassler Jr., *General George B. McClellan: Shield of the Union* (Baton Rouge: Louisiana State University Press, 1957), 109.
35. Robert G. Tanner, *Stonewall in the Valley: Thomas J. "Stonewall" Jack-*

son's Shenandoah Valley Campaign, Spring 1862 (Garden City, N.Y.: Doubleday, 1976), 226–33.
36. Sears, *To The Gates of Richmond,* 119.
37. *O.R.,* ser. I, vol. 11, part 3, 558.
38. Sears, *To The Gates of Richmond,* 124.
39. Ibid., 130.
40. Johnston, *Narrative of Military Operations,* 138.
41. Dowdey, *The Seven Days,* 127.
42. Chestnut, *Mary Chestnut's Civil War,* 378.
43. Fitzhugh Lee, *General Lee* (New York: D. Appleton, 1895).
44. Freeman, *R. E. Lee,* 2: 96–97.
45. John W. Thomason, Jr., *Jeb Stuart* (New York: Charles Scribner's Sons, 1930), 141–42.
46. Tanner, *Stonewall in the Valley.*
47. Sears, *To The Gates of Richmond.*
48. Ibid.
49. Emory M. Thomas, *Bold Dragoon: The Life of J. E. B. Stuart* (New York: Harper & Row, 1986), 139.
50. Burke Davis, *Jeb Stuart: The Last Cavalier* (New York: Rinehart, 1957), 151–52.
51. *O.R.,* ser. I, vol. 11, part 3, 657.
52. Thomas, *Bold Dragoon,* 140.
53. Ezra J. Warner, *Generals in Gray: Lives of the Confederate Commanders* (Baton Rouge: Louisiana State University Press, 1959), 296–97.
54. Robert E. Lee to Jefferson Davis, September 24, 1864, letter in possession of Clark B. Hall.
55. Alfred Hoyt Bill, *The Beleaguered City: Richmond, 1861–1865* (New York: Knopf, 1946), 140.
56. M. C. Butler to Maria Butler, August 8, 1862, Dalton Collection.
57. Wellman, *Giant in Gray,* 87.
58. John J. Hennessy, *Return to Bull Run: The Campaign and Battle of Second Manassas* (New York: Simon & Schuster, 1993).
59. M. C. Butler to Maria Butler, August 26, 1862, Dalton Collection.
60. M. C. Butler Personal File.

CHAPTER 5: SHARPSBURG
1. Freeman, *R. E. Lee,* 2: 350–651.
2. *The Wartime Papers of R. E. Lee,* ed. Clifford Dowdey and Louis H. Manarin (Boston: Little, Brown, 1961), 301.
3. James V. Murfin, *The Gleam of Bayonets: The Battle of Antietam and Robert E. Lee's Maryland Campaign, September 1862* (New York:

Thomas Yoseloff, 1965), 93.

4. *O.R.*, ser. I, vol. 19, part 1, 815.

5. Stephen W. Sears, *Landscape Turned Red: The Battle of Antietam* (New York: Ticknor & Fields, 1983), 85.

6. Freeman, *R. E. Lee*, 2: 359–60.

7. Heros von Borcke, *Memoirs of the Confederate War for Independence* (New York: Peter Smith, 1938), 1: 193.

8. William W. Blackford, *War Years with Jeb Stuart* (New York: Charles Scribner's Sons, 1945), 141.

9. Ibid.

10. Ibid., 142.

11. Freeman, *Lee's Lieutenants*, 2: 160.

12. Ibid., 161.

13. von Borcke, *Memoirs of the Confederate War*, 1: 203–4.

14. Ibid., 204.

15. Wellman, *Giant in Gray*, 90.

16. *O.R.*, ser. I, vol. 19, part 1, 823.

17. Ibid., 816.

18. Ibid., 823.

19. Edward J. Stackpole, *From Cedar Mountain to Antietam* (Harrisburg, Pa.: Stackpole, 1959), 346–47.

20. *O.R.*, ser. I, vol. 19, part 1, 824.

21. Murfin, *The Gleam of Bayonets*, 182.

22. Carl Sandberg, *Abraham Lincoln: The War Years* (New York: Harcourt, Brace & World, 1939), 2: 599.

23. Sears, *Landscape Turned Red*, 115.

24. Ibid., 150–51.

25. *O.R.*, ser. I, vol. 19, part 1, 824.

26. Shelby Foote, *The Civil War: A Narrative* (New York: Random House, 1958), 1: 688–92.

27. *O.R.*, ser. I, vol. 19, part 1, 824.

28. Sears, *Landscape Turned Red*, 238.

29. Ibid., 235–54.

30. Ibid., 258–89.

31. Ibid., 292.

32. *O.R.*, ser. I, vol. 19, part 1, 824.

CHAPTER 6: CHAMBERSBURG

1. George Cary Eggleston, *The History of the Confederate War: Its Causes and Its Conduct: A Narrative and Critical History* (New York: Sturgis & Walton, 1910), 2: 15.

2. David H. Donald, *Lincoln* (New York: Simon & Schuster, 1995), 375.
3. Gideon Welles, *Diary of Gideon Welles: Secretary of the Navy under Lincoln and Johnson* (Boston: Houghton Mifflin, 1911), 1: 150.
4. Donald, *Lincoln,* 377.
5. Elisabeth Cutting, *Jefferson Davis: Political Soldier* (New York: Dodd, Mead, 1930), 208.
6. Robert G. Hartje, *Van Dorn: The Life and Times of a Confederate General* (Nashville: Vanderbilt University Press, 1967), 221–33.
7. Kenneth A. Hafendorfer, *Perryville: Battle for Kentucky* (Utica, Ky.: McDowell, 1981).
8. *O.R.,* ser. I, vol. 19, part 2, 55.
9. Davis, *The Last Cavalier,* 211.
10. Ibid., 214.
11. *O.R.,* ser. I, vol. 19, part 2, 57.
12. Ibid.
13. Ibid.
14. Ibid., 52.
15. Brooks, *Butler and His Cavalry,* 80.
16. Freeman, *Lee's Lieutenants,* 2: 287.
17. *O.R.,* ser. I, vol. 19, part 2, 57.
18. Brooks, *Butler and His Cavalry,* 81.
19. *O.R.,* ser. I, vol. 19, part 2, 57.
20. Ibid., 52.
21. Ibid., 53.
22. Brooks, *Butler and His Cavalry,* 82.
23. *O.R.,* ser. I, vol. 19, part 2, 52–53.
24. Ibid., 59.
25. Ibid., 40.
26. Ibid., 29.
27. Ibid., 36.
28. Ibid., 41.
29. Ibid., 66.
30. Thomason, *Jeb Stuart,* 308–9.
31. Blackford, *War Years with Jeb Stuart,* 173.
32. *O.R.,* ser. I, vol. 19, part 2, 43.
33. Ibid., 38–39.
34. Ibid., 53.
35. Brooks, *Butler and His Cavalry,* 82–83.
36. Blackford, *War Years with Jeb Stuart,* 176–77.
37. Brooks, *Butler and His Cavalry,* 83.

38. Blackford, *War Years with Jeb Stuart*, 178.
39. Brooks, *Butler and His Cavalry*, 84.
40. *O.R.*, ser. I, vol. 19, part 2, 54.
41. Ibid., 54.

CHAPTER 7: A COLD WINTER

1. Wellman, *Giant in Gray*, 101.
2. Henry B. McClellan, *I Rode with Jeb Stuart: Life and Campaigns of Major General J. E. B. Stuart* (Bloomington: Indiana University, 1958), 167–68.
3. Brooks, *Butler and His Cavalry*, 99.
4. *Edgefield Advertiser*, June 19, 1861, 2.
5. Sears, *The Young Napoleon*, 336–37.
6. William M. Lamers, *The Edge of Glory: A Biography of General William S. Rosecrans, U.S.A.* (New York: Harcourt, Brace & World, 1961), 181.
7. Ben: Perley Poore, *The Life and Public Services of Ambrose E. Burnside: Soldier-Citizen-Statesman* (Providence: J. A. & R. A. Reid, 1882), 178–80.
8. M. C. Butler to Maria Butler, November 28, 1862, Dalton Collection.
9. Marvel, *Burnside*, 163–65.
10. Wellman, *Giant in Gray*, 102.
11. M. C. Butler to Maria Butler, November 28, 1862, Dalton Collection.
12. *O.R.*, ser. I, vol. 21, 16.
13. Brooks, *Butler and His Cavalry*, 85.
14. Ibid.
15. Ibid., 86.
16. M. C. Butler to Maria Butler, December 14, 1862, Dalton Collection.
17. Brooks, *Butler and His Cavalry*, 85.
18. Ibid., 87.
19. Edward J. Stackpole, *Drama on the Rappahannock: The Fredericksburg Campaign* (Harrisburg, Pa.: Stackpole, 1957).
20. *O.R.*, ser. I, vol. 21, 696.
21. Freeman, *Lee's Lieutenants*, 2: 400.
22. *O.R.*, ser. I, vol. 21, 736.
23. Freeman, *Lee's Lieutenants*, 2: 400.
24. Ibid., 402.
25. Brooks, *Butler and His Cavalry*, 89.

26. *O.R.*, ser. I, vol. 21, 737.
27. Ibid.
28. Freeman, *Lee's Lieutenants,* 2: 403.
29. *O.R.*, ser. I, vol. 21, 737.
30. Freeman, *Lee's Lieutenants,* 2: 405.
31. Ibid.
32. *O.R.*, ser. I, vol. 21, 734.
33. Ibid.
34. Ulysses R. Brooks, *Stories of the Confederacy* (Oxford, Miss.: Guild Bindery, 1991), 127.
35. Alexander F. Stevenson, *The Battle of Stone's River near Murfreeboro, Tennessee, December 30, 1862 to January 3, 1863* (Boston: James R. Osgood, 1884).
36. Ulysses S. Grant, *Personal Memoirs of U. S. Grant* (New York: Charles L. Webster, 1885), 1: 433.
37. William T. Sherman, *Personal Memoirs of General W. T. Sherman* (New York: Charles L. Webster, 1890) 1: 319–21.
38. *O.R.*, ser. I, vol. 21, 752.
39. Walter H. Hebert, *Fighting Joe Hooker* (Indianapolis: Bobbs-Merrill, 1944), 166.
40. *Edgefield Advertiser,* January 21, 1863, 2.
41. Brooks, *Stories of the Confederacy,* 129.
42. M. C. Butler to Maria Butler, March 1863, M. C. Butler Papers.
43. *O.R.*, ser. I, vol. 14, 269.
44. Ibid., 890.
45. *Edgefield Advertiser,* April 15, 1863.
46. M. C. Butler to Maria Butler, May 16, 1863, Dalton Collection.
47. Edward J. Stackpole, *Chancellorsville: Lee's Greatest Battle* (Harrisburg, Pa.: Stackpole, 1958), 147.
48. Jay Luvaas and Harold W. Nelson, eds., *The U.S. Army War College Guide to the Battles of Chancellorsville and Fredericksburg* (Carlisle: South Mountain, 1988).
49. Lenoir Chambers, *Stonewall Jackson* (New York: William Morrow, 1959), 2: 446–47.
50. Freeman, *R. E. Lee,* 3: 19.
51. *O.R.*, ser. I, vol. 25, part 2, 774.

CHAPTER 8: BRANDY STATION

1. William Woods Hassler, *A. P. Hill: Lee's Forgotten General* (Richmond: Garrett & Massie, 1962), 142–43.
2. Thomas, *Bold Dragoon,* 215–16.

3. Ibid., 217.
4. M. C. Butler to Maria Butler, May 21, 1863, Dalton Collection.
5. Ibid., June 1, 1863.
6. McClellan, *I Rode with Jeb Stuart,* 261.
7. Davis, *The Last Cavalier,* 304.
8. Ibid.
9. McClellan, *I Rode with Jeb Stuart,* 262.
10. Davis, *The Last Cavalier,* 305.
11. Marshall D. Krolick, "The Battle of Brandy Station," *The Civil War Quarterly* 7 (winter 1986): 56.
12. *O.R.,* ser. I, vol. 27, part 3, 27–28.
13. Krolick, "The Battle of Brandy Station," 56.
14. Fairfax Downey, *Clash of Cavalry: The Battle of Brandy Station* (New York: David McKay, 1959), 100.
15. Clark B. Hall, "The Battle of Brandy Station," *Civil War Times Illustrated* 29, no. 2 (May–June 1990): 38.
16. McClellan, *I Rode with Jeb Stuart,* 270.
17. Noble D. Preston, *History of the Tenth Regiment of Cavalry: New York State Volunteers* (New York: D. Appleton, 1892), 85.
18. Brooks, *Butler and His Cavalry,* 151–52.
19. Ibid., 152–53.
20. Ibid., 153.
21. Ibid., 154.
22. Downey, *Clash of Cavalry,* 115.
23. Brooks, *Butler and His Cavalry,* 153.
24. Ibid., 156.
25. Ibid., 155.
26. Ibid.
27. Robertson, "Gen. M. C. Butler as a Confederate," 110.
28. McClellan, *I Rode with Jeb Stuart,* 292.
29. Brooks, *Butler and His Cavalry,* 156.
30. Dr. T. M. Braskllien, "Annals of the War: Chapters of Unwritten History: A Sharp Cavalry Clash: The Personal Recollections of a South Carolina Trooper at Brandy Station: Butler at Stevensburg," *Phildelphia Weekly Times,* March 24, 1883.
31. Ibid.
32. Ibid.

CHAPTER 9: RECUPERATION

1. Brooks, *Butler and His Cavalry,* 160.
2. *O.R.,* ser. I, vol. 27, part 1, 950.

3. Downey, *Clash of Cavalry,* 142.
4. Braskllien, "Annals of the War."
5. Brooks, *Butler and His Cavalry,* 170.
6. *Edgefield Advertiser,* June 17, 1863, 2.
7. Brooks, *Butler and His Cavalry,* 173.
8. Mrs. Benjamin E. Nicholson, interview by author, Edgefield, South Carolina, October 6, 1996.
9. Samuel J. Martin, *Kill-Cavalry: The Life of Union General Hugh Judson Kilpatrick* (Rutherford, NJ: Fairleigh Dickinson University Press, 1996).
10. *O.R.,* ser. I, vol. 27, part 2, 692.
11. Clifford Dowdey, *Lee* (Boston: Little, Brown, 1965), 362.
12. Edwin B. Coddington, *The Gettysburg Campaign: A Study in Command* (New York: Charles Scribner's Sons, 1968).
13. Thomas, *Bold Dragoon,* 248.
14. Wellman, *Giant in Gray,* 120.
15. James S. Montgomery, *The Shaping of a Battle: Gettysburg* (Philadelphia: Chilton, 1959).
16. *South Carolina Genealogies,* 241.
17. Earl Schenck Miers, *The Web of Victory: Grant at Vicksburg* (New York: Knoft, 1955).
18. Lawrence L. Hewitt, *Port Hudson: Confederate Bastion on the Mississippi* (Baton Rouge: Louisiana State University Press, 1987).
19. Lawrence E. Friedman, M.D., *The Psychological Rehabilitation of the Amputee* (Springfield, Ill: Charles C. Thomas, 1978), 21.
20. Ibid.
21. M. C. Butler to Clara Maclean, December 21, 1864, Dalton Collection.
22. Clara Victoria Dargan Maclean Papers and Personal Diary, vol. 4, March 8, 1863, Special Collections Library, Duke University (hereafter cited as Maclean Papers).
23. *O.R.,* ser. I, vol. 29, part 2, 270.
24. Freeman, *Lee's Lieutenants,* 3: 215.
25. J. W. Ward, "General M. C. Butler of South Carolina," *Confederate Veteran* 3, no. 2 (February 1895): 42.
26. Wiley Sword, *Mountains Touched with Fire: Chattanooga Besieged, 1863* (New York: St. Martin's, 1995).
27. Stephen R. Wise, *Gate of Hell: Campaign for Charleston Harbor, 1863* (Columbia: University of South Carolina Press, 1994).
28. Wellman, *Giant in Gray,* 130.
29. *O.R.,* ser. I, vol. 29, part 2, 903.

30. Brian D. Kowell, "Pell-Mell Cavalry Chase," *America's Civil War* 5, no. 2 (July 1992): 74.
31. James Lee McDonough, *Chattanooga: A Death Grip on the Confederacy* (Knoxville: University of Tennessee Press, 1984).
32. Bruce Catton, *Grant Takes Command* (Boston: Little, Brown, 1968), 138.
33. *O.R.*, ser. I, vol. 29, part 2, 863.
34. Millard K. and Dean M. Bushong, *Fightin' Tom Rosser, C.S.A.* (Shippensburg, Pa.: Beidel Printing House, 1983), 65.
35. *O.R.*, ser. I, vol. 30, 1088–89.
36. Ibid., 1125.
37. Ibid., 1140.
38. Ibid., 1153.
39. Ibid., 1164.
40. Virgil Carrington Jones, *Eight Hours before Richmond* (New York: Henry Holt, 1957).
41. James E. B. Stuart, *The Letters of General J. E. B. Stuart,* ed. Adele H. Mitchell (Privately printed by the Stuart-Mosby Historical Society, 1990), 377.
42. *O.R.*, ser. I, vol. 30, 1230.
43. *O.R.*, ser. I, vol. 36, part 1, 1027.
44. "John Rutledge Family," *South Carolina Historical Magazine* 31, no. 1 (January 1930): 100.
45. Adelia A. Dunovant, "Gen. John Dunovant, Houston, Tex." *Confederate Veteran* 16, no. 1 (January 1908): 184.
46. Frank E. Vandiver, *Ploughshares into Swords: Josiah Gorgas and Confederate Ordnance* (Austin: University of Texas Press, 1952), 38.
47. *Winnsboro News and Herald,* May 25, 1910.
48. *O.R.*, ser. I, vol. 30, 1259.
49. M. C. Butler to Maria Butler, April 28, 1864, Dalton Collection.
50. Ibid., July 21, 1864, Dalton Collection.
51. Edward Steere, *The Wilderness Campaign* (Harrisburg, Pa.: Stackpole, 1960).
52. Phillip H. Sheridan, *Personal Memoirs of P. H. Sheridan* (New York: Charles L. Webster, 1888), 1: 371.
53. Davis, *The Last Cavalier,* 417.
54. William D. Matter, *If It Takes All Summer: The Battle of Spotsylvania* (Chapel Hill: University of North Carolina Press, 1988).
55. Freeman, *Lee's Lieutenants,* 3: 496–98.
56. Wellman, *Giant in Gray,* 142.
57. Edward L. Wells, *Hampton and His Cavalry in '64* (Richmond: Owens, 1991), 162.
58. Ibid., 166.

59. Brooks, *Butler and His Cavalry*, 210.
60. Wells, *Hampton and His Cavalry*, 170.

CHAPTER 10: TREVILIAN STATION

1. Brooks, *Butler and His Cavalry*, 273.
2. Freeman, *Lee's Lieutenants*, 3: 502.
3. Brooks, *Butler and His Cavalry*, 205–6.
4. Ibid., 205–6.
5. Ibid., 206.
6. Ibid.
7. M. C. Butler to Maria Butler, June 1, 1864, Dalton Collection.
8. Brooks, *Butler and His Cavalry*, 206.
9. Ibid., 227.
10. Noah Andre Trudeau, *Bloody Roads South: The Wilderness to Cold Harbor, May–June 1864* (Boston: Little, Brown, 1989), 298.
11. *O.R.*, ser. I, vol. 36, part 1, 186.
12. Freeman, *Lee's Lieutenants*, 3: 516.
13. Wells, *Hampton and His Cavalry*, 188.
14. Warner, *Generals in Gray*, 178.
15. Brooks, *Butler and His Cavalry*, 238.
16. C. M. Calhoun, *History of Greenwood* (Greenwood, SC: Index Job Print, n.d.), 65.
17. Matthew C. Butler, "The Cavalry Fight at Trevilian Station," in *Battles and Leaders of the Civil War*, ed. Robert U. Johnson and Clarence C. Buel (New York: Thomas Yoseloff, 1956), 4: 237.
18. Alice West Allen, "Recollections of War in Virginia," *Confederate Veteran* 23, no. 6 (June 1915), 268.
19. Brooks, *Butler and His Cavalry*, 239.
20. *O.R.*, ser. I, vol. 36, part 1, 1095.
21. Brooks, *Butler and His Cavalry*, 241.
22. Ibid., 243.
23. U. R. Brooks, "Memories of Battle," *Confederate Veteran* 22, no. 9 (September 1914), 408.
24. Butler, "The Cavalry Fight at Trevilian Station," 237.
25. Brooks, *Butler and His Cavalry*, 245.
26. Butler, "The Cavalry Fight at Trevilian Station," 238.
27. Ibid.
28. Brooks, *Butler and His Cavalry*, 247.
29. Butler, "The Cavalry Fight at Trevilian Station," 238.
30. Frank M. Myers, *The Comanches: A History of White's Battalion, Virginia Cavalry, Laurel Brigade, Hampton's Division, A.N.V., C.S.A.* (Marietta, GA: Continental, 1956), 302.

31. Butler, "The Cavalry Fight at Trevilian Station," 238.

32. Ibid.

33. Calhoun, *History of Greenwood,* 67–68.

34. *O.R.,* ser. I, vol. 36, part 1, 784.

35. Swank, *The Battle of Trevilian Station,* 74.

36. Myers, *The Comanches,* 304.

37. Butler, "The Cavalry Fight at Trevilian Station," 239.

38. Brooks, *Butler and His Cavalry,* 265.

39. Ibid., 254–55.

40. Myers, *The Comanches,* 304.

41. *Winnsboro News and Herald,* May 25, 1910.

42. Swank, *The Battle of Trevilian Station,* 26–27.

43. *O.R.,* ser. I, vol. 36, part 1, 797–98.

44. Myers, *The Comanches,* 306.

45. Clifford Dowdey, *Lee's Last Campaign: The Story of Lee and His Men against Grant* (Boston: Little, Brown, 1960), 317–18.

46. Richard J. Sommers, *Richmond Redeemed: The Siege at Petersburg* (Garden City, N.Y.: Doubleday, 1981), 2.

47. Stephen Z. Starr, *The Union Cavalry in the Civil War* (Baton Rouge: Louisiana State University Press, 1981), 2: 149.

48. *O.R.,* ser. I, vol. 36, part 1, 796–97.

49. James Harrison Wilson, *Under the Old Flag: Recollections of Military Operations in the War for the Union, the Spanish War, the Boxer Rebellion, etc.* (New York: D. Appleton, 1912), 1: 441.

50. *O.R.,* ser. I, vol. 36, part 1, 785.

51. Brooks, *Butler and His Cavalry,* 253.

CHAPTER 11. WILSON

1. Brooks, *Butler and His Cavalry,* 272.

2. Edward G. Longacre, *From Union Stars to Top Hat: A Biography of the Extraordinary General James Harrison Wilson* (Harrisburg, Pa.: Stackpole, 1972), 136–37.

3. Wilson, *Under the Old Flag,* 1: 459–64.

4. Wells, *Hampton and His Cavalry,* 237.

5. Wilson, *Under the Old Flag,* 1: 466.

6. Brooks, *Butler and His Cavalry,* 275.

7. *O.R.,* ser. I, vol. 40, part 1, 809.

8. Ibid.

9. Brooks, *Butler and His Cavalry,* 278.

10. Wells, *Hampton and His Cavalry,* 243.

11. Starr, *The Union Cavalry,* 2: 202.

12. Wilson, *Under the Old Flag,* 1: 473.

13. *O.R.,* ser. I, vol. 40, part 1, 629.
14. Ibid., 809.
15. Wellman, *Giant in Gray,* 151.
16. M. C. Butler to Maria Butler, July 3, 1864, Dalton Collection.
17. *O.R.,* ser. I, vol. 42, part 2, 1171.

CHAPTER 12: SIEGE

1. Frank E. Vandiver, *Jubal's Raid: General Early's Famous Attack on Washington in 1864* (New York: McGraw-Hill, 1960).
2. Albert Castel, *Decision in the West: The Atlanta Campaign of 1864* (Lawrence: University Press of Kansas, 1992).
3. Matthew C. Butler to Ulysses R. Brooks, April 19, 1908, Ulysses R. Brooks Papers, Special Collections Library, Duke University (hereafter cited as Brooks Papers).
4. Brooks, *Butler and His Cavalry,* 108.
5. *O.R.,* ser. I, vol. 40, part 1, 308–9.
6. Ibid., part 3, 809–15.
7. Nelson Morehouse Blake, *William Mahone of Virginia: Soldier and Political Insurgent* (Richmond: Garrett & Massie, 1935), 55.
8. Freeman Cleeves, *Meade of Gettysburg* (Norman: University of Oklahoma Press, 1960), 282.
9. Brooks, *Butler and His Cavalry,* 293.
10. Ibid., 301–2.
11. Millard K. Bushong, *Old Jube: A Biography of Geneal Jubal A. Early* (Boyce, Va.: Carr Publishing, 1955), 213.
12. Freeman, *Lee's Lieutenants,* 3: 571–72.
13. Roy Morris, Jr., *Sheridan: The Life and Wars of General Phil Sheridan* (New York: Crown Publishers, 1992), 180.
14. *O.R.,* ser. I, vol. 42, part 2, 1177.
15. *O.R.,* ser. I, vol. 42, part 1, 216–21.
16. Martin, *The Road to Glory,* 329–30.
17. Calhoun, *History of Greenwood,* 76–77.
18. Wells, *Hampton and His Cavalry,* 273.
19. *O.R.,* ser. I, vol. 42, part 1, 18.
20. Ibid.
21. Freeman, *Lee's Lieutenants,* 3: 588–89.
22. Myers, *The Comanches,* 322.
23. Ibid., 323–24.
24. Wellman, *Giant in Gray,* 155.
25. *O.R.,* ser. I, vol. 42, part 1, 942.
26. Myers, *The Comanches,* 325–26.

27. Calhoun, *History of Greenwood*, 80.
28. *O.R.*, ser. I, vol. 42, part 1, 228.
29. Brooks, *Butler and His Cavalry*, 306.
30. *O.R.*, ser. I, vol. 42, part 1, 228.
31. Brooks, *Butler and His Cavalry*, 307.
32. A. A. Hoehling, *Last Train from Atlanta* (New York: Bonanza, 1958).
33. M. C. Butler to Maria Butler, September 5, 1864, Dalton Collection.
34. M. C. Butler to Maria Butler, September 7, 1864, Dalton Collection.
35. Edward Boykin, *Beefsteak Raid* (New York: Funk & Wagnalls, 1960).
36. M. C. Butler Personal File.
37. Sifakis, *Who Was Who in the Confederacy*, 247.
38. Warner, *Generals in Gray*, 348.
39. Lynwood M. Hollad, *Pierce M. B. Young: The Warwick of the South* (Athens: University of Georgia Press, 1962), 94.
40. Thomas L. Rosser to Betty Winston Rosser, August 28, 1864, Thomas Lafayette Rosser Papers, Alderman Library, University of Virginia, Charlottesville, Virginia (hereafter cited as Rosser Papers).
41. Thomas L. Rosser to Betty Winston Rosser, September 6, 1864, Rosser Papers.
42. M. C. Butler to U. R. Brooks, December 18, 1905, Brooks Papers.

CHAPTER 13. MCDOWELL'S FARM

1. Freeman, *Lee's Lieutenants*, 3: 577–84.
2. Sommers, *Richmond Redeemed*, 28–49.
3. Ibid., 197.
4. Ibid., 198.
5. *O.R.*, ser. I, vol. 42, part 1, 634.
6. Ibid., part 2, 1106–7.
7. Brooks, *Butler and His Cavalry*, 196.
8. Ibid.
9. *O.R.*, ser. I, vol. 42, part 1, 947.
10. Sommers, *Richmond Redeemed*, 205.
11. Ibid.
12. Ibid., 240–267.
13. *O.R.*, ser. I, vol. 42, part 1, 947.
14. Sommers, *Richmond Redeemed*, 268–305.
15. Ibid., 321.
16. Brooks, *Butler and His Cavalry*, 325.
17. Sommers, *Richmond Redeemed*, 322.
18. Calhoun, *History of Greenwood*, 345.
19. Brooks, *Butler and His Cavalry*, 345.

20. Calhoun, *History of Greenwood,* 84.
21. Sommers, *Richmond Redeemed,* 324.
22. *O.R.,* ser. I, vol. 42, part 1, 635.
23. James I. Robertson, *General A. P. Hill: The Story of a Confederate Warrior* (New York: Random House, 1987), 304.
24. Sommers, *Richmond Redeemed,* 337.
25. Brooks, *Butler and His Cavalry,* 327.
26. Ibid.
27. Ibid., 330.
28. *O.R.,* ser. I, vol. 42, part 1, 948.
29. Brooks, *Butler and His Cavalry,* 331.
30. Ibid.
31. Dunovant, "Gen. John Dunovant, Houston, Tex.," 184.
32. Brooks, *Butler and His Cavalry,* 332.
33. *O.R.,* ser. I, vol. 42, part 1, 948.
34. Sommers, *Richmond Redeemed,* 350.
35. Brooks, *Butler and His Cavalry,* 333.
36. *O.R.,* ser. I, vol. 42, part 1, 635.
37. Sommers, *Richmond Redeemed,* 351.

CHAPTER 14: BURGESS' MILL

1. Wells, *Hampton and His Cavalry,* 352.
2. Wade Hampton to Mary Fisher Hampton, October 11, 1864, Wade Hampton Papers, South Caroliniana Library, University of South Carolina (hereafter cited as Hampton Papers).
3. Thomas A. Lewis, *The Guns of Cedar Creek* (New York: Harper & Row, 1988), 288.
4. Charles C. Osborne, *Jubal: The Life and Times of Jubal A. Early, C.S.A.* (Chapel Hill: Algonquin, 1992), 303.
5. H. J. Eckenrode and Bryan Conrad, *James Longstreet: Lee's War Horse* (Chapel Hill: University of North Carolina Press, 1936), 322.
6. *O.R.,* ser. I, vol. 42, part 1, 434.
7. Ibid., 548–49.
8. Ibid., 434–37.
9. Ibid., 438.
10. Wells, *Hampton and His Cavalry,* 329.
11. Brooks, *Stories of the Confederacy,* 53.
12. *O.R.,* ser. I, vol. 42, part 1, 949.
13. Ibid., 231.
14. Ibid.
15. Ibid., 949.
16. Ibid., 232–35.

17. Brooks, *Butler and His Cavalry,* 568–69.
18. Wellman, *Giant in Gray,* 161.
19. Brooks, *Butler and His Cavalry,* 569.
20. Wellman, *Giant in Gray,* 161.
21. *O.R.,* ser. I, vol. 42, part 1, 950.
22. Van Deusen, *William Henry Seward,* 398.
23. M. C. Butler to Daniel R. Durisoe, November 3, 1864, Dalton Collection.
24. Ulysses R. Brooks, "War Memories," *Confederate Veteran* 22, no. 11 (November 1914), 497.
25. George W. Nichols, *The Story of the Great March from the Diary of a Staff Officer* (New York: Harper & Brothers, 1865), 38.
26. Matthew C. Butler to Edward C. Anderson, November 1864, Wayne-Stites-Anderson Papers, Georgia Historical Society, Savannah.
27. *O.R.,* ser. I, vol. 42, part 1, 443.
28. Ibid., 444.
29. Calhoun, *History of Greenwood,* 91.
30. *O.R.,* ser. I, vol. 42, part 1, 444.
31. Calhoun, *History of Greenwood,* 91.
32. Brooks, *Butler and His Cavalry,* 348–49.
33. Ibid., 413.
34. Ibid., 386.
35. William Watts Ball, *The State That Forgot: South Carolina's Surrender to Democracy* (Indianapolis: Bobbs-Merrill, 1932), 240–41.
36. *O.R.,* ser. I, vol. 42, part 1, 445.
37. Brooks, *Butler and His Cavalry,* 387.
38. Ibid.
39. James Lee McDonough and Thomas L. Connelly, *Five Tragic Hours: The Battle of Franklin* (Knoxville: University of Tennessee Press, 1983).
40. Stanley F. Horn, *The Decisive Battle of Nashville* (Knoxville: University of Tennessee Press, 1978).
41. John M. Gibson, *Those 163 Days: A Southern Account of Sherman's March from Atlanta to Raleigh* (New York: Coward-McCann, 1961).
42. *The Wartime Papers of R. E. Lee,* 881.
43. Wells, *Hampton and His Cavalry,* 389.

CHAPTER 15: SOUTH CAROLINA

1. John G. Barrett, *Sherman's March through the Carolinas* (Chapel Hill: University of North Carolina Press, 1956), 44–46.
2. Ezra J. Warner, *Generals in Blue: Lives of the Union Commanders* (Baton Rouge: Louisiana State University Press, 1964), 442.

3. Barrett, *Sherman's March through the Carolinas,* 47–48.

4. Alfred Roman, *Military Operations of General Beauregard in the War between the States, 1861 to 1865: Including a Brief Personal Sketch and a Narrative of His Services in the War with Mexico, 1846–48* (New York: Harper & Brothers, 1884), 2: 338–39.

5. Brooks, *Butler and His Cavalry,* 403.

6. Calhoun, *History of Greenwood,* 93.

7. Ibid., 92.

8. *Edgefield Advertiser,* February 8, 1865, 2.

9. Bruce S. Allardice, *More Generals in Gray* (Baton Rouge: Louisiana State University Press, 1995), 239.

10. Ellison Capers, "South Carolina," in *Confederate Military History: A Library of Confedereate States History, in Thirteen Volumes, Written by Distinguished Men of the South and Edited by Gen. Clement A. Evans of Georgia* (Secaucus: Blue and Gray, n.d.), 411–12.

11. Wade Hampton, "The Battle of Bentonville," in *Battles and Leaders of the Civil War,* ed. Robert V. Johnson and Clarence C. Buel (New York: Thomas Yoseloff, 1956), 4: 701.

12. *O.R.,* ser. I, vol. 47, part 1, 1144.

13. Roman, *Operations of General Beauregard,* 2: 347–49.

14. Warner, *Generals in Gray,* 332–33.

15. *O.R.,* ser. I, vol. 47, part 2, 1207.

16. Clement Saussy, "Two Bridges Burned Near Columbia," *Confederate Veteran* 17, no. 11 (November 1909): 553.

17. Calhoun, *History of Greenwood,* 94.

18. Roman, *Operations of General Beauregard,* 2: 352.

19. Ibid., 366.

20. Ibid.

21. Mrs. Alfred P. Aldrich, "Barbarians in Barnwell," in *When Sherman Came: Southern Women and the "Great March,"* ed. Katherine M. Jones (Indianapolis: Bobbs-Merrill, 1964), 115.

22. Burke Davis, *Sherman's March* (New York: Random House, 1980), 192–93.

23. Gibson, *Those 163 Days,* 141.

24. Davis, *Sherman's March,* 167.

25. Calhoun, *History of Greenwood,* 95.

26. Matthew C. Butler, "Devoted South Carolina Confederates: Reunion of the Division U.C.V. at Chester, South Carolina," *Confederate Veteran* 8, no. 1 (January 1900): 29.

27. Ibid., 30.

28. Marion B. Lucas, *Sherman and His Burning of Columbia* (College Station: Texas A. & M. University Press, 1976).

29. Nathaniel Cheairs Hughes, *General William J. Hardee: Old Reliable* (Baton Rouge: Louisiana State University Press, 1965), 278.
30. Butler, "Devoted South Carolina Confederates," 30.
31. Brooks, *Butler and His Cavalry,* 467–68.
32. Calhoun, *History of Greenwood,* 96.
33. M. C. Butler to U. R. Brooks, March 6, 1906, Brooks Papers.
34. Butler, "Devoted South Carolina Confederates," 30.
35. Johnston, *Narrative of Military Operations,* 371.
36. M. C. Butler to U. R. Brooks, March 6, 1906, Brooks Papers.
37. Brooks, *Butler and His Cavalry,* 469.
38. Butler, "Devoted South Carolina Confederates," 31.
39. M. C. Butler to U. R. Brooks, March 6, 1906, Brooks Papers.
40. Butler, "Devoted South Carolina Confederates," 31.
41. Brooks, *Butler and His Cavalry,* 471.
42. *O.R.,* ser. I, vol. 47, part 2, 546.
43. Ibid., 596.
44. Ulysses R. Brooks, "Hampton and Butler: Some Pages of Heretofore Unwritten History," ed. R. A. Brock, *Southern Historical Society Papers* 23 (January–December 1895): 29.
45. Calhoun, *History of Greenwood,* 97.
46. Hughes, *Old Reliable,* 278.
47. Butler, "Devoted South Carolina Confederates," 32.
48. Ibid.
49. Brooks, *Butler and His Cavalry,* 473.
50. Ibid.
51. Butler, "Devoted South Carolina Confederates," 32.
52. Ibid.
53. Ibid., 33.
54. Calhoun, *History of Greenwood,* 99.
55. Davis, *Sherman's March,* 196.
56. *O.R.,* ser. I, vol. 47, part 2, 1329.
57. John F. Marszalek, *Sherman: A Soldier's Passion for Order* (New York: Free Press, 1993), 286.

CHAPTER 16: NORTH CAROLINA

1. Sherman, *Personal Memoirs,* 2: 272.
2. Rod Gragg, *Confederate Goliath: The Battle of Fort Fisher* (New York: HarperCollins, 1991).
3. John M. Schofield, *Forty-Six Years in the Army* (New York: Century, 1897), 346.
4. Marvel, *Burnside,* 76.

5. James Lee McDonough, *Schofield: Union General in the Civil War and Reconstruction* (Tallahassee: Florida State University Press, 1972), 156.
6. Barrett, *Sherman's March through the Carolinas,* 115.
7. Johnston, *Narrative of Military Operations,* 378–80.
8. *O.R.,* ser. I, vol. 47, part 2, 1320.
9. Joseph Wheeler, "Alabama," in *Confederate Military History: A Library of Confederate States History, Written by Distinguished Men of the South, and Edited by Gen. Clement A. Evans of Georgia* (Secaucus: Blue and Gray, n.d.), 423–24.
10. Mark L. Bradley, *Last Stand in the Carolinas: The Battle of Bentonville* (Campbell, Calif.: Savas Woodbury, 1996), 379.
11. Butler, "Devoted South Carolina Confederates," 33.
12. Calhoun, *History of Greenwood,* 98.
13. *O.R.,* ser. I, vol. 47, part 1, 861.
14. Matthew C. Butler to Edward L. Wells, March 27, 1900, Edward L. Wells Papers, Charleston Library Society (hereafter cited as Wells Papers).
15. Brooks, "Hampton and Butler," 31.
16. Calhoun, *History of Greenwood,* 101.
17. M. C. Butler to Edward Wells, March 27, 1900, Wells Papers.
18. Ibid.
19. Ibid.
20. Calhoun, *History of Greenwood,* 104.
21. M. C. Butler to Edward Wells, March 27, 1900, Wells Papers.
22. C. M. Calhoun, "Credit to Wheeler Claimed for Others," *Confederate Veteran* 20, no. 2 (February 1912): 82.
23. M. C. Butler to Edward Wells, March 27, 1900, Wells Papers.
24. Edward L. Wells, "A Morning Call on General Kilpatrick," *Southern Historical Society Papers* 12 (January–December 1884): 126.
25. Calhoun, *History of Greenwood,* 103.
26. Wells, "A Morning Call on General Kilpatrick," 126.
27. Davis, *Sherman's March,* 214.
28. Don C. Seitz, *Braxton Bragg: General of the Confederacy* (Columbia: State, 1924), 514.
29. Barrett, *Sherman's March through the Carolinas,* 133.
30. Wells, *Hampton and His Cavalry,* 33–34.
31. Barrett, *Sherman's March through the Carolinas,* 133.
32. Johnston, *Narrative of Military Operations,* 382.
33. Calhoun, *History of Greenwood,* 113.
34. Hughes, *Old Reliable,* 284.
35. Foote, *The Civil War,* 3: 828.

36. Hampton, "The Battle of Bentonville," 4: 701.
37. Johnston, *Narrative of Military Operations*, 386.
38. Hampton, "The Battle of Bentonville," 4: 702.
39. Ibid., 703.
40. Barrett, *Sherman's March through the Carolinas*, 164–65.
41. Mark L. Bradley, *Last Stand in the Carolinas*, 154.
42. *O.R.*, ser. I, vol. 47, part 1, 1056.
43. Ibid.
44. Johnston, *Narrative of Military Operations*, 386–87.
45. Evander M. Law to John G. Stokes, March 26, 1865, Evander McIvor Law Papers, Virginia Historical Society, Richmond.
46. *O.R.*, ser. I, vol. 47, part 3, 737.

CHAPTER 17: THE END OF THE WAR

1. Bradley, *Last Stand in the Carolinas*, 343.
2. Barrett, *Sherman's March through the Carolinas*, 178.
3. *O.R.*, ser. I, vol. 47, part 1, 1056.
4. Bradley, *Last Stand in the Carolinas*, 352.
5. Ibid., 379.
6. Hampton, "The Battle of Bentonville," 705.
7. Sherman, *Personal Memoirs*, 2: 315.
8. B. H. Liddell Hart, *Sherman: Soldier, Realist, American* (New York: Dodd, Mead, 1929), 386.
9. Freeman, *R. E. Lee*, 4: 59–60.
10. George Ward Nichols, *The Story of the Great March*, 285.
11. Thomas Lawrence Connelly, *Autumn of Glory: The Army of Tennessee, 1862–1865* (Baton Rouge: Louisiana State University Press, 1971), 531.
12. Johnston, *Narrative of Military Operations*, 400.
13. *O.R.*, ser. I, vol. 47, part 23, 777.
14. Jefferson C. Davis, *The Rise and Fall of the Confederate Government* (New York: D. Appleton, 1881), 2: 679.
15. Johnston, *Narrative of Military Operations*, 397.
16. Ibid., 399–400.
17. Sherman, *Personal Memoirs*, 2: 347.
18. Ibid., 349.
19. Johnston, *Narrative of Military Operations*, 405–7.
20. Sherman, *Personal Memoirs*, 2: 344.
21. Johnston, *Narrative of Military Operations*, 408.
22. Wade Hampton to Hugh Judson Kilpatrick, April 20, 1865, Wade Hampton Papers, Special Collections Library, Duke University, Durham, North Carolina.

23. Wellman, *Giant in Gray,* 183.
24. John P. Dyer, *"Fightin'" Joe Wheeler* (Baton Rouge: Louisiana State University Press, 1941), 229.
25. Stanley F. Horn, *The Army of Tennessee: A Military History* (Indianapolis: Bobbs-Merrill, 1941), 427.
26. Calhoun, *History of Greenwood,* 106.
27. Dyer, *"Fightin'" Joe Wheeler,* 230.
28. Butler, "Devoted South Carolina Confederates," 33.
29. Ibid.
30. Ibid.
31. *Edgefield Advertiser,* May 5, 1865.
32. Myrta Lockett Avary, *Dixie after the War* (Boston: Houghton Mifflin, 1937), 161.

CHAPTER 18: GOVERNOR ORR

1. Francis Butler Simkins and Robert H. Woody, *South Carolina During Reconstruction* (Chapel Hill: University of North Carolina Press, 1932), 29.
2. Welles, *Diary of Gideon Welles,* 2: 234.
3. Joel Williamson, *After Slavery: The Negro in South Carolina during Reconstruction, 1861–1877* (Chapel Hill: University of North Carolina Press, 1965), 32.
4. *Edgefield Advertiser,* June 14, 1865.
5. Williamson, *After Slavery,* 34.
6. Ball, *The State That Forgot,* 128.
7. Williamson, *After Slavery,* 35.
8. Milledge Luke Bonham, "Around 1865," *Edgefield Advertiser,* centennial edition, December 16, 1936.
9. Matthew Calbraith Butler and LeRoy Youmans Legal Papers, South Caroliniana Library, University of South Carolina.
10. John S. Reynolds, *Reconstruction in South Carolina: 1865–1877* (Columbia: State, 1905), 7.
11. Ibid., 8–9.
12. Ibid., 14.
13. Lloyd Paul Stryker, *Andrew Johnson: A Study in Courage* (New York: MacMillan, 1930), 222.
14. Reynolds, *Reconstruction in South Carolina,* 13–14.
15. *Edgefield Advertiser,* August 9, 1865.
16. Reynolds, *Reconstruction in South Carolina,* 17–20.
17. Simkins and Woody, *South Carolina during Reconstruction,* 37.
18. *Edgefield Advertiser,* October 25, 1865.
19. Sifakis, *Who Was Who in the Confederacy,* 212.

20. Robert Selph Henry, *The Story of Reconstruction* (Indianapolis: Bobbs-Merrill, 1938), 107.

21. Reynolds, *Reconstruction in South Carolina,* 23–24.

22. John William DeForest, *A Union Officer in the Reconstruction,* ed. James H. Croushore and David M. Potter (New Haven: Yale University Press, 1948), xxiii–iv.

23. Henry, *The Story of Reconstruction,* 108.

24. Newspaper article (unidentified), Butler Family Scrapbook.

25. Matthew C. Butler, "Negro and White Man: Irrepressible Conflict between the Two Classes," letter to newspaper (unidentified), September 13, 1899, Butler Family Scrapbook.

26. Newspaper (unidentified), Butler Family Scrapbook.

27. James A. Woodburn, *The Life of Thaddeus Stevens: A Study of American Political History, Especially in the Period of the Civil War and Reconstruction* (Indianapolis: Bobbs-Merrill, 1913), 340.

28. Reynolds, *Reconstruction in South Carolina,* 42–43.

29. Ibid., 43.

30. Newspaper clipping (unidentified), Butler Family Scrapbook.

31. Warner, *Generals in Blue,* 446–47.

32. Simkins and Woody, *South Carolina during Reconstruction,* 57.

33. Oliver O. Howard, *Autobiography of Oliver Otis Howard: Major General United States Army* (New York: Baker & Taylor, 1907), 2: 215.

34. Hodding Carter, *The Angry Scar: The Story of Reconstruction* (Garden City: Doubleday, 1959), 57.

35. *Edgefield Advertiser,* November 1, 1865.

36. Ibid., December 20, 1865.

37. *The Random House Dictionary of the English Language: The Unabridged Edition* (New York: Random House, 1967), 1939–40.

38. *Edgefield Advertiser,* July 25, 1866.

39. M. C. Butler to Maria Butler, July 4, 1866, M. C. Butler Papers.

40. Ibid.

41. Ibid., July 14, 1866.

42. Simkins and Woody, *South Carolina during Reconstruction,* 60.

43. Claude G. Bowers, *The Tragic Era: The Revolution after Lincoln* (Cambridge: Riverside, 1929), 123.

44. Newspaper clipping (unidentified), Butler Family Scrapbook.

45. *Edgefield Advertiser,* September 12, 1866.

46. Ibid., September 19, 1866.

47. Butler Family Bible.

48. Henry, *The Story of Reconstruction,* 198.

49. *Edgefield Advertiser,* December 12, 1866.

50. Simkins and Woody, *South Carolina during Reconstruction,* 63.

51. *Edgefield Advertiser,* March 6, 1867.

52. Reynolds, *Reconstruction in South Carolina,* 53.

53. Carter, *The Angry Scar,* 126.

54. *Edgefield Advertiser,* May 1, 1867.

55. Ibid., May 22, 1867.

56. Hampton M. Jarrell, *Wade Hampton and the Negro: The Road Not Taken* (Columbia: University of South Carolina Press, 1949), 16.

57. Henry, *The Story of Reconstruction,* 226.

58. Simkins and Woody, *South Carolina during Reconstruction,* 88.

59. M. C. Butler to B. H. Rutledge, July 25, 1867, M. C. Butler Papers.

60. W. A. Swanberg, *Sickles the Incredible* (New York: Charles Scribner's Sons, 1956), 291.

61. Warner, *Generals in Blue,* 67–68.

62. *Edgefield Advertiser,* September 11, 1867.

63. Ibid., November 6, 1867.

64. Simkins and Woody, *South Carolina during Reconstruction,* 89.

65. Reynolds, *Reconstruction in South Carolina,* 78.

66. *Edgefield Advertiser,* December 18, 1867.

67. Simkins and Woody, *South Carolina during Reconstruction,* 91.

68. Jarrell, *Wade Hampton and the Negro,* 23.

69. Henry T. Thompson, *Ousting the Carpetbagger from South Carolina* (New York: Negro Universities Press, 1969), 29.

70. Simkins and Woody, *South Carolina during Reconstruction,* 109.

71. *Edgefield Advertiser,* April 22, 1868.

72. Ibid., May 13, 1868.

73. Stryker, *Andrew Johnson,* 572–736.

74. *Edgefield Advertiser,* April 29, 1868.

75. Ibid., June 3, 1868.

76. Ibid., July 8, 1868.

77. Ibid.

78. Reynolds, *Reconstruction in South Carolina,* 98.

79. Simkins and Woody, *South Carolina during Reconstruction,* 109.

CHAPTER 19: GOVERNOR SCOTT

1. Warner, *Generals in Blue,* 428–29.

2. Reynolds, *Reconstruction in South Carolina,* 87.

3. Michael E. Thompson, "Blacks, Carpetbaggers, and Scalawags: A Study of the Membership of the South Carolina Legislature, 1868–1870" (Ph.D. diss., Washington State University, 1975), 39–44.

4. Ibid., 110–18.
5. Stewart Mitchell, *Horatio Seymour of New York* (Cambridge: Harvard University Press, 1939), 418.
6. *Edgefield Advertiser,* August 5, 1868.
7. Ibid., August 19, 1868.
8. Ibid., August 26, 1868.
9. Herbert Shapiro, "The Ku Klux Klan During Reconstruction: The South Carolina Episode," *Journal of Negro History* 49, no. 1 (January 1964): 36.
10. Albion Winegar Tourgee, *The Invisible Empire* (Baton Rouge: Louisiana State University Press, 1989), 27–28.
11. Francis B. Simkins, "The Ku Klux Klan in South Carolina, 1868–1871," *Journal of Negro History* 12, no. 4 (October 1927): 609.
12. Allen W. Trelease, *White Terror: The Ku Klux Klan Conspiracy and Southern Reconstruction* (New York: Harper & Row, 1971), 115.
13. Simkins, "The Ku Klux Klan in South Carolina," 610.
14. Trelease, *White Terror,* 116.
15. Ibid., 364.
16. Reynolds, *Reconstruction in South Carolina,* 114.
17. Ibid., 115.
18. Simkins and Woody, *South Carolina during Reconstruction,* 208–9.
19. Ibid., 142.
20. Burton, *In My Father's House,* 130.
21. Williamson, *After Slavery,* 261.
22. *Edgefield Advertiser,* December 5, 1868.
23. Edmunds, *Francis W. Pickens,* 180.
24. Butler Family Bible.
25. Burton, *In My Father's House,* 231.
26. Edgefield County/RMC (Deeds): Grantor (Direct) Index to Conveyances 1869–1905. South Carolina Department of Archives and History, Columbia.
27. Carol K. Rothrock Bleser, *The Promised Land: The History of the South Carolina Land Commission, 1869–1890* (Columbia: University of South Carolina Press, 1969), 55–56.
28. U.S. House and Senate Joint Select Committee, *The Ku Klux Klan: Testimony Taken by the Joint Select Committee to Inquire into the Conditions of Affairs in the Late Insurrectionary States,* 42nd Cong., 2nd sess., 1872, 1192.
29. Bettis Rainsford, interview by author, Edgefield, South Carolina, October 6, 1995.
30. M. C. Butler to Maria Butler, March 27, 1870, M. C. Butler Papers.

31. *The Ku Klux Klan Testimony,* 1216–17.
32. R. H. Woody, "The South Carolina Election of 1870," *North Carolina Historical Review* 8, no. 2 (April) 1931: 172.
33. Peggy Lamson, *The Glorious Failure: Black Congressman Robert Brown Elliott and the Reconstruction in South Carolina* (New York: W. W. Norton, 1973), 103.
34. Ibid.
35. Ibid., 104.
36. U.S. *Senate Journal, 41st Cong.* 2nd sess., December 6, 1869.
37. Bowers, *The Tragic Era,* 360.
38. Lamson, *The Glorious Failure,* 88.
39. *The Ku Klux Klan Testimony,* 1190.
40. Ibid., 1188.
41. Ibid., 1198.
42. Richard Nelson Current, *Those Terrible Carpetbaggers: A Reinterpretation* (New York: Oxford University Press, 1988), 226.
43. *The Ku Klux Klan Testimony,* 1190.
44. Reynolds, *Reconstruction in South Carolina,* 155.
45. Ibid., 158.
46. Trelease, *White Terror,* 352.
47. *The Ku Klux Klan Testimony,* 1208.
48. Oliver B. Burton, "Race and Reconstruction in Edgefield County," *Journal of Social History* 12, (Fall) 1978: 37.
49. Butler Family Bible.
50. Shapiro, "The Ku Klux Klan During Reconstruction," 41.
51. *Edgefield Advertiser,* May 25, 1871.
52. Shapiro, "The Ku Klux Klan During Reconstruction," 45.
53. *Edgefield Advertiser,* April 6, 1871.
54. Ibid., May 25, 1871.
55. Ibid., June 29, 1871.
56. Ibid., July 13, 1871.
57. Ibid., August 24, 1871.
58. William A. Sheppard, *Red Shirts Remembered: Southern Brigadiers of the Reconstruction Period* (Atlanta: Ruralist Press, 1940), 313.
59. Rainsford, interview.
60. Matthew C. Butler to Rosa Mills, June 29, 1871, James W. Foster Papers, Rosa Mills File, Maryland Historical Society, Baltimore (hereafter cited as Foster Papers).
61. 1870 Federal Census of Maryland, Wards 4–5, Baltimore City, Maryland Historical Society, Baltimore.
62. M. C. Butler to Rosa Mills, no date, Foster Papers.

63. Rosa Mills to M. C. Butler, March 8, 1879, Foster Papers.
64. Burton, *In My Father's House,* 141.
65. Ellen Iredell Butler, interview by author, Columbia, S.C., March 4, 1997.
66. Bowers, *The Tragic Era,* 355.
67. Reynolds, *Reconstruction in South Carolina,* 160–62.
68. Simkins and Woody, *South Carolina during Reconstruction,* 153.
69. Ibid., 154–55.
70. *Proceedings of the Tax-Payers Convention of South Carolina Held at Columbia Beginning May 9th and Ending May 12, 1871* (Charleston: Edward Perry, 1871), 17.
71. Ibid., 103–4.
72. Ibid.
73. Williamson, *After Slavery,* 384.
74. Simkins and Woody, *South Carolina during Reconstruction,* 159.
75. *Edgefield Advertiser,* May 5, 1871.
76. Reynolds, *Reconstruction in South Carolina,* 466.
77. Simkins and Woody, *South Carolina during Reconstruction,* 204–06.
78. Ibid., 207.
79. Ibid., 213.
80. Ibid., 215.
81. *Edgefield Advertiser,* January 25, 1872.
82. Mark Wahlgren Summers, *The Era of Good Stealing* (New York: Oxford University Press, 1993), 81.
83. Simkins and Woody, *South Carolina during Reconstruction,* 217–22.
84. *Edgefield Advertiser,* June 8, 1871.
85. *The Ku Klux Klan Testimony,* 1211.
86. Trelease, *White Terror,* 403–7.
87. *The Ku Klux Klan Testimony,* 1194.
88. *Edgefield Advertiser,* November 23, 1871.
89. Ibid., February 22, 1872.
90. Ibid., April 11, 1872.
91. *The Ku Klux Klan Testimony,* 1191.
92. *Edgefield Advertiser,* November 16, 1871.
93. Claude M. Fuess, *Carl Schurz Reformer* (New York: Dodd, Mead, 1932), 193–97.
94. *Edgefield Advertiser,* August 15, 1872.
95. Reynolds, *Reconstruction in South Carolina,* 224.
96. Ibid., 225.
97. Simkins and Woody, *South Carolina during Reconstruction,* 467.
98. *Edgefield Advertiser,* September 5, 1872.

99. Ibid., November 14, 1872.
100. Walter Allen, *Governor Chamberlain's Administration in South Carolina: A Chapter of Reconstruction in the Southern States* (New York: Negro Universities Press, 1969), 7.

CHAPTER 20: GOVERNOR MOSES

1. Thompson, "Blacks, Carpetbaggers and Scalawags," 205–6.
2. Simkins and Woody, *South Carolina during Reconstruction,* 126.
3. Ibid., 127.
4. Reynolds, *Reconstruction in South Carolina,* 226.
5. Ibid., 228.
6. *Edgefield Advertiser,* January 9, 1873.
7. Ibid., February 13, 1873.
8. Ibid., May 8, 1873.
9. Ibid., July 17, 1873.
10. Reynolds, *Reconstruction in South Carolina,* 229.
11. Oakley H. Coburn, letter to author, February 13, 1998.
12. Col. J. P. Thomas to M. C. Butler, April 9, 1885, M. C. Butler Papers.
13. Ellen Iredell Butler, interview by author, March 25, 1997.
14. *Edgefield Advertiser,* October 16, 1873.
15. William S. McFeely, *Grant: A Biography* (New York: Norton, 1981), 392.
16. *Edgefield Advertiser,* October 30, 1873.
17. Ibid., November 6, 1873.
18. Butler Family Bible.
19. Thompson, *Ousting the Carpetbagger,* 62.
20. Ibid., 63.
21. Reynolds, *Reconstruction in South Carolina,* 250.
22. Ibid., 247.
23. *Edgefield Advertiser,* April 9, 1874.
24. Ibid.
25. Reynolds, *Reconstruction in South Carolina,* 264.
26. Simkins and Woody, *South Carolina during Reconstruction,* 184.
27. Butler Family Bible.
28. Benjamin R. Tillman Papers, "Autobiography," South Caroliniana Library, University of South Carolina (hereafter cited as "Autobiography").
29. Burton, "Race and Reconstruction," 41.
30. Julian L. Mims, "Radical Reconstruction in Edgefield County, 1868–1877 (master's thesis, University of South Carolina, 1969), 62.

31. Francis Butler Simkins, *The Tillman Movement in South Carolina* (Durham: Duke University Press, 1926), 41.
32. Burton, "Race and Reconstruction," 41.
33. George C. Rable, *But There Was No Peace: The Role of Violence in the Politics of Reconstruction* (Athens: University of Georgia Press, 1984), 165.
34. Simkins and Woody, *South Carolina during Reconstruction*, 471.
35. Allen, *Governor Chamberlain's Administraiton*, 8.
36. Ibid.
37. Simkins and Woody, *South Carolina during Reconstruction*, 472.
38. *Edgefield Advertiser*, October 22, 1874.
39. Allen, *Governor Chamberlain's Administraiton*, 9.
40. Newspaper article (unidentified), Butler Family Scrapbook.
41. Reynolds, *Reconstruction in South Carolina*, 302.
42. Burton, "Race and Reconstruction," 41.
43. Mims, "Radical Reconstruction in Edgefield County," 63.
44. Simkins and Woody, *South Carolina during Reconstruction*, 486.

CHAPTER 21: RED SHIRTS
1. Thompson, *Ousting the Carpetbagger*, 3.
2. Carter, *The Angry Scar*, 222.
3. Alfred B. Williams, "Hampton and Chamberlain Sketched As They Were When the Campaign Began," *Charleston Evening Post*, September 19, 1926.
4. Reynolds, *Reconstruction in South Carolina*, 284–86.
5. Ibid.
6. Ibid., 289.
7. Allen, *Governor Chamberlain's Administration*, 128.
8. Anthony Harrigan, "The Houses of Edgefield," *South Carolina Magazine* 16, no. 11 (November 1952), 18.
9. Mrs. Benjamin E. Nicholson, interview by author, Edgefield, South Carolina, October 6, 1995.
10. Butler Family Bible.
11. Bowers, *The Tragic Era*, 452–57.
12. Simkins and Woody, *South Carolina during Reconstruction*, 478.
13. Reynolds, *Reconstruction in South Carolina*, 327–28.
14. Ibid., 337–38.
15. Simkins and Woody, *South Carolina during Reconstruction*, 481.
16. *Edgefield Advertiser*, May 4, 1876.
17. Reynolds, *Reconstruction in South Carolina*, 342.
18. Simkins and Woody, *South Carolina during Reconstruction*, 482.

19. Reynolds, *Reconstruction in South Carolina,* 343.
20. Brooks, *Butler and His Cavalry,* 55–56.
21. M. C. Butler to Matt Whittaker Ransom, June 4, 1876, Matt Whittaker Ransom Papers, Southern Historical Collection, University of North Carolina.
22. M. C. Butler, letter to the editor, *Augusta Chronicle and Sentinel,* July 13, 1876 (hereafter cited as letter to the editor).
23. Rable, *But There Was No Peace,* 166–67.
24. *Augusta Chronicle and Sentinel,* July 7, 1876.
25. Francis W. P. Butler to Daniel H. Chamberlain, July 6, 1918, Dalton Collection.
26. M. C. Butler, letter to the editor.
27. Ibid.
28. *Augusta Chronicle and Sentinel,* July 9, 1876.
29. Ibid.
30. M. C. Butler, letter to the editor.
31. *Augusta Chronicle and Sentinel,* July 9, 1876.
32. Ibid.
33. *Augusta Chronicle and Sentinel,* July 11, 1876.
34. Ibid.
35. Current, *Those Terrible Carpetbaggers,* 349.
36. Tillman, "Autobiography," 18.
37. Alfred B. Williams, "Hamburg Lights Consuming Flame," *Charleston Evening Post,* August 8, 1926.
38. *Augusta Chronicle and Sentinel,* July 9, 1876.
39. Ibid.
40. Tillman, "Autobiography," 20.
41. *Official Records Concerning the Hamburgh, South Carolina, Massacre of 1876, and the Parties Connected Therewith: Reply of Hon. S. H. Miller of Pennsylvania in the House of Representatives, Tuesday, July 25, 1882, to Remarks of Hon. M. C. Butler of South Carolina, Delivered in the Senate of the United States, Friday, July 21, 1882* (Washington, D.C.: Government Printing Office, 1882), 9.
42. *Augusta Chronicle and Sentinel,* July 9, 1876.
43. *Augusta Chronicle and Sentinel,* July 10, 1876.
44. Tillman, "Autobiography," 21.
45. *Reply of Hon. S. H. Miller,* 9.
46. Tillman, "Autobiography," 22–23.
47. *Augusta Chronicle and Sentinel,* July 13, 1876.
48. *Reply of Hon. S. H. Miller,* 9.
49. Francis W. P. Butler to Daniel H. Chamberlain, July 6, 1918, Dalton Collection.

50. *Augusta Chronicle and Sentinel*, July 13, 1876.
51. Francis W. P. Butler to Daniel H. Chamberlain, July 6, 1918, Dalton Collection.
52. Alfred B. Williams, *Hampton and His Red Shirts: South Carolina's Deliverance in 1876* (Charleston: Walker, Evans & Cogswell, 1935), 34.
53. Simkins and Woody, *South Carolina during Reconstruction*, 566–67.
54. Francis W. P. Butler to Daniel H. Chamberlain, July 6, 1918, Dalton Collection.
55. *Edgefield Advertiser*, August 10, 1876.
56. Reynolds, *Reconstruction in South Carolina*, 360–61.
57. *Congressional Record*, 44th Cong., 2nd sess. appendix, H. Rept. 175, part 2, 242.
58. Ibid.
59. Francis W. P. Butler to Daniel H. Chamberlain, July 6, 1918, Dalton Collection.
60. Wellman, *Giant in Gray*, 249.
61. Wade Hampton to James Conner, September 5, 1878, Hampton Papers.
62. Reynolds, *Reconstruction in South Carolina*, 353.
63. Wade Hampton to James Conner, September 5, 1878, Hampton Papers.
64. Alfred B. Williams, "Red Shirts Appear in Charleston," *Charleston Evening Post*, September 26, 1926.
65. Ibid.
66. Ibid.
67. Francis W. P. Butler to Daniel H. Chamberlain, July 6, 1918, Dalton Collection.
68. Ibid., 67.
69. Williams, *Hampton and His Red Shirts*, 52.
70. Ball, *The State That Forgot*, 159–62.
71. *Edgefield Advertiser*, August 24, 1876.
72. Alfred B. Wiliams, "Call Reaches Hampton in Cashiers Valley," *Charleston Evening Post*, August 22, 1926.
73. Reynolds, *Reconstruction in South Carolina*, 366.
74. Allen, *Governor Chamberlain's Administration*, 378.
75. Ibid., 379.
76. Thompson, *Outsting the Carpetbagger*, 121.
77. Alfred B. Williams, "October '76, Critical for Carolina," *Charleston Evening Post*, December 12, 1926.
78. H.R. 175, part 2, 242.
79. Richard Zuczek, *State of Rebellion: Reconstruction in South Carolina* (Columbia: University of South Carolina Press, 1996), 174–78.

80. Allen, *Governor Chamberlain's Administration*, 407.
81. *Congressional Record*, 44th Congress, 2nd sess., February 21, 1877, 218.
82. Ibid.
83. Simkins and Woody, *South Carolina during Reconstruction*, 514.
84. Ibid., 522.

CHAPTER 22: REDEMPTION DAY
1. Reynolds, *Reconstruction in South Carolina*, 410.
2. Benjamin Massey to his son, November 28, 1876, Benjamin Harper Massey Papers, Caroliniana Society, University of South Carolina.
3. Avery, *Dixie after the War*, 367.
4. Simkins and Woody, *South Carolina during Reconstruction*, 526–27.
5. *Edgefield Advertiser*, November 30, 1876.
6. Avery, *Dixie after the War*, 370.
7. Wellman, *Giant in Gray*, 284–85.
8. Simkins and Woody, *South Carolina during Reconstruction*, 528–29.
9. Ibid., 532–33.
10. Richard M. Zuczek, "The Last Campaign of the Civil War: South Carolina and the Revolution of 1876," *Civil War History* 42, no. 1 (March 1996), 29–30.
11. Reynolds, *Reconstruction in South Carolina*, 433–35.
12. Researcher (unidentified) notes, Hampton Family Papers, South Caroliniana Library, University of South Carolina.
13. H. J. Eckenrode, *Rutherford B. Hayes: Statesman of Reunion* (New York: Dodd, Mead, 1930), 223.
14. Ibid., 211–12.
15. Ibid., 212.
16. Carter, *The Angry Scar*, 337.
17. Allen B. Tankersley, *John B. Gordon: A Study in Gallantry* (Atlanta: Whitehall, 1955), 286.
18. James M. Morgan, *Recollections of a Rebel Reefer* (Boston: Houghton Mifflin, 1917), 372–73.
19. *Congressional Record*, spec. sess., 45th Cong., March 5, 1877, 2.
20. Wellman, *Giant in Gray*, 291–92.
21. *Edgefield Advertiser*, May 31, 1877.
22. Ibid., August 2, 1877.
23. Ellen Iredell Butler, interview by author, March 25, 1997.
24. *Congressional Record*, 1st sess., 45th Cong., November 20, 1877, 556–57.
25. Ibid., 644.
26. Ball, *The State That Forgot*, 241.
27. *Congressional Record*, 1st sess., 45th Cong., November 20, 1877, 556–57.

28. Ibid., 557.

29. Ibid., November 26, 1877, 641.

30. Ibid., 644.

31. Ibid.

32. Ibid.

33. Ibid., 712.

34. Ibid., November 29, 1877, 761.

35. *Edgefield Advertiser,* May 17, 1877.

36. *Congressional Record,* 1st sess., 45th Cong., November 29, 1877, 756.

37. Ibid., November 30, 1877, 797.

38. Ibid., December 6, 1877, 40.

39. M. C. Butler to Edward Wells, May 6, 1855, Wells Papers.

40. *Congressional Record,* 1st sess., 45th Cong., December 15, 1877, 236.

CHAPTER 23: U.S. SENATOR

1. *Boyd's Directory of the District of Columbia, Together with a Compedium of Its Government, Institutions, and Trades, to Which is Added a Complete Business Directory, a Street Directory, and a Congressional Directory,* Washington, D.C.: Compiled and published by William H. Boyd, 1878–1890.

2. M. C. Butler to George B. Lorning, July 13, 1882, M. C. Butler Papers.

3. M. C. Butler to Harry Hammond, January 22, 1880, Hammond, Bryan, and Cummings Papers, South Caroliniana Library, University of South Carolina (hereafter cited as Hammond, Bryan, Cummings Papers).

4. *Edgefield Advertiser,* July 4, 1878.

5. Newspaper (unidentified) article, Butler Family Scrapbook.

6. William G. Temple to E. W. Seibels, April 25, 1884, Seibels Family Papers, South Caroliniana Library, University of South Carolina.

7. Ellen Iredell Butler, interview by author, March 4, 1997.

8. M. C. Butler to Martin W. Gary, April 3, 1878, Martin Witherspoon Gary Papers, South Caroliniana Library, University of South Carolina.

9. *Edgefield Advertiser,* July 25, 1878.

10. Ibid., November 7, 1878.

11. Wellman, *Giant in Gray,* 301–4.

12. Ibid., 304–05.

13. *Boyd's Directory of the District of Columbia.*

14. *Congressional Record,* 3rd sess., 45th Cong., December 3, 1878, 12.

15. Ibid., December 16, 1878, 200–205.

16. *Edgefield Advertiser,* August 28, 1879.

17. *Congressional Record,* 1st sess., 46th Cong., March 3, 1879, 15.

18. Ibid., April 22–23, 1879, 672–73, 732–33.

19. Oakley H. Coburn, letter to author, February 13, 1998.
20. Carl Esche, letter to author, February 25, 1998.
21. *Boyd's Directory of the District of Columbia.*
22. *Congressional Record,* 2nd sess., 46th Cong., February 3, 1880, 670.
23. Ibid., May 28, 1880, 3859.
24. *Congressional Record,* index, 46th Cong., 2nd sess., 39–40.
25. M. C. Butler to John J. Dargan, March 24, 1880, John Julius Dargan Papers, South Caroliniana Library, University of South Carolina.
26. Glenn Tucker, *Hancock the Superb* (Indianapolis: Bobbs-Merrill, 1960), 300.
27. Theodore Clarke-Smith, *The Life and Letters of James Abram Garfield* (New Haven: Yale University Press, 1925), 2: 983.
28. Tucker, *Hancock the Superb,* 303.
29. Ball, *The State That Forgot,* 179.
30. *Congressional Record,* index, 46th Cong., 3rd sess., 29.
31. *Edgefield Advertiser,* March 3, 1881.
32. Ibid., January 13, 1881.
33. Blake, *William Mahone of Virginia,* 172–82.
34. Ibid., 206.
35. *Congressional Record,* spec. sess., 47th Cong., April 20, 1881, 356.
36. Ibid., April 28, 1881, 426.
37. Ibid., May 2, 1881, 431.
38. *Edgefield Advertiser,* June 30, 1881.
39. Ibid., December 7, 1882.
40. Ibid., June 6, 1881.
41. Bushong and Bushong, *Fightin' Tom Rosser,* 193.
42. *Edgefield Advertiser,* January 27, 1881.
43. Clarke-Smith, *James Abram Garfield,* 2: 1184.
44. Ibid., 2: 1180
45. Ibid., 2: 1201.
46. Joseph Nathan Kane, *Facts about the Presidents: A Compilation of Biographical and Historical Information* (New York: H. W. Wilson, 1989), 126–28.
47. *Edgefield Advertiser,* July 28, 1881.
48. Ibid., June 30, 1881.
49. *Boyd's Directory of the District of Columbia.*
50. *Congressional Record,* spec. sess., 47th Cong., October 25, 1881, 525.
51. Ibid., index, 1st sess., 47th Cong., 57–58.
52. Assistant Adjutant General's Office to Matthew Calbraith Butler II, June 23, 1882, War Department Letters and Telegrams Sent Relating to the United States Military Academy from 1867 to 1904, National Archives, RG 94, Washington, D.C.

53. Ball, *The State That Forgot,* 180.
54. *Edgefield Advertiser,* December 7, 1882.

CHAPTER 24: SECOND TERM

1. *Edgefield Advertiser,* March 1, 1883.
2. Holland, *Pierce M. B. Young,* 187.
3. *Congressional Record,* 2nd sess., 47th Cong., 605–614.
4. *Edgefield Advertiser,* January 4, 1883.
5. Ibid.
6. Ibid., January 17, 1884.
7. Ibid.
8. Ibid., March 1, 1883.
9. Ibid.
10. *Boyd's Directory of the District of Columbia.*
11. *Decennial Record of the Class of '83 of Princeton College, N.J., 1883–1893,* Comp. and ed. Edward Huntting Rudd (Princeton: Princeton College Press, n.d.), 17.
12. *Congressional Record,* 1st sess., 48th Cong., 49.
13. *Edgefield Advertiser,* January 31, 1884.
14. *Congressional Record,* 1st sess., 48th Cong., 881–83.
15. Ibid., 1012.
16. Ibid., 1384.
17. Ibid., 1385.
18. Ibid., 1394.
19. Ibid., 2289.
20. *Edgefield Advertiser,* April 24, 1884.
21. Ibid.
22. M. C. Butler to John C. Haskell, June 16, 1884, John C. Haskell Papers, Southern Historical Collection, University of North Carolina.
23. Allen Nevins, *Grover Cleveland: A Study in Courage* (New York: Dodd, Mead, 1944), 144–46.
24. Ibid.
25. Ibid., 155.
26. *Edgefield Advertiser,* June 12, 1884.
27. Ellen Iredell Butler, interview by author, March 25, 1997.
28. *Official Register of the Officers and Cadets of the U.S. Military Academy* (New York: West Point, 1884), 18.
29. *Edgefield Advertiser,* October 9, 1884.
30. *Boyd's Directory of the District of Columbia.*
31. Maclean Papers.
32. M. C. Butler to Clara Maclean, December 21, 1884, Maclean Papers.
33. Ibid., May 10, 1885.

34. *Congressional Record,* 48th Cong., 2nd sess., 1835–36.
35. Ibid., 1839.
36. Nevins, *Grover Cleveland,* 208.
37. Ellen Iredell Butler, interview by author, March 25, 1997.
38. *Official Register of the Officers and Cadets of the U.S. Military Academy,* 1885, 19.
39. *Decennial Record of the Class of '83 of Princeton College,* 17.
40. William W. Butler to M. C. Butler, December 31, 1885, M. C. Butler Papers.
41. Ibid.
42. William W. Butler to M. C. Butler, June 8, 1885, M. C. Butler Papers.
43. *Boyd's Directory of the District of Columbia.*
44. William W. Butler to M. C. Butler, December 31, 1885, M. C. Butler Papers.
45. Francis Butler Simkins, *Pitchfork Ben Tillman: South Carolinian* (Baton Rouge: Louisiana State University Press, 1944), 93.
46. *Congressional Record,* 49th Cong., 1st sess., 244–46.
47. Ibid., 949–51.
48. Ibid., 1090.
49. Ibid., 1158.
50. Ibid., 1090.
51. Ibid., 3256–57.
52. Ibid., 3314–16.
53. Ibid., 3316.
54. Ibid., 7138.
55. Ibid.,
56. Ibid., 7139.
57. William W. Butler to M. C. Butler, December 31, 1885, M. C. Butler Papers.
58. William W. Butler to M. C. Butler, January 13, 1885, M. C. Butler Papers.
59. Catherine E. Forrest Weber, "Editing the Civil War Commanders: Robert Underwood Johnson and the Century," *Traces of Indiana and Midwestern History* 10, no. 3 (summer 1998), 8.
60. William W. Butler to M. C. Butler, December 23, 1885, Dalton Collection.
61. Ibid.
62. William W. Butler to M. C. Butler, June 8, 1886, Dalton Collection.
63. Ibid.
64. Ibid.
65. Ibid.

66. William W. Butler to M. C. Butler, June 28, 1886, Dalton Collection.
67. William W. Butler to M. C. Butler, July 13, 1886, Dalton Collection.
68. Susan Elise Butler to M. C. Butler, July 1886, Dalton Collection.
69. William W. Butler to M. C. Butler, July 1, 1886, Dalton Collection.
70. *Congressional Record,* 50th Cong., spec. sess., 927.
71. J. C. Garlington, *Men of the Time* (Spartanburg: Reprint, 1972), 66.
72. *Official Register of the Officers and Cadets of the U.S. Military Academy,* 1886, 16.
73. *Decennial Record of the Class of '83 of Princeton College,* 18.
74. *Boyd's Directory of the District of Columbia.*
75. *Congressional Record,* 49th Cong., 2nd sess., 728.
76. Ibid., 1145.
77. Ibid., 1148.
78. Ibid.
79. Ibid., 1154.
80. Ibid., 1760.
81. Ibid., 1903.
82. Ibid., 2189.
83. Ibid.
84. Simkins, *Pitchfork Ben Tillman,* 97.
85. Ibid., 104.
86. Ibid., 107–8.
87. Ibid., 120.
88. Judith A. Sibly, letter to author, February 26, 1998.
89. *Boyd's Directory of the District of Columbia.*
90. *Congressional Record,* 50th Cong., 1st sess., 126.
91. Ellen Iredell Butler, interview by author, March 4, 1997.
92. *Edgefield County Deed Book,* Edgefield County, South Carolina, vol. 10, 718.
93. *Congressional Record,* 50th Cong., 1st sess., 2833.
94. Nevins, *Grover Cleveland,* 397–98.
95. *Official Register of the Officers and Cadets of the U.S. Military Academy,* 1888, 11.
96. Newspaper article (unidentified), Adams Family Scrapbook, in possession of Ellen Adams Gutow, Highland, Maryland.
97. Bvt. Maj. Gen. George W. Cullum, *Biographical Register of the Officers and Graduates of the U.S. Military Academy at West Point, N.Y.: From Its Establishment in 1802 to 1890: With the Early History of the United States Military Academy* (Boston and New York: Riverside Press, 1891), vol. 3, nos. 2001–3384, 423.
98. Matthew C. Butler to Francis W. Dawson, May 3, 1888, Francis W. Dawson Correspondence, 1881–1888, Charleston Library Society.

99. *Congressional Record,* 50th Cong., 1st sess., 6180.
100. Simkins, *Pitchfork Ben Tillman,* 132–33.
101. *Congressional Record,* 50th Cong., 1st sess., 8678–79.
102. Nevins, *Grover Cleveland,* 362–63.
103. Ibid., 439.
104. Simkins, *Pitchfork Ben Tillman,* 133–34.

CHAPTER 25: THIRD TERM

1. Margaret Leech, *In the Days of McKinley* (New York: Harper & Brothers, 1959), 43.
2. *Boyd's Directory of the District of Columbia.*
3. *Congressional Record,* 50th Cong., 2nd sess., 780–81.
4. Ibid., 2142.
5. M. C. Butler to Bradley T. Johnson, May 5, 1889, M. C. Butler Papers.
6. *Boyd's Directory of the District of Columbia;* Author's observations. This dwelling was razed years ago to make space for an apartment complex, but it was no doubt similar to the old buildings that still remain in this area. Each butts into its neighbors, is three stories high, built of brick. The roof line, facing the street, has ornate trim along the leading edge. Steep steps rise to the front door, which opens to the second floor. The width of these similar homes is quite narrow, scarcely enough to accommodate a single room.
7. Cullum, *Biographical Register,* vol. 3, nos. 2001–3384, 423.
8. Garlington, *Men of the Time,* 66.
9. *Congressional Record,* 51st Cong., 1st sess., 7.
10. Ibid., 622–30.
11. M. C. Butler to Harry Hammond, March 12, 1890, Hammond, Bryan, Cummings Papers.
12. *Congressional Record,* 51st Cong., 1st sess., 3712–21.
13. Ibid., 7068, 7166.
14. Ibid., 8334–40.
15. *The American Almanac of American History,* ed. Arthur M. Schlesinger Jr. (New York: Bison Books, 1983), 371.
16. Simkins, *Pitchfork Ben Tillman,* 145.
17. Ibid., 155.
18. Ibid., 186.
19. *Congressional Record,* 51st Cong., 2nd sess., 375.
20. Ibid., 584–87.
21. Ibid., 1566–67.
22. Ibid., 3317–18.

23. Nevins, *Grover Cleveland,* 343.

24. *Congressional Record,* 51st Cong., 2nd sess., 3318.

25. Simkins, *Pitchfork Ben Tillman,* 193.

26. John Chapman, *History of Edgefield* (Newberry, S.C.: Elbert H. Aull, 1897), 370.

27. Newspaper article (unidentified) Butler Family Scrapbook.

28. *The Princetonian* 16, no. 59 (December 4, 1891).

29. H. B. McBae to M. C. Butler, December 2, 1891, M. C. Butler Papers.

30. Garlington, *Men of the Time,* 66.

31. *Congressional Record,* 51st Cong., 2nd sess., 375.

32. Ibid., 52nd Cong., 1st sess., 73–74.

33. Ibid., 2302–3.

34. Ibid., 3486–87.

35. Ibid., 4315–16, 4356–58.

36. *The American Almanac of American History,* 374.

37. Simkins, *Pitchfork Ben Tillman,* 210.

38. Ibid., 264.

39. Ibid., 214.

40. Ibid., 216.

41. *The American Almanac of American History,* 375.

42. *Congressional Record,* 52nd Cong., 1st sess., 785–90.

43. Ibid., 1138.

44. Ibid., 1332–33, 1364–65.

45. *Congressional Record,* 53rd Cong., spec. sess., 17.

46. Garlington, *Men of the Time,* 66.

47. Cullum, *Biographical Register,* 423.

48. *The American Almanac of American History,* 374.

49. Ibid., 376.

50. Ibid.

51. *Edgefield Advertiser,* October 26, 1893.

52. *Congressional Record,* 53rd Cong., 1st sess., 2106–10.

53. Ibid., 2204–9.

54. Nevins, *Grover Cleveland,* 545–46.

CHAPTER 26: DEFEAT

1. *Edgefield Advertiser,* October 26, 1893.

2. Ibid., November 9, 1893.

3. Ibid., December 7, 1893.

4. Simkins, *Pitchfork Ben Tillman,* 266.

5. *Edgefield Advertiser,* February 2, 1894.

6. *Spartanburg Herald,* Febraury 21, 1894.
7. Nevins, *Grover Cleveland,* 550–52.
8. *Congressional Record,* 53rd Cong., 2nd sess., 313–17.
9. Nevins, *Grover Cleveland,* 561.
10. *Edgefield Advertiser,* March 7, 1894.
11. *Congressional Record,* 53rd Cong., 2nd sess., 3182.
12. *Edgefield Advertiser,* April 4, 1894.
13. Simkins, *Pitchfork Ben Tillman,* 247–54.
14. *Edgefield Advertiser,* April 11, 1894.
15. Ibid.
16. Ibid., April 18, 1894.
17. Ibid., May 2, 1894.
18. *Congressional Record,* 53rd Cong., 2nd sess., 4875.
19. Simkins, *Pitchfork Ben Tillman,* 266–67.
20. *Edgefield Advertiser,* June 20, 1894.
21. Simkins, *Pitchfork Ben Tillman,* 266.
22. *Edgefield Advertiser,* June 20, 1894.
23. Ibid.
24. Ibid.
25. Ibid., June 27, 1894.
26. Simkins, *Pitchfork Ben Tillman,* 268–69.
27. Ibid., 270.
28. *Edgefield Advertiser,* July 4, 1894.
29. Ibid., July 25, 1894.
30. Ibid., August 8, 1894.
31. Ibid.
32. Ibid., September 19, 1894.
33. Ibid., August 29, 1894.
34. Simkins, *Pitchfork Ben Tillman,* 272.
35. *Edgefield Advertiser,* September 19, 1894.
36. Simkins, *Pitchfork Ben Tillman,* 272.
37. Newspaper article (unidentified), Butler Family Scrapbook.
38. *Edgefield Advertiser,* December 19, 1894.
39. *Congressional Record,* 53rd Cong., 3rd sess., 625.
40. *Edgefield Advertiser,* January 30, 1895.
41. Simkins, *Pitchfork Ben Tillman,* 272.
42. *Congressional Record,* 53rd Cong., 3rd sess., 2624–29.
43. "A Synopsis of the Public Service of General M. C. Butler, as U.S. Senator from South Carolina, from 1877 to 1894," loose article, M. C. Butler Papers.

CHAPTER 27: MAJOR GENERAL

1. Mrs. Benjamin E. Nicholson, interview by author, October 6, 1995.
2. M. C. Butler to W. Gordon McCabe, July 24, 1896, M. C. Butler Papers.
3. Ellen Adams Gutow, interview by author, November 7, 1998.
4. *Edgefield Advertiser,* May 22, 1895.
5. Ibid., June 5, 1895.
6. *Points and Authorities Showing the Unconstitutionality and Illegality of Pending Legislation before Congress Touching the Five Civilized Tribes of Indians* (Washington: Gibson Bros., Printers and Bookbinders, 1896).
7. *The American Almanac of American History,* 382.
8. *New York Times,* July 5, 1896.
9. *The American Almanac of American History,* 382.
10. *New York Times,* July 1, 1896.
11. Newspaper articles (unidentified), Adams Family Scrapbook, in possession of Ellen Adams Gutow, Highland, Maryland.
12. *Edgefield Advertiser,* November 6, 1896.
13. G. J. A. O'Toole, *The Spanish War: An American Epic, 1898* (New York: W. W. Norton, 1984), 50.
14. Ibid., 55.
15. Ibid., 56–57.
16. Ibid., 78.
17. Ibid., 103.
18. David F. Trask, *The War with Spain in 1898* (New York: Macmillan, 1981), 24–28.
19. O'Toole, *The Spanish War,* 148.
20. Ibid., 169.
21. Ibid., 171.
22. Ibid., 195–96.
23. Trask, *The War with Spain,* 150–52.
24. Matthew C. Butler Papers, File 698, Adjutant General's Office, National Archives (hereafter cited as File 698).
25. Newspaper article (unidentified), Butler Family Scrapbook.
26. Ibid.
27. *Correspondence Relating to the War With Spain Including the Insurrection in the Philippine Islands and the China Relief Expedition, April 15, 1898– July 30, 1902* (Washington: Center for Military History, United States Army, 1993), 1: 521.
28. File 698.
29. Newspaper article (unidentified), Butler Family Scrapbook.
30. O'Toole, *The Spanish War,* 184.

31. Trask, *The War with Spain,* 104.
32. Ibid., 383–85.
33. O'Toole, *The Spanish War,* 173.
34. Trask, *The War with Spain,* 116.
35. O'Toole, *The Spanish War,* 221.
36. Trask, *The War with Spain,* 180.
37. Ibid., 252.
38. *Charleston News and Courier,* May 31, 1898.
39. Newspaper article (unidentified), Butler Family Scrapbook.
40. Cullum, *Biographical Register,* 473.
41. Newspaper article (unidentified), Butler Family Scrapbook.
42. Trask, *The War with Spain,* 191.
43. Newspaper article (unidentified), Butler Family Scrapbook.
44. O'Toole, *The Spanish War,* 300–322.
45. Trask, *The War with Spain,* 262–64.
46. Ibid., 353–58.
47. Wilson, *Under the Old Flag,* 2:442–49.
48. Trask, *The War with Spain,* 427–35.
49. Newspaper article (unidentified), Butler Family Scrapbook.
50. File 698.
51. Newspaper article (unidentified), Butler Family Scrapbook.
52. M. C. Butler to Francis W. P. Butler, September 16, 1898, M. C. Butler Papers.
53. Ibid.
54. M. C. Butler to Lilian Butler, n.d., Dalton Collection.
55. Ibid., September 27, 1898.
56. Ibid.
57. M. C. Butler to Russell A. Alger, September 26, 1898, Dalton Collection.
58. Petition, File 698.
59. Cullum, *Biographical Register,* 473.
60. M. C. Butler to Henry C. Corbin, November 5, 1898, Record Group 59, National Archives, Washington, D.C. (hereafter cited as RG 59).
61. Henry C. Corbin to M. C. Butler, November 15, 1898, RG 59.
62. M. C. Butler to Henry C. Corbin, November 19, 1898, RG 59.
63. Henry C. Corbin to M. C. Butler, November 21, 1898, RG 59.
64. M. C. Butler to Russell A. Alger, December 19, 1898, File 698.
65. M. C. Butler to Walter Wyman, October 24, 1898, Dalton Collection.
66. RG59.

67. Ibid.

68. Leech, *In the Days of McKinley,* 317–20.

CHAPTER 28: THE FINAL DAYS

1. Newspaper article (unidentified), Butler Family Scrapbook.

2. Ibid.

3. *The American Almanac of American History,* 396.

4. *New York Times,* September 27, 1900.

5. *Columbia State,* October 1, 1900.

6. Newspaper article (unidentified), Butler Family Scrapbook.

7. Stanley Karnow, *In Our Image: America's Empire in the Philippines* (New York: Random House, 1989), 139–40.

8. Newspaper article (unidentified), Butler Family Scrapbook.

9. Ibid.

10. Marie Butler McNeeley to Lilian Butler, March 21, 1903, Lilian Butler Papers, South Caroliniana Library, University of South Carolina (hereafter cited as Lilian Butler Papers).

11. Ellen Adams Gutow, interview by author, November 27, 1998.

12. Leech, *In the Days of McKinley,* 595–96.

13. Simkins, *Pitchfork Ben Tillman,* 9.

14. Newspaper article (unidentified), Butler Family Scrapbook.

15. M. C. Butler to Lilian Butler, April 15, 1902, Lilian Butler Papers.

16. Ibid., March 31, 1902.

17. Ibid., April 14, 1902.

18. Ibid., September 23, 1902.

19. *United States Reports, Cases Adjudged in the Supreme Court at the October Term, 1905* (New York: Banks Law, 1906), 202: 101–02.

20. Ibid.

21. M. C. Butler to Lill B. Stowe, December 27, 1905, M. C. Butler Papers.

22. *United States Reports,* 202:120–23.

23. *Eastern Cherokee Applications of the U.S. Court of Claims, 1906–1909,* National Archives Microfilm Publications, pamphlet M1104 (Washington: National Archives Trust Fund Board, National Archives and Records Service, 1981), 2.

24. M. C. Butler to Ulysses Brooks, May 12, 1905, Brooks Papers.

25. *Edgefield Advertiser,* January 12, 1903.

26. Newspaper article (unidentified), Butler Family Scrapbook.

27. Ellen Iredell Butler, interview by author, March 25, 1997.

28. David Parker, letter to author, July 23, 1998.

29. *Edgefield Advertiser,* July 17, 1906.

30. *Columbia State,* November 20, 1906.
31. "Matthew Calbraith Butler," *The Bald Eagle* (Sons of Confederate Veterans, Brig. General Martin Witherspoon Gary Camp #1532, Edgefield, South Carolina) 6, no. 3 (March 1998): 2.
32. *Edgefield Advertiser,* October 5, 1903.
33. Edgefield County Clerk of Courts, book 20, Edgefield County Courthouse, Edgefield, South Carolina, 77.
34. Ellen Adams Gutow, interview by author, November 27, 1998.
35. *The American Almanac of American History,* 410–11.
36. Daniel E. Sutherland, *The Confederate Carpetbaggers* (Baton Rouge: Louisiana State University Press, 1988), 290.
37. Newspaper article (unidentified), Butler Family Scrapbook.
38. Lawrence S. Rowland, Alexander Moore, and George C. Rogers, *The History of Beaufort County, South Carolina, 1514 to 1861* (Columbia: University of South Carolina Press, 1996), 1:376–77.
39. *Our Family Circle,* ed. Annie Elizabeth Miller (Landen, Tenn: Continental Book, 1975), 313.
40. *O.R.,* ser. I, vol. 6, 37.
41. Ibid., vol. 35, part 2, 425.
42. Ibid., vol. 46, part 2, 1174.
43. *Our Family Circle,* 315–16.
44. Newspaper article (unidentified), Butler Family Scrapbook.
45. Ibid.
46. Ibid.
47. Ellen Adams Gutow, interview by author, November 27, 1998.
48. Ibid.
49. Newspaper article (unidentified), Butler Family Scrapbook.
50. Cullum, *Biographical Register,* 428.
51. Butler Family Bible.
52. *Edgefield Advertiser,* January 3, 1906.
53. Newspaper article (unidentified), Butler Family Scrapbook.
54. Newspaper article (unidentified), courtesy of David Parker.
55. Newspaper article (unidentified), Butler Family Scrapbook.
56. Brooks, *Butler and His Cavalry,* 61.
57. Newspaper article (unidentified), Butler Family Scrapbook.
58. Ibid.
59. Ibid.
60. Newspaper article (unidentified), Courtesy of David Parker.
61. Ibid.
62. Newspaper article (unidentified), Butler Family Scrapbook.

PRIMARY SOURCES
Manuscripts/Official Documents

Brooks, Ulysses R. Papers. Special Collections Library. Duke University, Durham, North Carolina

Butler Family Bible, South Caroliniana Library, University of South Carolina.

Butler, Lilian. Papers. South Caroliniana Library, University of South Carolina.

Butler, Matthew C. Papers. Harry L. and Mary K. Dalton Collection. Special Collections Library. Duke University, Durham, North Carolina.

————. Papers. South Caroliniana Library. University of South Carolina.

————. Papers. RG59. National Archives.

————. Personal File. RG94. National Archives.

————. Papers. File 698. Adjutant General's Office. National Archives.

Butler, Matthew C., and LeRoy Youmans. Legal Papers. South Carolinina Library. University of South Carolina.

Butler II, Matthew C. Papers. RG 94. National Archives.

Congressional Record. 1876–1894. Washington, D.C.

Correspondence Relating to the War with Spain Including the Insurrection in the Philippine Islands and the China Relief Expedition, April 15, 1898–July 30, 1902. Volume 1, Washington, D.C.: Center for Military History, U.S. Army, 1993.

Dargan, John Julius. Papers. South Carolinina Library. University of South Carolina.

Dawson, Francis W. Correspondence, 1881–1888. Charleston Library Society.

Decennial Record of the Class of '83 of Princeton College, N.J., 1883–1893. Comp. and ed. Edward Huntting Rudd. Princeton: Princeton College Press, n.d.

Eastern Cherokee Applications of the U.S. Court of Claims, 1906–1909. National Archives Microfilm Publications, pamphlet M1104, Washington: National Archives Trust Fund Board, National Archives and Records Service, 1981.

Edgefield County Clerk of Courts. Book 20. Edgefield County Courthouse, Edgefield, South Carolina.

Edgefield County Deed Book. Edgefield County, South Carolina.

Edgefield County/RMC (Deeds): Grantor (Direct) Index to Conveyances 1869–1906. South Carolina Department of Archives and History, Columbia, South Carolina.

Edgefield Marriage Records. Ed. Carlee T. McClendon. Columbia, S.C.: R. L. Bryan, 1970.

1870 Federal Census of Maryland, Baltimore City. Maryland Historical Society, Baltimore.

Foster, James W. Papers. Rosa Mills File. Maryland Historical Society, Baltimore.

Gary, Martin Witherspoon. Papers. South Caroliniana Library. University of South Carolina.

Hammond, Bryan, and Cummings Papers. South Caroliniana Library. University of South Carolina.

Hampton Family Papers. South Caroliniana Library. University of South Carolina.

Hampton, Wade. Papers. Special Collections Library. Duke University. Durham, North Carolina.

———. Papers. South Caroliniana Library. University of South Carolina.

Haskell, John C. Papers. Southern Historical Collection. University of North Carolina.

Law, Evander McIvor. Papers. Virginia Historical Society, Richmond.

Maclean, Clara Victoria Dargan. Papers and Personal Diary. Special Collections Library. Duke University, Durham, North Carolina.

Massey, Benjamin Harper. Papers. Caroliniana Society, University of South Carolina.

Points and Authorities Showing the Unconstitutionality and Illegality of Pending Legislation before Congress Touching the Five Civilized Tribes of Indians. Washington: Gibson Bros., Printers and Bookbinders, 1896.

Official Records Concerning the Hamburgh, South Carolina, Massacre of 1876, and the Parties Connected Therewith: Reply of Hon. S. H. Miller of Pennsylvania in the House of Representatives, Tuesday, July 25, 1882, to Remarks of Hon. M. C. Butler of South Carolina, Delivered in the Senate of the United States, Friday, July 21, 1882, Washington, D.C., Government Printing Office, 1882.

Official Register of the Officers and Cadets of the U.S. Military Academy. New York: West Point.

Proceedings of the Tax-Payers Convention of South Carolina Held at Columbia Beginning May 9th and Ending May 12, 1871. Charleston: Edward Perry, 1871.

Ransom, Matt Whittaker. Papers. Southern Historical Collection. University of North Carolina.

Rosser, Thomas Lafayette. Papers. Alderman Library. University of Virginia.

Seibels Family Papers. South Caroliniana Library. University of South Carolina.

Tillman, Benjamin R. "Autobiography." Papers. South Caroliniana Library. University of South Carolina.

Tillman, M. N. Collection. Magnolia Dale. Edgefield Historical Society, Edgefield, South Carolina.

U.S. House and Senate Joint Select Committee. The Ku Klux Klan: Testimony Taken by the Joint Select Committee to Inquire into the Conditions of Affairs in the Late Insurrection States, 42nd Cong., 2nd sess., 1872.

United States Reports, Cases Adjudged in the Supreme Court at the October Term, 1905. Vol. 202. New York: Banks Law, 1906.

U.S. Senate Journal. 41st Cong., 2nd sess., December 6, 1869. War Department Letters and Telegrams Sent Relating to the United States Military Academy from 1867 to 1904. Adjutant General's Office. RG94. National Archives.

War of the Rebellion: A Compilation of the Official Records of the Union and Confederate Armies. 128 vols. Washington, D.C.: Government Printing Office, 1880–1900.

Wayne-Stites-Anderson Papers, Georgia Historical Society, Savannah.

Wells, Edward L. Papers. Charleston Library Society.

Regimental Histories

Brooks, U. R. *Butler and His Cavalry in the War of Secession, 1861–1865.* Germantown, Tenn.: Guild Bindery, 1994.

Myers, Frank M. *The Comanches: A History of White's Battalion, Virginia Cavalry, Laurel Brigade, Hampton's Division, A.N.V., C.S.A.* Marietta, Ga.: Continental, 1956.

Preston, Noble D. *History of the Tenth Regiment of Cavalry, New York State Volunteers.* New York: D. Appleton, 1892.

Wells, Edward L. *Hampton and His Cavalry in '64.* Richmond: Owens, 1991.

Printed Correspondence and Diaries

Chesnut, Mary. *Mary Chesnut's Civil War.* Ed. C. Vann Woodward. New Haven: Yale University Press, 1981.

Conner, James. *Letters of General James Conner, C.S.A.* Ed. Mary Conner Moffett. Columbia: R. L. Bryan, 1950.

Gaston, John T. *Confederate War Diary of John T. Gaston.* Ed. Alifaire G. Walden. Columbia: Vogue, 1960.

Griffin, James B. *A Gentleman and an Officer: A Military and Social History of James B. Griffin.* Ed. Judith V. McArthur and Orville Vernon Burton. New York: Oxford University Press, 1996.

Hammond, James Henry. *Secret and Sacred: The Diaries of James Henry Hammond, a Southern Slaveholder.* Ed. Carol Bleser. New York: Oxford University Press, 1988.

Nichols, George Ward. *The Story of the Great March from the Diary of a Staff Officer.* New York: Harper & Brothers, 1865.

Stuart, James E. B. *The Letters of General J. E. B. Stuart.* Ed. Adele H. Mitchell. Privately printed by the Stuart-Mosby Historical Society, 1990.

The Wartime Papers of R. E. Lee. Ed. Clifford Dowdey and Louis H. Manarin. Boston: Little, Brown, 1961.

Welles, Gideon. *Diary of Gideon Welles: Secretary of the Navy under Lincoln and Johnson.* 3 vols. Boston: Houghton Mifflin, 1911.

Memoirs, Reminiscences, and Recollections

Alexander, Edward Porter. *Fighting for the Confederacy: The Personal Recollections of General Edward Porter Alexander.* Ed. Gary W. Gallagher. Chapel Hill: University of North Carolina Press, 1989.

Battles and Leaders of the Civil War. Ed. Robert U. Johnson and Clarence C. Buel. New York: Thomas Yoseloff, 1956.

Blackford, William W. *War Years with Jeb Stuart.* New York: Charles Scribner's Sons, 1945.

Brooks, Ulysses R. *Stories of the Confederacy.* Oxford, Miss.: Guild Bindery, 1991.

Butler, Matthew C. "The Cavalry Fight at Trevilian Station." In *Battles and Leaders of the Civil War,* ed. Robert U. Johnson and Clarence C. Buel. vol. 4. New York: Thomas Yoseloff, 1956, 237–39.

Calhoun, C. M. *History of Greenwood.* Greenwood, S.C.: Index Job Print, n.d.

Davis, Jefferson C. *The Rise and Fall of the Confederate Government.* 2 vols. New York: D. Appleton, 1881.

DeForest, John William. *A Union Officer in the Reconstruction.* Ed. James H.

Croushore and David M. Potter. New Haven: Yale University Press, 1948.

Early, Jubal A. *Autiobiographical Sketch and Narrative of the War Between the States.* Philadelphia: J. B. Lippincott, 1912.

Grant, Ulysses S. *Personal Memoirs of U. S. Grant.* 2 vols. New York: Charles L. Webster, 1885.

Hampton, Wade. "The Battle of Bentonville." In *Battles and Leaders of the Civil War,* ed. Robert J. Johnson and Clarence C. Buel. Vol. 4. New York: Thomas Yoseloff, 1956, 700–705.

Howard, Oliver O. *Autobiography of Oliver Otis Howard: Major General United States Army.* 2 vols. New York: Baker & Taylor, 1907.

Johnston, Joseph E. *Narrative of Military Operations: Directed during the Late War between the States.* New York: D. Appleton, 1874.

McClellan, George B. *McClellan's Own Story: The War for the Union: The Soldiers Who Fought It; The Civilians Who Directed It; and His Relations to It and Them.* New York: Charles L. Webster, 1887.

McClellan, Henry B. *I Rode with Jeb Stuart: Life and Campaigns of Major-General J.E.B. Sutart.* Bloomington: Indiana University, 1958.

Morgan, James M. *Recollections of a Rebel Reefer.* Boston: Houghton Mifflin, 1917.

Recollections and Reminiscences, 1861–1865, through World War I. Columbia: South Carolina Division, Daughters of the Confederacy, 1991.

Roman, Alfred. *Military Operations of General Beauregard in the War between the States, 1861 to 1865: Including a Brief Personal Sketch and a Narrative of His Services in the War with Mexico, 1856–48.* 2 vols. New York: Harper & Brothers, 1884.

Schofield, John M. *Forty-Six Years in the Army.* New York: Century, 1897.

Sherman, William T. *Personal Memoirs of General W. T. Sherman.* 2 vols. New York: Charles L. Webster, 1890.

Sheridan, Phillip H. *Personal Memoirs of P. H. Sheridan.* 2 vols. New York: Charles L. Webster, 1888.

von Borcke, Heros. *Memoirs of the Confederate War for Independence.* 2 vols. New York: Peter Smith, 1938.

When Sherman Came: Southern Women and the "Great March." Ed. Katherine M. Jones. Indianapolis: Bobbs-Merrill, 1964.

Wilson, James Harrison. *Under the Old Flag: Recollections of Military Operations in the War for the Union, the Spanish War, the Boxer Rebellion, etc.* 2 vols. New York: D. Appleton, 1912.

Newspapers and Magazines

Adams Family Scrapbook (unidentified articles), Ellen Adams Gutow, Highland, Maryland

America's Civil War
Augusta Chronicle and Sentinel
Bald Eagle, The
Butler Family Scrapbook (unidentified articles), South Caroliniana Library,
    University of South Carolina
Charleston Evening Post
Charleston News and Courier
Civil War History
Civil War Quarterly, The
Civil War Times Illustrated
Columbia State
Confederate Veteran
Edgefield Advertiser
Journal of Negro History
Journal of Social History
New York Times
North Carolina Historical Review
Philadelphia Weekly Times
Princetonian, The
South Carolina Historical Magazine
South Carolina Magazine
Southern Historical Society Papers
Traces of Indiana and Midwestern History
Winnsboro News and Herald

SECONDARY SOURCES

Books

Aldrich, Mrs. Alfred P. "Barbarians in Barnwell." In *When Sherman Came:
    Southern Women and the "Great March."* Ed. Katherine M. Jones. Indi-
    anapolis: Bobbs-Merrill, 1964, 114–21.
Allardice, Bruce S. *More Generals in Gray.* Baton Rouge: Louisiana State
    University Press, 1995.
Allen, Walter. *Governor Chamberlain's Administration in South Carolina: A
    Chapter of Reconstruction in the Southern States.* New York: Negro Uni-
    versities Press, 1969.
American Almanac of American History, The. Ed. Arthur M. Schlesinger Jr.
    New York: Bison Books, 1983.
Avary, Myrta Lockett. *Dixie after the War.* Boston: Houghton Mifflin, 1937.
Ball, William Watts. *The State That Forgot: South Carolina's Surrender to
    Democracy.* Indianapolis: Bobbs-Merrill, 1932.

Barrett, John G. *Sherman's March through the Carolinas.* Chapel Hill: University of North Carolina Press, 1956.

Bill, Alfred Hoyt. *The Beleaguered City: Richmond, 1861–1865.* New York: Knopf, 1946.

Biographical Directory of the South Carolina House of Representatives. Ed. Walter B. Edger. Columbia: University of South Carolina Press, 1974.

Blake, Nelson Morehouse. *William Mahone of Virginia: Soldier and Political Insurgent.* Richmond: Garrett & Massie, 1935.

Bleser, Carol K. Rothrock. *The Promised Land: The History of the South Carolina Land Commission, 1869–1890.* Columbia: University of South Carolina Press, 1969.

Bowers, Claude G. *The Tragic Era: The Revolution after Lincoln.* Cambridge: Riverside, 1929.

Boyd's Directory of the District of Columbia, Together with a Compedium of Its Governments, Institutions, and Trades, to Which is Added a Complete Business Directory, a Street Directory, and a Congressional Directory. Washington, D.C.: Compiled and published by William H. Boyd, 1878–1890.

Boykin, Edward. *Beefsteak Raid.* New York: Funk & Wagnalls, 1960.

Bradley, Mark L. *Last Stand in the Carolinas: The Battle of Bentonville.* Campbell, Calif.: Savas Woodbury, 1996.

Burton, Oliver Vernon. *In My Father's House Are Many Mansions.* Chapel Hill: University of North Carolina Press, 1985.

Bushong, Millard K. *Old Jube: A Biography of General Jubal A. Early.* Boyce, Va.: Carr, 1955.

Bushong, Millard K. and Dean M. Bushong. *Fightin' Tom Rosser, C.S.A.* Shippensburg, Pa.: Beidel, 1983.

Capers, Ellison. "South Carolina." *Confederate Military History: A Library of Confederate States History, in Thirteen Volumes, Written by Distinguished Men of the South and Edited by Gen. Clement A. Evans of Georgia.* Secaucus: Blue & Gray, n.d.

Capers, Henry D. *The Life and Times of C. G. Memminger.* Richmond: Everett Waddey, 1893.

Carter, Hodding. *The Angry Scar: The Story of Reconstruction.* Garden City: Doubleday, 1959.

Castel, Albert. *Decision in the West: The Atlanta Campaign of 1864.* Lawrence: University Press of Kansas, 1992.

Catton, Bruce. *Grant Takes Command.* Boston: Little, Brown, 1968.

Chambers, Lenoir. *Stonewall Jackson.* 2 vols. New York: William Morrow, 1959.

Chapman, John. *History of Edgefield.* Newberry, S.C.: Elbert H. Aull, 1897.

Clarke-Smith, Theodore. *The Life and Letters of James Abram Garfield.* 2 vols. New Haven: Yale University Press, 1925.

Cleeves, Freeman. *Meade of Gettysburg.* Norman: University of Oklahoma Press, 1960.

Coddington, Edwin B. *The Gettysburg Campaign: A Study in Command.* New York: Charles Scribner's Sons, 1968.

Connelly, Thomas Lawrence. *Autumn of Glory: The Army of Tennessee, 1862–1865.* Baton Rouge: Louisiana State University Press, 1971.

Cullum, Bvt. Maj. Gen. George W. *Biographical Register of the Officers and Graduates of the U.S. Military Academy at West Point, N.Y.: From Its Establishment in 1802 to 1890: With the Early History of the United States Military Academy.* Vol. 3, nos. 2001–3384. Boston and New York: Riverside, 1891.

Current, Richard Nelson. *Those Terrible Carpetbaggers: A Reinterpretation.* New York: Oxford University Press, 1988.

Cutting, Elisabeth. *Jefferson Davis: Political Soldier.* New York: Dodd, Mead, 1930.

Davis, Burke. *Jeb Stuart: The Last Cavalier.* New York: Rinehart, 1957.

———. *Sherman's March.* New York: Random House, 1980.

Davis, William C. *Battle at Bull Run: A History of the First Major Campaign of the Civil War.* Garden City, N.Y.: Doubleday, 1977.

———. *Duel between the First Ironclads.* Garden City, N.Y.: Doubleday, 1975.

Donald, David H. *Lincoln.* New York: Simon & Schuster, 1995.

———. *Charles Sumner and the Coming of the Civil War.* New York: Knopf, 1961.

Dowdey, Clifford. *Lee.* Boston: Little, Brown, 1965.

———. *The Seven Days: The Emergence of Lee.* Boston: Little, Brown, 1964.

———. *Lee's Last Campaign: The Story of Lee and His Men against Grant.* Boston: Little, Brown, 1960.

Downey, Fairfax. *Clash of Cavalry: The Battle of Brandy Station.* New York: David McKay, 1959.

Dyer, John P. *"Fightin'" Joe Wheeler.* Baton Rouge: Louisiana State University Press, 1941.

Eckenrode, H. J. *Rutherford B. Hayes: Statesman of Reunion.* New York: Dodd, Mead, 1930.

Eckenrode, H. J., and Bryan Conrad. *James Longstreet: Lee's War Horse.* Chapel Hill: University of North Carolina Press, 1936.

Edmunds, John B., Jr. *Francis W. Pickens and the Politics of Destruction.* Chapel Hill: University of North Carolina Press, 1986.

Eggleston, George Cary. *The History of the Confederate War: Its Cause and Its*

Conduct: A Narrative and Critical History. 2 vols. New York: Sturgis & Walton, 1910.

Foote, Shelby. *The Civil War: A Narrative.* 3 vols. New York: Random House, 1958.

Freeman, Douglas Southall. *Lee's Lieutenants: A Study in Command.* 3 vols. New York: Charles Scribner's Sons, 1942.

———. *R. E. Lee: A Biography.* 4 vols. New York: Charles Scribner's Sons, 1934.

Friedmann, Lawrence E., M.D. *The Psychological Rehabilitation of the Amputee.* Springfield, Ill.: Charles C. Thomas, 1978.

Fuess, Claude M. *Carl Schurz Reformer.* New York: Dodd, Mead, 1932.

Garlington, J. C. *Men of the Time.* Spartanburg: Reprint, 1972.

Gibson, John M. *Those 163 Days: A Southern Account of Sherman's March from Atlanta to Raleigh.* New York: Coward-McCann, 1961.

Govan, Gilbert E., and James W. Livingood. *A Different Valor: The Story of Joseph E. Johnston, C.S.A.* Indianapolis: Bobbs-Merrill, 1956.

Gragg, Rod. *Confederate Goliath: The Battle of Fort Fisher.* New York: HarperCollins, 1991.

Hafendorfer, Kenneth A. *Perryville: Battle for Kentucky.* Utica, Ky.: McDowell, 1981.

Hamilton, James. *The Battle of Fort Donelson.* New York: Thomas Yoseloff, 1968.

Hart, B. H. Liddell. *Sherman: Soldier, Realist, American.* New York: Dodd, Mead, 1929.

Hartje, Robert G. *Van Dorn: The Life and Times of a Confederate General.* Nashville: Vanderbilt University Press, 1967.

Hassler, Warren W., Jr. *General George B. McClellan: Shield of the Union.* Baton Rouge: Louisiana State University Press, 1957.

Hassler, William Woods. *A. P. Hill: Lee's Forgotten General.* Richmond: Garrett & Massie, 1962.

Hattaway, Herman. *General Stephen D. Lee.* Jackson: University of Mississippi Press, 1976.

Hebert, Walter H. *Fighting Joe Hooker.* Indianapolis: Bobbs-Merrill, 1944.

Hennessy, John J. *Return to Bull Run: The Campaign and Battle of Second Manassas.* New York: Simon & Schuster, 1993.

Henry, Robert Selph. *The Story of the Confederacy.* Indianapolis: Bobbs-Merrill, 1931.

———. *The Story of Reconstruction.* Indianapolis: Bobbs-Merrill, 1938.

Hewitt, Lawrence L. *Port Hudson: Confederate Bastion on the Mississippi.* Baton Rouge: Louisiana State University Press, 1987.

Hoehling, A. A. *Last Train from Atlanta.* New York: Bonanza, 1958.

Holland, Lynwood M. *Pierce M. B. Young: The Warwick of the South.* Athens: University of Georgia Press, 1962.

Horn, Stanley F. *The Army of Tennessee: A Military History.* Indianapolis: Bobbs-Merrill, 1941.

————. *The Decisive Battle of Nashville.* Knoxville: University of Tennessee Press, 1978.

Hughes, Nathaniel Cheairs. *General William J. Hardee: Old Reliable.* Baton Rouge: Louisiana State University Press, 1965.

Jarrell, Hampton M. *Wade Hampton and the Negro: The Road Not Taken.* Columbia: University of South Carolina Press, 1949.

Johannsen, Robert W. *Stephen A. Douglas.* New York: Oxford University Press, 1973.

Johnson, Bradley T. *A Memoir of the Life and Public Service of Joseph E. Johnston.* Baltimore: R. H. Woodward, 1891.

Jones, Virgil Carrington. *Eight Hours before Richmond.* New York: Henry Holt, 1957.

Kane, Joseph Nathan. *Facts about the Presidents: A Compilation of Biographical and Historical Information.* New York: H. W. Wilson, 1989.

Karnow, Stanley. *In Our Image: America's Empire in the Philippines.* New York: Random House, 1989.

Lamers, William M. *The Edge of Glory: A Biography of General William S. Rosecrans, U.S.A.* New York: Harcourt, Brace & World, 1961.

Lamson, Peggy. *The Glorious Failure: Black Congressman Robert Brown Elliott and the Reconstruction in South Carolina.* New York: W. W. Norton, 1973.

Lee, Fitzhugh. *General Lee.* New York: D. Appleton, 1895.

Leech, Margaret. *In the Days of McKinley.* New York: Harper & Brothers, 1959.

Lewis, Thomas A. *The Guns of Cedar Creek.* New York: Harper & Row, 1988.

Long, E. B., and Barbara Long. *The Civil War Day by Day: An Almanac, 1861–1865.* Garden City, N.Y.: Doubleday, 1971.

Longacre, Edward G. *From Union Stars to Top Hat: A Biography of the Extraordinary General James Harrison Wilson.* Harrisburg, Pa.: Stackpole, 1972.

Lucas, Marion B. *Sherman and His Burning of Columbia.* College Station: Texas A. & M. University Press, 1976.

Luvaas, Jay, and Harold W. Nelson, eds. *The U.S. Army War College Guide to the Battles of Chancellorsville and Fredericksburg.* Carlisle: South Mountain, 1988.

Marszalek, John F. *Sherman: A Soldier's Passion for Order.* New York: Free Press, 1993.

Martin, Samuel J. *Kill-Cavalry: The Life of Union General Hugh Judson Kilpatrick*. Rutherford, N.J.: Fairleigh Dickinson University Press, 1996.

—————. *The Road to Glory: The Life of Confederate General Richard S. Ewell*. Indianapolis: Guild Press of Indiana, 1991.

Marvel, William. *Burnside*. Chapel Hill: University of North Carolina Press, 1991.

Matter, William D. *If It Takes All Summer: The Battle of Spotsylvania*. Chapel Hill: University of North Carolina Press, 1988.

McDonough, James Lee. *Chattanooga: A Death Grip on the Confederacy*. Knoxville: University of Tennessee Press, 1984.

—————. *Schofield: Union General in the Civil War and Reconstruction*. Tallahassee: Florida State University Press, 1972.

McDonough, James Lee, and Thomas L. Connelly. *Five Tragic Hours: The Battle of Franklin*. Knoxville: University of Tennessee Press, 1983.

McFeely, William S. *Grant: A Biography*. New York: Norton, 1981.

McPherson, James M. *Battle Cry of Freedom: The Civil War Era*. New York: Oxford University Press, 1988.

Miers, Earl Schenck. *The Web of Victory: Grant at Vicksburg*. New York: Knopf, 1955.

Milton, George Fort. *The Eve of Conflict: Stephen A. Douglas and the Needless War*. Boston: Houghton and Mifflin, 1934.

Mitchell, Stewart. *Horatio Seymour of New York*. Cambridge: Harvard University Press, 1938.

Montgomery, James S. *The Shaping of a Battle: Gettysburg*. Philadelphia: Chilton, 1959.

Morison, Samuel Eliot. *"Old Bruin": Commodore Matthew C. Perry, 1794–1858*. Boston: Little, Brown, 1967.

Morris, Roy Jr. *Sheridan: The Life and Wars of General Phil Sheridan*. New York: Crown, 1992.

Murfin, James V. *The Gleam of Bayonets: The Battle of Antietam and Robert E. Lee's Maryland Campaign, September 1862*. New York: Thomas Yoseloff, 1965.

Nevins, Allen. *Grover Cleveland: A Study in Courage*. New York: Dodd, Mead, 1944.

Osborne, Charles C. *Jubal: The Life and Times of General Jubal A. Early, C.S.A.* Chapel Hill: Algonquin, 1992.

O'Toole, G. J. A. *The Spanish War: An American Epic, 1898*. New York: W. W. Norton, 1984.

Our Family Circle. Ed. Annie Elizabeth Miller. Landen, Tenn.: Continental Book, 1975.

Perry, Rev. Calbraith Bourn. *The Perrys of Rhode Island and Tales of Silver*

Creek: The Bosworth-Bourn-Perry Homestead. New York: Tobias A. Wright, 1913.

Pollard, Edward. *The Early Life, Campaigns, and Public Services of Robert E. Lee: With a Record of the Campaigns and Heroic Deeds of His Companions in Arms, "Names the World Will Not Willingly Let Die."* New York: E. B. Treat, 1871.

Poore, Ben: Perley. *The Life and Public Services of Ambrose E. Burnside: Soldier–Citizen–Statesman*. Providence: J. A. & R. A. Reid, 1882.

Rable, George C. *But There Was No Peace: The Role of Violence in the Politics of Reconstruction*. Athens: University of Georgia Press, 1984.

Random House Dictionary of the English Language: The Unabridged Edition. New York: Random House, 1967.

Reynolds, John S. *Reconstruction in South Carolina: 1865–1877*. Columbia: State, 1905.

Robertson, Mrs. C. E. "Seth Thorton Prior." In *Recollections and Reminiscences, 1861–1865 through World War I*. Columbia: South Carolina Division, Daughters of the Confederacy, 1991, 436–37.

Robertson, James I. *General A. P. Hill: The Story of a Confederate Warrior*. New York: Random House, 1987.

Rowland, Lawrence S., Alexander Moore, and George C. Rogers. *The History of Beaufort County, South Carolina, 1514 to 1861*. Vol. 1. Columbia: University of South Carolina Press, 1996.

Sandberg, Carl. *Abraham Lincoln: The War Years*. 4 vols. New York: Harcourt, Brace & World, 1939.

Sears, Stephen W. *To the Gates of Richmond: The Peninsula Campaign*. New York: Ticknor & Fields, 1992.

———. *George M. McClellan: The Young Napoleon*. New York: Ticknor & Fields, 1988.

———. *Landscape Turned Red: The Battle of Antietam*. New York: Ticknor & Fields, 1983.

Seitz, Don C. *Braxton Bragg: General of the Confederacy*. Columbia: State, 1924.

Shea, William L., and Earl J. Hess. *Pea Ridge: Civil War Campaign in the West*. Chapel Hill: University of North Carolina Press, 1992.

Sheppard, William A. *Red Shirts Remembered: Southern Brigadiers of the Reconstruction Period*. Atlanta: Ruralist Press, 1940.

Sifakis, Stewart. *Who Was Who in the Confederacy: A Biographical Encyclopedia of More than 1,000 Confederate Participants*. New York: Facts on File, 1988.

Simkins, Francis Butler. *Pitchfork Ben Tillman: South Carolinian*. Baton Rouge: Louisiana State University Press, 1944.

————. *The Tillman Movement in South Carolina*. Durham: Duke University Press, 1926.

Simkins, Francis Butler, and Robert H. Woody. *South Carolina during Reconstruction*. Chapel Hill: University of North Carolina Press, 1932.

Sommer, Richard J. *Richmond Redeemed: The Siege at Petersburg*. Garden City, N.Y.: Doubleday, 1981.

South Carolina Genealogies. Spartanburg, S.C.: Reprint, 1983.

Stackpole, Edward J. *Chancellorsville: Lee's Greatest Battle*. Harrisburg, Pa.: Stackpole, 1958.

————. *Drama on the Rappahannock: The Fredericksburg Campaign*. Harrisburg, Pa.: Stackpole, 1957.

————. *From Cedar Mountain to Antietam*. Harrisburg, Pa.: Stackpole, 1959.

Starr, Stephen Z. *The Union Cavalry in the Civil War*. 3 vols. Baton Rouge: Louisiana State University Press, 1991.

Steere, Edward. *The Wilderness Campaign*. Harrisburg, Pa.: Stackpole, 1960.

Stevenson, Alexander F. *The Battle of Stone's River near Murfreesboro, Tennessee, December 30, 1862 to Januuary 3, 1863*. Boston: James R. Osgood, 1884.

Stryker, Lloyd Paul. *Andrew Johnson: A Study in Courage*. New York: Macmillan, 1930.

Summers, Mark Wahlgren. *The Era of Good Stealing*. New York: Oxford University Press, 1993.

Sutherland, Daniel E. *The Confederate Carpetbaggers*. Baton Rouge: Louisiana State University Press, 1988.

Swanberg, W. A. *First Blood: The Story of Fort Sumter*. New York: Charles Scribner's Sons, 1957.

————. *Sickles the Incredible*. New York: Charles Scribner's Sons, 1956.

Swank, Walbrook Davis. *The Battle of Trevilian Station: The Civil War's Greatest and Bloodiest of All Cavalry Battles*. Shippensburg, Pa.: Burd Street, 1994.

Sword, Wiley. *Mountain Touched With Fire: Chattanooga Besieged, 1863*. New York: St. Martin's, 1995.

————. *Shiloh: Bloody April*. New York: William Morrow, 1974.

Tankersley, Allen B. *John B. Gordon: A Study in Gallantry*. Atlanta: Whitehall, 1955.

Tanner, Robert G. *Stonewall in the Valley: Thomas J. "Stonewall" Jackson's Shenandoah Valley Campaign, Spring 1862*. Garden City, N.Y.: Doubleday, 1976.

Thomas, Benjamin P. *Abraham Lincoln: A Biography*. New York: Knopf, 1952.

Thomas, Emory M. *Bold Dragoon: The Life of J. E. B. Stuart*. New York: Harper & Row, 1986.

Thomason, John W., Jr. *Jeb Stuart*. New York: Charles Scribner's Sons, 1930.

Thompson, Jr., Henry T. *Ousting the Carpetbagger from South Carolina*. New York: Negro Universities Press, 1969.

Tourgee, Albion Winegar. *The Invisible Empire*. Baton Rouge: Louisiana State University Press, 1989.

Trask, David F. *The War with Spain in 1898*. New York: Macmillan, 1981.

Trelease, Allen W. *White Terror: The Ku Klux Klan Conspiracy and Southern Reconstruction*. New York: Harper & Row, 1971.

Trudeau, Noah Andre. *Bloody Roads South: The Wilderness to Cold Harbor, May–June 1864*. Boston: Little, Brown, 1989.

Tucker, Glenn. *Hancock the Superb*. Indianapolis: Bobbs-Merrill, 1960.

Van Deusen, Glyndon G. *William Henry Seward: Lincoln's Secretary of State: The Negotiator of the Alaska Purchase*. New York: Oxford University Press, 1967.

Vandiver, Frank E. *Jubal's Raid: General Early's Famous Attack on Washington in 1864*. New York: McGraw-Hill, 1960.

——. *Ploughshares into Swords: Josiah Gorgas and Confederate Ordnance*. Austin: University of Texas Press, 1952.

——. *Their Tattered Flags: The Epic of the Confederacy*. New York: Harper's Magazine, 1970.

Warner, Ezra J. *Generals in Blue: Lives of the Union Commanders*. Baton Rouge: Louisiana State University Press, 1954.

——. *Generals in Gray: Lives of the Confederate Commanders*. Baton Rouge: Louisiana State University Press, 1959.

Wellman, Manly Wade. *Giant in Gray: A Biography of Wade Hampton of South Carolina*. New York: Charles Scribner's Sons, 1949.

Wheeler, Joseph. "Alabama." In *Confederate Military History: A Library of Confederate States History, Written by Distinguished Men of the South, and Edited by Gen. Clement A. Evans of Georgia*. Secaucus: Blue and Gray, n.d.

Williams, Alfred B. *Hampton and His Red Shirts: South Carolina's Deliverance in 1876*. Charleston: Walker, Evans & Cogswell, 1935.

Williamson, Joel. *After Slavery: The Negro in South Carolina during Reconstruction, 1861–1877*. Chapel Hill: University of North Carolina Press, 1965.

Wise, Stephen R. *Gate of Hell: Campaign for Charleston Harbor, 1863*. Columbia: University of South Carolina Press, 1994.

Woodburn, James A. *The Life of Thaddeus Stevens: A Study of American Political History, Especially in the Period of the Civil War and Reconstruction*. Indianapolis: Bobbs-Merrill, 1913.

Woodson, Hortense. *Companies from Edgefield in Confederate Service*. Edgefield, S.C.: Edgefield Advertiser, 1960.

Woodworth, Steven E. *Jefferson Davis and His Generals.* Lawrence: University Press of Kansas, 1990.

Zuczek, Richard. *State of Rebellion: Reconstruction in South Carolina.* Columbia: University of South Carolina Press, 1996.

Articles in Newspapers/Journals

Allen, Alice West, "Recollections of War in Virginia." *Confederate Veteran* 23, no. 6 (June 1915): 268–69.

Bonham, Milledge Luke. "Around 1865." *Edgefield Advertiser,* centennial edition, December 16, 1936.

Braskllien, Dr. T. M. "Annals of the War: Chapters of Unwritten History: A Sharp Cavalry Clash: The Personal Recollections of a South Carolina Trooper at Brandy Station: Butler at Stevensburg." *Philadelphia Weekly Times,* March 24, 1883.

Brooks, Ulysses R. "Memories of Battles." *Confederate Veteran* 22, no. 9 (September 1914): 408–10.

———, "Hampton and Butler: Some Pages of Heretofore Unwritten History." Ed. R. A. Brock. *Southern Historical Society Papers* 23 (January–December 1895): 25–37.

———, "War Memories," *Confederate Veteran* 22, no. 11 (November 1914): 497–99.

Burton, Oliver B. "Race and Reconstruction in Edgefield County." *Journal of Social History* 12 (fall 1978): 31–56.

"Matthew Calbraith Butler." *The Bald Eagle* (Sons of Confederate Veterans, Brig. General Martin Witherspoon Gary Camp #1532, Edgefield, South Carolina) 6, no. 3 (March 1998): 1–2.

Matthew C. Butler. "Devoted South Carolina Confederates: Reunion of the Division U. C. V. at Chester, South Carolina." *Confederate Veteran* 8, no. 1 (January 1900): 28–33.

Calhoun, C. M. "Credit to Wheeler Claimed for Others." *Confederate Veteran* 20, no. 2 (February 1912): 82.

Coxe, John. "The Battle of First Manassas." *Confederate Veteran* 23, no. 1 (January 1915): 24–26.

Dunovant, Adelia A. "Gen. John Dunovant, Houston, Tex." *Confederate Veteran* 16, no. 1 (January 1908): 183–84.

Hall, Clark B. "The Battle of Brandy Station." *Civil War Times Illustrated* 20, no. 2 (May–June 1990): 32–42, 45.

Harrigan, Anthony. "The Houses of Edgefield." *South Carolina Magazine* 16, no. 11 (November 1952): 16–18.

"John Rutledge Family." *South Carolina Historical Magazine* 31, no. 1 (January 1930): 98–105.

Kowell, Brian D. "Pell-Mell Cavalry Chase." *America's Civil War* 5, no. 2 (July 1992): 39–45, 72–74.

Krolick, Marshall D. "The Battle of Brandy Station." *The Civil War Quarterly* 7 (winter 1986): 52–65.

Rhett, Claudine. "Generous Action of a Comrade." *Confederate Veteran* 3, no. 1 (January 1895): 7.

Robertson, Mrs. A. I. "Gen. M. C. Butler as a Confederate." *Confederate Veteran* 8, no. 3 (March 1900): 110–11.

Saussy, Clement. "Two Bridges Burned Near Columbia." *Confederate Veteran* 17, no. 11 (November 1909): 553–54.

Shapiro, Herbert. "The Ku Klux Klan during Reconstruction: The South Carolina Episode." *Journal of Negro History* 49, no. 1 (January 1964): 35–55.

Simkins, Francis B. "The Ku Klux Klan in South Carolina, 1868–1871." *Journal of Negro History* 12, no. 4 (October 1927): 607–647.

"A Synopsis of the Public Service of General M. C. Butler as U.S. Senator from South Carolina, from 1877 to 1894." Loose article, M. C. Butler Papers, South Caroliniana Library, 1–6.

Ward, J. W. "General M. C. Butler of South Carolina." *Confederate Veteran* 3 no. 2 (February 1895): 42.

Weber, Catherine E. Forrest. "Editing the Civil War Commanders: Robert Underwood Johnson and the *Century.*" *Traces of Indiana and Midwestern History* 10, no. 3 (summer 1998): 3–12.

Wells, Edward L. "A Morning Call on General Kilpatrick." *Southern Historical Society Papers* 12 (January–December 1884): 123–130.

Wilkins, John Grimball. "Gen. Matthew Calbraith Butler, C.S.A." *Confederate Veteran* 35, no. 3 (March 1927): 89.

Williams, Alfred B. "Call Reaches Hampton in Cahsiers Valley." *Charleston Evening Post,* August 22, 1926.

———. "Hamburg Lights Consuming Flame." *Charleston Evening Post,* August 8, 1926.

———. "Hampton and Chamberlain Sketched as They Were When the Campaign Began." *Charleston Evening Post,* September 19, 1926.

———. "King Street Sees Wild Rioting." *Charleston Evening Post,* October 10, 1926.

———. "October '76, Critical for Carolina." *Charleston Evening Post,* December 12, 1926.

———. "Red Shirts Appear in Charleston." *Charleston Evening Post,* September 26, 1926.

Williams, Jack Kenny. "The Code of Honor in Ante-Bellum South Carolina." *South Carolina Historical Magazine* 54, no. 3 (July 1953): 113–128.

Woody, R. H. "The South Carolina Election of 1870." *North Carolina Historical Review* 8, no. 2 (April 1931): 169–185.

Zuczek, Richard M. "The Last Campaign of the Civil War: South Carolina and the Revolution of 1876." *Civil War History* 42, no. 1 (March 1996): 18–31.

UNPUBLISHED MATERIAL
Dissertations

Channing, Steven A. "Crisis of Fear: Secession in South Carolina." Ph.D. diss., University of North Carolina, 1968.

Mims, Julian L. "Radical Reconstruction in Edgefield County, 1868–1877." Master's thesis, University of South Carolina, 1969.

Thompson, Michael E. "Blacks, Carpetbaggers, and Scalawags: A Study of the Membership of the South Carolina Legislature, 1868–1870." Ph.D. diss., Washington State University, 1975.

Letters/Interviews

Butler, Ellen Iredell (Matthew C. Butler's granddaughter). Interview by author. March 4, 1997 and March 25, 1997. Columbia, South Carolina.

Coburn, Oakley H. (Librarian, Wofford College, Spartanburg, South Carolina). Letter to author, February 13, 1998.

Esche, Carl (Special Collections Assistant, Seeley G. Mudd Library, Princeton University). Letter to author, February 25, 1998.

Gutow, Ellen Adams (Matthew C. Butler's great-granddaughter). Interview by author. November 27, 1998. Highland, Md.

Nicholson, Mrs. Benjamin E. (owner of "East Hill"). Interview by author. October 6, 1995. Edgefield, South Carolina.

Parker, David (relative of Matthew C. Butler). Letter to author, July 23, 1998. Edgefield, South Carolina.

Rainsford, Bettis (relative to Matthew C. Butler). Interview by author. October 6, 1995. Edgefield, South Carolina.

Sibly, Judith A. (Archives curator, Special Collections and Archives Division, U.S. Military Academy, West Point, New York). Letter to author, February 26, 1998.

INDEX

Adams, Doc, 207–210

Aiken, Col. Hugh K.: background, 83; commands Dunovant's Brigade, 123; killed at Big Lynch's Creek, 146; photo, 83; returns to the 6th South Carolina, 137; at Trevilian Station, 93; wounded, 93

Aldrich, Sen. Nelson W., 261, 263–64

Alexander, Sarah Wallace, 3–4, 6

Alger, Sec. of War Russell A., 293, 296–97

Allison, Sen. William B., 230, 237–38

Ames, Gen. Adelbert: at Brandy Station, 71; governor of Mississippi, 205; orders the arrest of Edgefield leading citizens, 170

Anderson, Gen. Richard H., 35, 89, 114

Arthur, Pres. Chester A., 233, 235

Averell, Gen. William W., 56, 80, 107

Banks, Gen. Nathaniel P., 30, 37, 78

Beauregard, Gen. Pierre G. T.: commands at Charleston, 18; defends Charleston, 79; —, Manassas, 18–20; —, Petersburg, 97; —, South Carolina, 136–38; leaves Columbia, 139; meets with President Davis, 161; promotes Hampton, 139; refuses to release his cavalry, 80–81, retreats to Charlotte, 141; turns command over to Johnston, 143

Birney, Gen. David B., 107, 114

Blackburn, Sen. Joseph C. S., 266–67

Blackford, Lieut. William W., 46, 56–57

Blaine, Sen. James G.: introduces resolution on voting restrictions in the South, 229–31; nominated for president, 242; opposes Butler's inquiry request, 225; quoted, 225, 229, 231

Blair, Sen. Henry W.: attacks Southern school systems, 241; castigates President Cleveland, 255; defends foreign labor bill, 244; opposes Butler's proposal to resettle blacks, 259; quoted, 241, 244, 255, 259; scorned by Butler, 255

Bostick, Benjamin, 306

Bragg, Gen. Braxton: defeated at Chattanooga, 80; —, at Murfreesboro, 65; —, at Kinston (NC), 154; fights under Johnston at Bentonville, 156–57; invades Kentucky, 52; mentioned, 60, 139, 150; resumes field command in North Carolina, 150; routs Rosencrans at Chickamauga Creek, 79

Breckinridge, Gen. John C., 12, 161

Brooks, Ulysses R., 77, 307

Brown, John, 11–12, 42

Bryan, William Jennings, 287, 300

Buell, Gen. Don Carlos, 52, 60

Burnside, Gen. Ambrose E.: commands Army of the Potomac, 60; defends

377

93, 101, 108, 121–22; attends Democratic National Convention, 206–7, 232, 242, 254; attitude toward blacks, 128, 169, 177, 258–60; Blue Ridge Railroad, 181–82, 189–90, 195; boyhood, 4–5; born, 1; calls on President Roosevelt, 302–3; campaigns for Cleveland, 243; —, John Green, 200; —, Hampton, 214; —, lieutenant governor, 184–85; —, U.S. Senate, 275–83; —, Seymour, 180; castigates Chamberlain, 212; challenges to duel, 9–10, 280, 282; in charge of Red Shirts, 219; Cherokee Case, 303–4; Columbia and Greenville Railroad, 195; comments about President Johnson, 173; commissioned U.S. major general, 289; confronts black militia, 198, 200–201; converts to Catholic faith, 307–8; coolness under pressure, 57–58, 65, 93, 96, 109, 151–52, 281; court martial duty, 298; defeated for Senate, 185, 283; defends Southern election methods, 229–30, 238, 262–63; descriptions, 6, 88, 228, 238, 265, 290–91, 300; discouraged by Civil War, 110–11; Dispensary, 276–77; East Hill home, 203–4, 276, 302, 305; Edgefield murder, 169–70; elected to U.S. Senate, 219–20, 236, 256; —, state representative, 12, 167; entrapped by Radicals, 221–22; fights at Brandy Station, ix–x, 71– 75; —, Burgess' Mill, 125–28; —, McDowell's Farm, 115–22; —, "Morning Call" on Kilpatrick, 151– 53; —, Trevilian Station, 91–96; has financial difficulties, 164, 173, 182, 188, 191, 195, 237, 242, 245; frees his slaves, 165; funeral, 308–10; Hamburg Massacre, 207–11, 224, 280–

81; house burned, 200; Immigration Society, 177, 187; induces Hampton to accept nomination for governor, 211–13; joins Hampton Legion, 15; Ku Klux Klan, 181, 186, 191; Land Commission, 182– 83; law practice, 9, 12, 166, 172, 174–75, 195, 206–7, 234, 286, 303–4; leads charge at Frederick City, 47–48; —, McDowell's Farm, 115; —, Seven Pines, 39; —, Trevilian Station, 91–93; —, Urbana, 47; —, Williamsburg, 33–34; Lottery Plan, 187, 190–91, 193, 195; lobbyist, 286; marries, 11, 306; Mexican mines, 305; named to Cuban Evacuation Commission, 295; nominated for South Carolina lieutenant governor, 184; —, U.S. Senator, 185, 219; obtains Federal funds for South Carolina, 226–28, 231, 284–85; oratory skills, 177, 206, 234; organizes Democratic Clubs, 180, 206, 274; parties, 19, 42, 46, 52, 59; personal bravery, 89, 108; plan for Cuban militia, 296–97; photos, frontispiece, 7, 10, 227, 291; presented with horse, 293; promoted CSA major, 20; —, CSA colonel, 43; —, CSA brigadier general, 79; CSA major general, 111; proposes debtor relief for South Carolina, 299–300; provides relief for Cubans, 296, 298; —, Edgefield poor, 174; purchases Edgefield law office, 254; —, Washington home, 258; raids Chambersburg, 52–55; —, Dumfries, 61–63; —, Occoquan, 64–65; —, below Washington, 44–46, 48; Red Shirt Campaign, 213–17; relations with his troops, 35, 63, 102, 104–5, 129, 131, 154–55; rents quarters in Washington, 221–22, 226, 229, 231–32, 235, 239, 243, 245, 253,

faith in Fitz Lee, 103; mentioned,
ix, x, 17, 48, 53, 59, 66, 77, 114,
115, 129, 143, 150, 158, 161, 229,
242, 310; named division cavalry
commander, 79; —, temporary head
of Lee's cavalry corps, 90; names
Butler as chief of Legion cavalry, 42;
—, temporary division chief, 94;
nominated for governor, 213; objects to Stuart's reorganization plans,
81; offers friendship to blacks, 174;
orders Butler to Charlotte, 141; —,
to leave South Carolina, 147; organizes Hampton Legion, 15, 17–18;
photo, 16; proposes reelection plan
for Butler, 274; praises Butler, 48,
96; promotes Butler to division
command, 111; quoted, 15, 24, 26,
48, 55, 70, 81, 83, 96, 123, 127–28,
145, 147, 163, 174, 213, 274, 289;
raids Chambersburg, 52–53, 55; —,
Dumfries, 61–63; —, Occoquan,
63–64; recommends Butler as Spanish-American War general, 284;
recuperates in South Carolina, 79;
refuses to surrender, 163–64;
replaced in Senate by Irby, 262;
requests keeping veterans as scouts,
83; retreats to Peninsula, 50; returns
to duty after Gettysburg wounding,
80; —, to South Carolina to defend
Charleston, 67; —, Columbia, 132,
137–39; runs for reelection, 228;
seizes control of South Carolina,
219–20; selects Edgefield Hussars for
Legion, 15; son killed/son wounded, 127–28; stands up to Lee, 42;
supplies Legion officers with swords
/uniforms, 18; threatens Hood, 70;
—, Sherman, 145; wounded at Gettysburg, 79; writes his wife, 24
Hancock, Gen. Winfield Scott: fights at
Burgess' Mill, 124–28; —, Deep
Bottom, 105–6; —, Jarratt's Station,
129; —, New Market Road, 107;

—, Peninsula, 35; —, Reams' Station, 108–10; nominated for U.S.
President, 232; quoted, 109; refuses
to campaign, 232
Hardee, Gen. William J.: arrives in
North Carolina, 147; fights at Averasborough, 155; —, Bentonville,
156–57, 160; heads toward North
Carolina, 141; meets Butler at Cheraw, 146–47; mentioned, 150–51,
154, 161; moves out of Charleston
to block Sherman's advance, 136;
quoted, 146, 155, 160
Harrison, Pres. Benjamin: debates with
Butler on South Dakota statehood,
245–46; —, Montana statehood,
247; defeated for second term, 269;
elected, 256; nominated, 255; renominated, 269; signs statehood bill,
260
Haskell, Alexander C., 214, 262
Hayes, Pres. Rutherford B.: agrees to
deal that gives him Presidency, 220;
election disputed, 217; meets with
Butler, 222; —, Chamberlain, 222;
mentioned, 220–21, 226, 232; takes
oath of office, 221
Heth, Gen. Henry, 106, 108–9, 117,
125
Hill, Gen. Ambrose Powell: fights at
McDowell's Farm, 117–19; —,
Mechanicsville, 40; —, Sharpsburg,
50; Reams' Station, 109; mentioned, 102, 117, 124–25; promoted to
corps command, 69
Hill, Gen. Daniel H.: fights at Seven
Pines, 37–38; —, Sharpsburg, 49;
—, South Mountain, 48; mention-
ed, 29, 31, 47; secret orders lost, 48
Hiscock, Sen. Frank, 257–58, 261
Hoar, Sen. George F.: accuses Butler of
abusing blacks, 238; attempts to stop
Butler's filibuster, 264; objects to
Butler's black deportation plan, 259;
supports Lodge's Force bill, 262